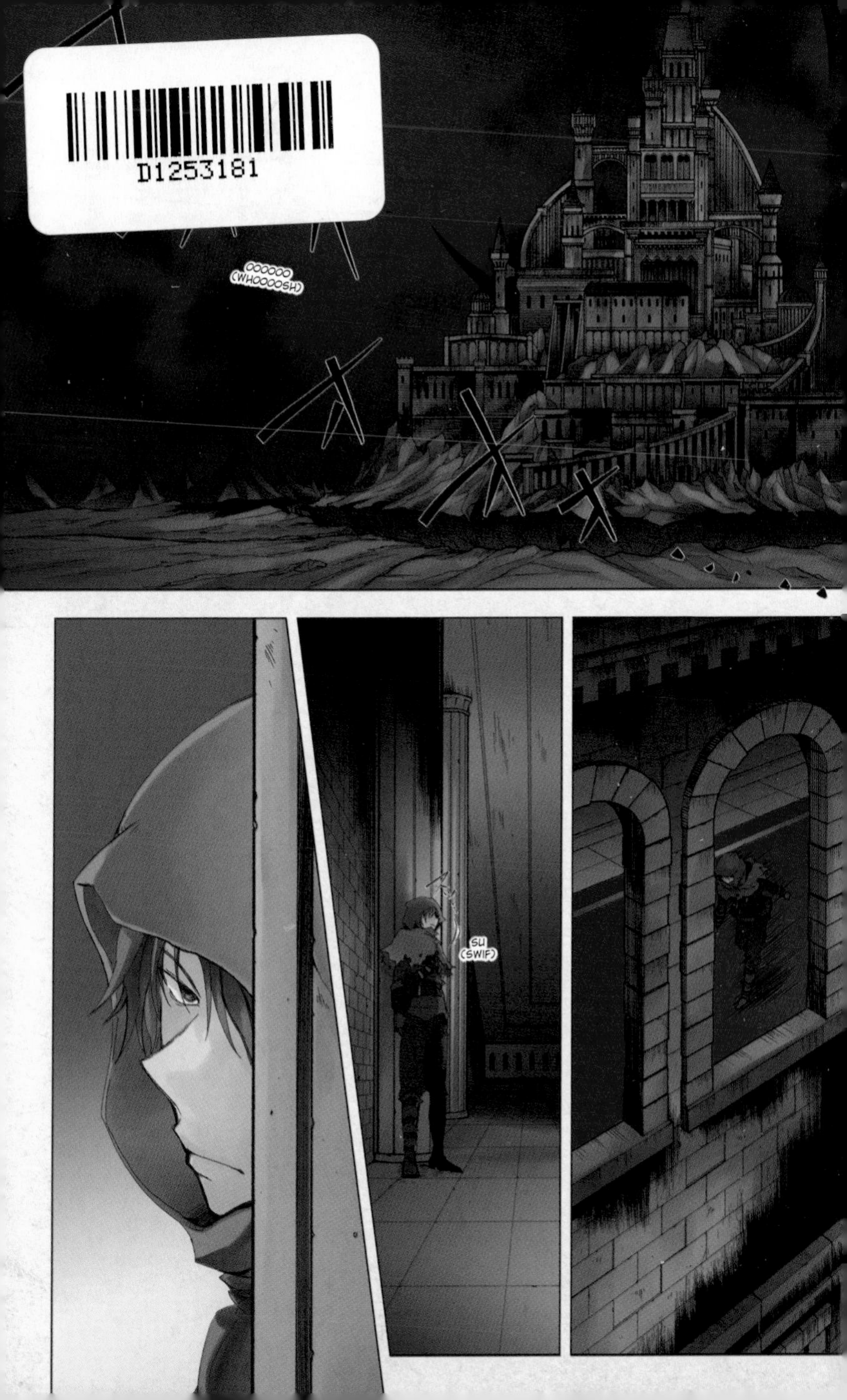
OOOOOO
(WHOOOOSH)
SU
(SWIF)

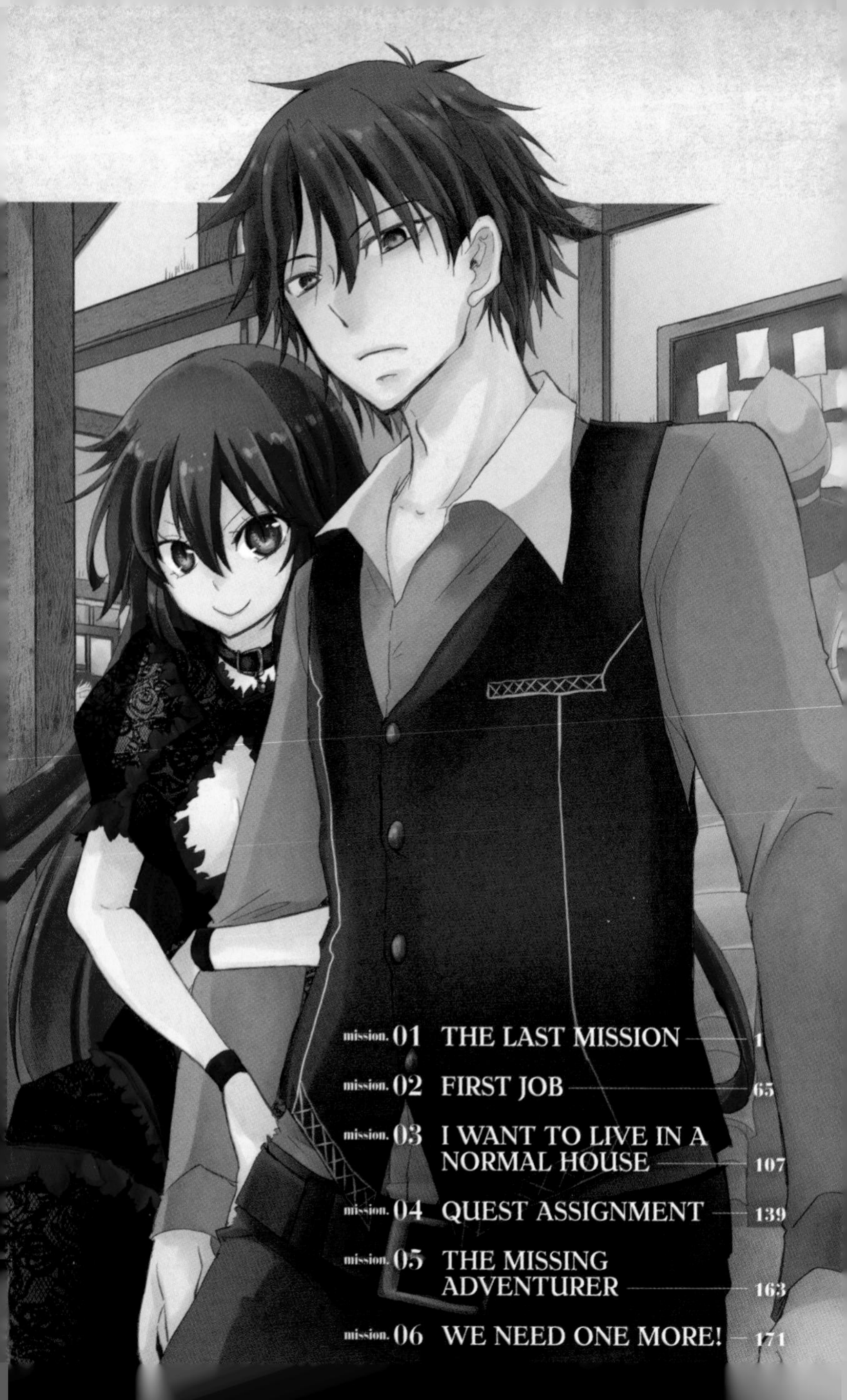

HAZURE SKILL

THE GUILD MEMBER WITH A WORTHLESS SKILL IS ACTUALLY A LEGENDARY ASSASSIN

Fuh Araki ORIGINAL STORY Kennoji CHARACTER DESIGN KWKM

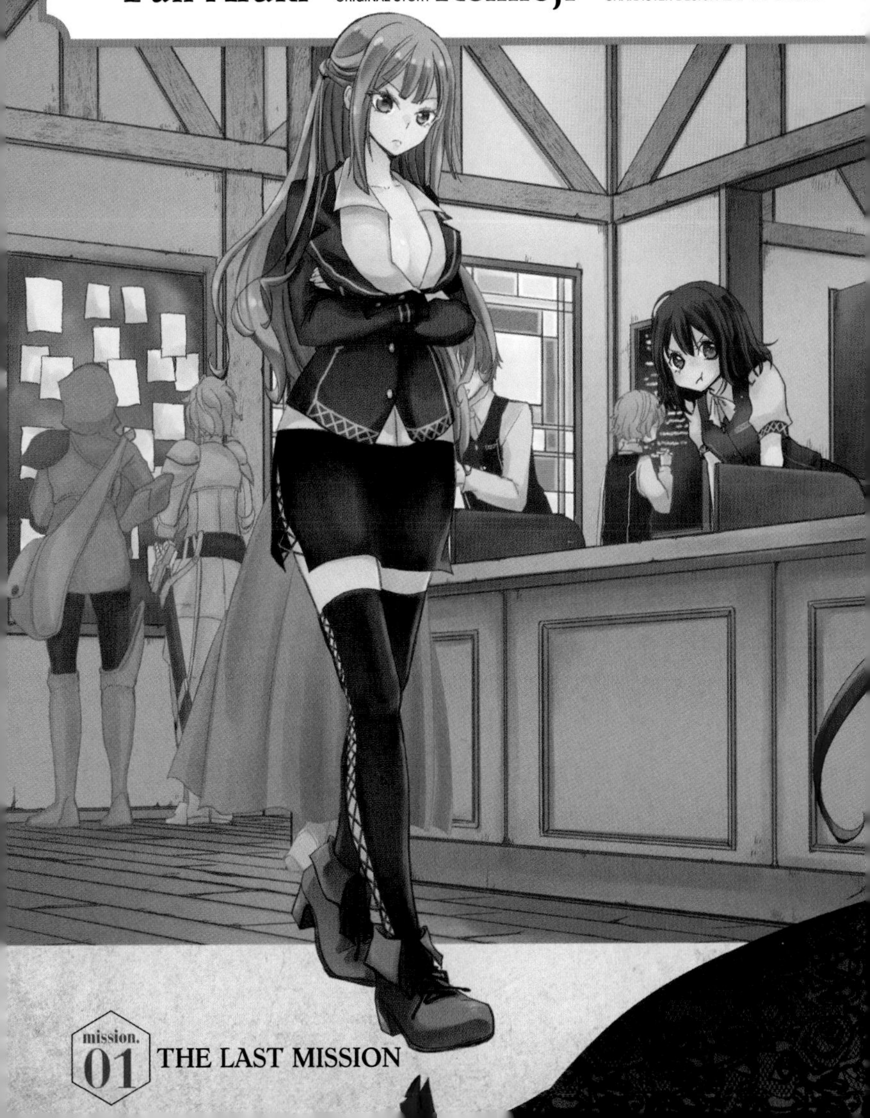

mission. 01 THE LAST MISSION

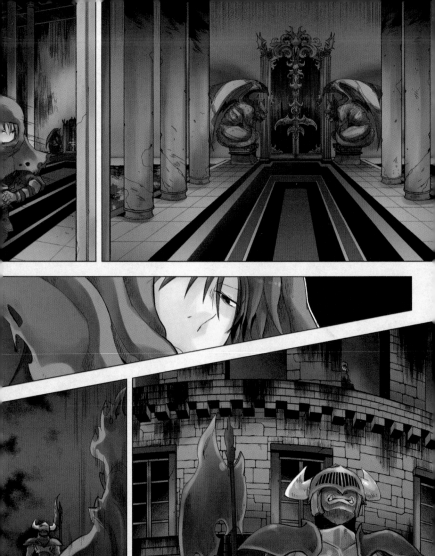

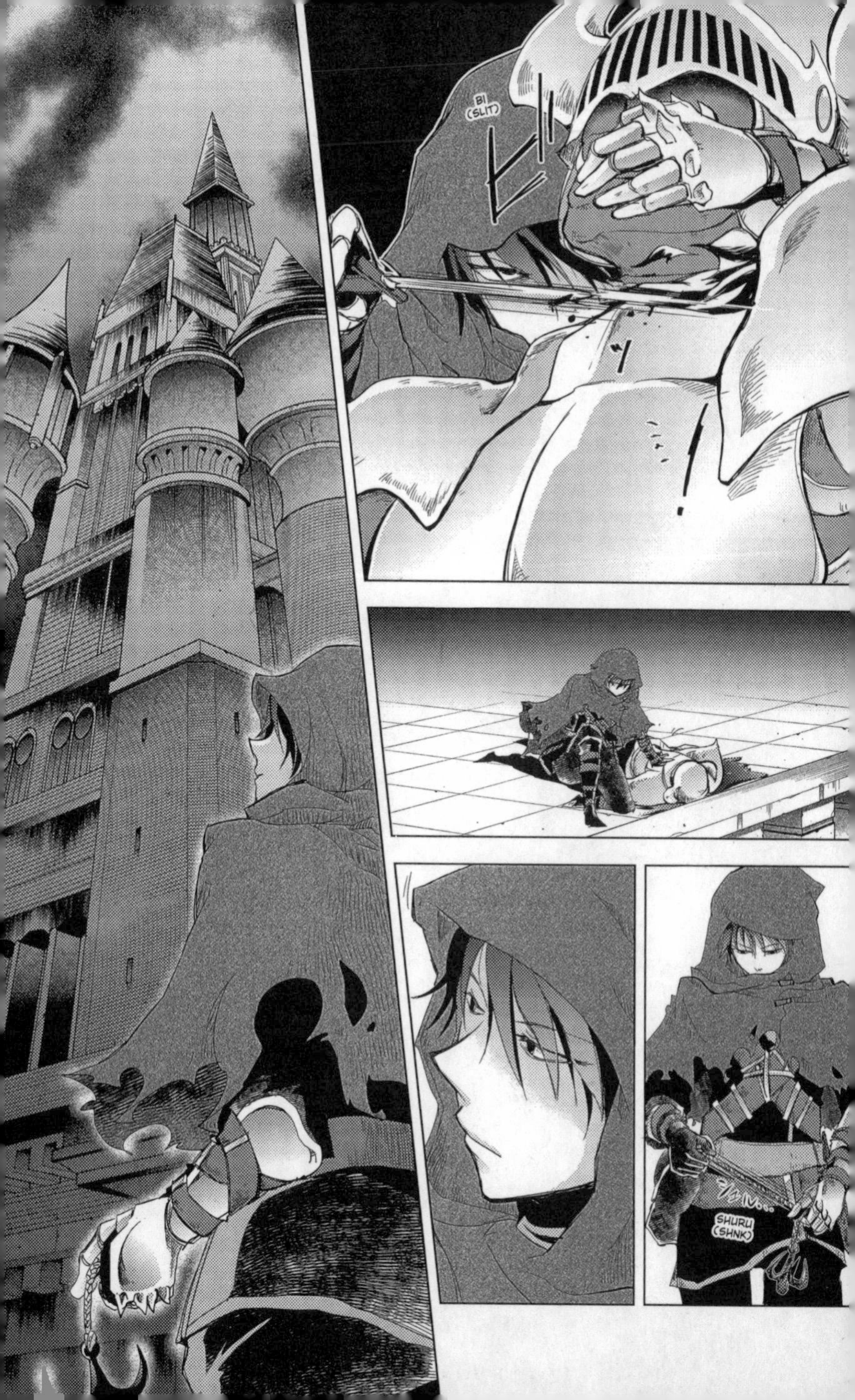
BI (SLIT)
SHURU (SHNK)

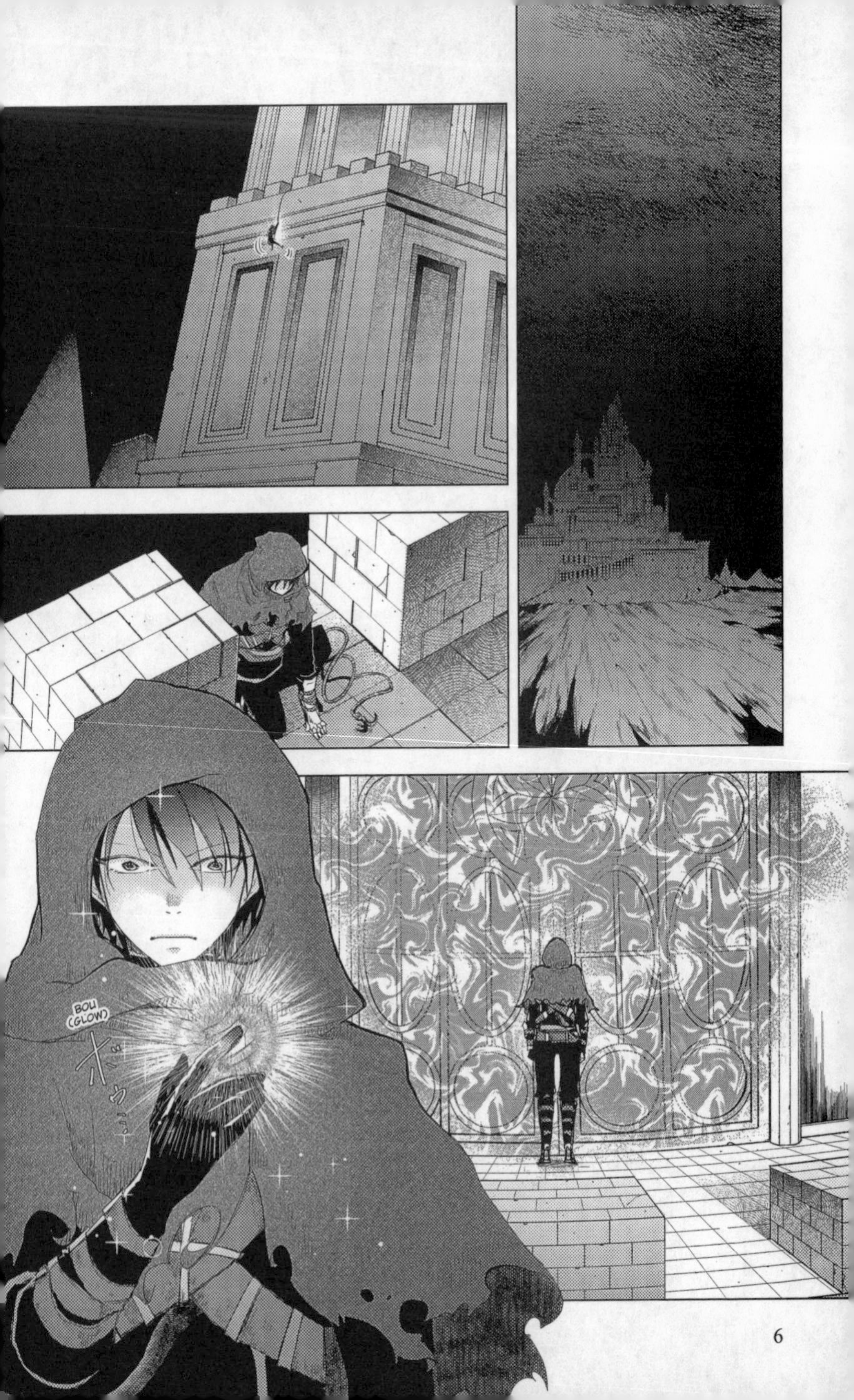
BOU (GLOW)

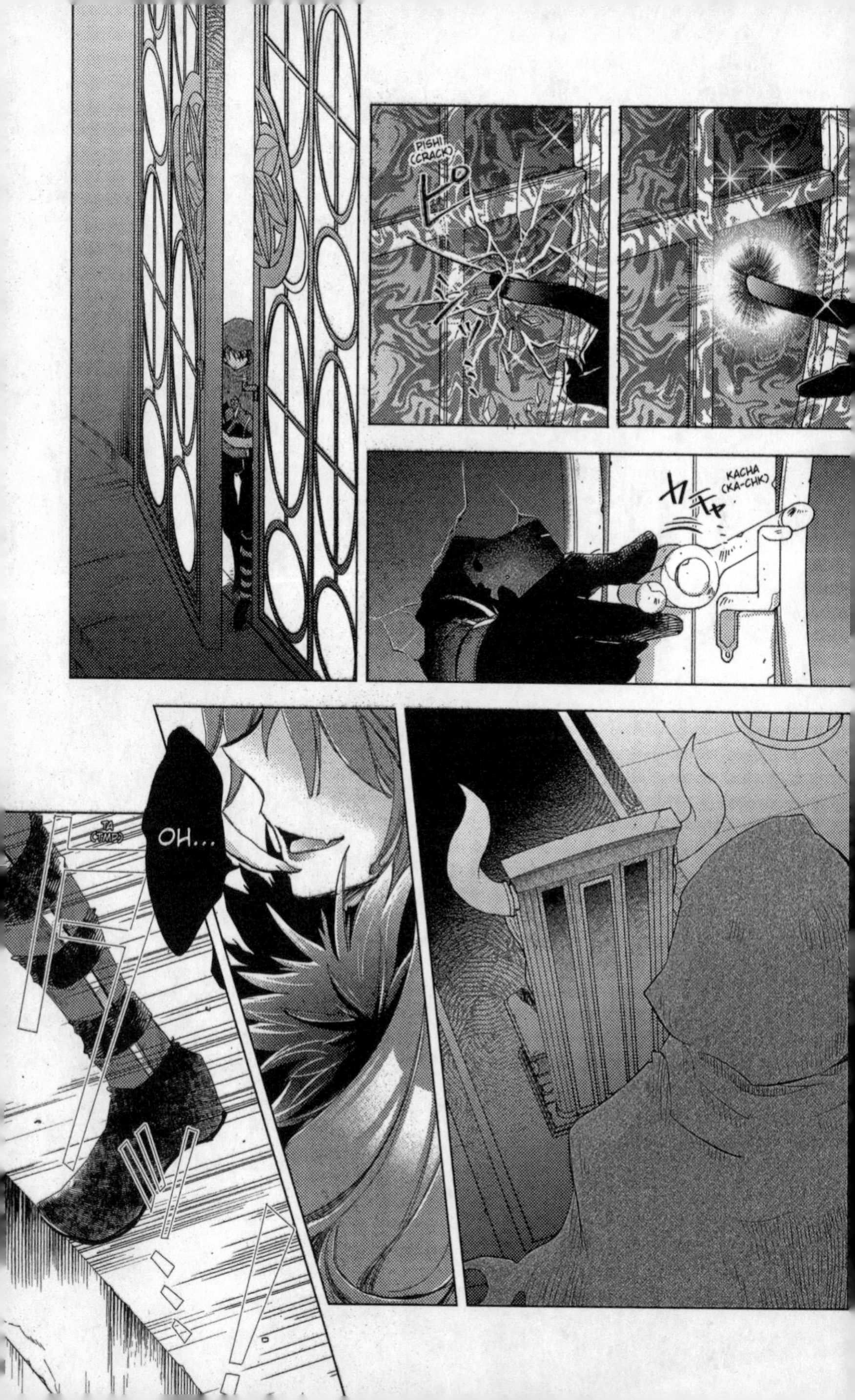
PISHI (CRACK)
KACHA (KA-CHK)
TA (TMP)
OH...

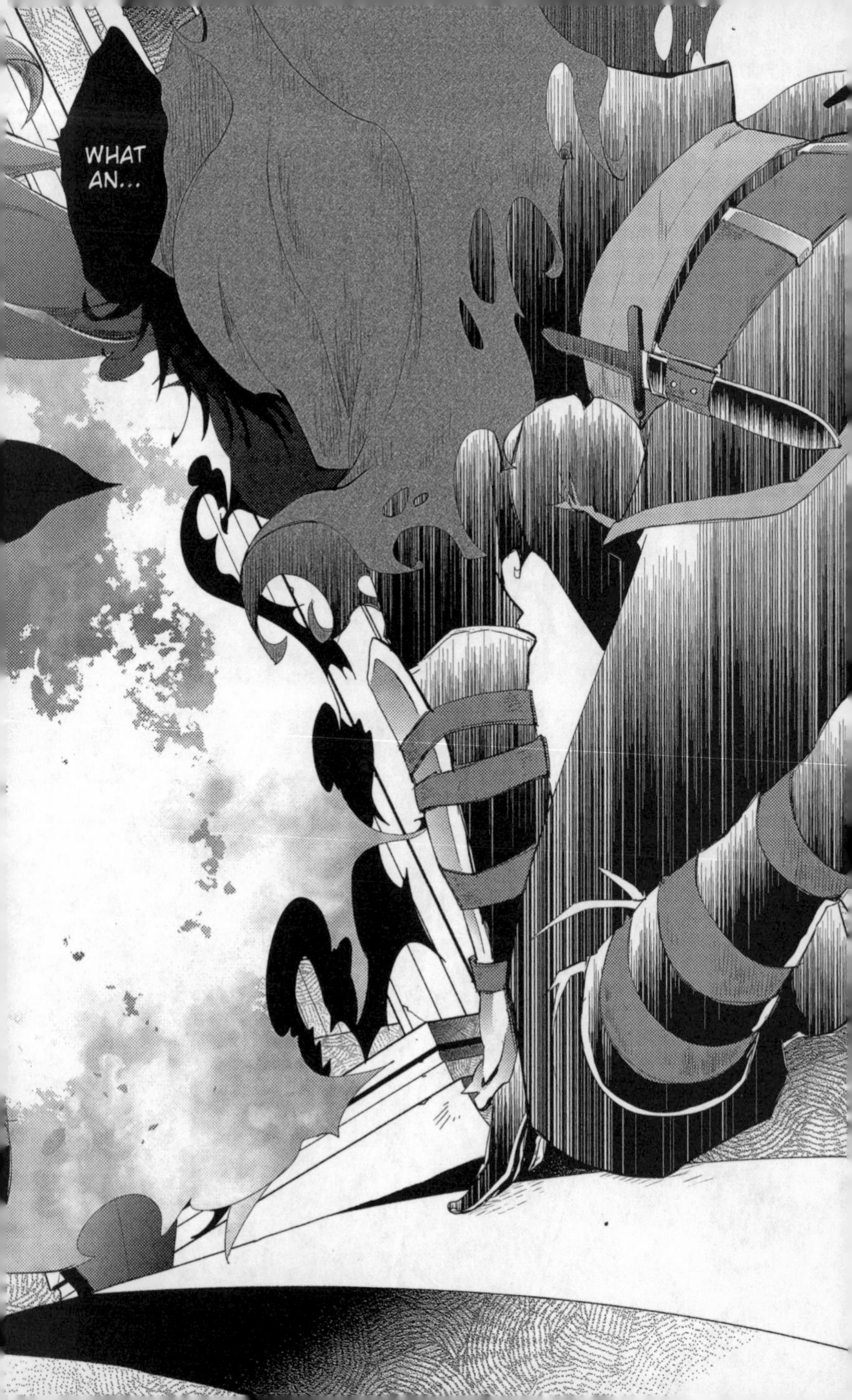
WHAT AN...

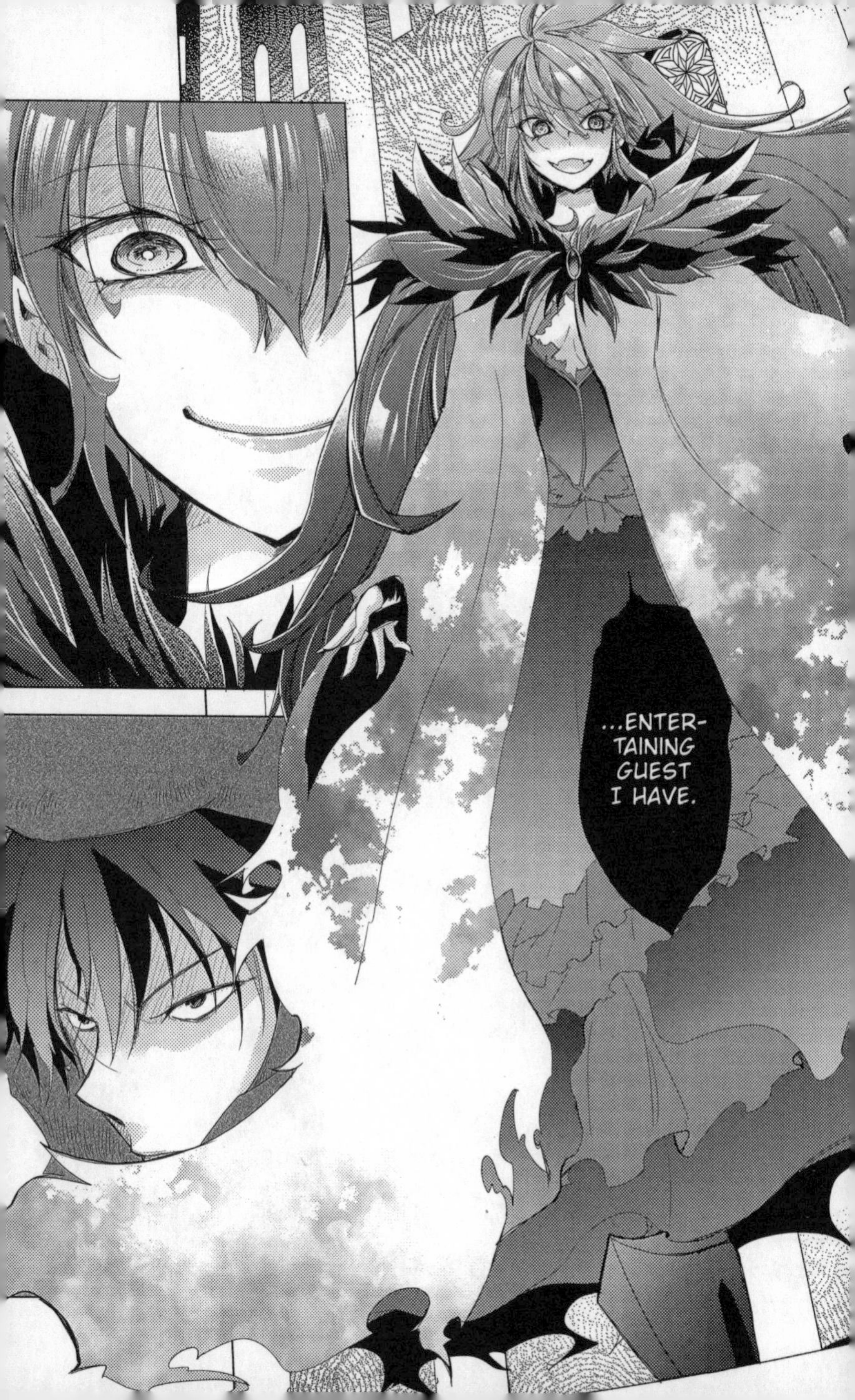
...ENTER-TAINING GUEST I HAVE.

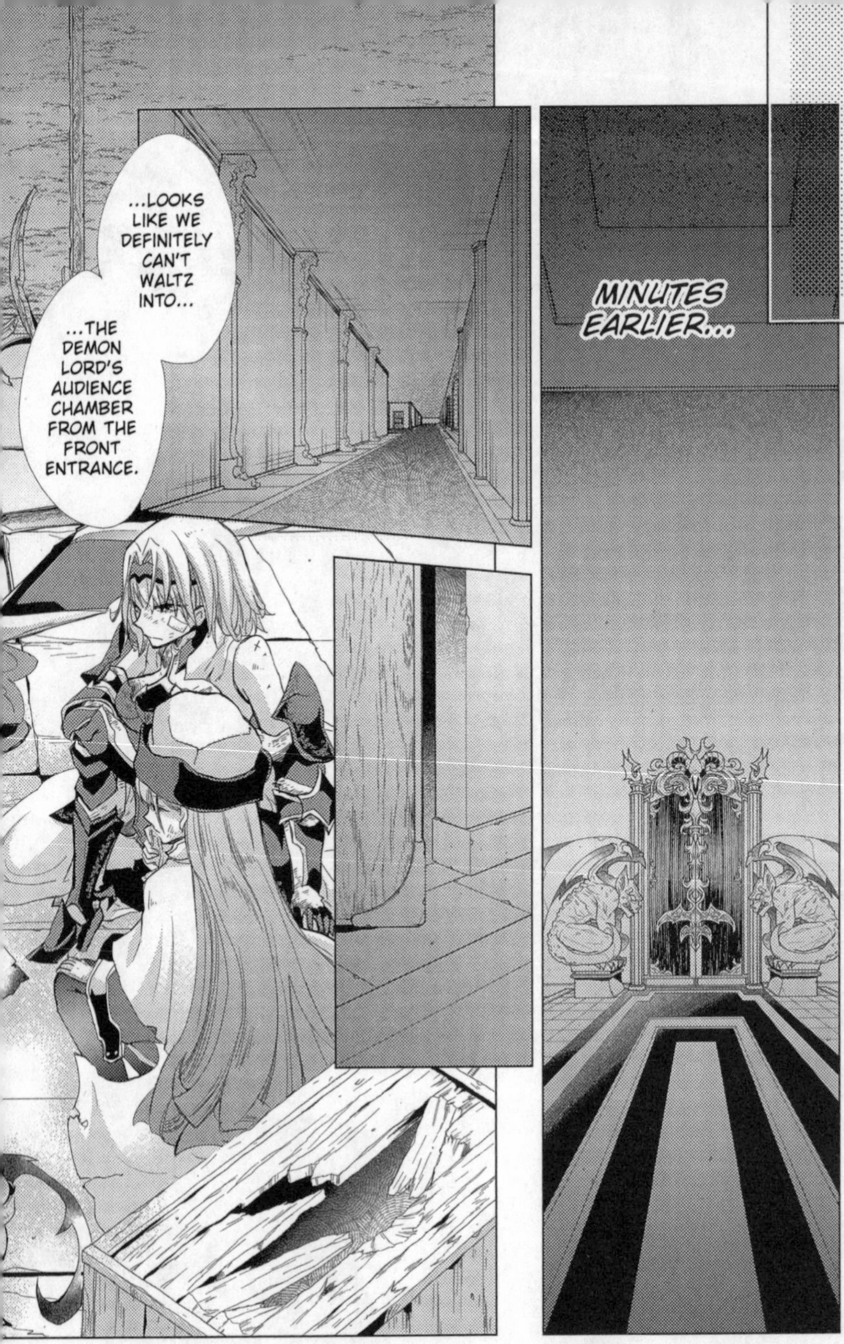
MINUTES EARLIER...
...LOOKS LIKE WE DEFINITELY CAN'T WALTZ INTO...
...THE DEMON LORD'S AUDIENCE CHAMBER FROM THE FRONT ENTRANCE.

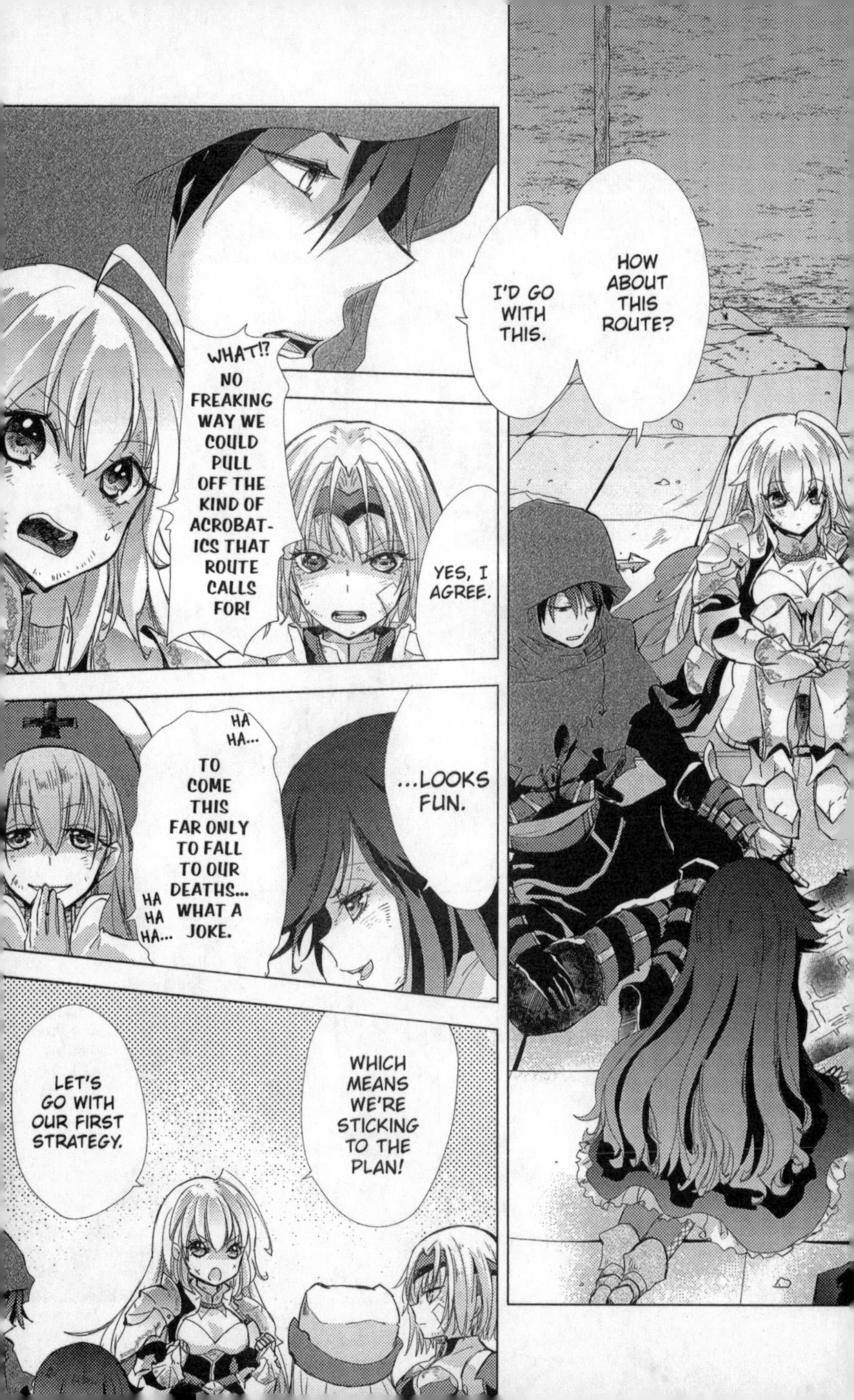
HOW ABOUT THIS ROUTE?
I'D GO WITH THIS.
WHAT!? NO FREAKING WAY WE COULD PULL OFF THE KIND OF ACROBAT-ICS THAT ROUTE CALLS FOR!
YES, I AGREE.
...LOOKS FUN.
HA HA... TO COME THIS FAR ONLY TO FALL TO OUR DEATHS... WHAT A JOKE.
HA HA HA...
WHICH MEANS WE'RE STICKING TO THE PLAN!
LET'S GO WITH OUR FIRST STRATEGY.

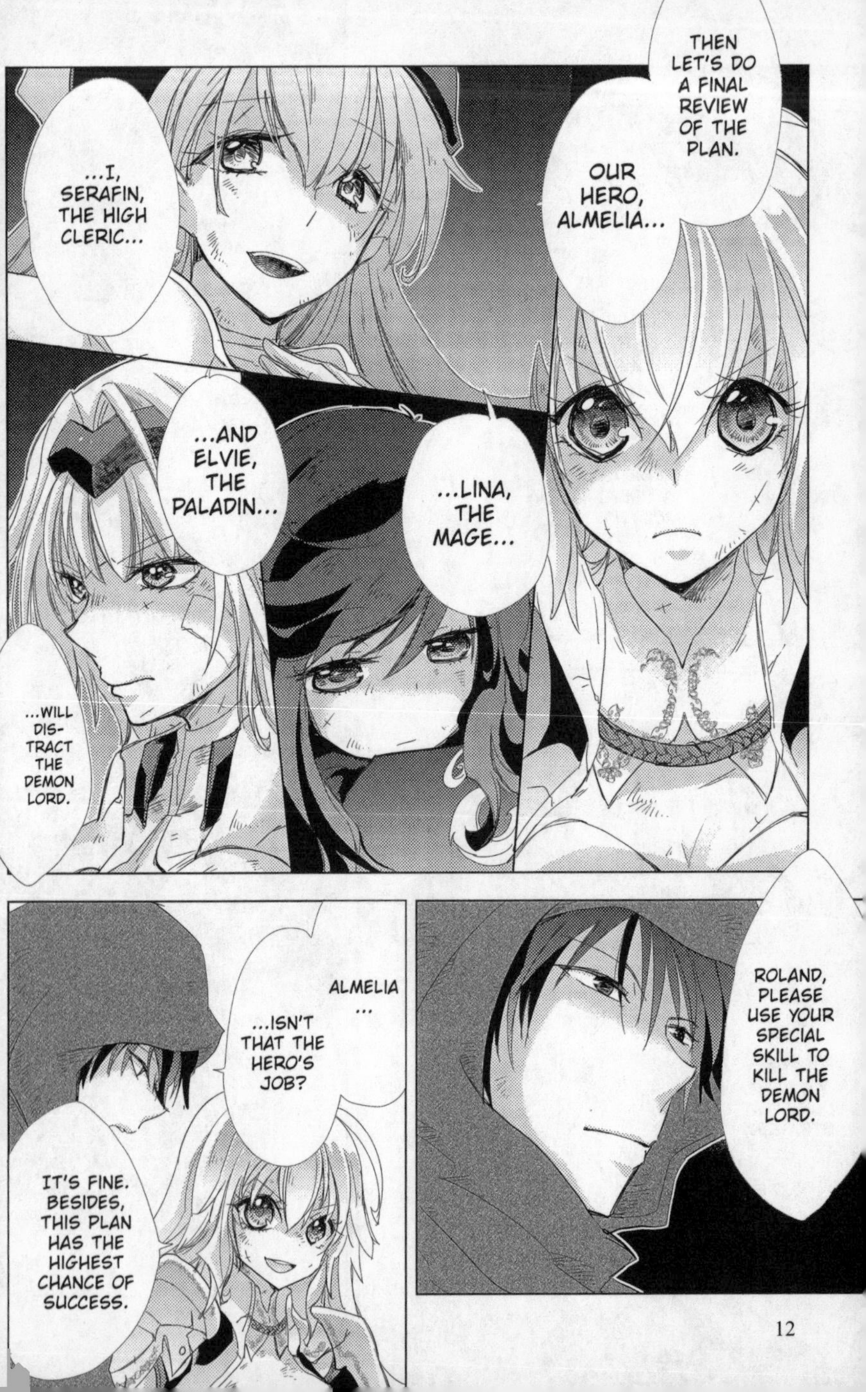
THEN LET'S DO A FINAL REVIEW OF THE PLAN.
OUR HERO, ALMELIA...
...I, SERAFIN, THE HIGH CLERIC...
...LINA, THE MAGE...
...AND ELVIE, THE PALADIN...
...WILL DIS-TRACT THE DEMON LORD.
ROLAND, PLEASE USE YOUR SPECIAL SKILL TO KILL THE DEMON LORD.
ALMELIA...
...ISN'T THAT THE HERO'S JOB?
IT'S FINE. BESIDES, THIS PLAN HAS THE HIGHEST CHANCE OF SUCCESS.

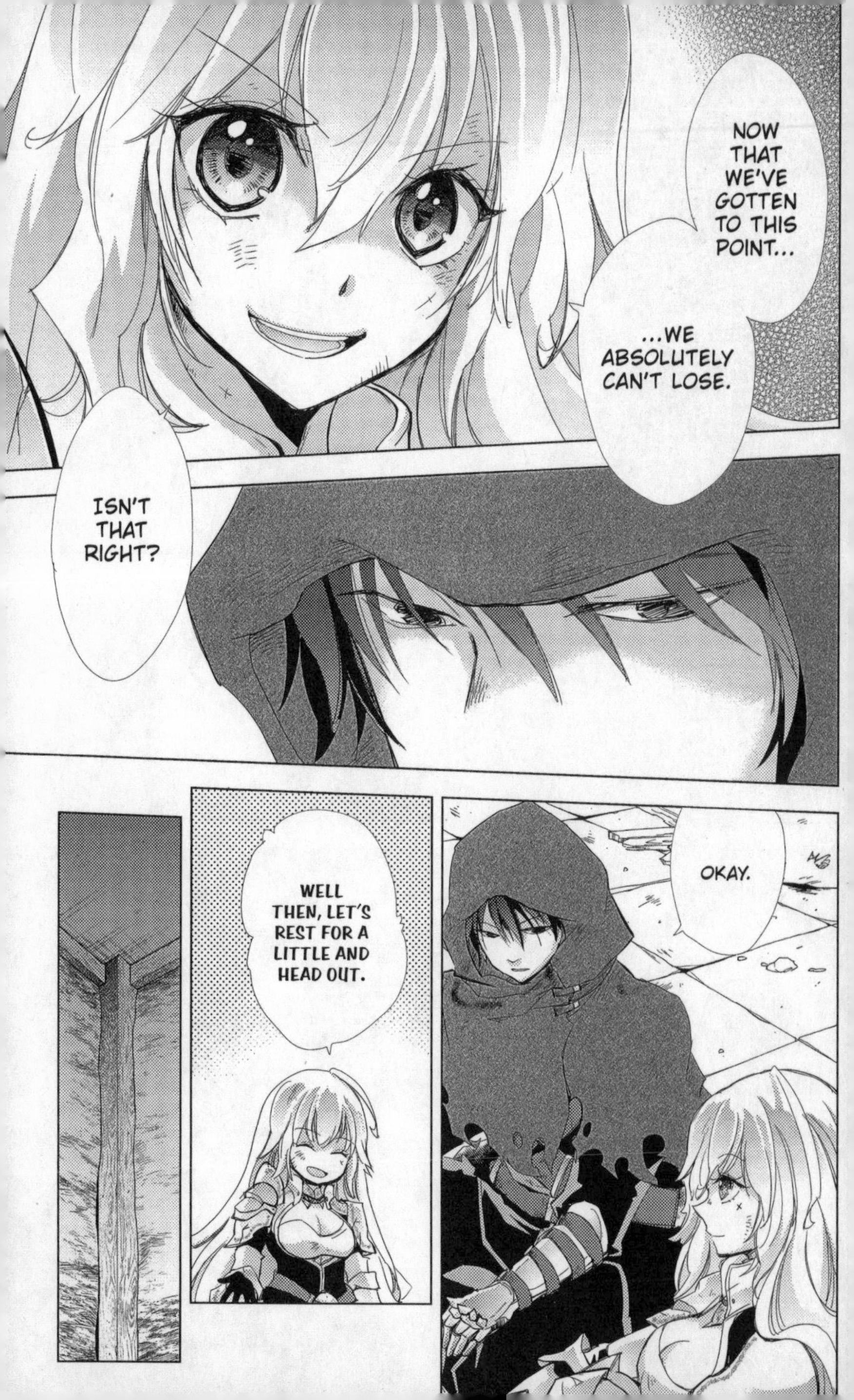
NOW THAT WE'VE GOTTEN TO THIS POINT...
...WE ABSOLUTELY CAN'T LOSE.
ISN'T THAT RIGHT?
OKAY.
WELL THEN, LET'S REST FOR A LITTLE AND HEAD OUT.

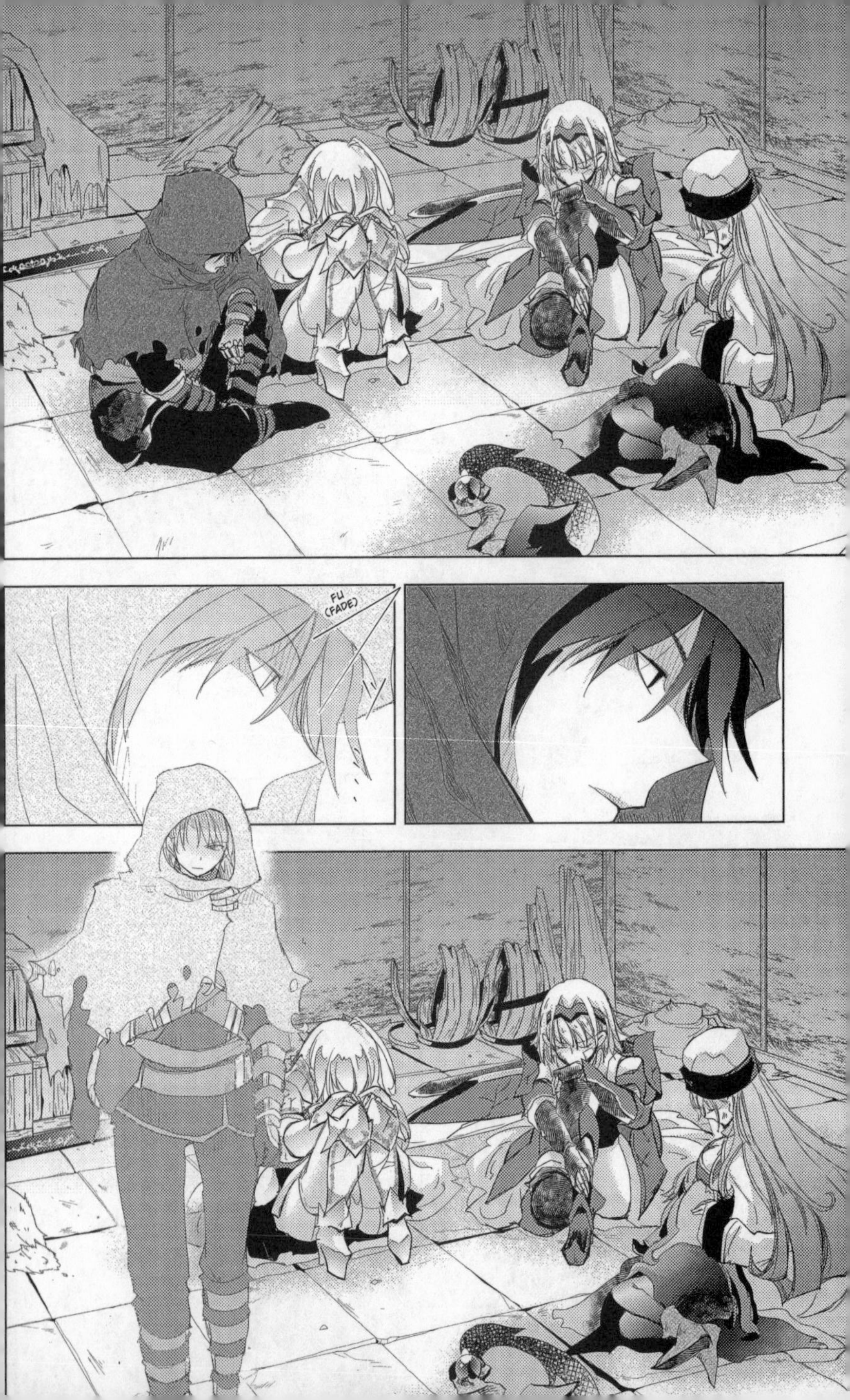
FU
(FADE)

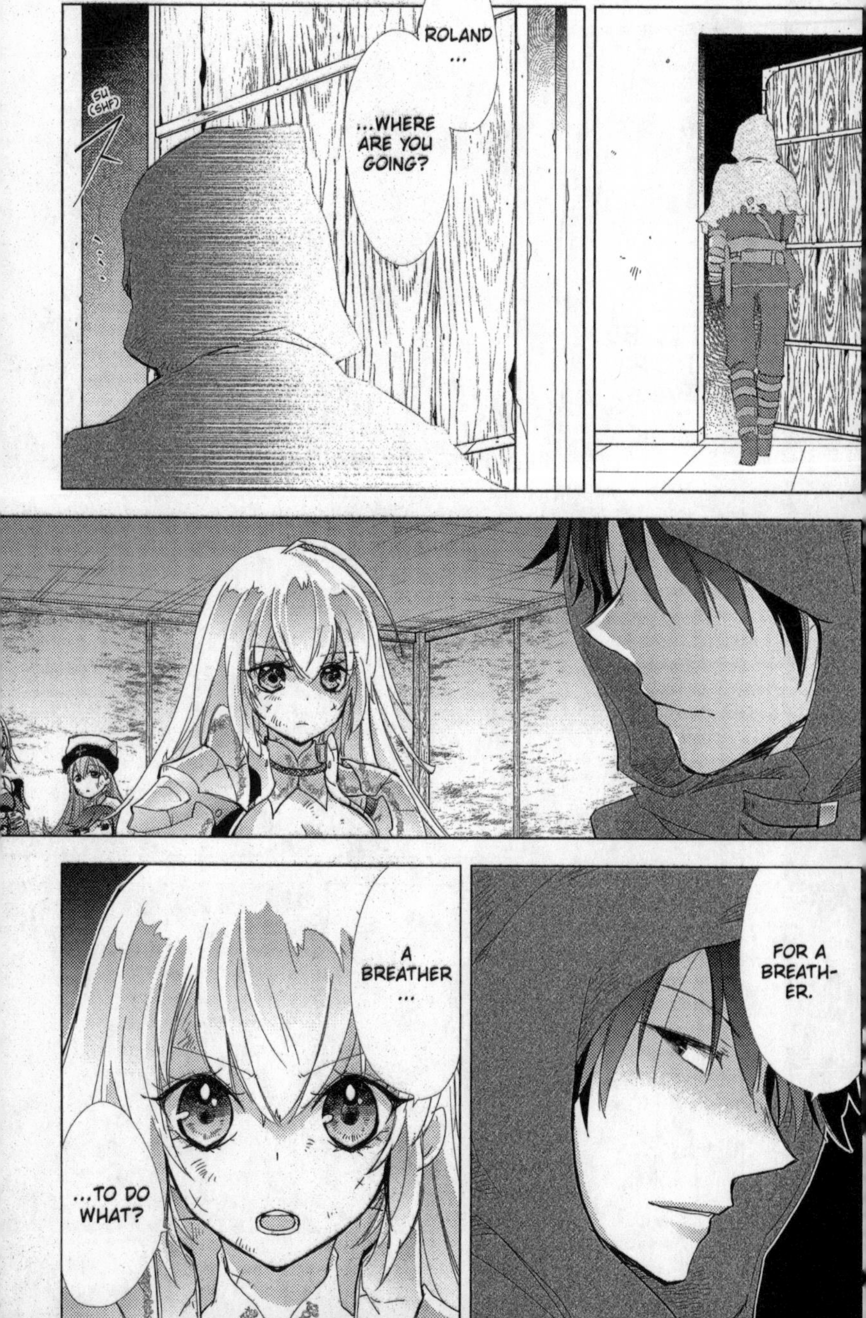
ROLAND...
...WHERE ARE YOU GOING?
SU (SHF)
FOR A BREATHER.
A BREATHER...
...TO DO WHAT?

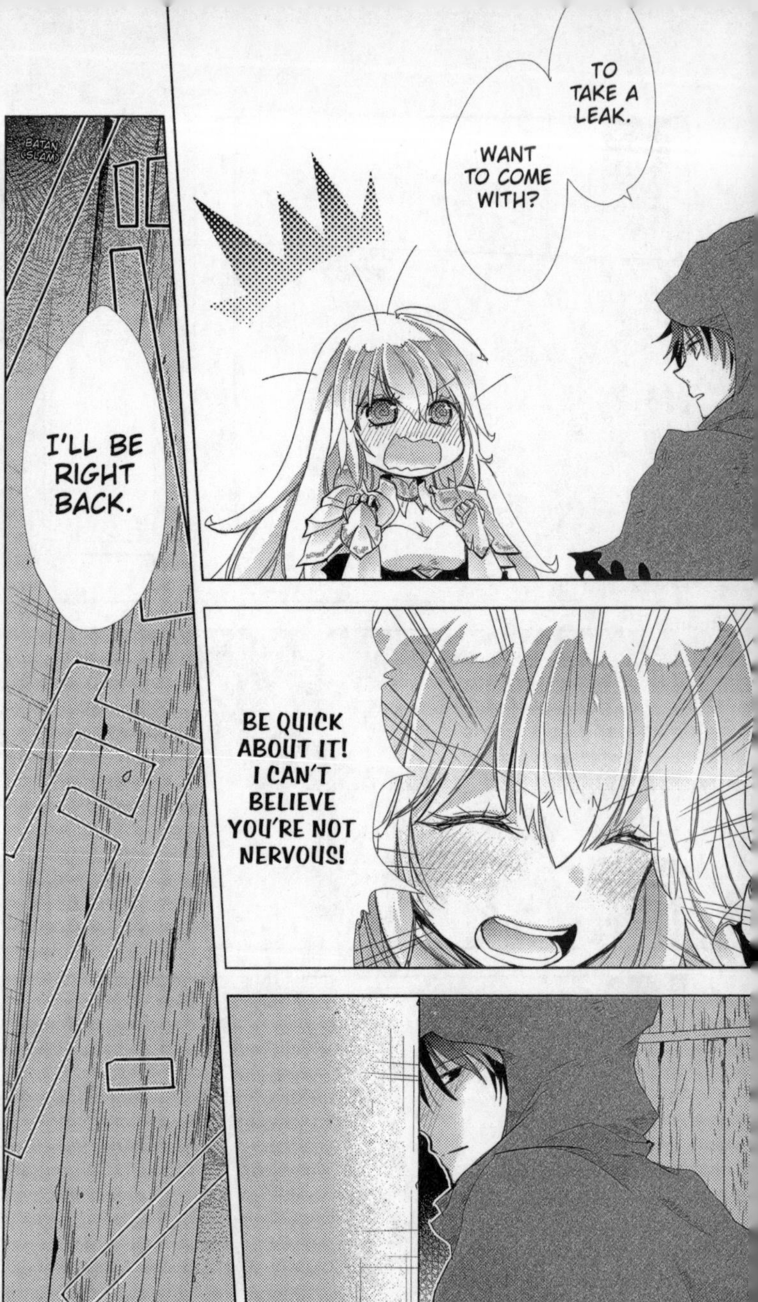
TO TAKE A LEAK.
WANT TO COME WITH?
BE QUICK ABOUT IT! I CAN'T BELIEVE YOU'RE NOT NERVOUS!
BATAN (SLAM)
I'LL BE RIGHT BACK.

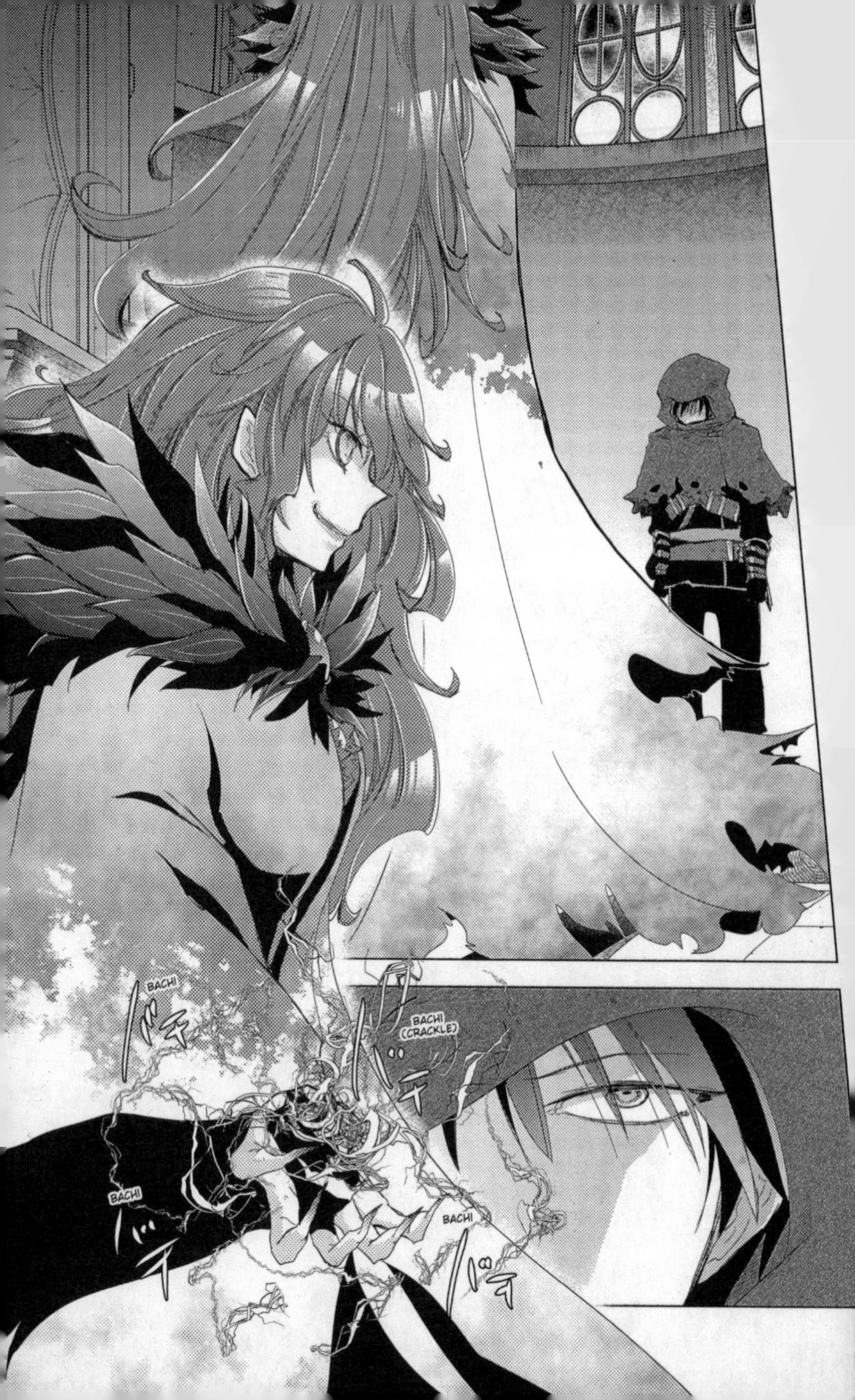
BACHI (CRACKLE)
BACHI
BACHI
BACHI

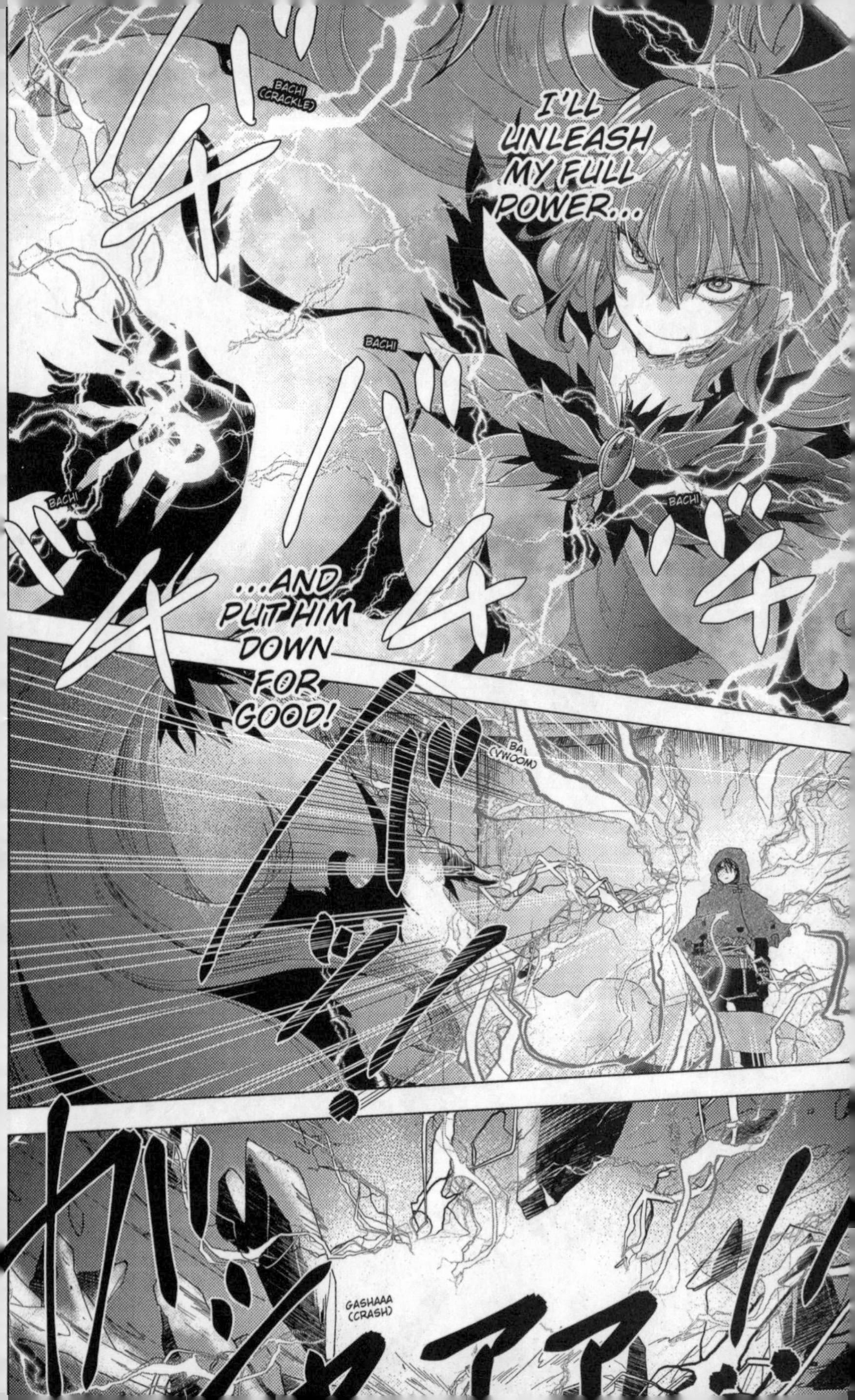
I'LL UNLEASH MY FULL POWER...
BACHI
BACHI
BACHI (CRACKLE)
BACHI
...AND PUT HIM DOWN FOR GOOD!
BA (VWOOM)
GASHAAA (CRASH)

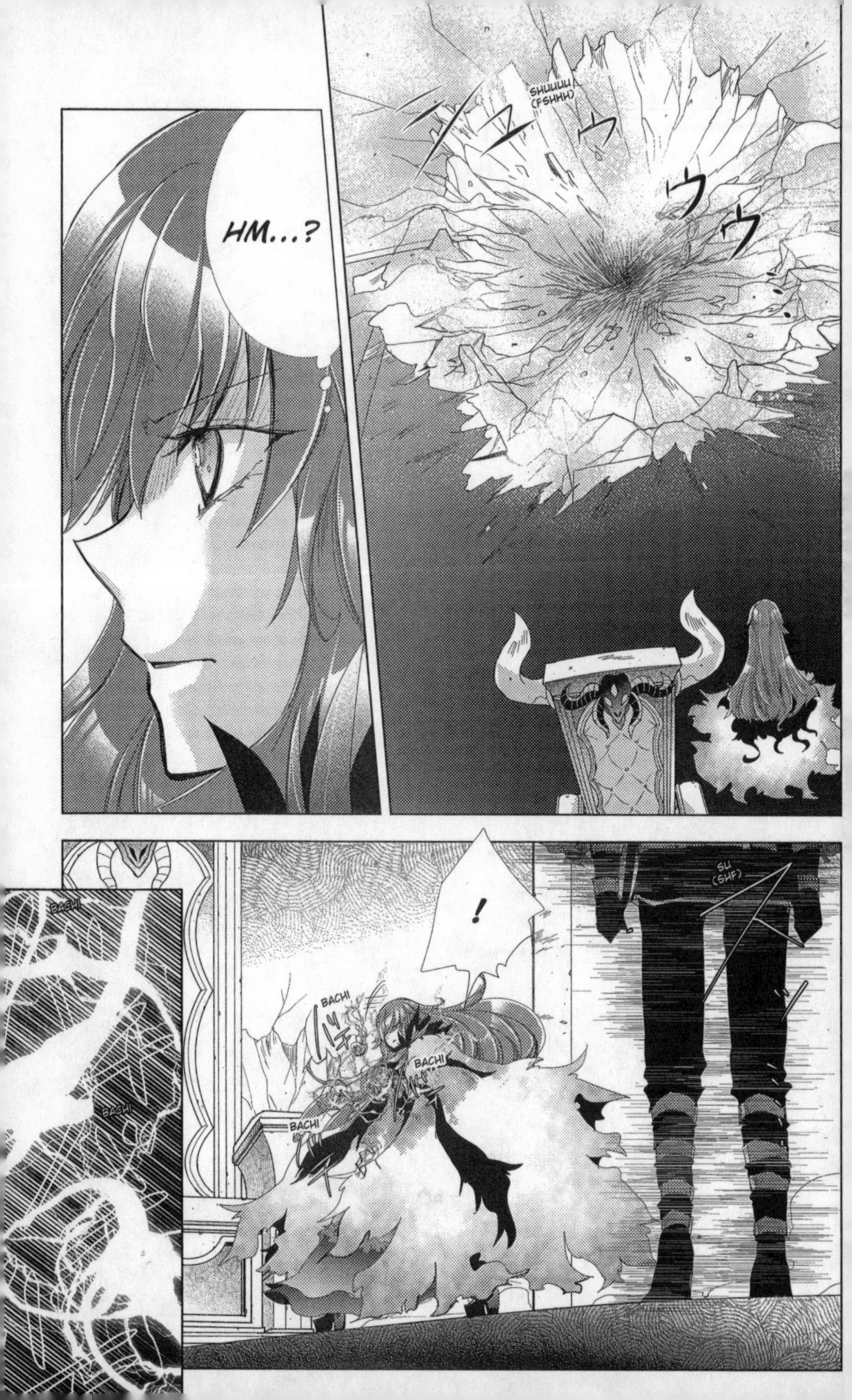
SHUUUU (FSHHH)
HM...?
SU (SHF)
!
BACHI
BACHI
BACHI
BACHI
BACHI

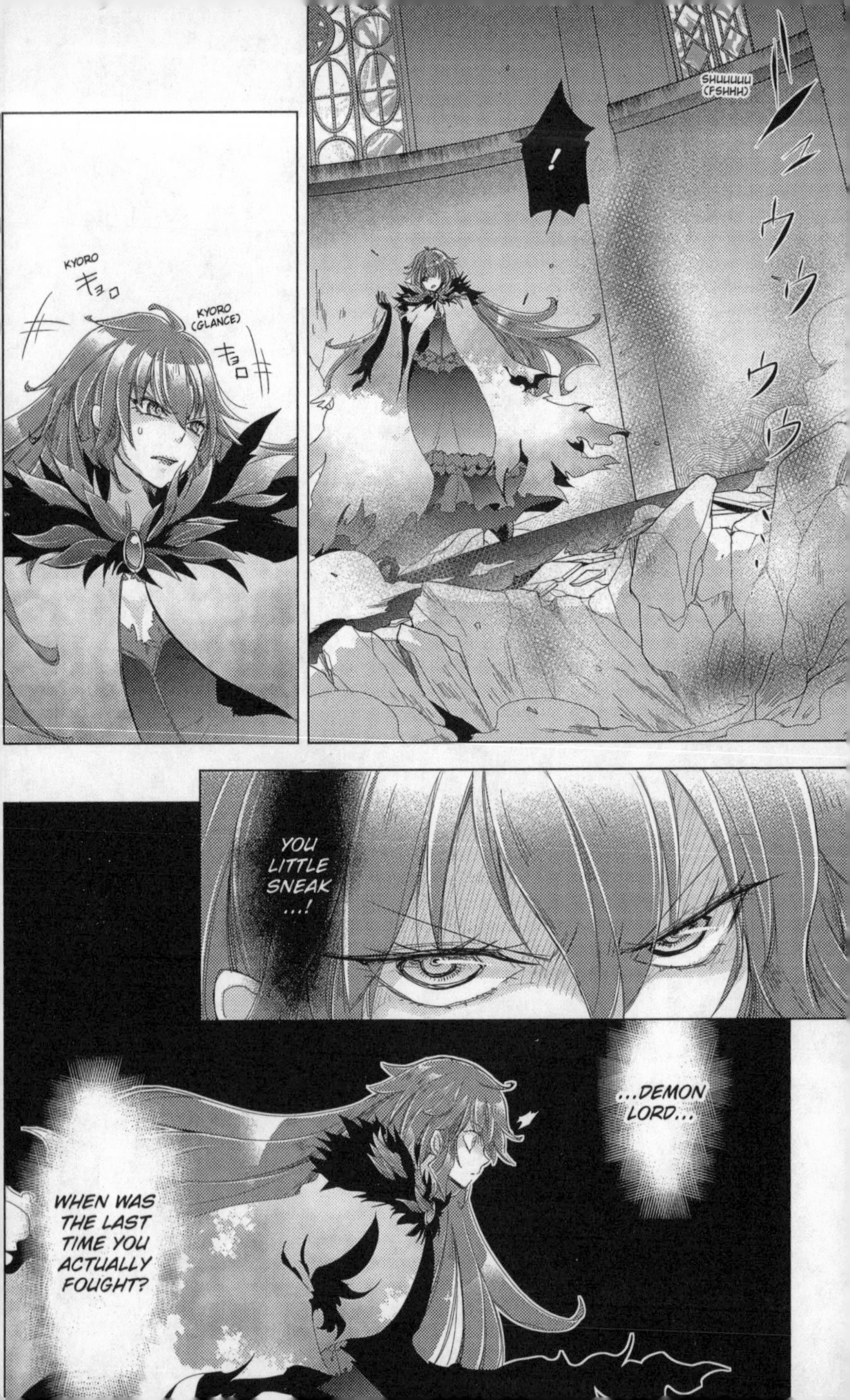
SHUUUUU
(FSHHH)
!
KYORO
キョロ
KYORO
(GLANCE)
キョロ
YOU LITTLE SNEAK ...!
...DEMON LORD...
WHEN WAS THE LAST TIME YOU ACTUALLY FOUGHT?

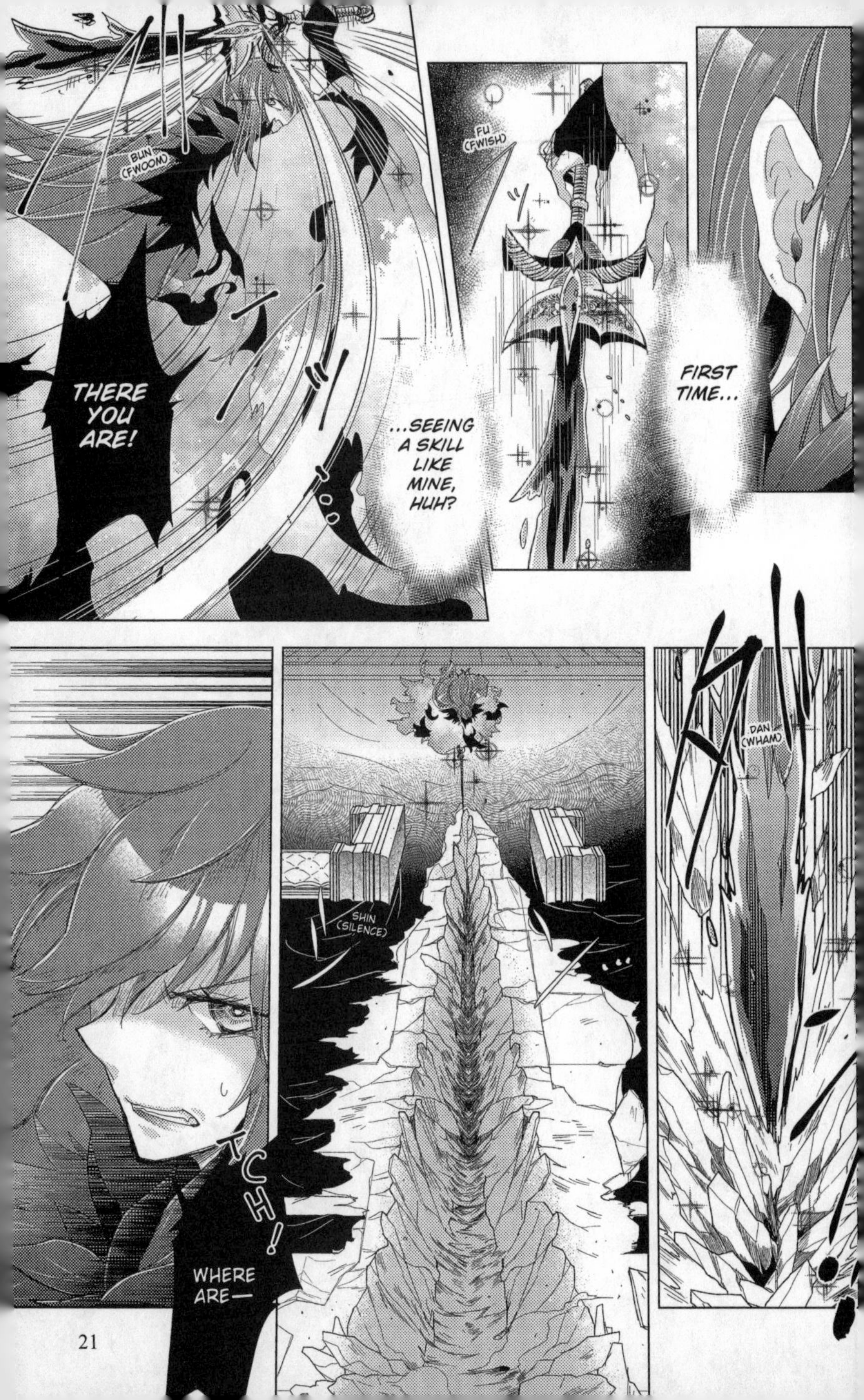
FIRST TIME...
FU (FWISH)
...SEEING A SKILL LIKE MINE, HUH?
BUN (FWOOM)
THERE YOU ARE!
DAN (WHAM)
SHIN (SILENCE)
TCH!
WHERE ARE—

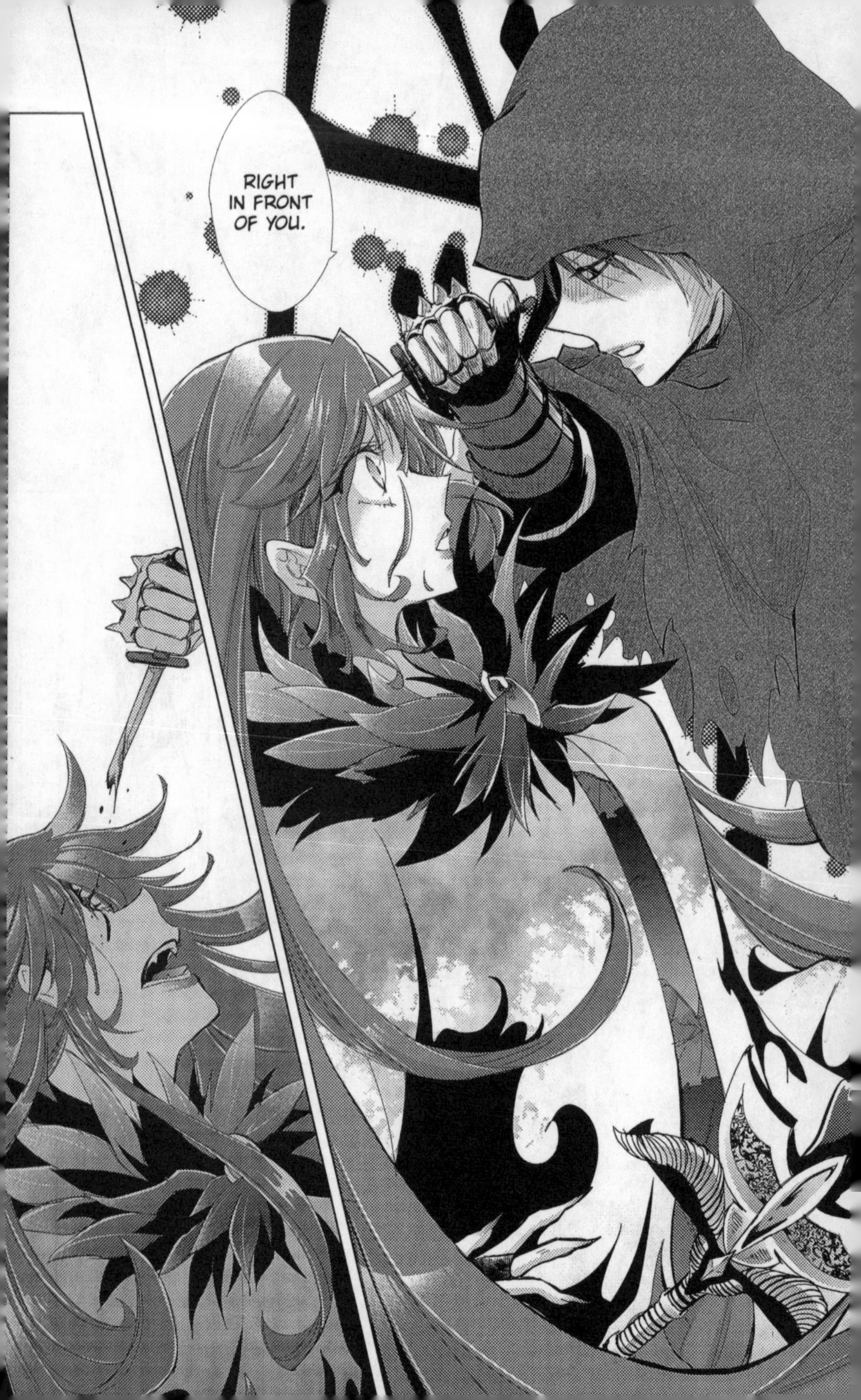
RIGHT IN FRONT OF YOU.

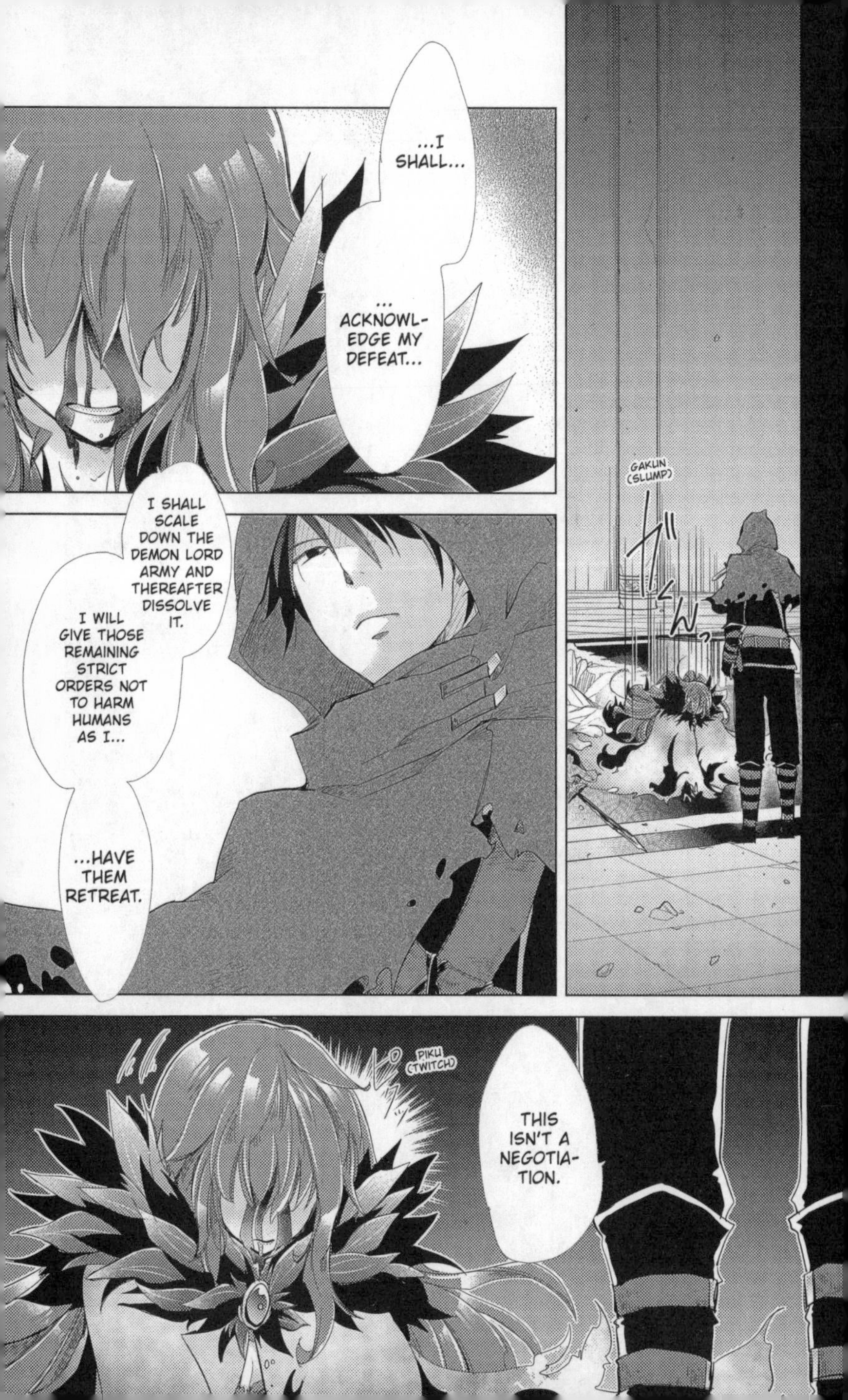
GAKUN (SLUMP)
...I SHALL...
...ACKNOWL-EDGE MY DEFEAT...
I SHALL SCALE DOWN THE DEMON LORD ARMY AND THEREAFTER DISSOLVE IT.
I WILL GIVE THOSE REMAINING STRICT ORDERS NOT TO HARM HUMANS AS I...
...HAVE THEM RETREAT.
PIKU (TWITCH)
THIS ISN'T A NEGOTIA-TION.

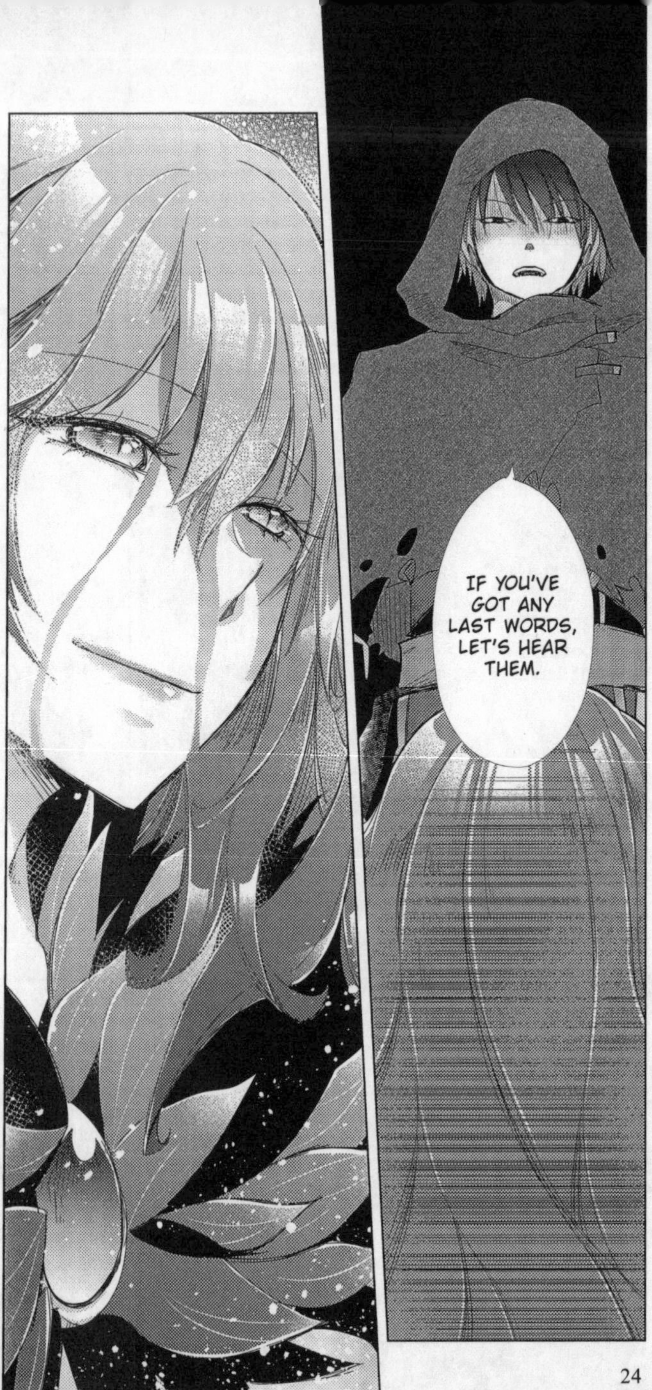
IF YOU'VE GOT ANY LAST WORDS, LET'S HEAR THEM.

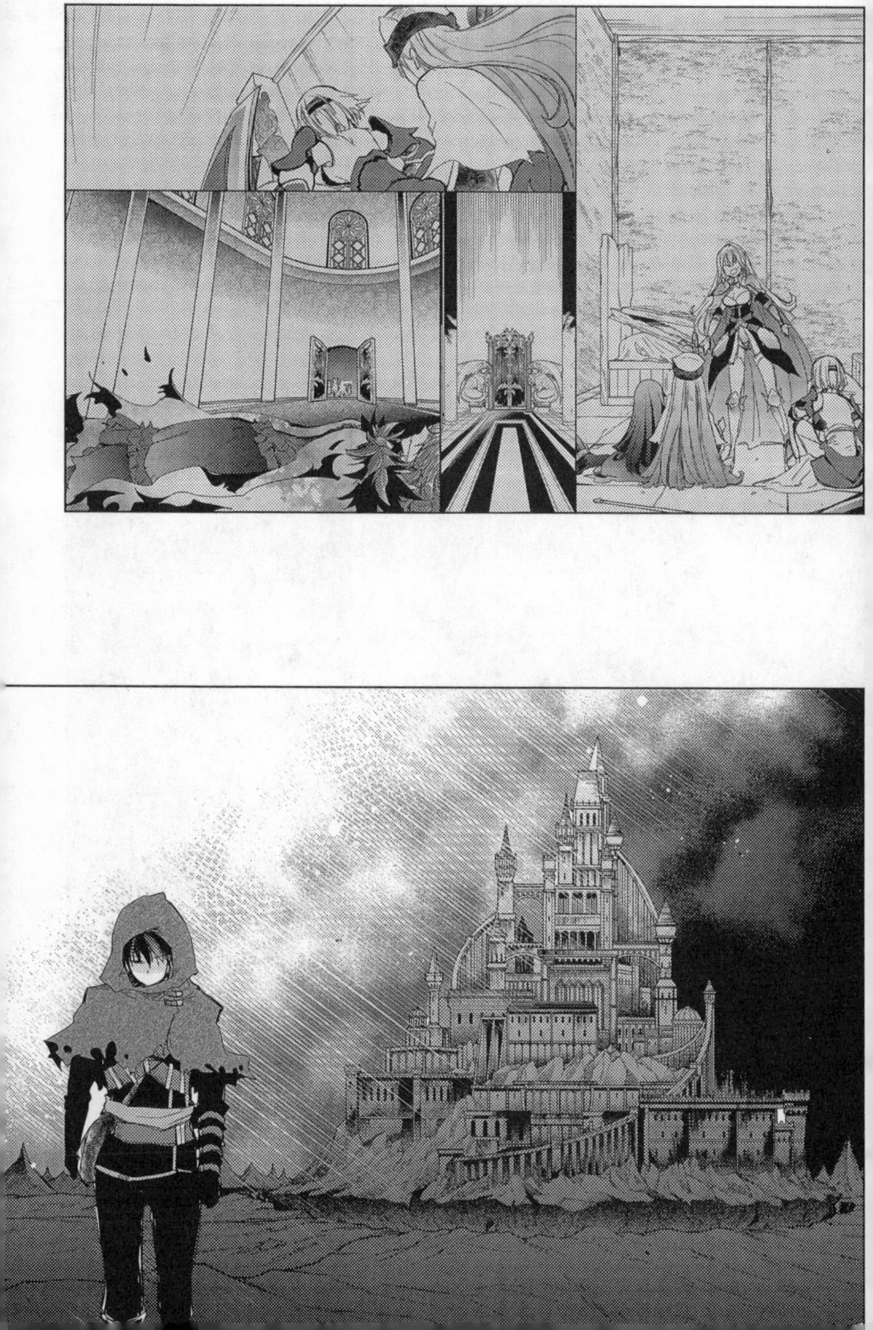

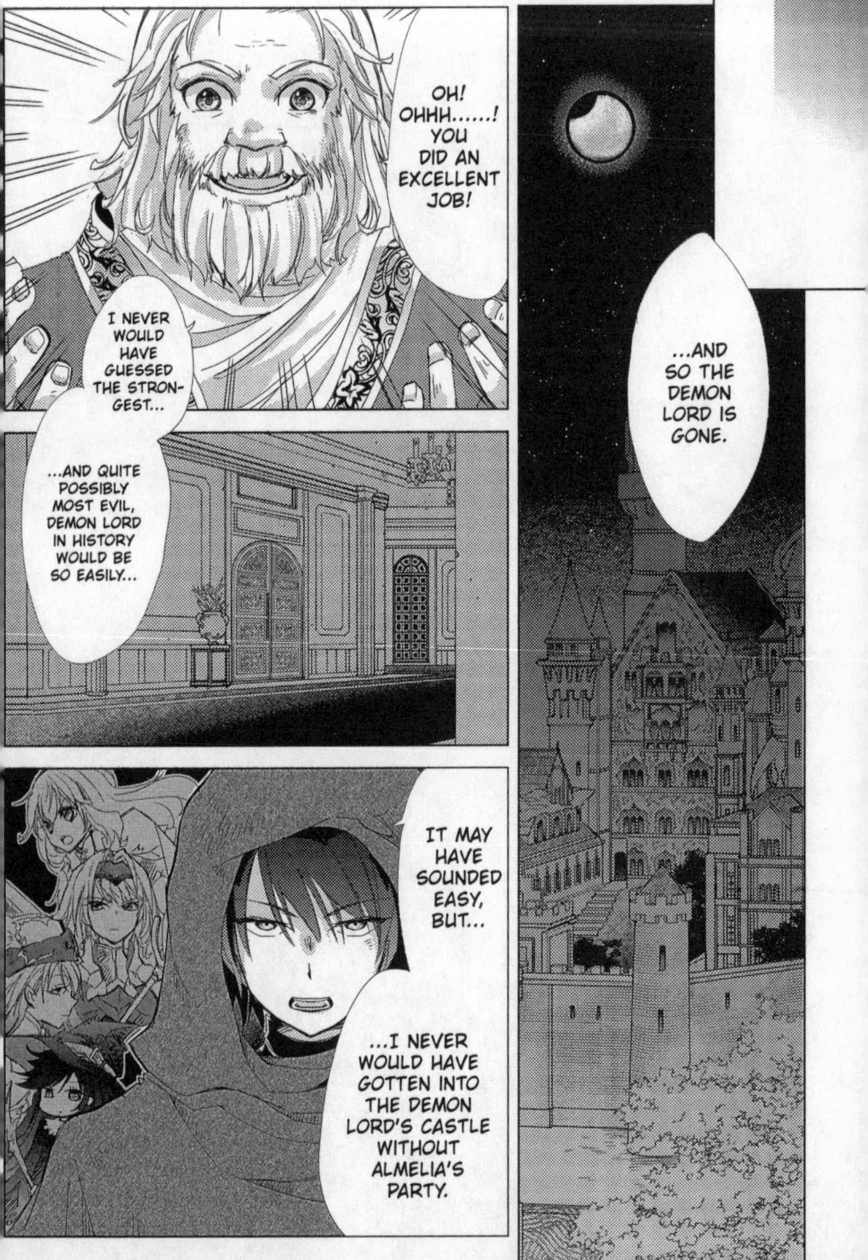
...AND SO THE DEMON LORD IS GONE.
OH! OHHH......! YOU DID AN EXCELLENT JOB!
I NEVER WOULD HAVE GUESSED THE STRONG-GEST...
...AND QUITE POSSIBLY MOST EVIL, DEMON LORD IN HISTORY WOULD BE SO EASILY...
IT MAY HAVE SOUNDED EASY, BUT...
...I NEVER WOULD HAVE GOTTEN INTO THE DEMON LORD'S CASTLE WITHOUT ALMELIA'S PARTY.

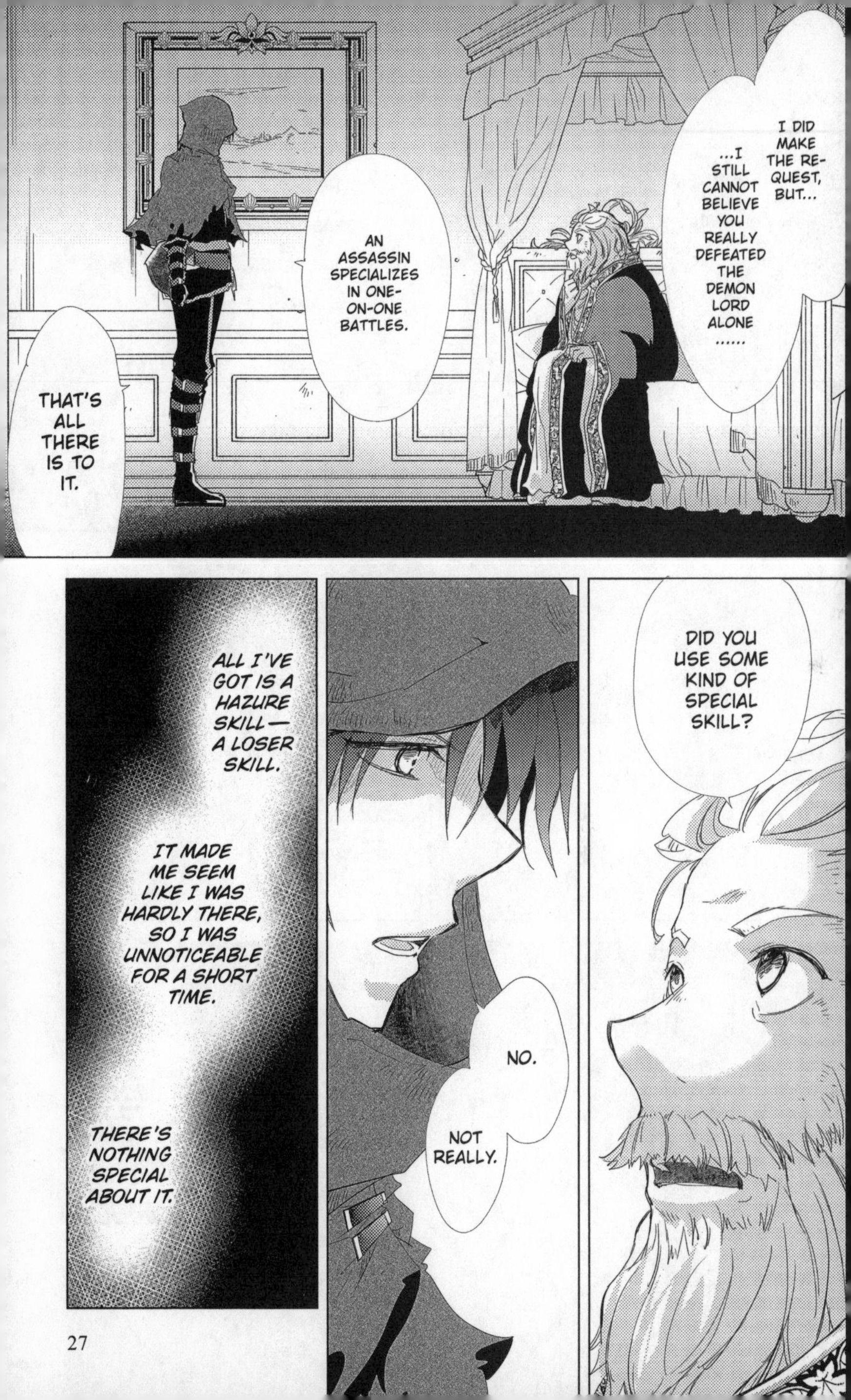
I DID MAKE THE RE-QUEST, BUT...
...I STILL CANNOT BELIEVE YOU REALLY DEFEATED THE DEMON LORD ALONE ......
AN ASSASSIN SPECIALIZES IN ONE-ON-ONE BATTLES.
THAT'S ALL THERE IS TO IT.
DID YOU USE SOME KIND OF SPECIAL SKILL?
NO.
NOT REALLY.
ALL I'VE GOT IS A HAZURE SKILL—A LOSER SKILL.
IT MADE ME SEEM LIKE I WAS HARDLY THERE, SO I WAS UNNOTICEABLE FOR A SHORT TIME.
THERE'S NOTHING SPECIAL ABOUT IT.

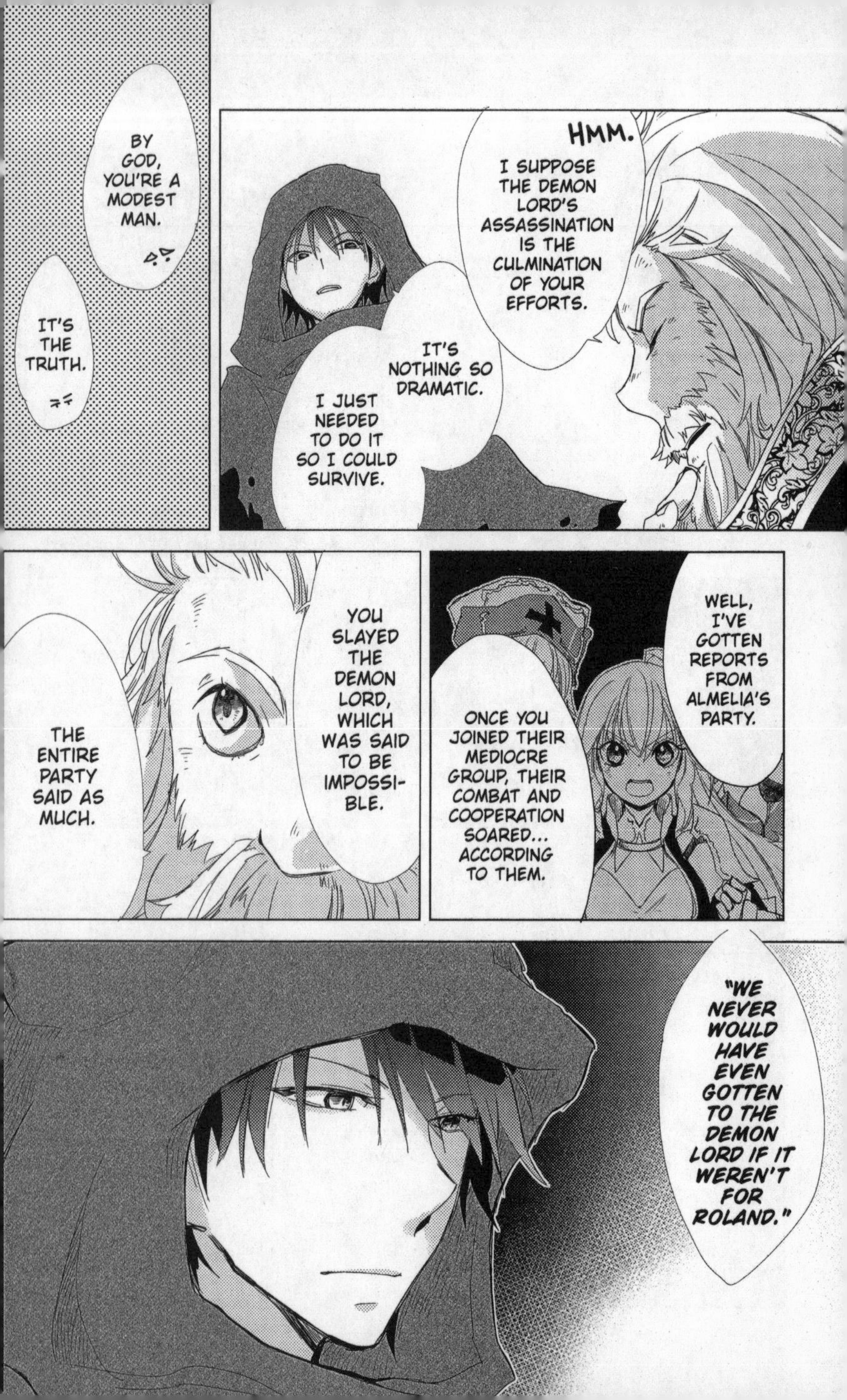
HMM.
I SUPPOSE THE DEMON LORD'S ASSASSINATION IS THE CULMINATION OF YOUR EFFORTS.
IT'S NOTHING SO DRAMATIC.
I JUST NEEDED TO DO IT SO I COULD SURVIVE.
BY GOD, YOU'RE A MODEST MAN.
IT'S THE TRUTH.
WELL, I'VE GOTTEN REPORTS FROM ALMELIA'S PARTY.
ONCE YOU JOINED THEIR MEDIOCRE GROUP, THEIR COMBAT AND COOPERATION SOARED... ACCORDING TO THEM.
YOU SLAYED THE DEMON LORD, WHICH WAS SAID TO BE IMPOSSIBLE.
THE ENTIRE PARTY SAID AS MUCH.
"WE NEVER WOULD HAVE EVEN GOTTEN TO THE DEMON LORD IF IT WEREN'T FOR ROLAND."

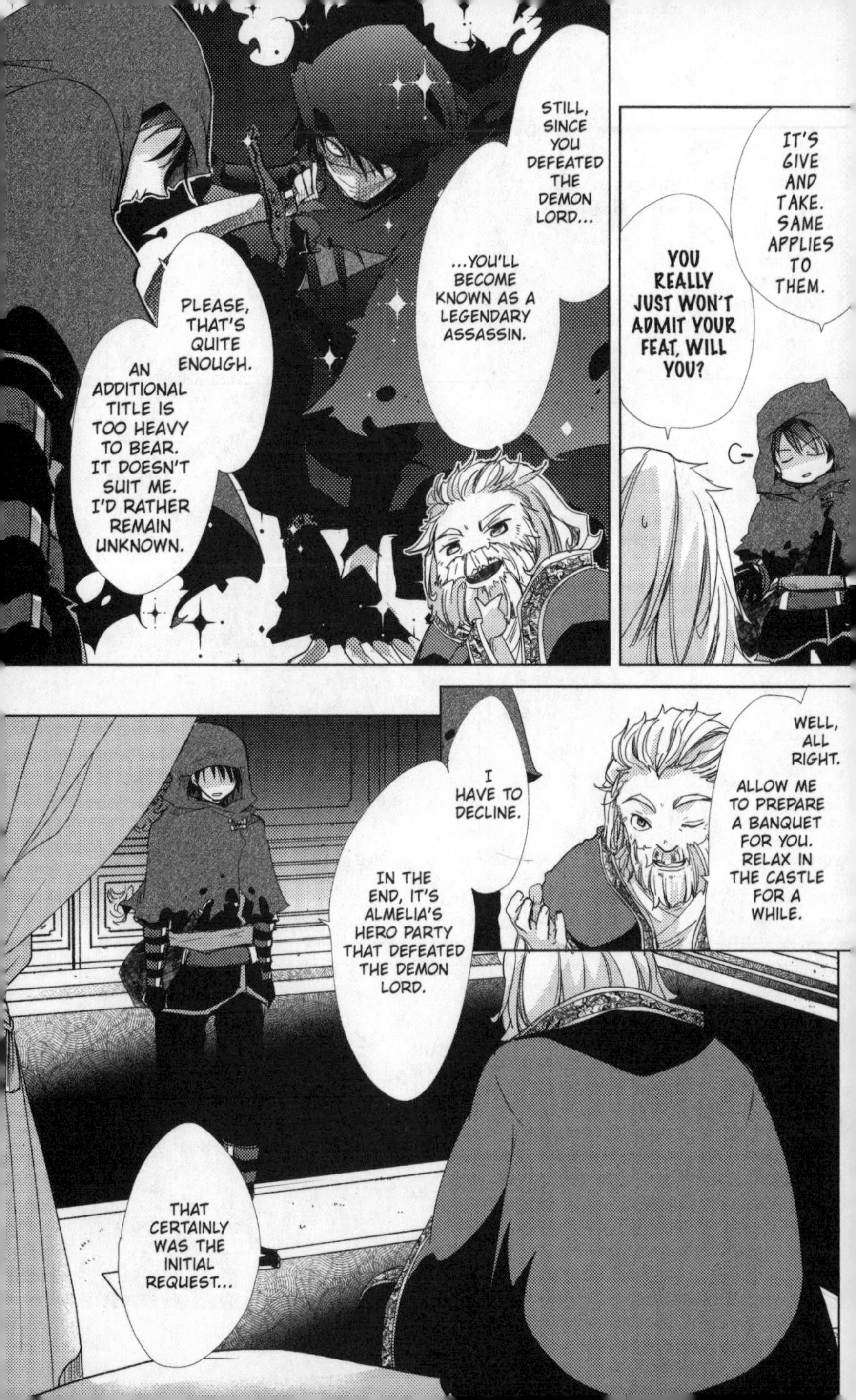
IT'S GIVE AND TAKE. SAME APPLIES TO THEM.
YOU REALLY JUST WON'T ADMIT YOUR FEAT, WILL YOU?
STILL, SINCE YOU DEFEATED THE DEMON LORD...
...YOU'LL BECOME KNOWN AS A LEGENDARY ASSASSIN.
PLEASE, THAT'S QUITE ENOUGH.
AN ADDITIONAL TITLE IS TOO HEAVY TO BEAR. IT DOESN'T SUIT ME. I'D RATHER REMAIN UNKNOWN.
WELL, ALL RIGHT.
ALLOW ME TO PREPARE A BANQUET FOR YOU. RELAX IN THE CASTLE FOR A WHILE.
I HAVE TO DECLINE.
IN THE END, IT'S ALMELIA'S HERO PARTY THAT DEFEATED THE DEMON LORD.
THAT CERTAINLY WAS THE INITIAL REQUEST...

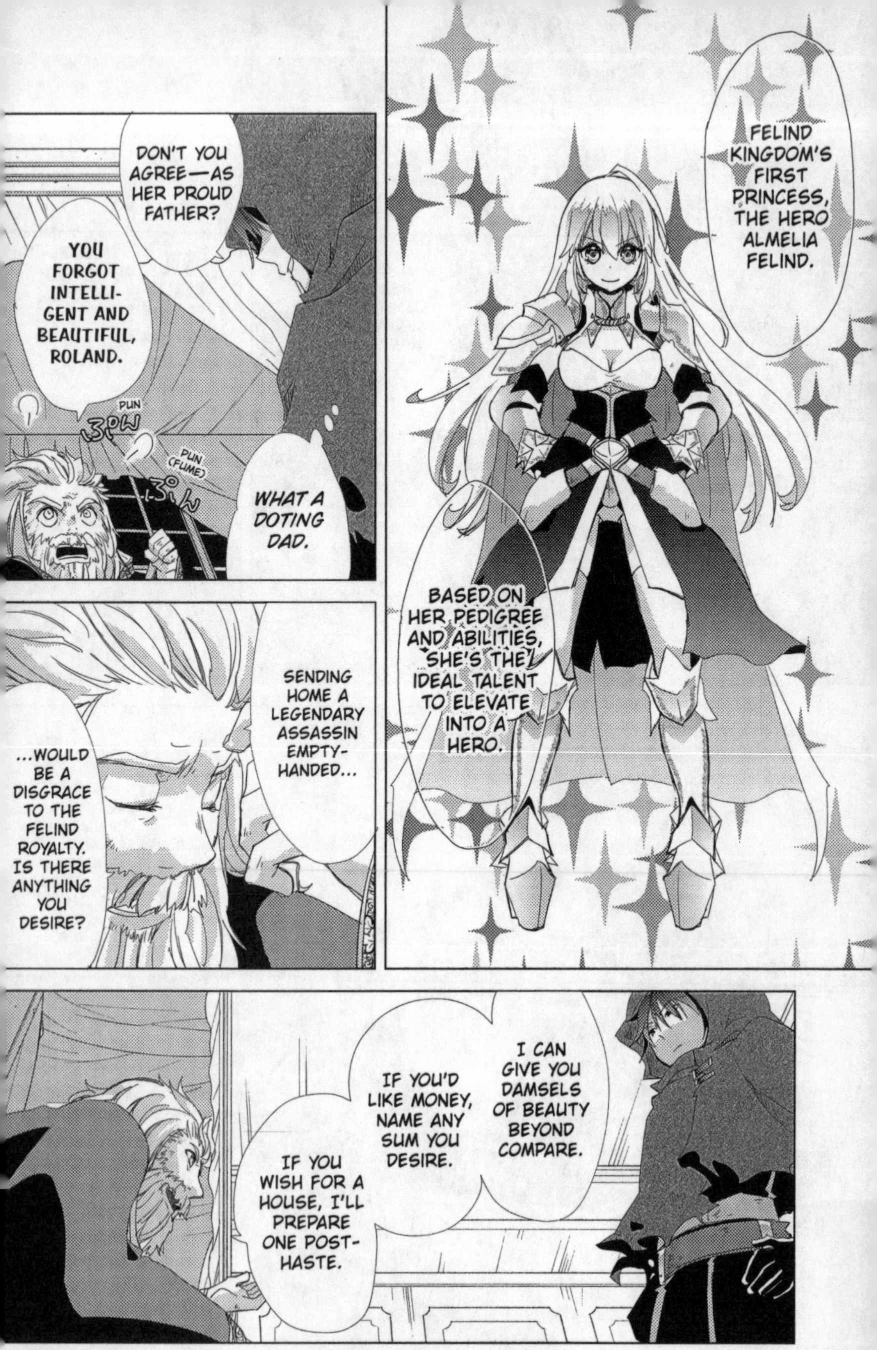
FELIND KINGDOM'S FIRST PRINCESS, THE HERO ALMELIA FELIND.
BASED ON HER PEDIGREE AND ABILITIES, SHE'S THE IDEAL TALENT TO ELEVATE INTO A HERO.
DON'T YOU AGREE—AS HER PROUD FATHER?
YOU FORGOT INTELLIGENT AND BEAUTIFUL, ROLAND.
PUN
PUN (FUME)
WHAT A DOTING DAD.
SENDING HOME A LEGENDARY ASSASSIN EMPTY-HANDED...
...WOULD BE A DISGRACE TO THE FELIND ROYALTY. IS THERE ANYTHING YOU DESIRE?
I CAN GIVE YOU DAMSELS OF BEAUTY BEYOND COMPARE.
IF YOU'D LIKE MONEY, NAME ANY SUM YOU DESIRE.
IF YOU WISH FOR A HOUSE, I'LL PREPARE ONE POST-HASTE.

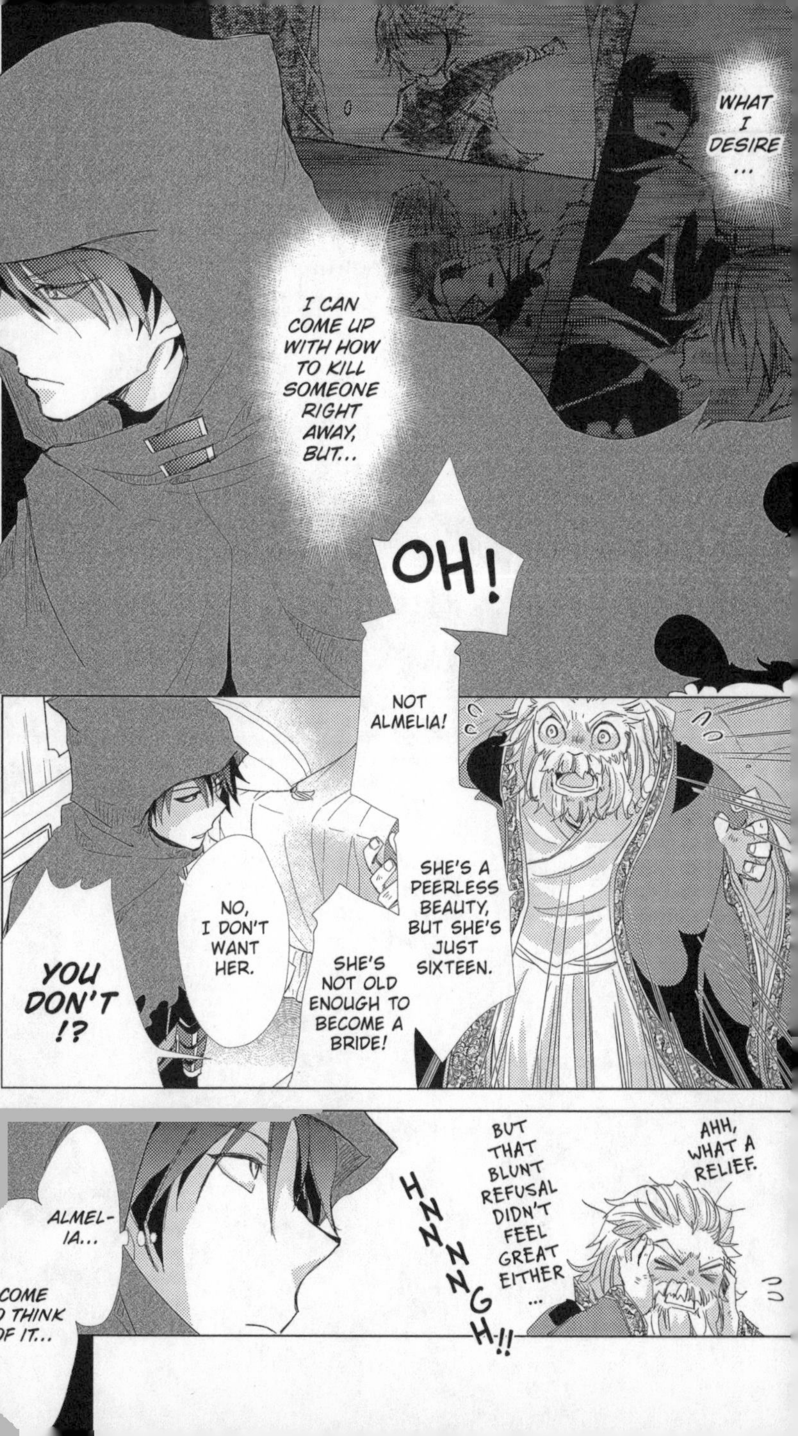
WHAT I DESIRE...
I CAN COME UP WITH HOW TO KILL SOMEONE RIGHT AWAY, BUT...
OH!
NOT ALMELIA!
SHE'S A PEERLESS BEAUTY, BUT SHE'S JUST SIXTEEN.
SHE'S NOT OLD ENOUGH TO BECOME A BRIDE!
NO, I DON'T WANT HER.
YOU DON'T!?
AHH, WHAT A RELIEF.
BUT THAT BLUNT REFUSAL DIDN'T FEEL GREAT EITHER...
HNNNNGH!!
ALMEL-IA...
COME TO THINK OF IT...

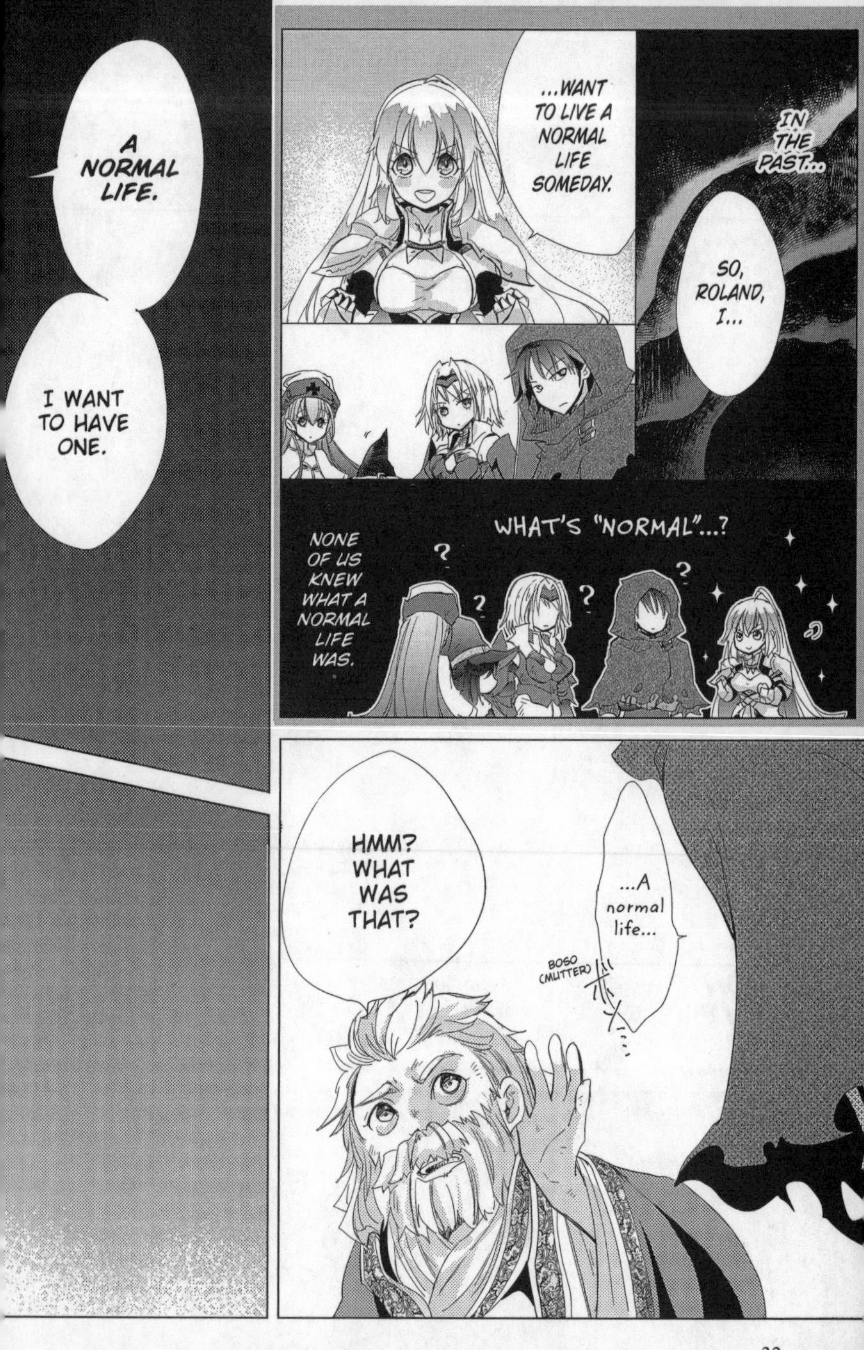
IN THE PAST...
SO, ROLAND, I...
...WANT TO LIVE A NORMAL LIFE SOMEDAY.
WHAT'S "NORMAL"...?
NONE OF US KNEW WHAT A NORMAL LIFE WAS.
A NORMAL LIFE.
I WANT TO HAVE ONE.
...A normal life...
BOSO (MUTTER)
HMM? WHAT WAS THAT?

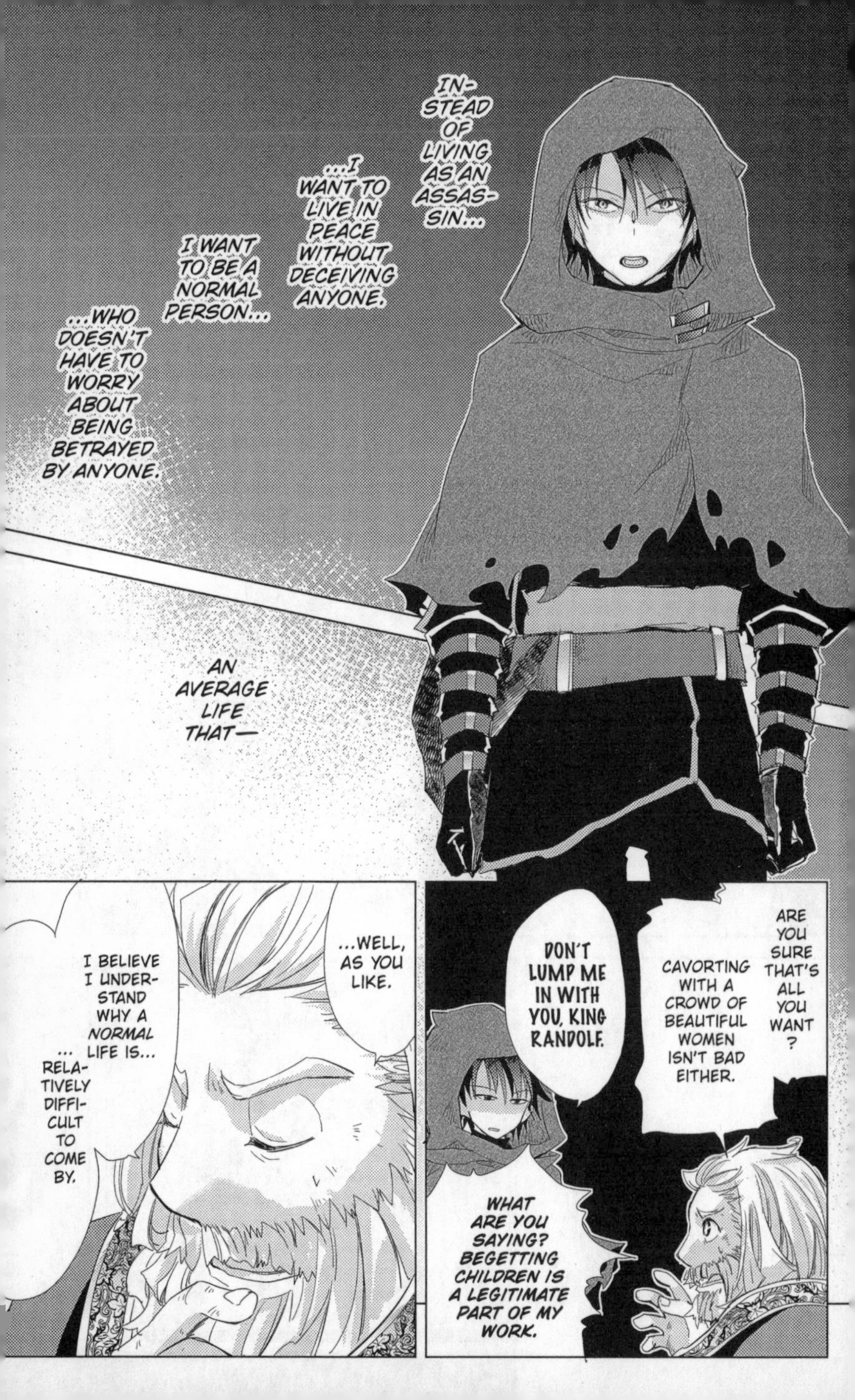
INSTEAD OF LIVING AS AN ASSASSIN...
...I WANT TO LIVE IN PEACE WITHOUT DECEIVING ANYONE.
I WANT TO BE A NORMAL PERSON...
...WHO DOESN'T HAVE TO WORRY ABOUT BEING BETRAYED BY ANYONE.
AN AVERAGE LIFE THAT—
ARE YOU SURE THAT'S ALL YOU WANT?
CAVORTING WITH A CROWD OF BEAUTIFUL WOMEN ISN'T BAD EITHER.
DON'T LUMP ME IN WITH YOU, KING RANDOLF.
WHAT ARE YOU SAYING? BEGETTING CHILDREN IS A LEGITIMATE PART OF MY WORK.
...WELL, AS YOU LIKE.
I BELIEVE I UNDERSTAND WHY A NORMAL LIFE IS... ...RELATIVELY DIFFICULT TO COME BY.

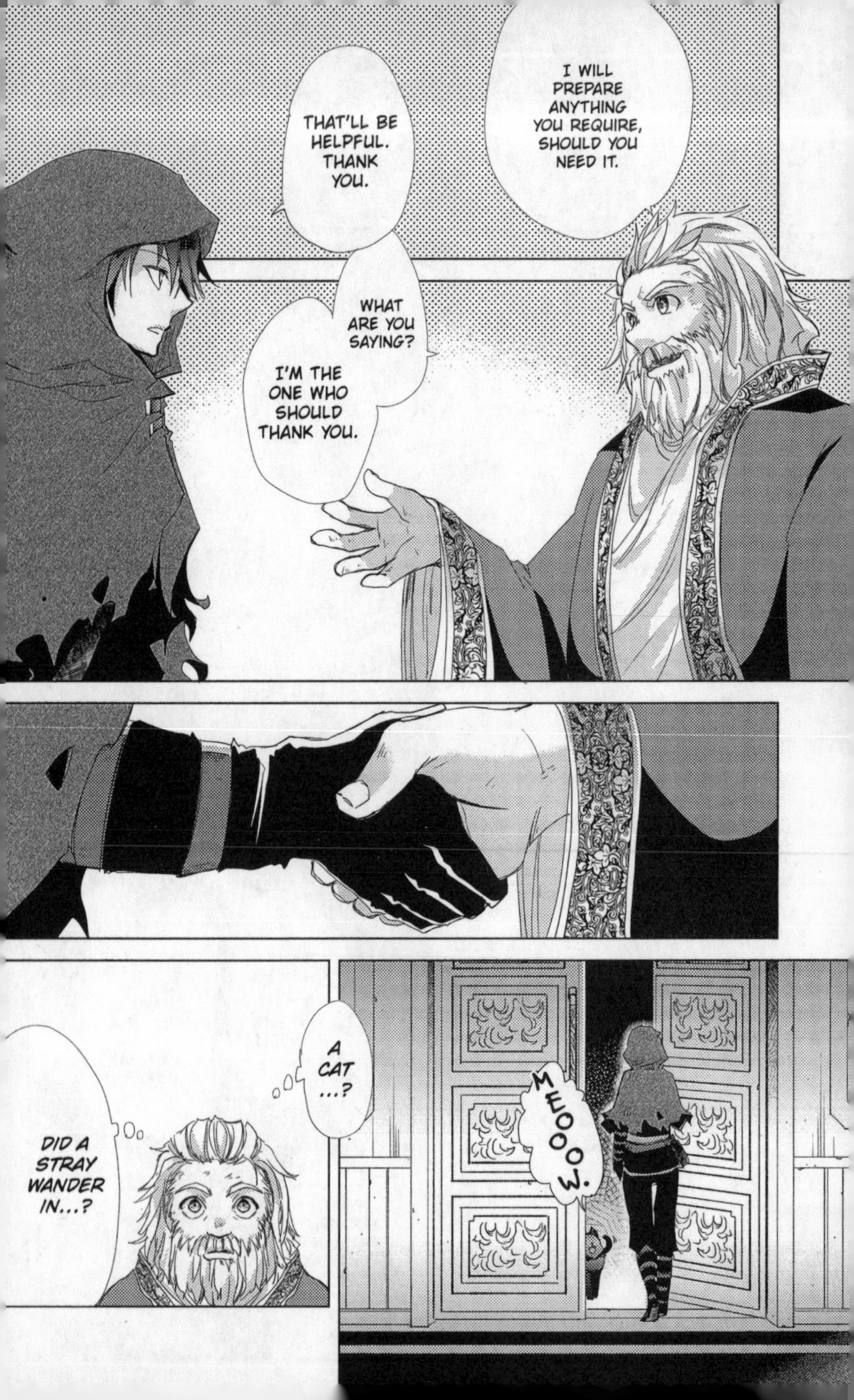
I WILL PREPARE ANYTHING YOU REQUIRE, SHOULD YOU NEED IT.
THAT'LL BE HELPFUL. THANK YOU.
WHAT ARE YOU SAYING?
I'M THE ONE WHO SHOULD THANK YOU.
MEOOOW.
A CAT ...?
DID A STRAY WANDER IN...?

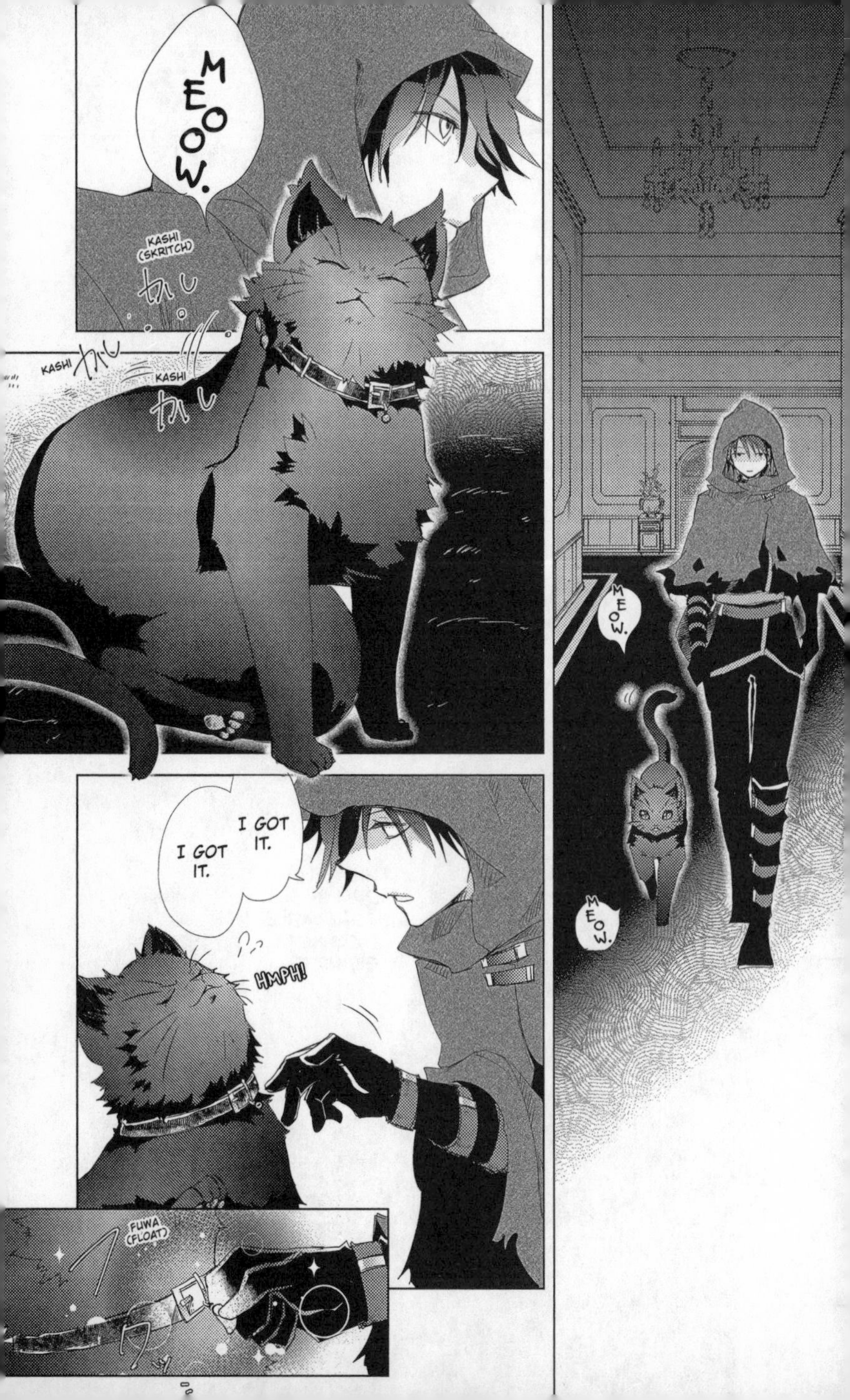
MEOW.
MEOW.
MEOOW.
KASHI (SKRITCH)
KASHI
KASHI
I GOT IT.
I GOT IT.
HMPH!
FUWA (FLOAT)

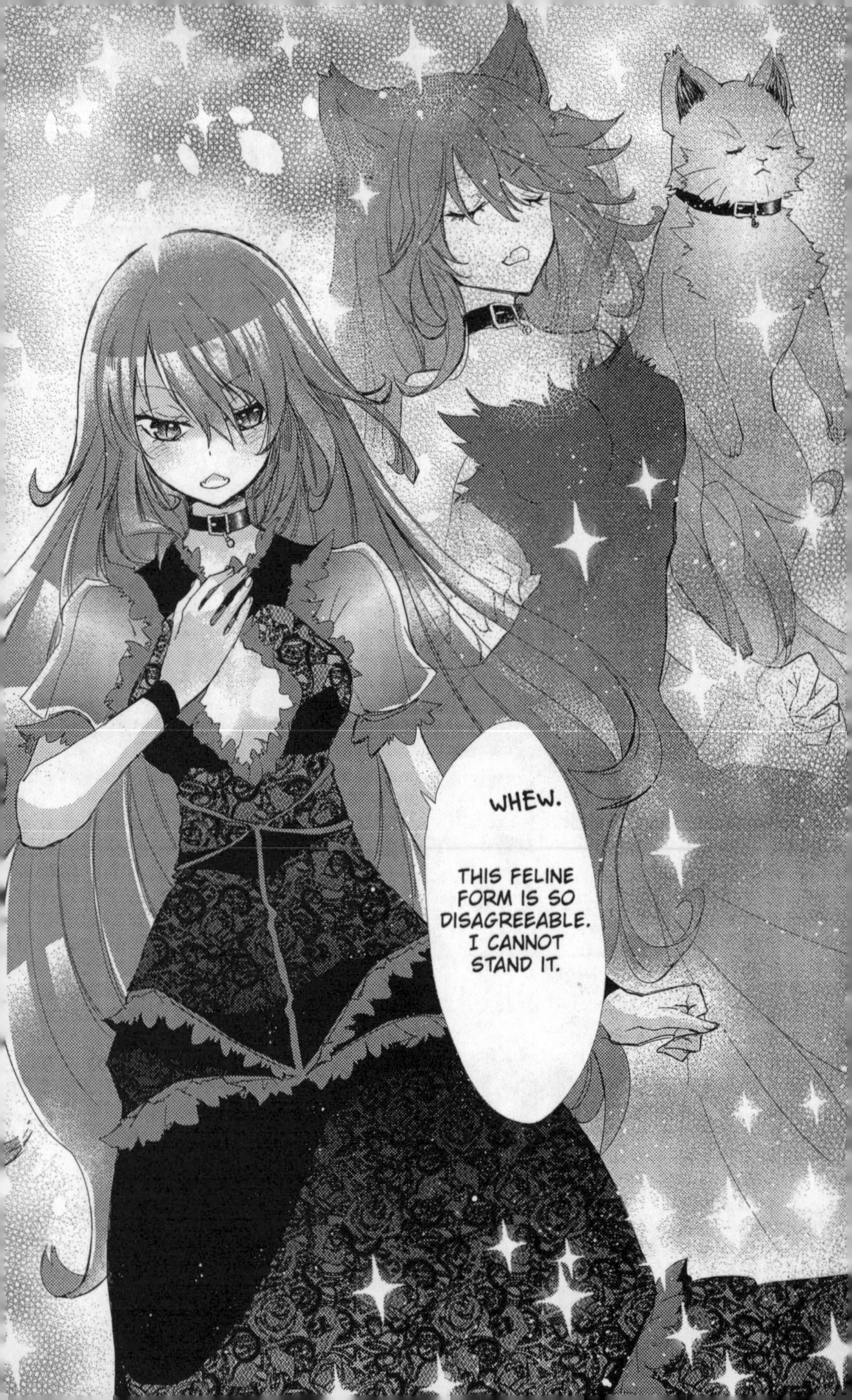
WHEW.
THIS FELINE FORM IS SO DISAGREEABLE. I CANNOT STAND IT.

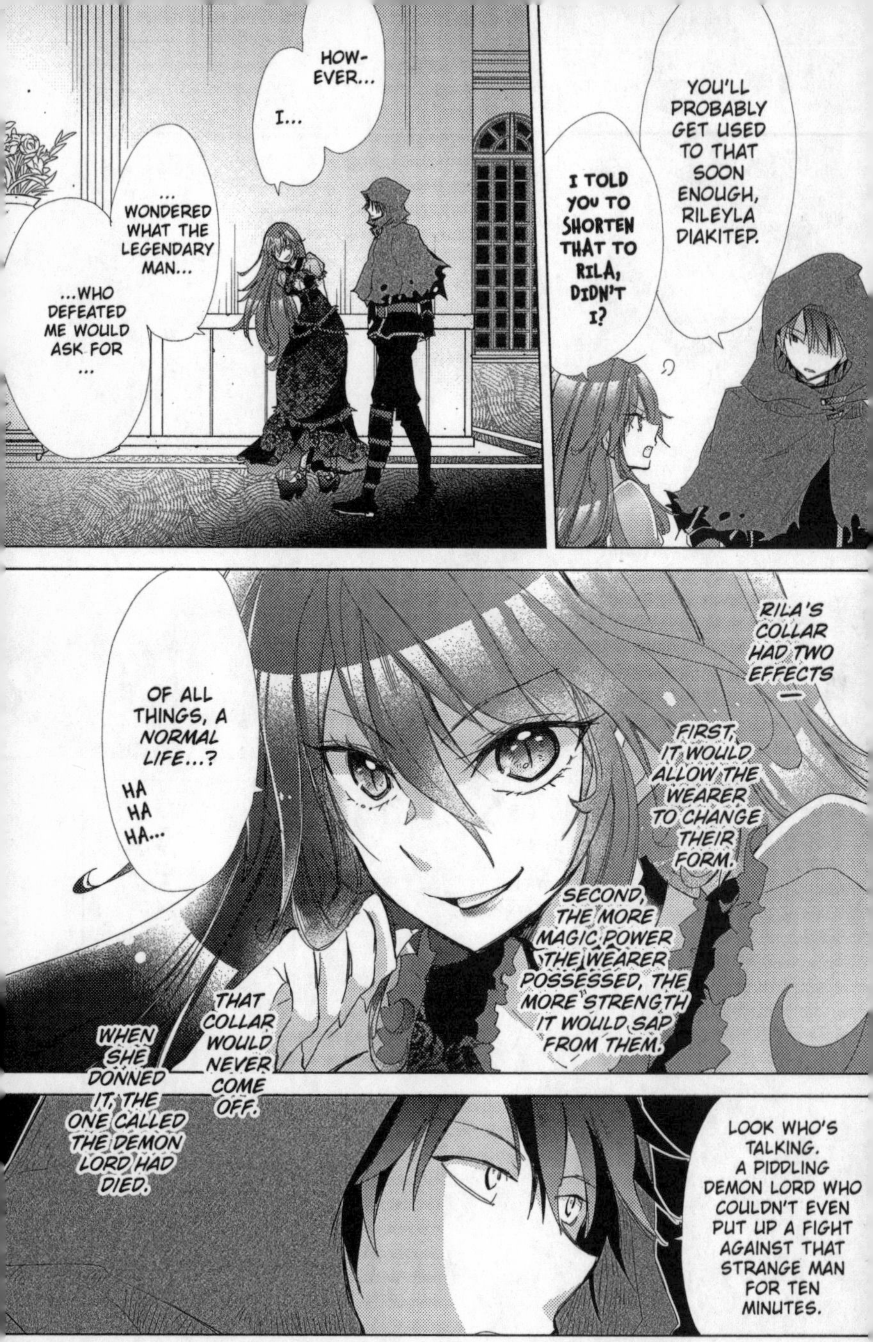
YOU'LL PROBABLY GET USED TO THAT SOON ENOUGH, RILEYLA DIAKITEP.
I TOLD YOU TO SHORTEN THAT TO RILA, DIDN'T I?
HOW-EVER... I...
...WONDERED WHAT THE LEGENDARY MAN...
...WHO DEFEATED ME WOULD ASK FOR...
RILA'S COLLAR HAD TWO EFFECTS—
FIRST, IT WOULD ALLOW THE WEARER TO CHANGE THEIR FORM.
SECOND, THE MORE MAGIC POWER THE WEARER POSSESSED, THE MORE STRENGTH IT WOULD SAP FROM THEM.
OF ALL THINGS, A NORMAL LIFE...?
HA HA HA...
THAT COLLAR WOULD NEVER COME OFF.
WHEN SHE DONNED IT, THE ONE CALLED THE DEMON LORD HAD DIED.
LOOK WHO'S TALKING. A PIDDLING DEMON LORD WHO COULDN'T EVEN PUT UP A FIGHT AGAINST THAT STRANGE MAN FOR TEN MINUTES.

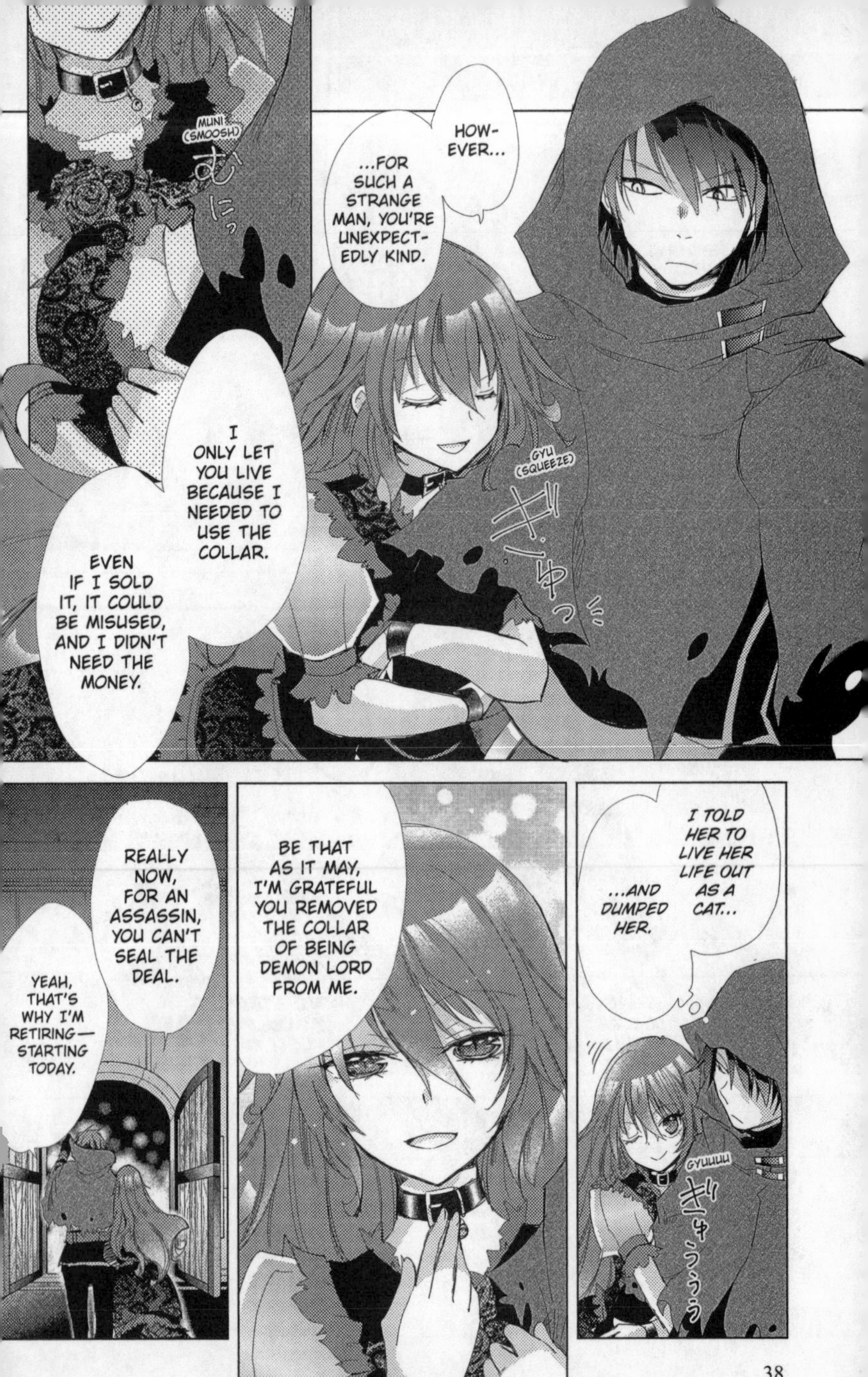
HOW-EVER...
...FOR SUCH A STRANGE MAN, YOU'RE UNEXPECTEDLY KIND.
MUNI (SMOOSH)
GYU (SQUEEZE)
I ONLY LET YOU LIVE BECAUSE I NEEDED TO USE THE COLLAR.
EVEN IF I SOLD IT, IT COULD BE MISUSED, AND I DIDN'T NEED THE MONEY.
I TOLD HER TO LIVE HER LIFE OUT AS A CAT...
...AND DUMPED HER.
GYUUUU
BE THAT AS IT MAY, I'M GRATEFUL YOU REMOVED THE COLLAR OF BEING DEMON LORD FROM ME.
REALLY NOW, FOR AN ASSASSIN, YOU CAN'T SEAL THE DEAL.
YEAH, THAT'S WHY I'M RETIRING— STARTING TODAY.

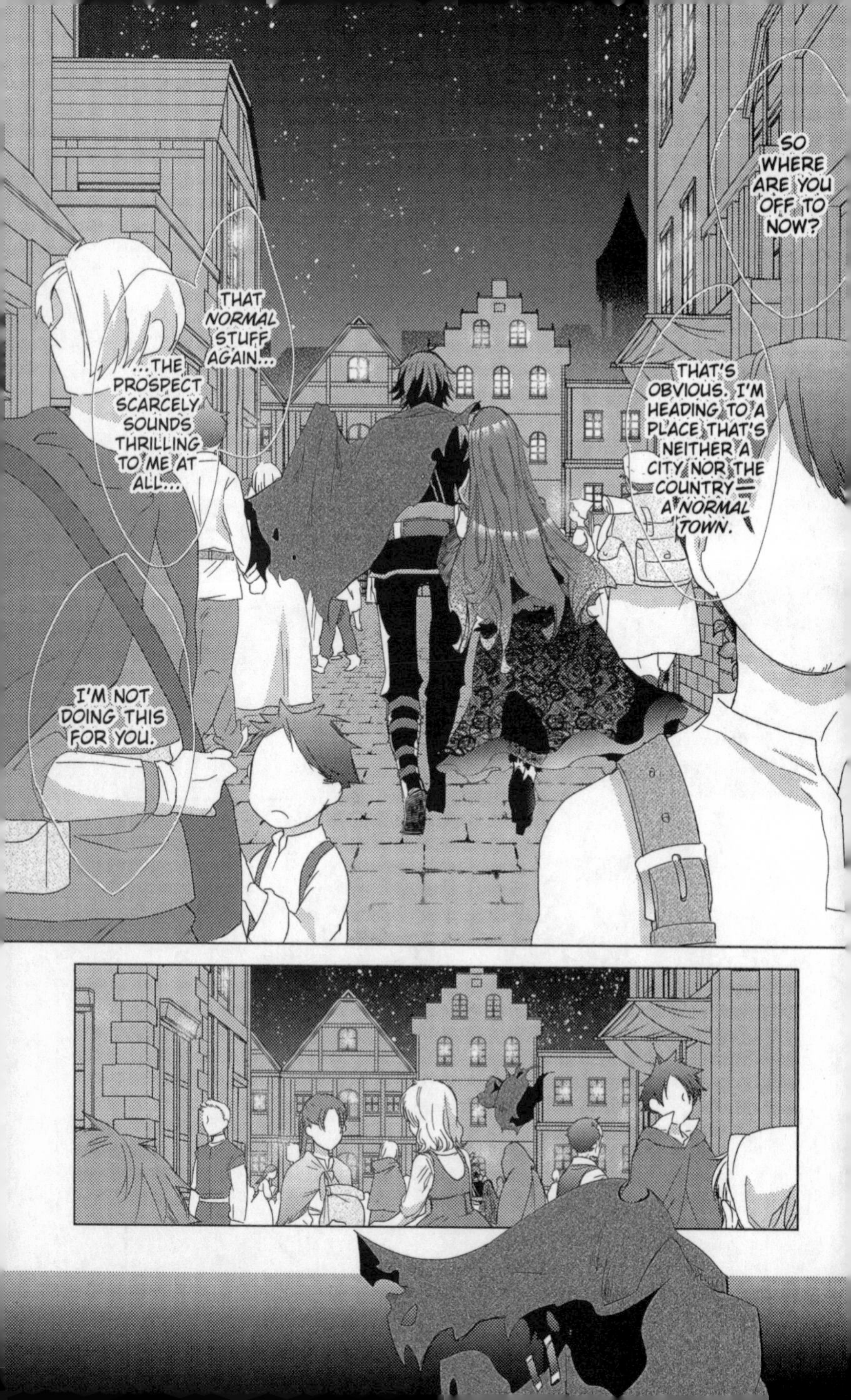
SO WHERE ARE YOU OFF TO NOW?
THAT'S OBVIOUS. I'M HEADING TO A PLACE THAT'S NEITHER A CITY NOR THE COUNTRY—A *NORMAL* TOWN.
THAT *NORMAL* STUFF AGAIN...
...THE PROSPECT SCARCELY SOUNDS THRILLING TO ME AT ALL...
I'M NOT DOING THIS FOR YOU.

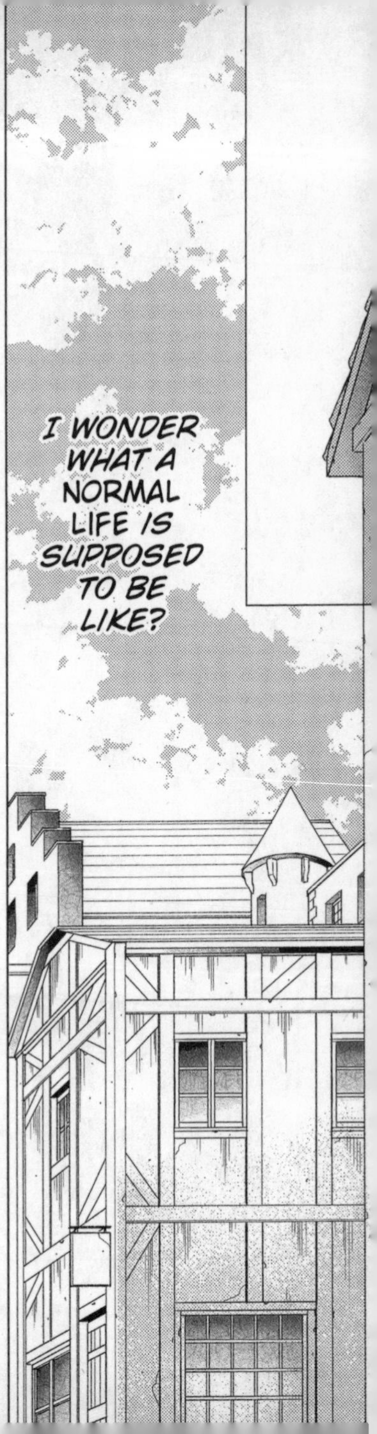
I WONDER WHAT A NORMAL LIFE IS SUPPOSED TO BE LIKE?
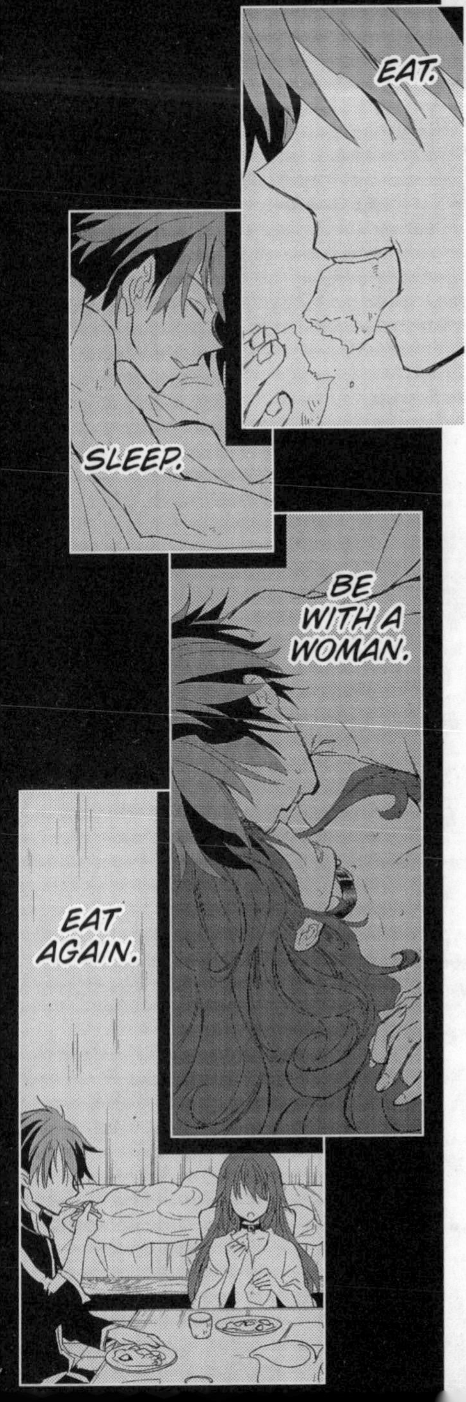
EAT.
SLEEP.
BE WITH A WOMAN.
EAT AGAIN.

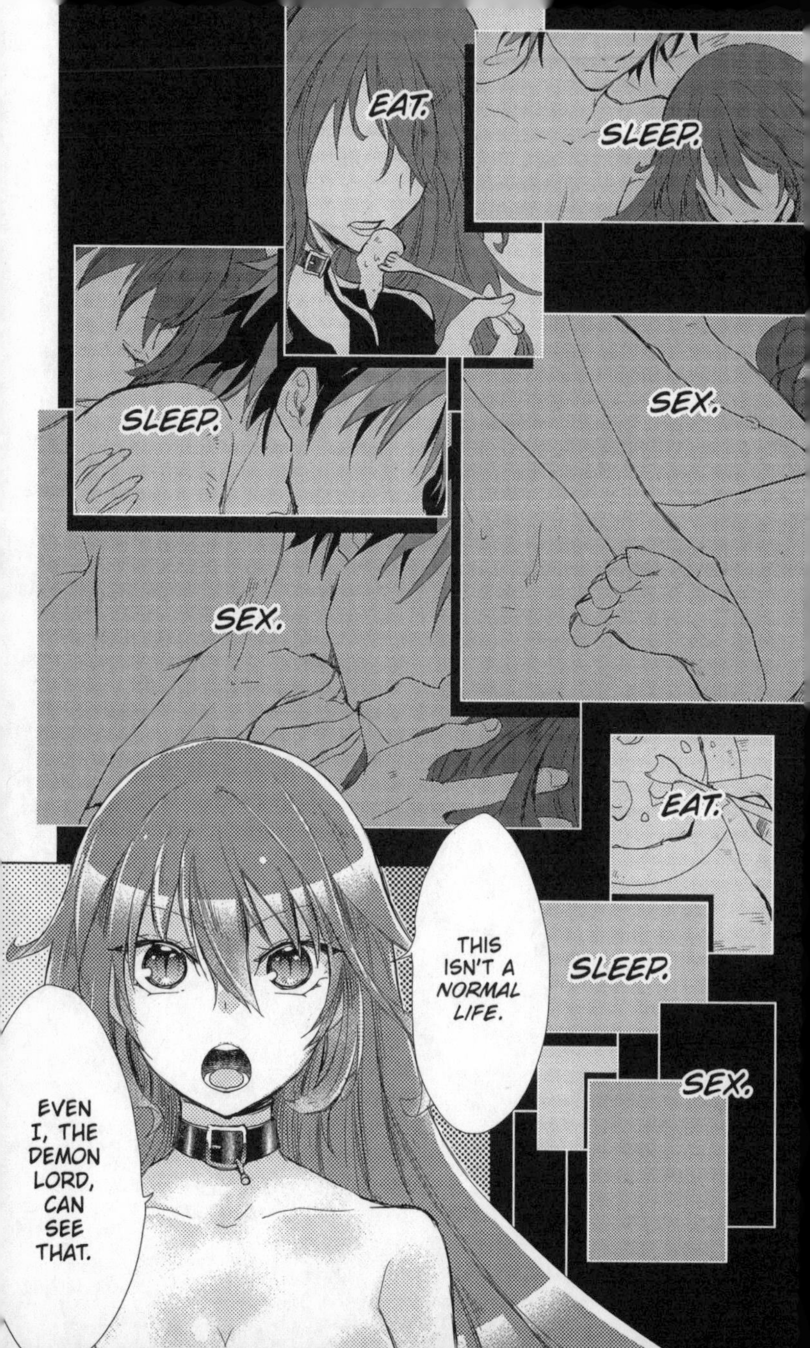
SLEEP.
EAT.
SEX.
SLEEP.
SEX.
EAT.
SLEEP.
SEX.
THIS ISN'T A NORMAL LIFE.
EVEN I, THE DEMON LORD, CAN SEE THAT.

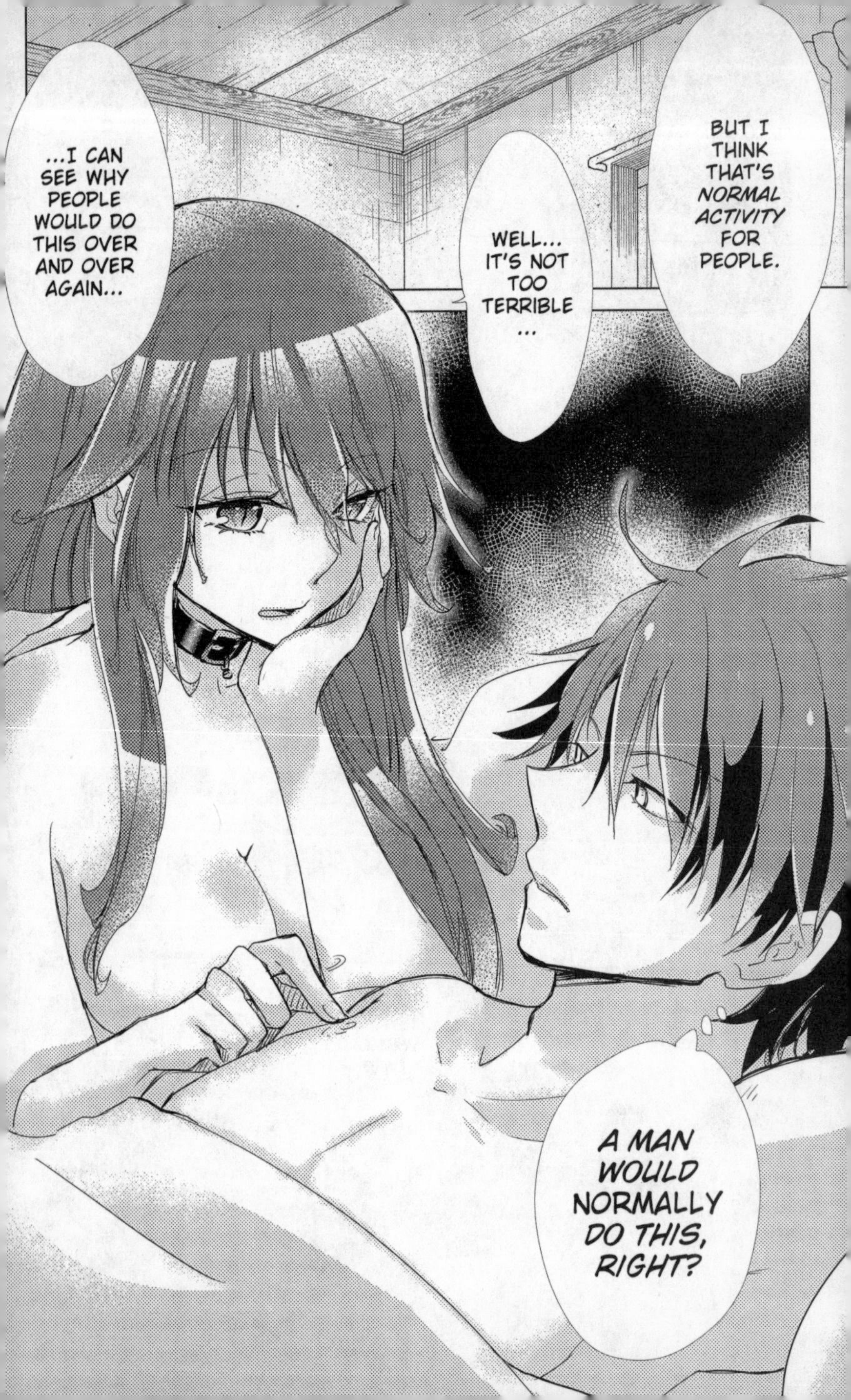
BUT I THINK THAT'S NORMAL ACTIVITY FOR PEOPLE.
WELL... IT'S NOT TOO TERRIBLE...
...I CAN SEE WHY PEOPLE WOULD DO THIS OVER AND OVER AGAIN...
A MAN WOULD NORMALLY DO THIS, RIGHT?

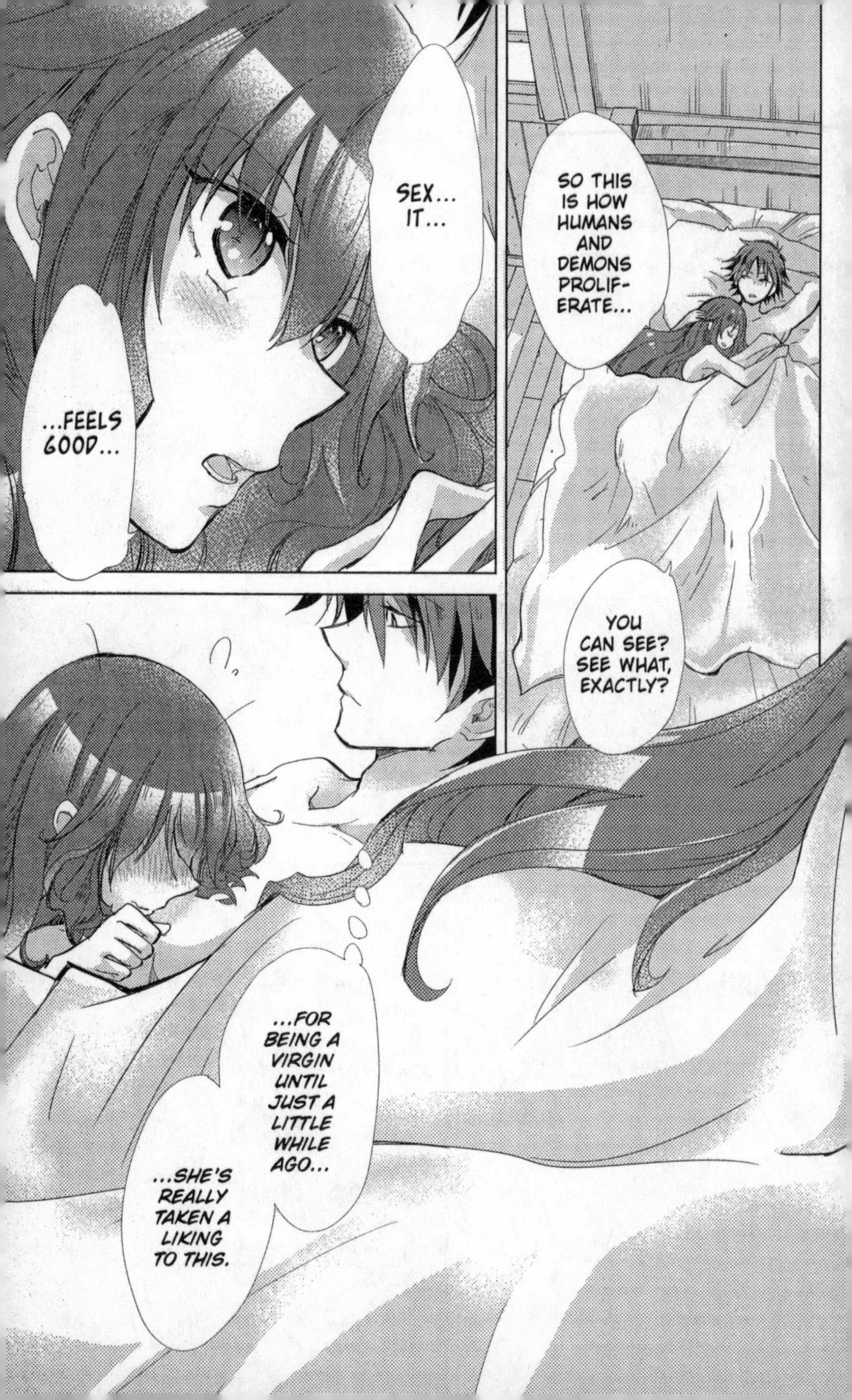
SO THIS IS HOW HUMANS AND DEMONS PROLIF-ERATE...
YOU CAN SEE? SEE WHAT, EXACTLY?
SEX... IT...
...FEELS GOOD...
...FOR BEING A VIRGIN UNTIL JUST A LITTLE WHILE AGO...
...SHE'S REALLY TAKEN A LIKING TO THIS.

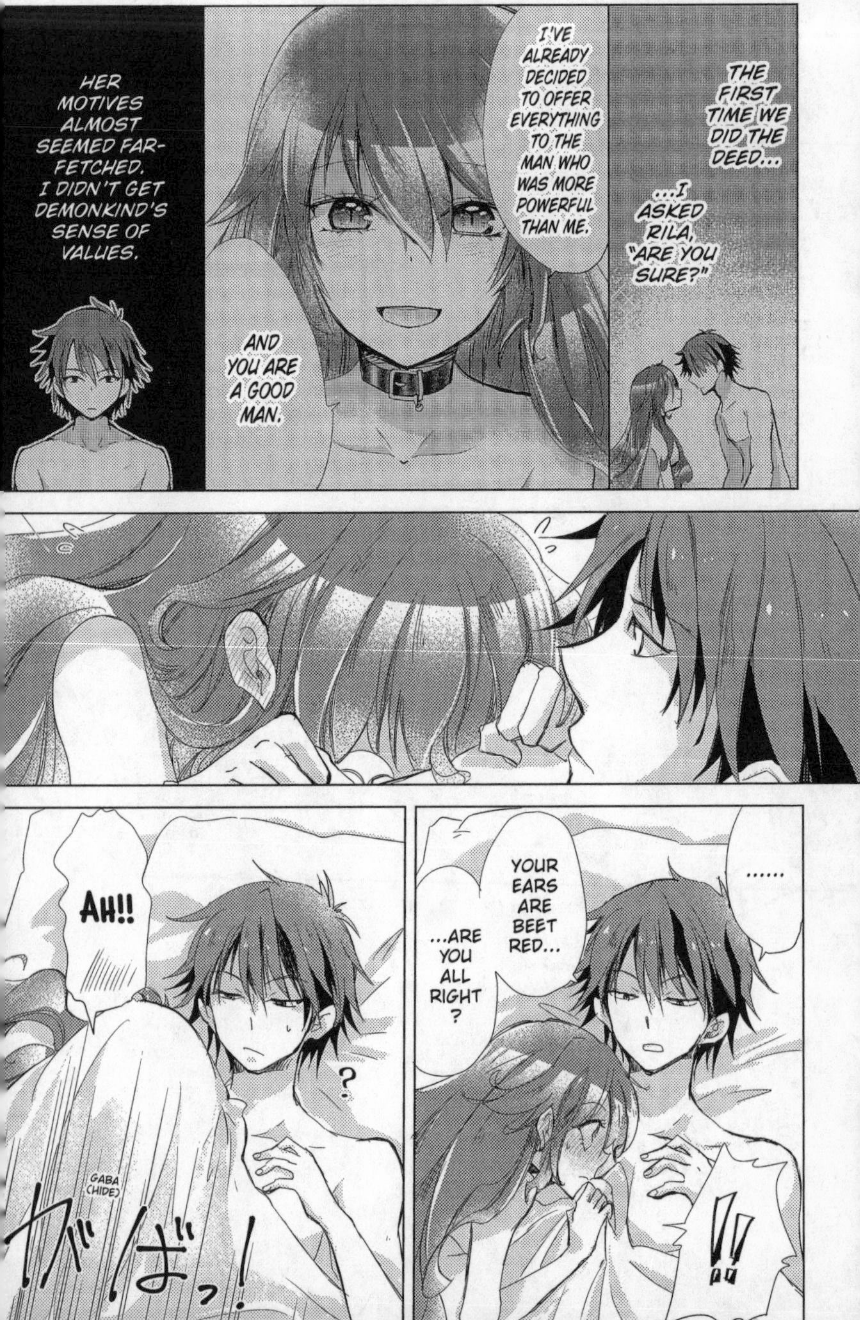
THE FIRST TIME WE DID THE DEED...
...I ASKED RILA, "ARE YOU SURE?"
I'VE ALREADY DECIDED TO OFFER EVERYTHING TO THE MAN WHO WAS MORE POWERFUL THAN ME.
AND YOU ARE A GOOD MAN.
HER MOTIVES ALMOST SEEMED FAR-FETCHED. I DIDN'T GET DEMONKIND'S SENSE OF VALUES.
......
YOUR EARS ARE BEET RED...
...ARE YOU ALL RIGHT?
!!
AH!!
?
GABA (HIDE)
がばっ!

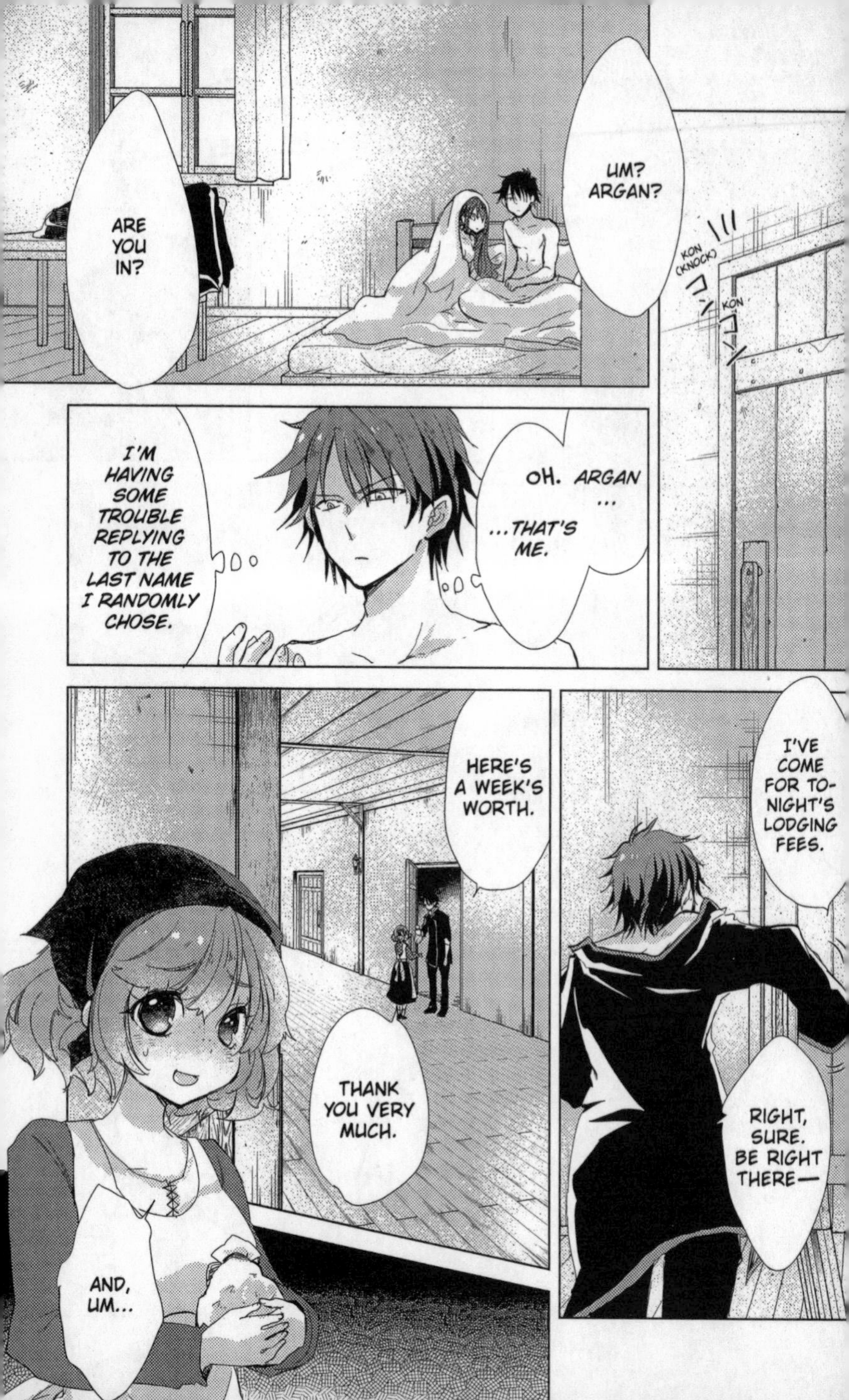
KON (KNOCK)
KON
UM? ARGAN?
ARE YOU IN?
OH. ARGAN...
...THAT'S ME.
I'M HAVING SOME TROUBLE REPLYING TO THE LAST NAME I RANDOMLY CHOSE.
I'VE COME FOR TO-NIGHT'S LODGING FEES.
RIGHT, SURE. BE RIGHT THERE—
HERE'S A WEEK'S WORTH.
THANK YOU VERY MUCH.
AND, UM...

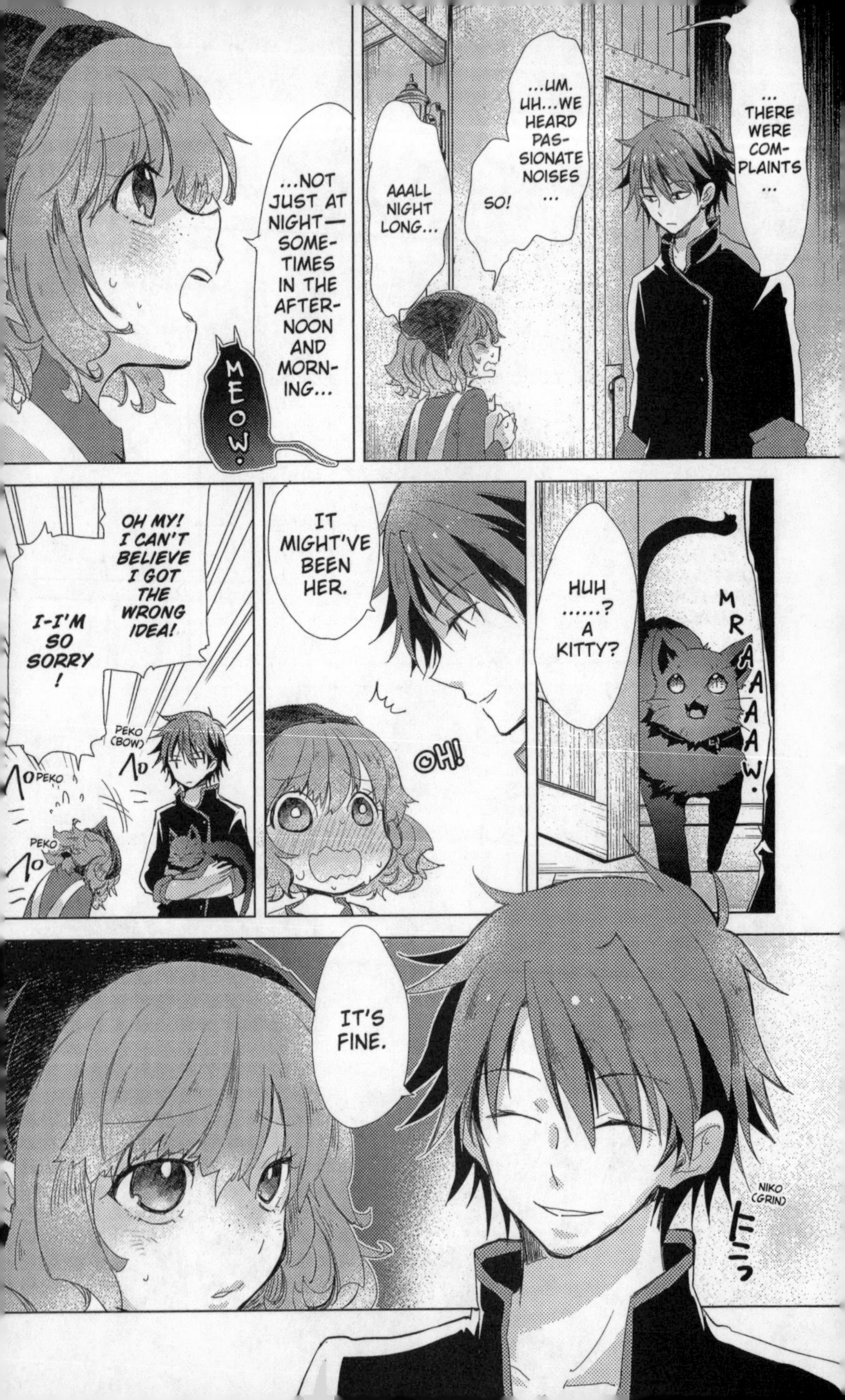
...THERE WERE COMPLAINTS...
...UM. UH...WE HEARD PASSIONATE NOISES...
SO!
AAALL NIGHT LONG...
...NOT JUST AT NIGHT—SOMETIMES IN THE AFTERNOON AND MORNING...
MEOW.
MRAAAAAW.
HUH ......? A KITTY?
IT MIGHT'VE BEEN HER.
OH!
OH MY! I CAN'T BELIEVE I GOT THE WRONG IDEA!
I-I'M SO SORRY!
PEKO (BOW)
PEKO
PEKO
IT'S FINE.
NIKO (GRIN)

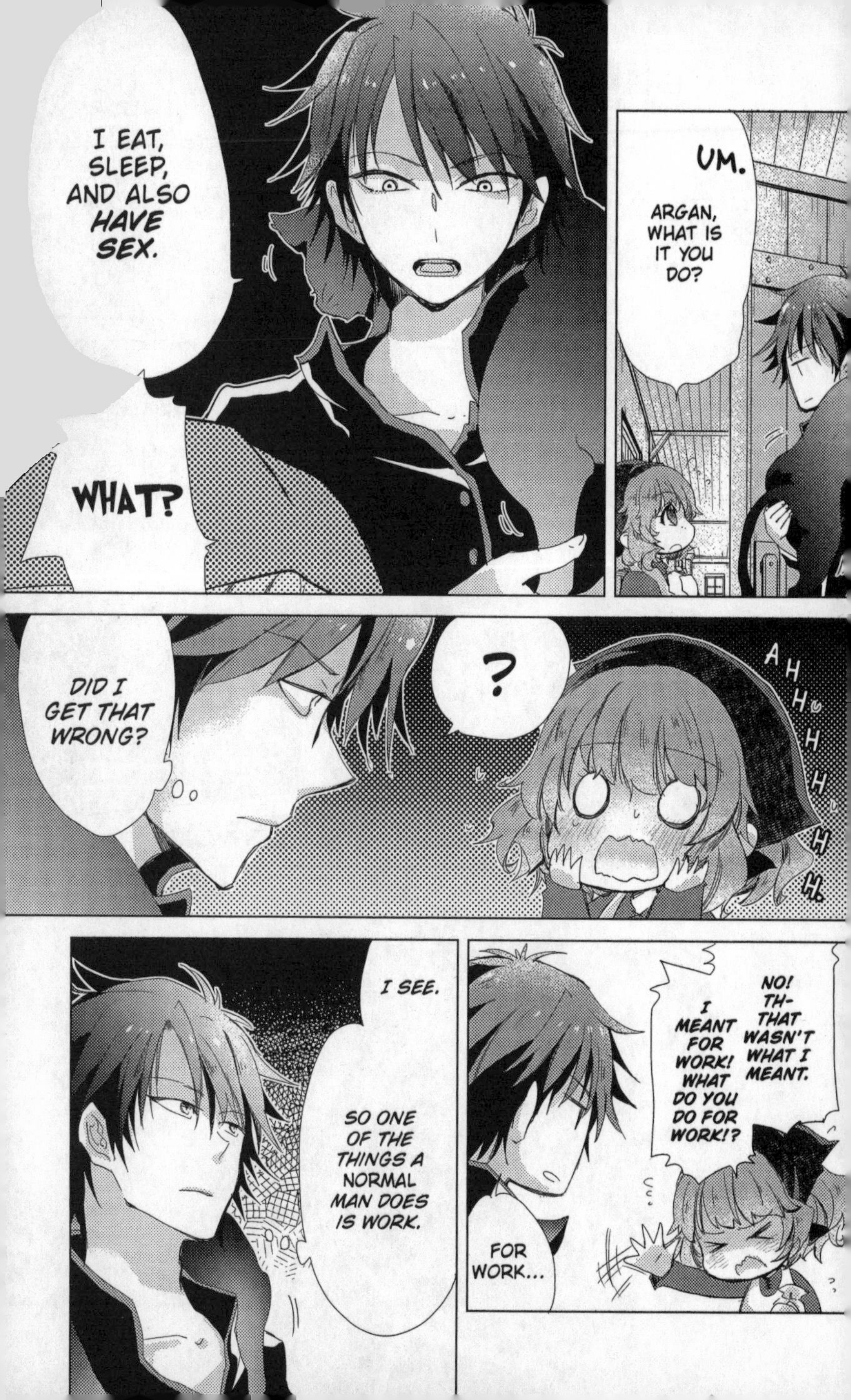
UM.
ARGAN, WHAT IS IT YOU DO?
I EAT, SLEEP, AND ALSO *HAVE SEX.*
WHAT?
AHHHHHHH
?
DID I GET THAT WRONG?
NO! TH-THAT WASN'T WHAT I MEANT.
I MEANT FOR WORK! WHAT DO YOU DO FOR WORK!?
FOR WORK...
I SEE.
SO ONE OF THE THINGS A NORMAL MAN DOES IS WORK.

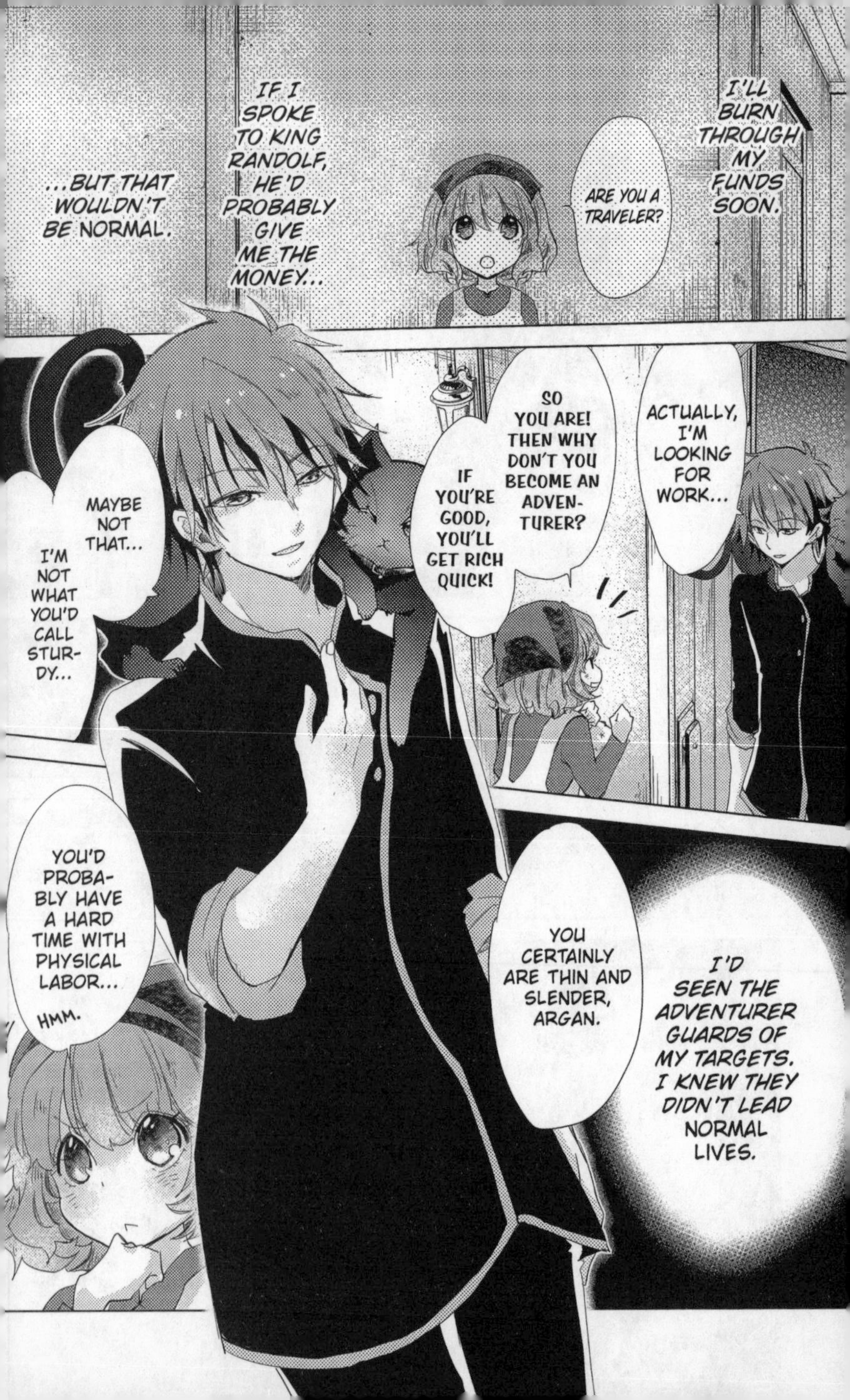
I'LL BURN THROUGH MY FUNDS SOON.
ARE YOU A TRAVELER?
IF I SPOKE TO KING RANDOLF, HE'D PROBABLY GIVE ME THE MONEY...
...BUT THAT WOULDN'T BE NORMAL.
ACTUALLY, I'M LOOKING FOR WORK...
SO YOU ARE! THEN WHY DON'T YOU BECOME AN ADVEN-TURER?
IF YOU'RE GOOD, YOU'LL GET RICH QUICK!
MAYBE NOT THAT...
I'M NOT WHAT YOU'D CALL STUR-DY...
I'D SEEN THE ADVENTURER GUARDS OF MY TARGETS. I KNEW THEY DIDN'T LEAD NORMAL LIVES.
YOU CERTAINLY ARE THIN AND SLENDER, ARGAN.
YOU'D PROBA-BLY HAVE A HARD TIME WITH PHYSICAL LABOR...
HMM.

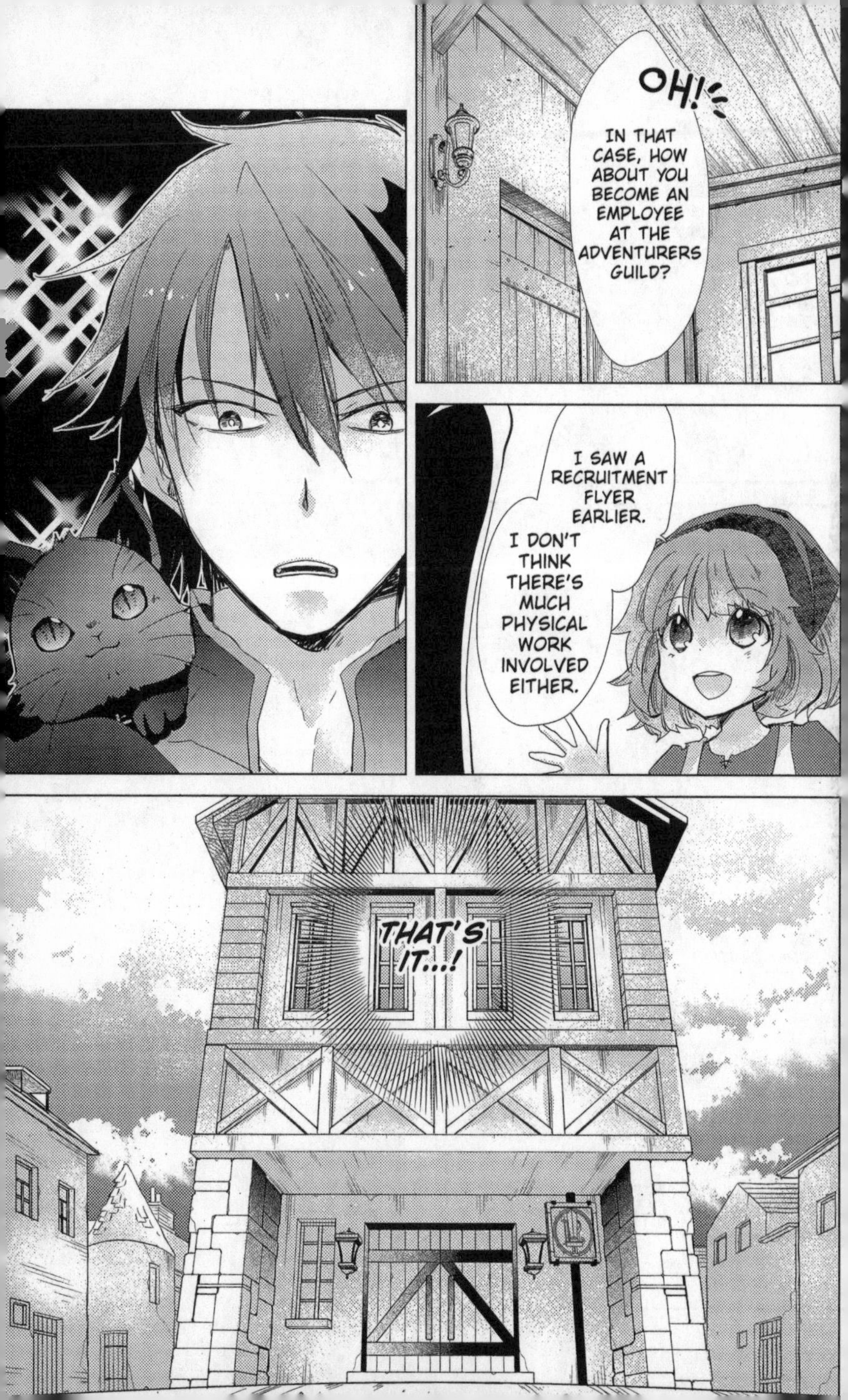
OH!
IN THAT CASE, HOW ABOUT YOU BECOME AN EMPLOYEE AT THE ADVENTURERS GUILD?
I SAW A RECRUITMENT FLYER EARLIER.
I DON'T THINK THERE'S MUCH PHYSICAL WORK INVOLVED EITHER.
THAT'S IT...!

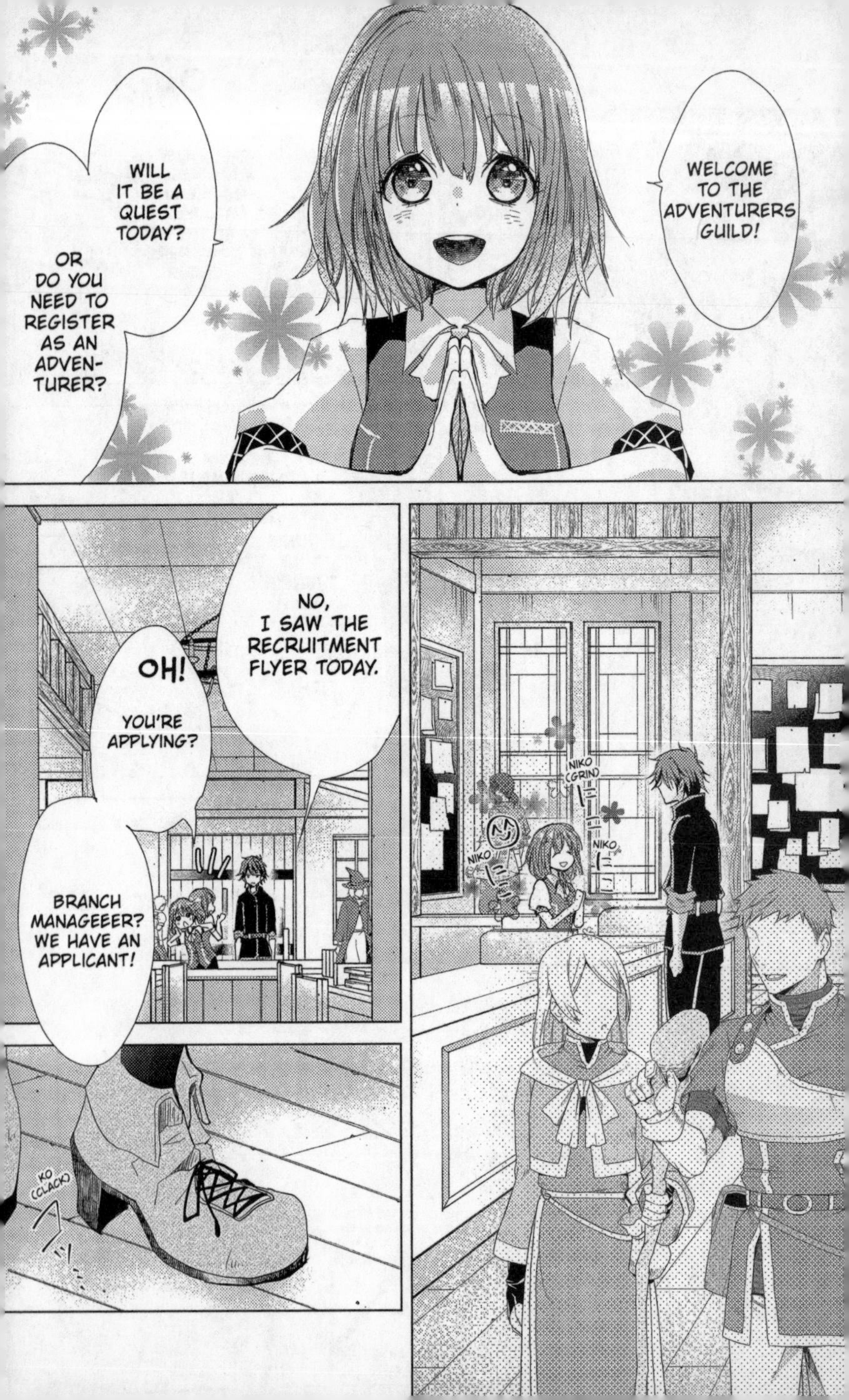
WELCOME TO THE ADVENTURERS GUILD!
WILL IT BE A QUEST TODAY?
OR DO YOU NEED TO REGISTER AS AN ADVEN-TURER?
NIKO (GRIN)
NIKO
NIKO
NO, I SAW THE RECRUITMENT FLYER TODAY.
OH!
YOU'RE APPLYING?
BRANCH MANAGEEER? WE HAVE AN APPLICANT!
KO (CLACK)

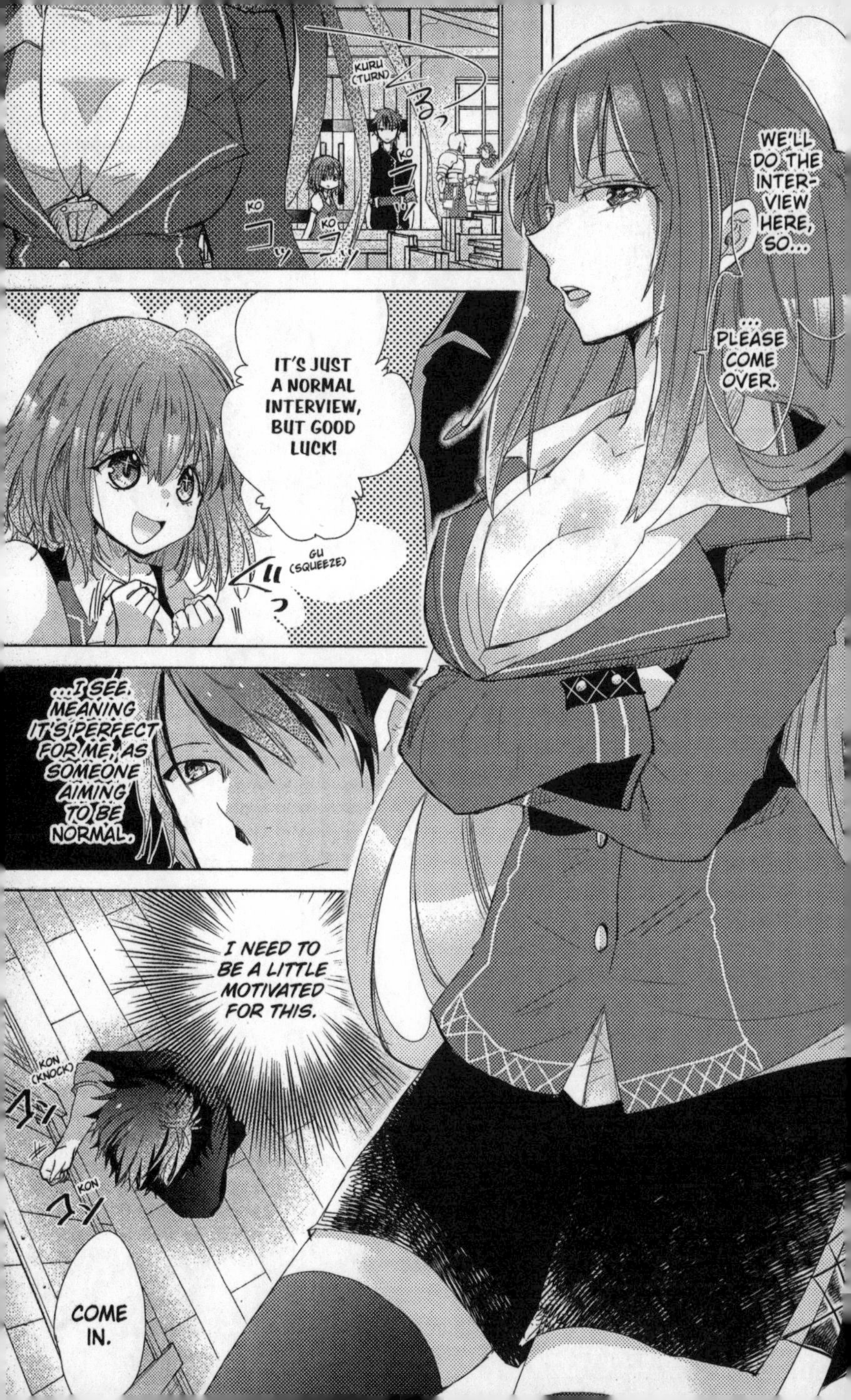

WE'LL DO THE INTER-VIEW HERE, SO...
...PLEASE COME OVER.
KURU (TURN)
KO
KO
KO
IT'S JUST A NORMAL INTERVIEW, BUT GOOD LUCK!
GU (SQUEEZE)
...I SEE. MEANING IT'S PERFECT FOR ME, AS SOMEONE AIMING TO BE NORMAL.
I NEED TO BE A LITTLE MOTIVATED FOR THIS.
KON (KNOCK)
KON
COME IN.

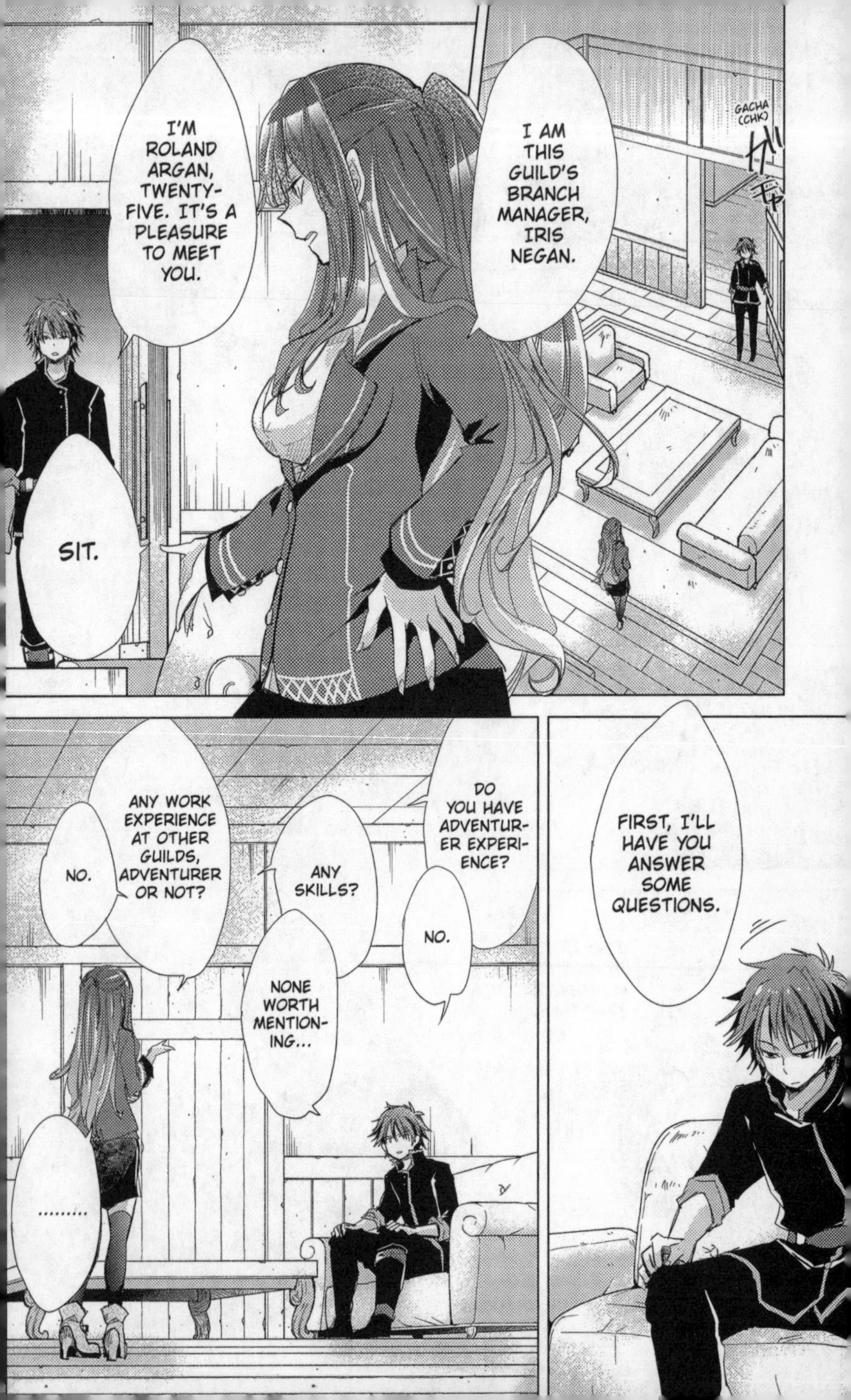
GACHA (CHK)
ガチャ
I AM THIS GUILD'S BRANCH MANAGER, IRIS NEGAN.
I'M ROLAND ARGAN, TWENTY-FIVE. IT'S A PLEASURE TO MEET YOU.
SIT.
FIRST, I'LL HAVE YOU ANSWER SOME QUESTIONS.
DO YOU HAVE ADVENTURER EXPERIENCE?
NO.
ANY SKILLS?
NONE WORTH MENTIONING...
ANY WORK EXPERIENCE AT OTHER GUILDS, ADVENTURER OR NOT?
NO.
....

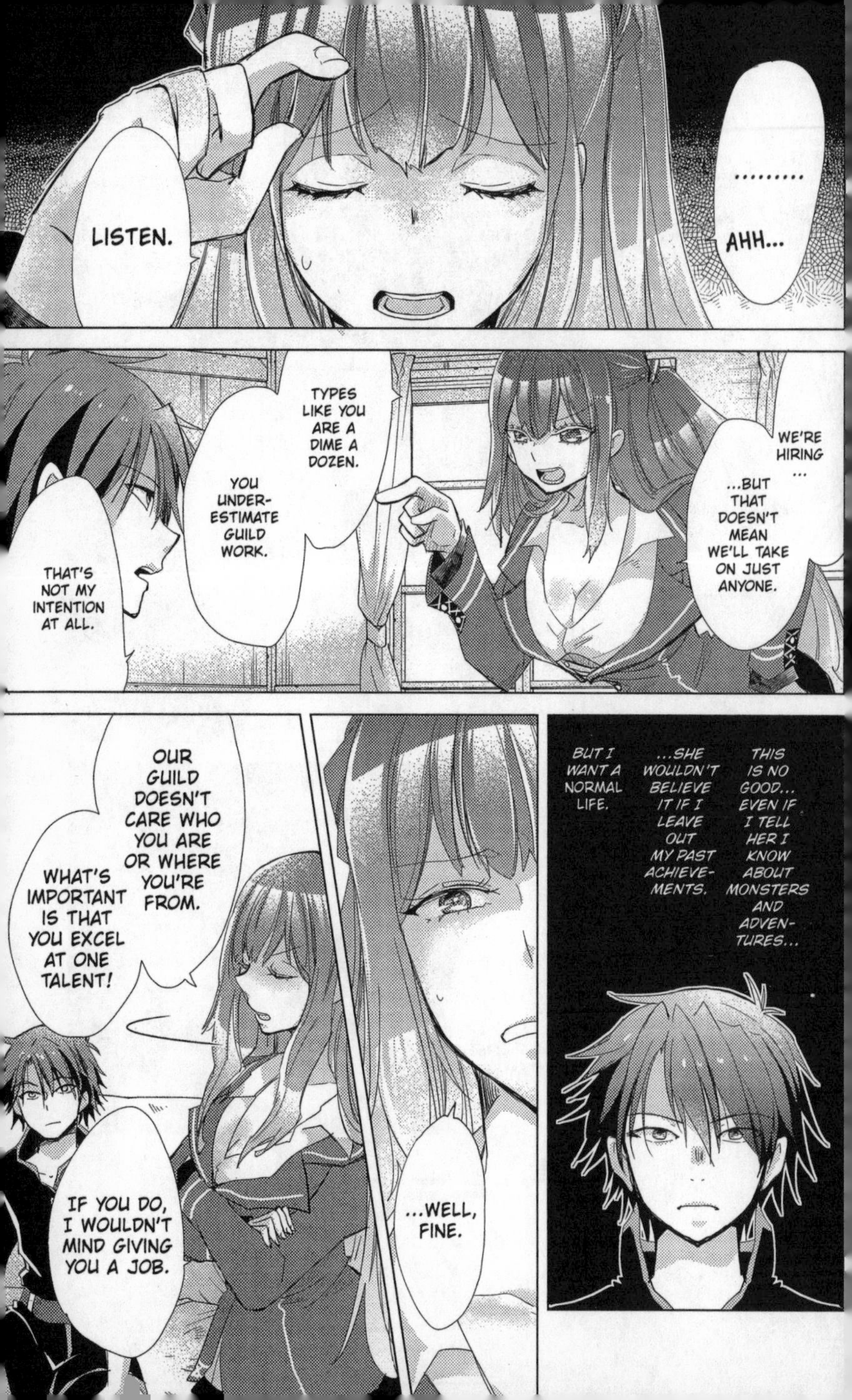

....
AHH...
LISTEN.
WE'RE HIRING...
...BUT THAT DOESN'T MEAN WE'LL TAKE ON JUST ANYONE.
TYPES LIKE YOU ARE A DIME A DOZEN.
YOU UNDER-ESTIMATE GUILD WORK.
THAT'S NOT MY INTENTION AT ALL.
THIS IS NO GOOD... EVEN IF I TELL HER I KNOW ABOUT MONSTERS AND ADVEN-TURES...
...SHE WOULDN'T BELIEVE IT IF I LEAVE OUT MY PAST ACHIEVE-MENTS.
BUT I WANT A NORMAL LIFE.
...WELL, FINE.
OUR GUILD DOESN'T CARE WHO YOU ARE OR WHERE YOU'RE FROM.
WHAT'S IMPORTANT IS THAT YOU EXCEL AT ONE TALENT!
IF YOU DO, I WOULDN'T MIND GIVING YOU A JOB.

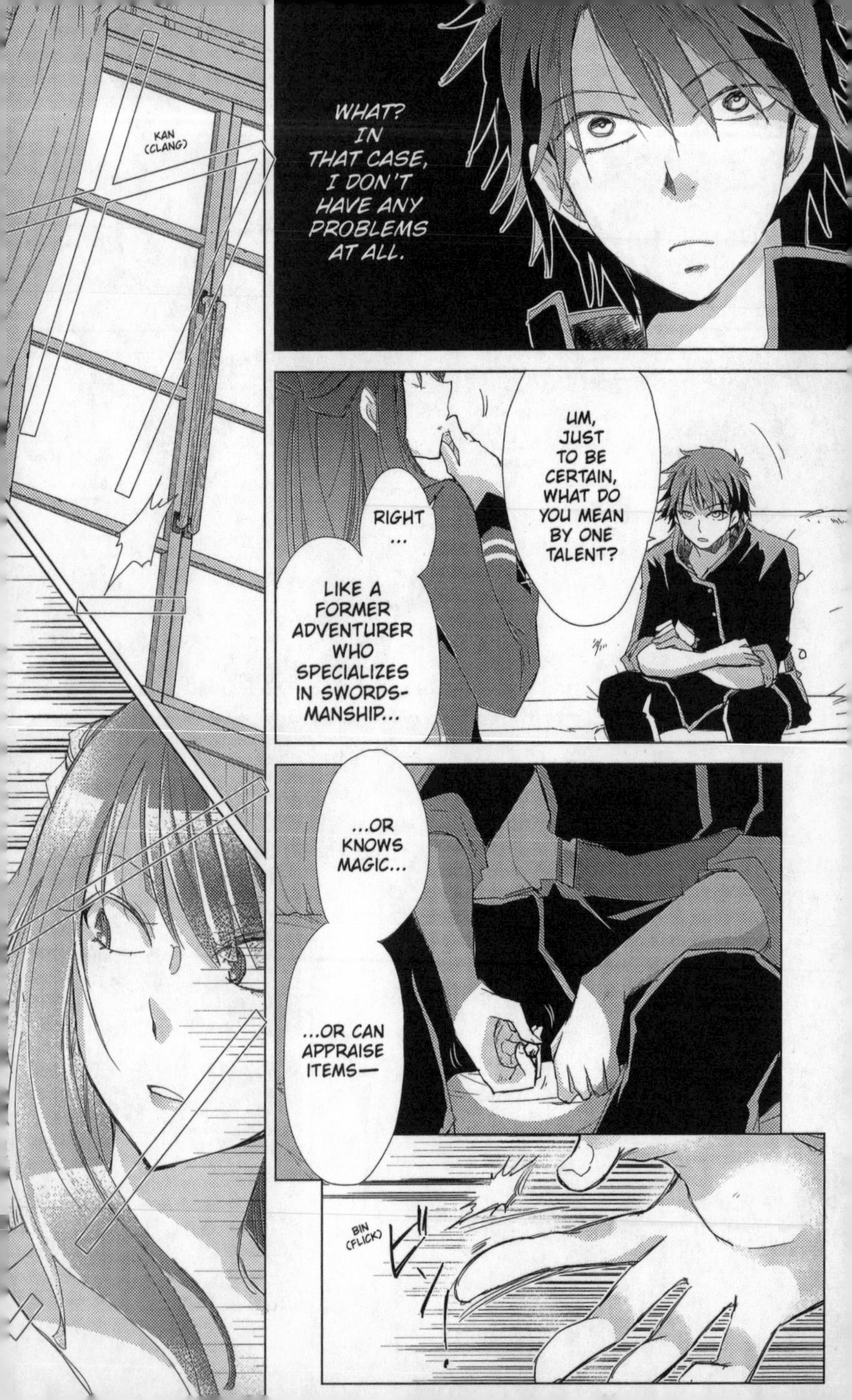
WHAT? IN THAT CASE, I DON'T HAVE ANY PROBLEMS AT ALL.
UM, JUST TO BE CERTAIN, WHAT DO YOU MEAN BY ONE TALENT?
RIGHT...
LIKE A FORMER ADVENTURER WHO SPECIALIZES IN SWORDS-MANSHIP...
...OR KNOWS MAGIC...
...OR CAN APPRAISE ITEMS—
BIN (FLICK)
KAN (CLANG)

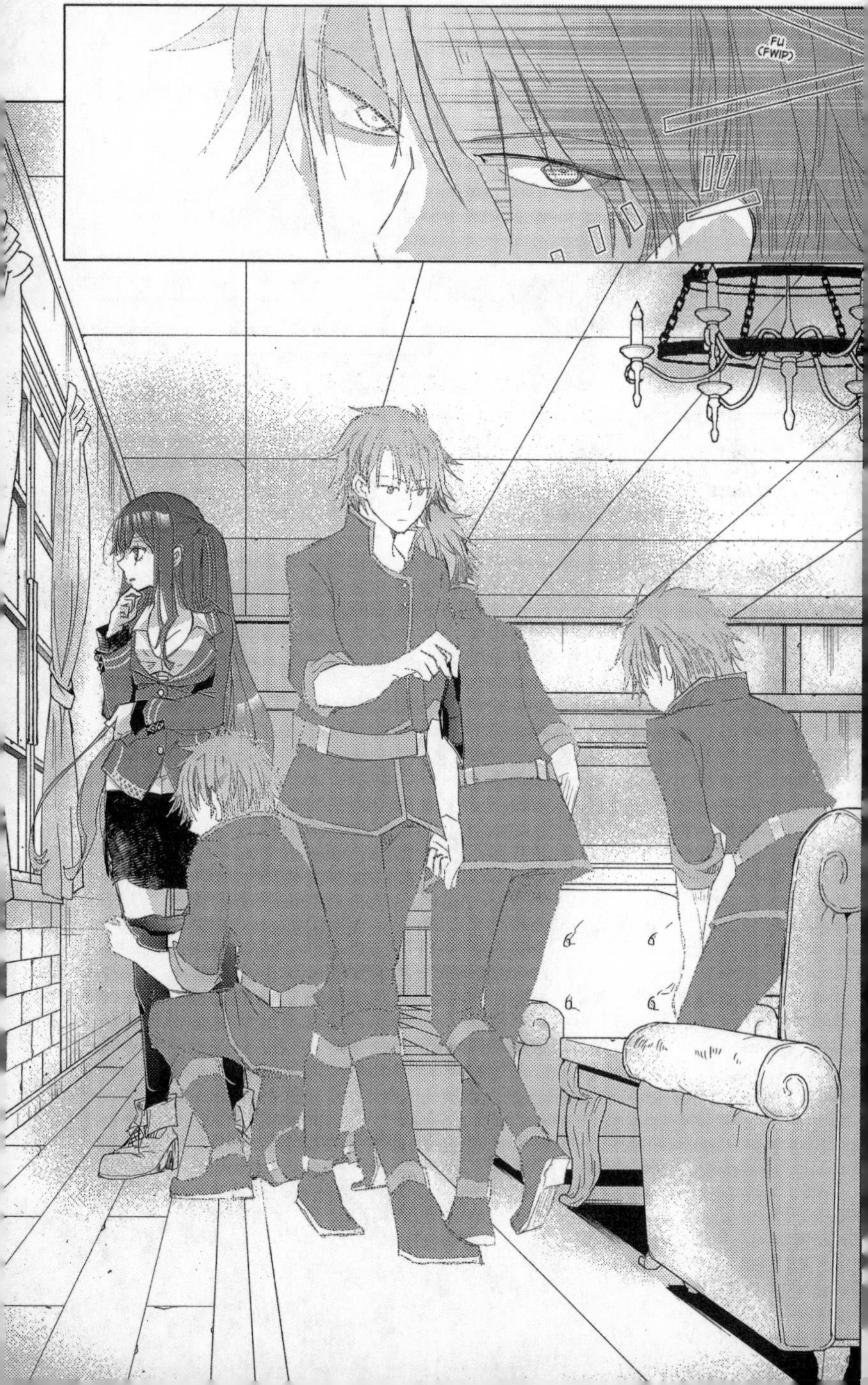
FU
(FWIP)

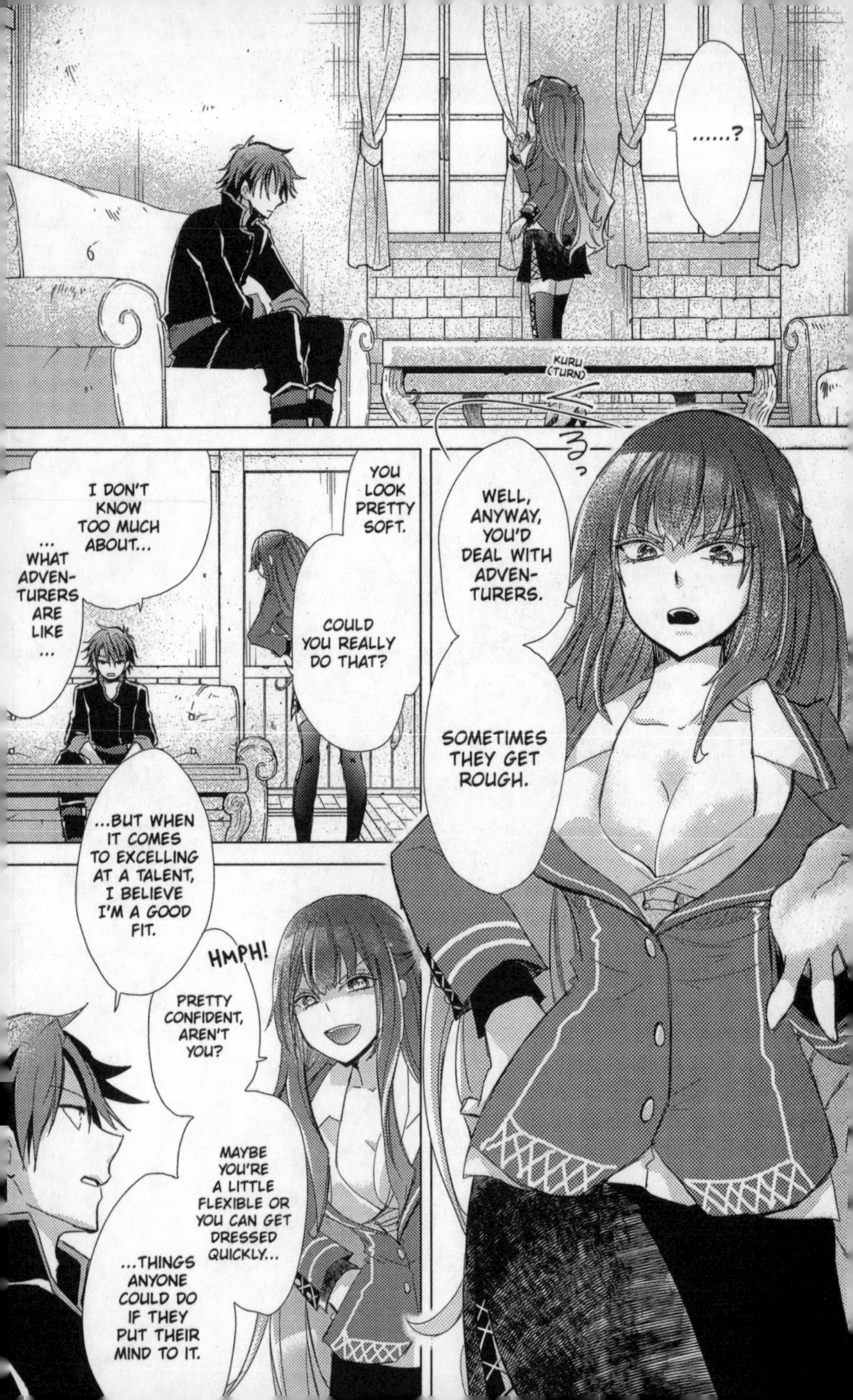
......?
KURU (TURN)
WELL, ANYWAY, YOU'D DEAL WITH ADVEN-TURERS.
SOMETIMES THEY GET ROUGH.
YOU LOOK PRETTY SOFT.
COULD YOU REALLY DO THAT?
I DON'T KNOW TOO MUCH ABOUT...
...WHAT ADVEN-TURERS ARE LIKE...
...BUT WHEN IT COMES TO EXCELLING AT A TALENT, I BELIEVE I'M A GOOD FIT.
HMPH!
PRETTY CONFIDENT, AREN'T YOU?
MAYBE YOU'RE A LITTLE FLEXIBLE OR YOU CAN GET DRESSED QUICKLY...
...THINGS ANYONE COULD DO IF THEY PUT THEIR MIND TO IT.

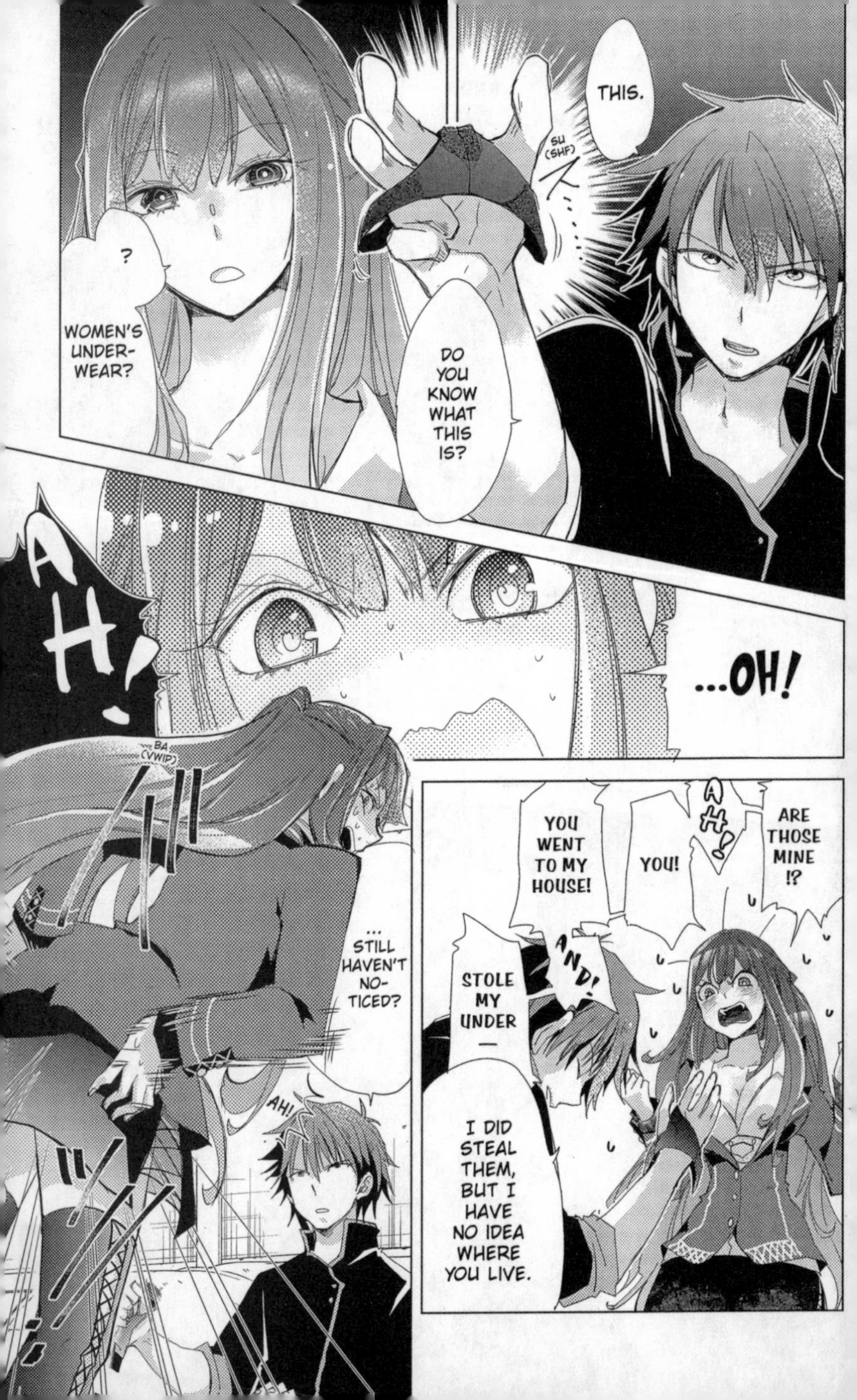
THIS.
SU (SHF)
DO YOU KNOW WHAT THIS IS?
?
WOMEN'S UNDER-WEAR?
...OH!
AH!
ARE THOSE MINE!?
AH!
YOU!
YOU WENT TO MY HOUSE!
AND!
STOLE MY UNDER—
I DID STEAL THEM, BUT I HAVE NO IDEA WHERE YOU LIVE.
BA (VWIP)
... STILL HAVEN'T NO-TICED?
AH!

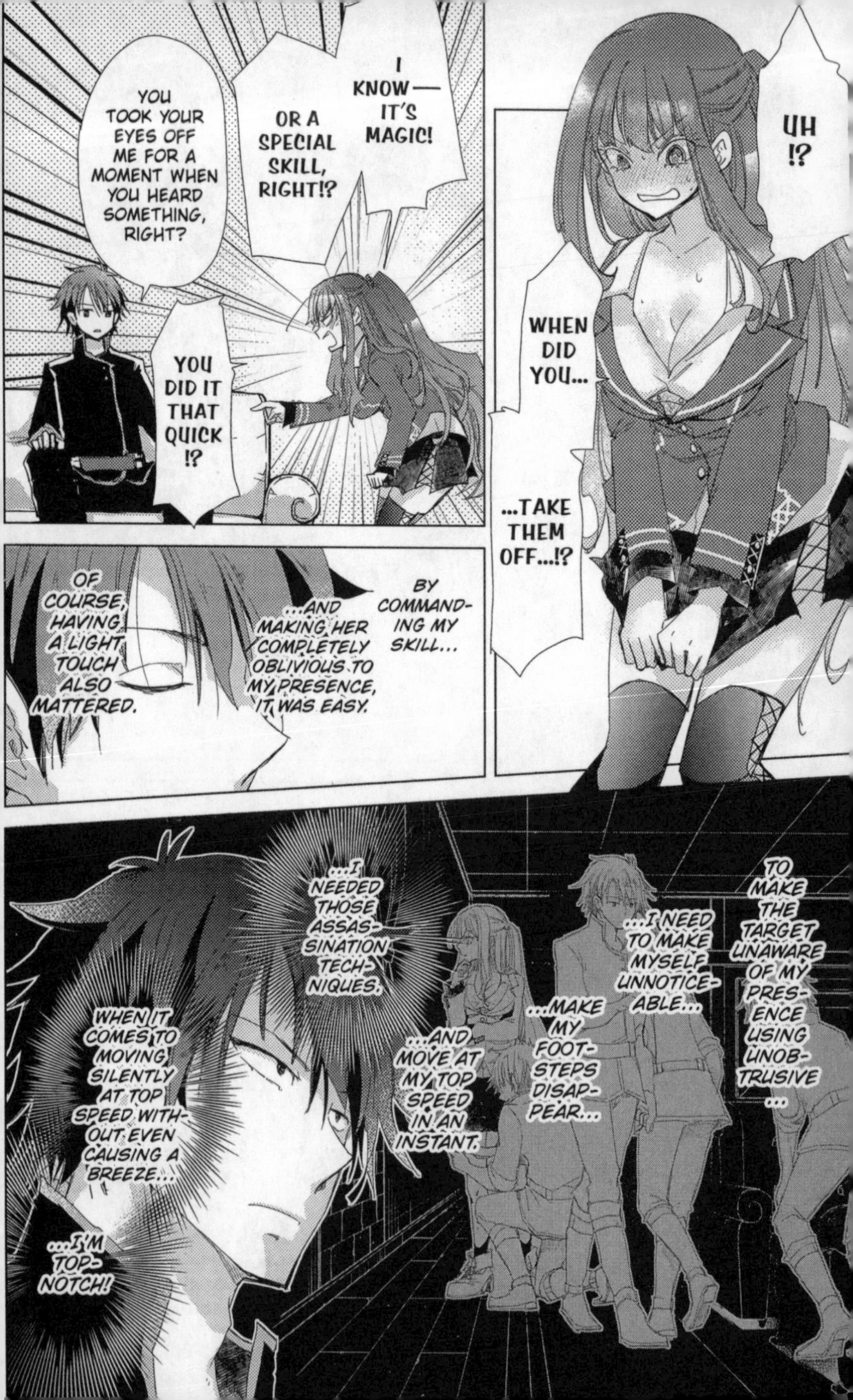
UH !?
WHEN DID YOU...
...TAKE THEM OFF...!?
I KNOW— IT'S MAGIC!
OR A SPECIAL SKILL, RIGHT!?
YOU TOOK YOUR EYES OFF ME FOR A MOMENT WHEN YOU HEARD SOMETHING, RIGHT?
YOU DID IT THAT QUICK !?
BY COMMAND-ING MY SKILL...
...AND MAKING HER COMPLETELY OBLIVIOUS TO MY PRESENCE, IT WAS EASY.
OF COURSE, HAVING A LIGHT TOUCH ALSO MATTERED.
TO MAKE THE TARGET UNAWARE OF MY PRES-ENCE USING UNOB-TRUSIVE ...
...I NEED TO MAKE MYSELF UNNOTICE-ABLE...
...MAKE MY FOOT-STEPS DISAP-PEAR...
...AND MOVE AT MY TOP SPEED IN AN INSTANT.
...I NEEDED THOSE ASSAS-SINATION TECH-NIQUES.
WHEN IT COMES TO MOVING SILENTLY AT TOP SPEED WITH-OUT EVEN CAUSING A BREEZE...
...I'M TOP-NOTCH!

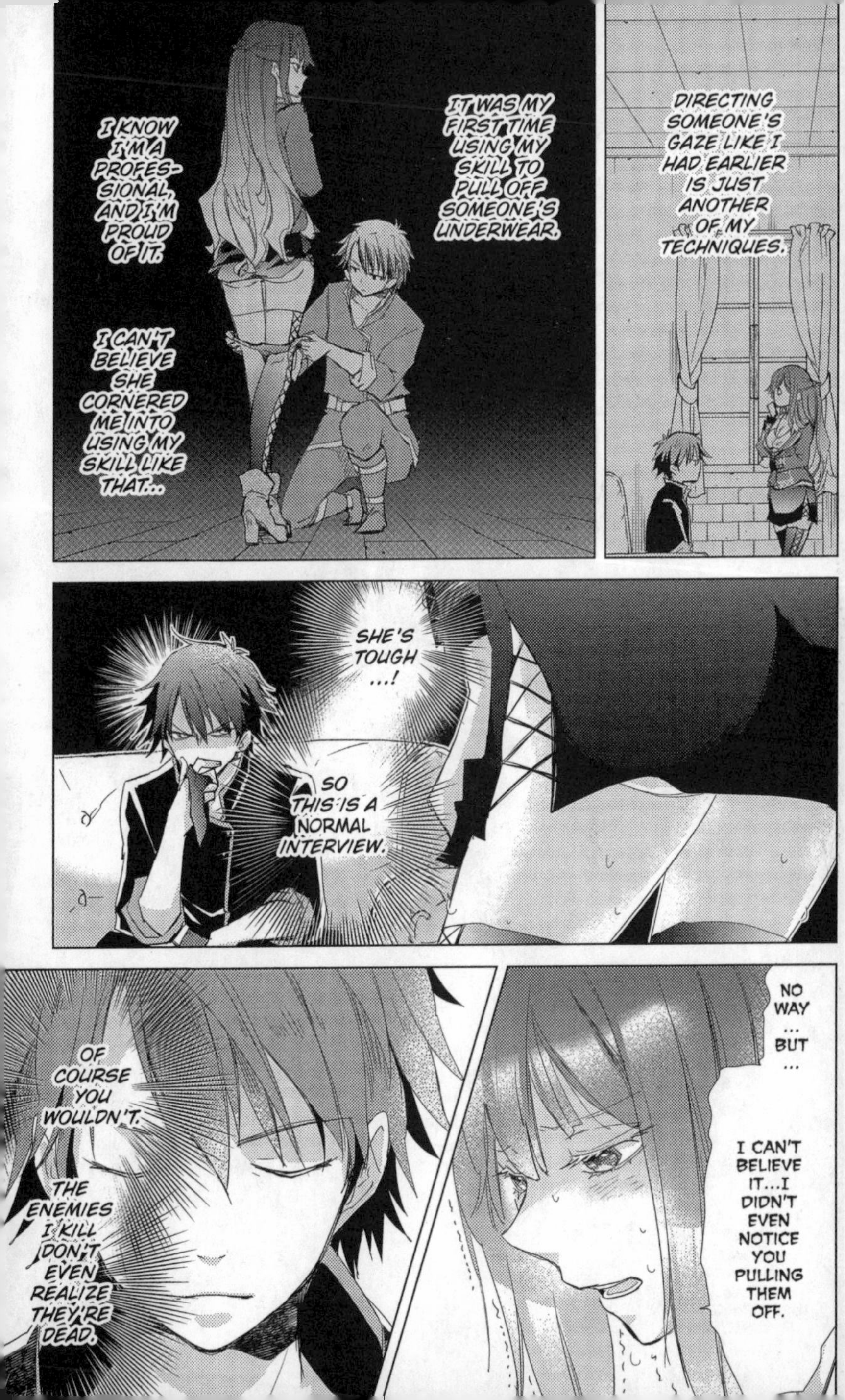
DIRECTING SOMEONE'S GAZE LIKE I HAD EARLIER IS JUST ANOTHER OF MY TECHNIQUES.
IT WAS MY FIRST TIME USING MY SKILL TO PULL OFF SOMEONE'S UNDERWEAR.
I KNOW I'M A PROFES-SIONAL, AND I'M PROUD OF IT.
I CAN'T BELIEVE SHE CORNERED ME INTO USING MY SKILL LIKE THAT...
SHE'S TOUGH...!
SO THIS IS A NORMAL INTERVIEW.
NO WAY... BUT...
I CAN'T BELIEVE IT...I DIDN'T EVEN NOTICE YOU PULLING THEM OFF.
OF COURSE YOU WOULDN'T.
THE ENEMIES I KILL DON'T EVEN REALIZE THEY'RE DEAD.

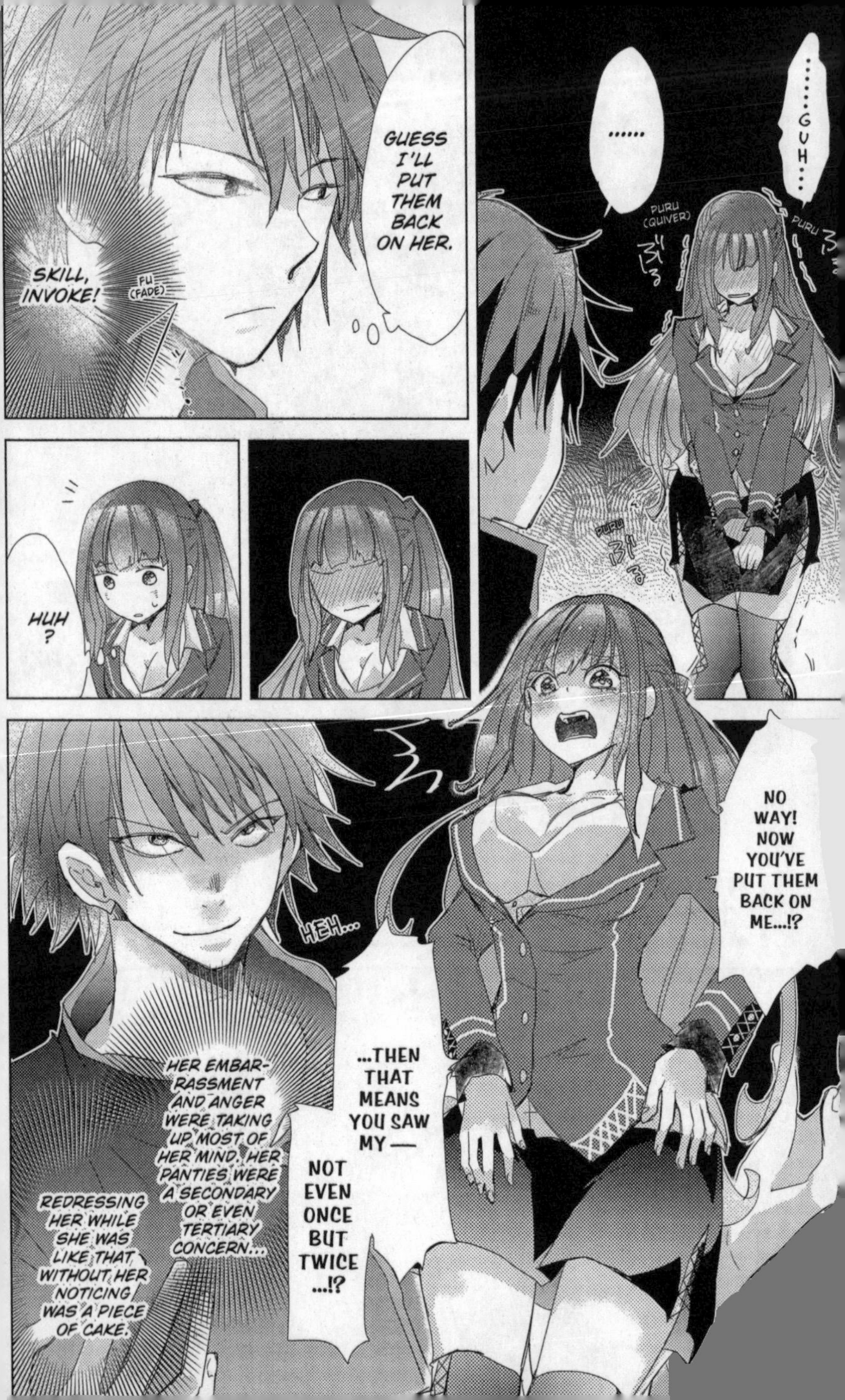
......GUH......
......
PURU (QUIVER)
PURU
PURU
GUESS I'LL PUT THEM BACK ON HER.
FU (FADE)
SKILL, INVOKE!
HUH?
NO WAY! NOW YOU'VE PUT THEM BACK ON ME...!?
...THEN THAT MEANS YOU SAW MY—
NOT EVEN ONCE BUT TWICE...!?
HEH...
HER EMBARRASSMENT AND ANGER WERE TAKING UP MOST OF HER MIND. HER PANTIES WERE A SECONDARY OR EVEN TERTIARY CONCERN...
REDRESSING HER WHILE SHE WAS LIKE THAT WITHOUT HER NOTICING WAS A PIECE OF CAKE.

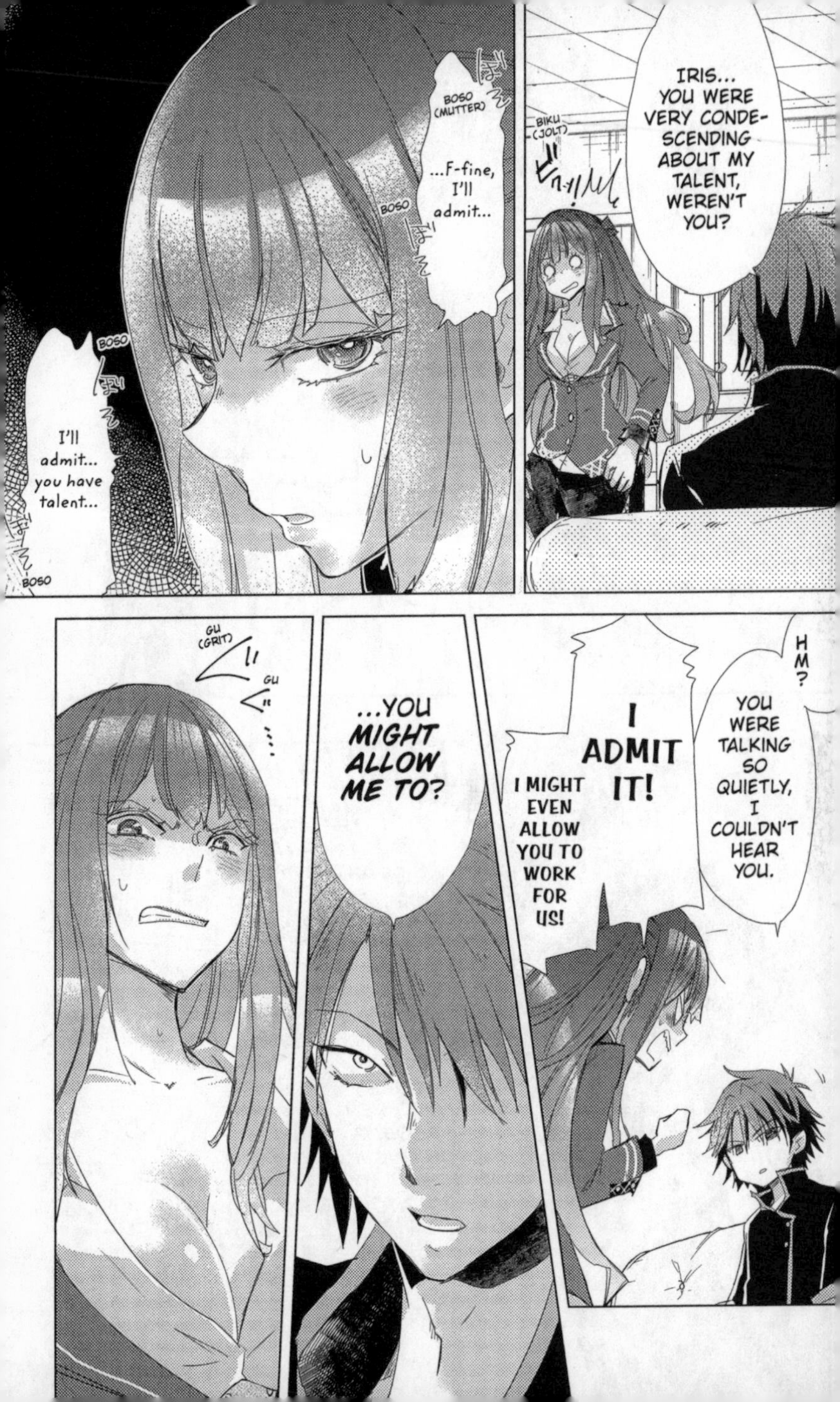
IRIS... YOU WERE VERY CONDE-SCENDING ABOUT MY TALENT, WEREN'T YOU?
BIKU (JOLT)
BOSO (MUTTER)
...F-fine, I'll admit...
BOSO
BOSO
I'll admit... you have talent...
BOSO
HM? YOU WERE TALKING SO QUIETLY, I COULDN'T HEAR YOU.
I ADMIT IT!
I MIGHT EVEN ALLOW YOU TO WORK FOR US!
...YOU MIGHT ALLOW ME TO?
GU (GRIT)
GU

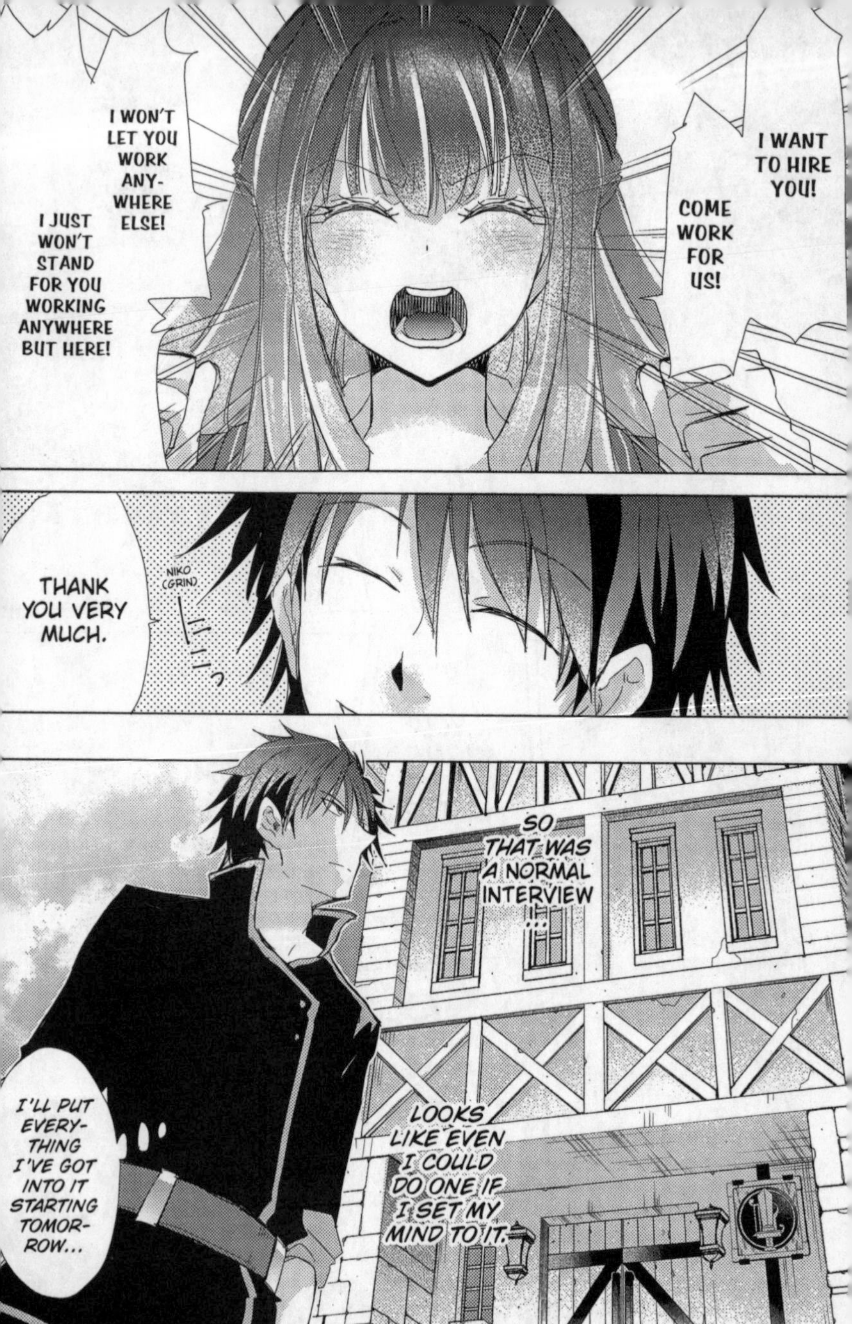
I WANT TO HIRE YOU!
COME WORK FOR US!
I WON'T LET YOU WORK ANY-WHERE ELSE!
I JUST WON'T STAND FOR YOU WORKING ANYWHERE BUT HERE!
NIKO (GRIN)
THANK YOU VERY MUCH.
SO THAT WAS A NORMAL INTERVIEW ...
LOOKS LIKE EVEN I COULD DO ONE IF I SET MY MIND TO IT.
I'LL PUT EVERY-THING I'VE GOT INTO IT STARTING TOMOR-ROW...

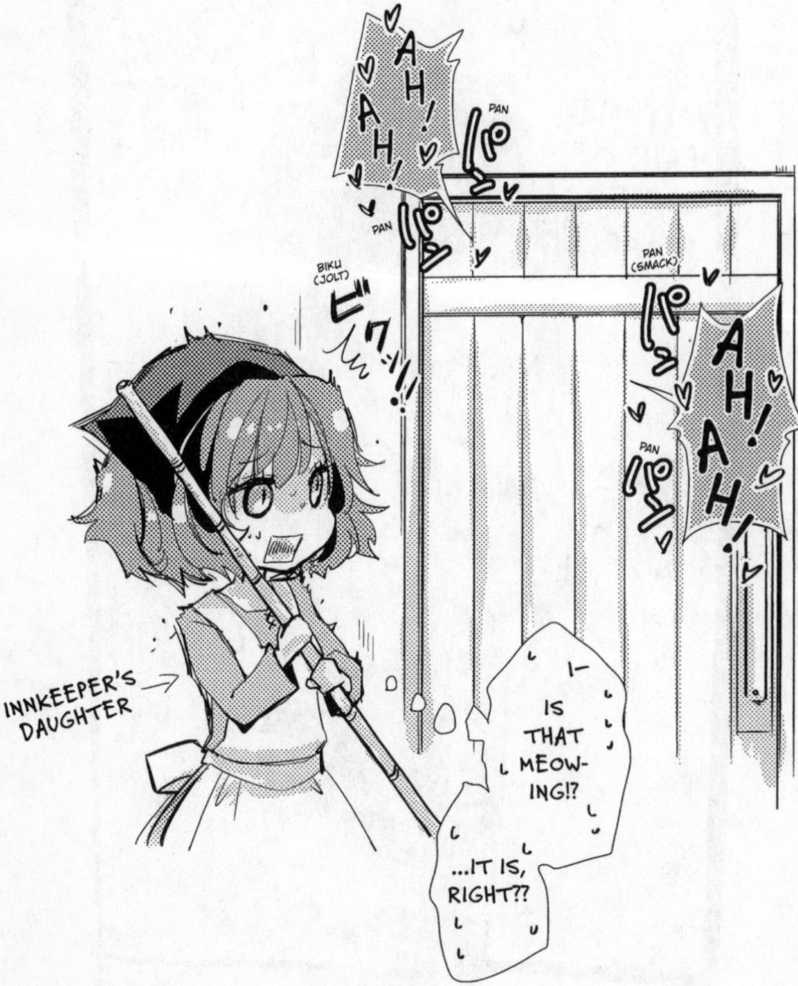
PAN (SMACK)
AH! AH! AH!
PAN
AH! AH!
PAN
PAN
BIKU (JOLT)
I- IS THAT MEOWING!?
...IT IS, RIGHT??
INNKEEPER'S DAUGHTER

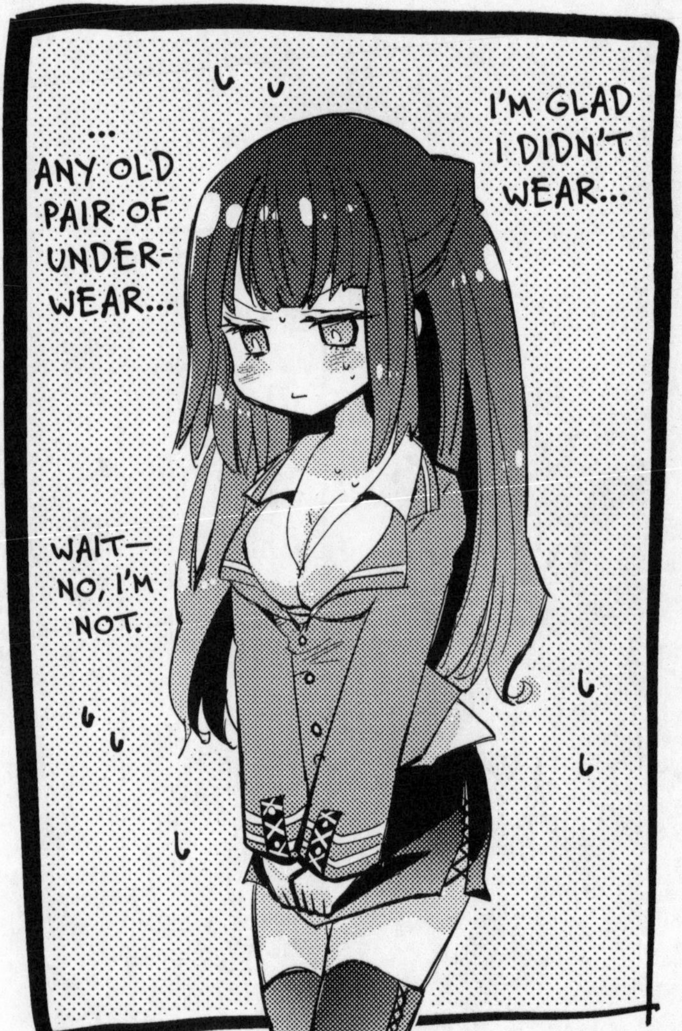
I'M GLAD I DIDN'T WEAR...
... ANY OLD PAIR OF UNDER-WEAR...
WAIT— NO, I'M NOT.

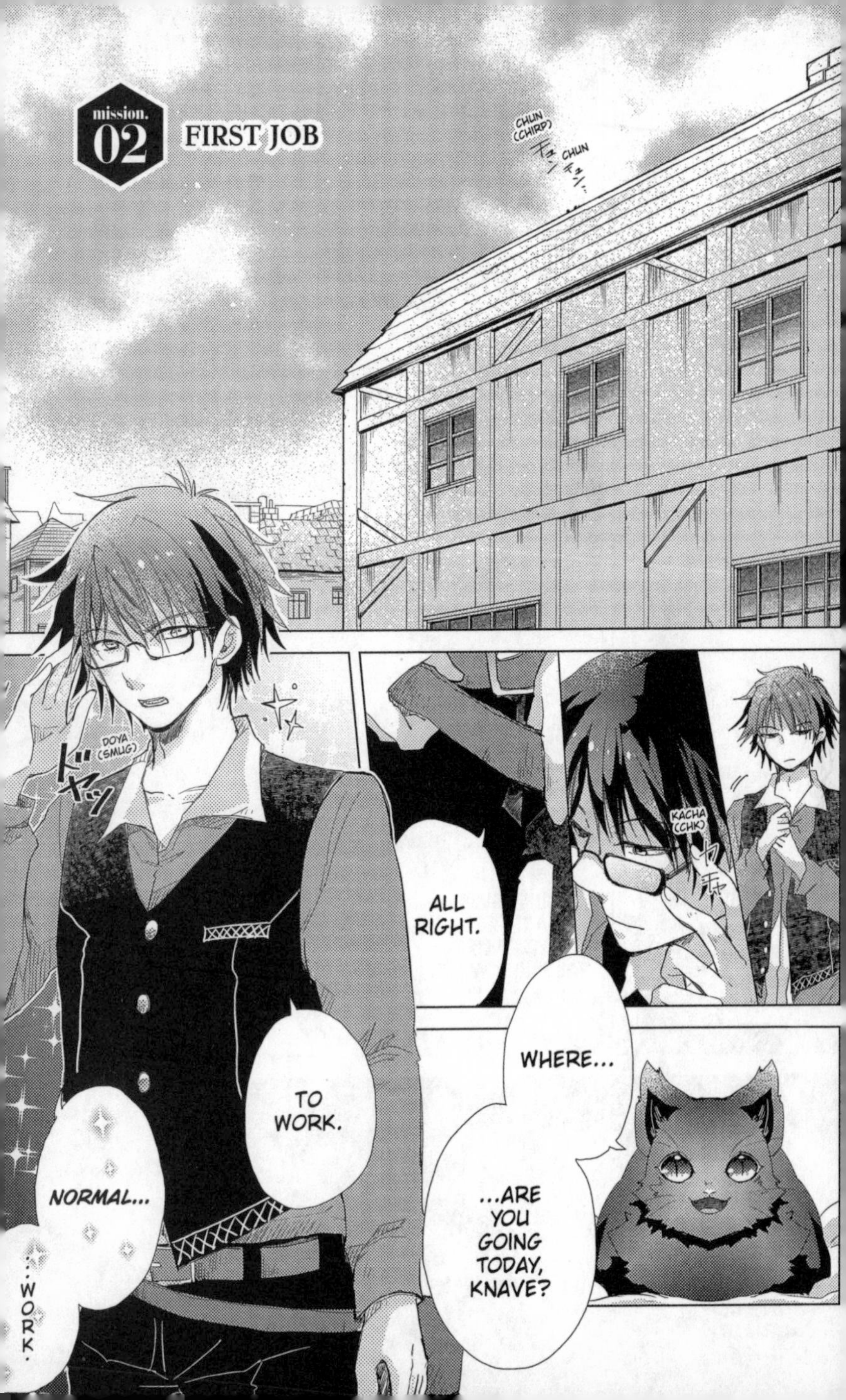
mission. 02
FIRST JOB
CHUN (CHIRP)
CHUN
KACHA (CHK)
ALL RIGHT.
WHERE...
...ARE YOU GOING TODAY, KNAVE?
DOYA (SMUG)
TO WORK.
NORMAL...
...WORK.

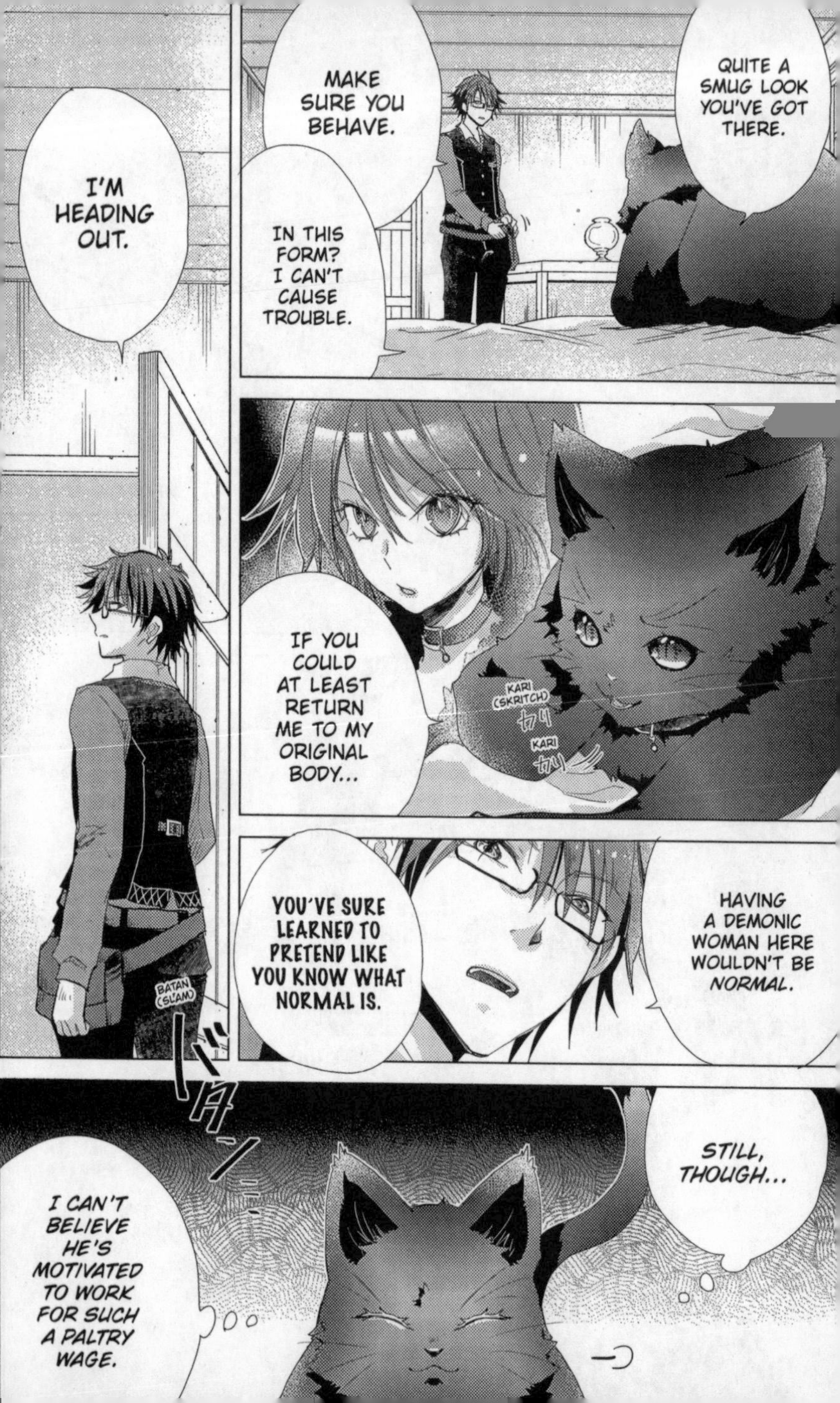
QUITE A SMUG LOOK YOU'VE GOT THERE.
MAKE SURE YOU BEHAVE.
IN THIS FORM? I CAN'T CAUSE TROUBLE.
IF YOU COULD AT LEAST RETURN ME TO MY ORIGINAL BODY...
KARI (SKRITCH)
KARI
HAVING A DEMONIC WOMAN HERE WOULDN'T BE NORMAL.
YOU'VE SURE LEARNED TO PRETEND LIKE YOU KNOW WHAT NORMAL IS.
I'M HEADING OUT.
BATAN (SLAM)
STILL, THOUGH...
I CAN'T BELIEVE HE'S MOTIVATED TO WORK FOR SUCH A PALTRY WAGE.

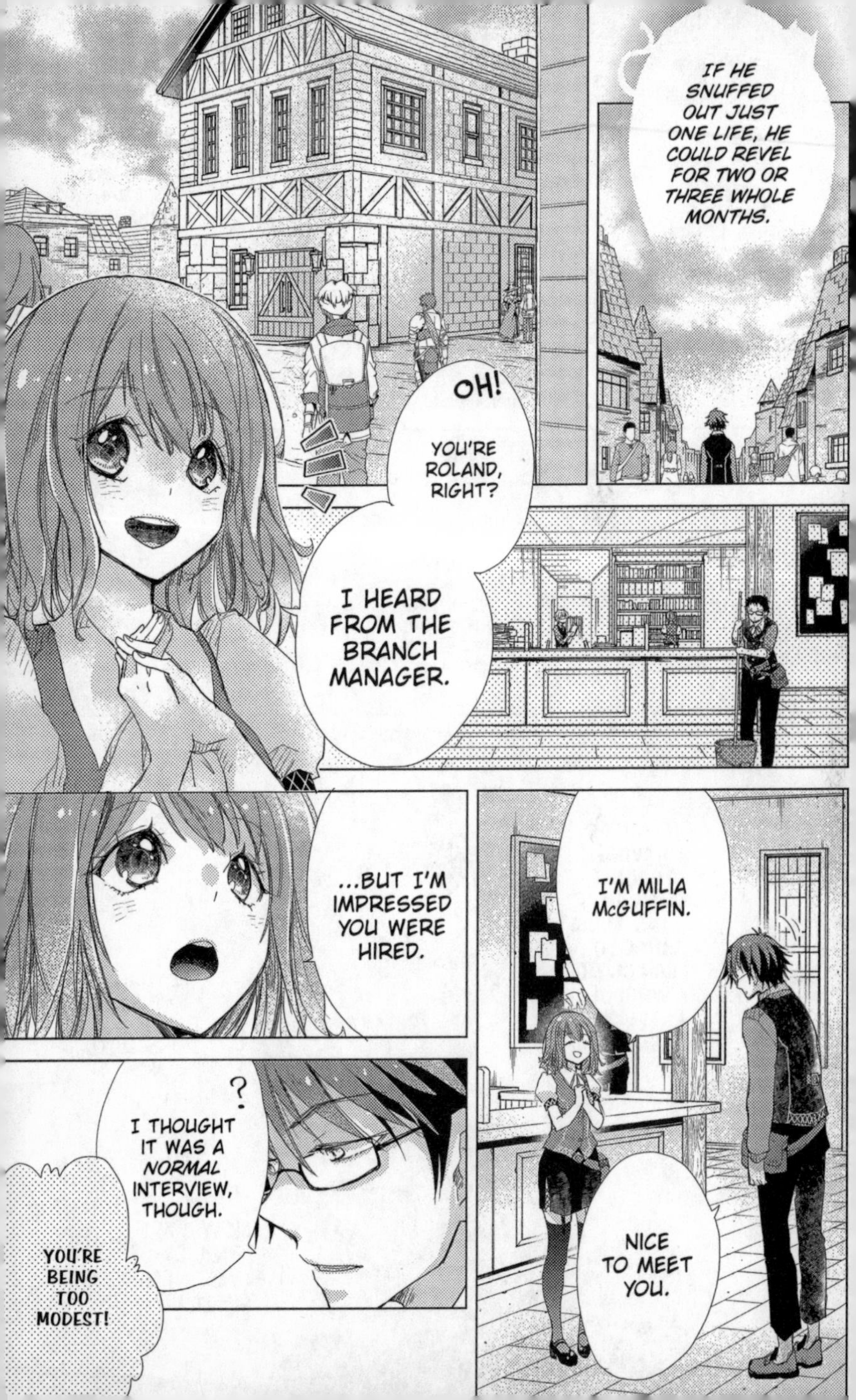
IF HE SNUFFED OUT JUST ONE LIFE, HE COULD REVEL FOR TWO OR THREE WHOLE MONTHS.
OH!
YOU'RE ROLAND, RIGHT?
I HEARD FROM THE BRANCH MANAGER.
I'M MILIA McGUFFIN.
NICE TO MEET YOU.
...BUT I'M IMPRESSED YOU WERE HIRED.
?
I THOUGHT IT WAS A *NORMAL* INTERVIEW, THOUGH.
YOU'RE BEING TOO MODEST!

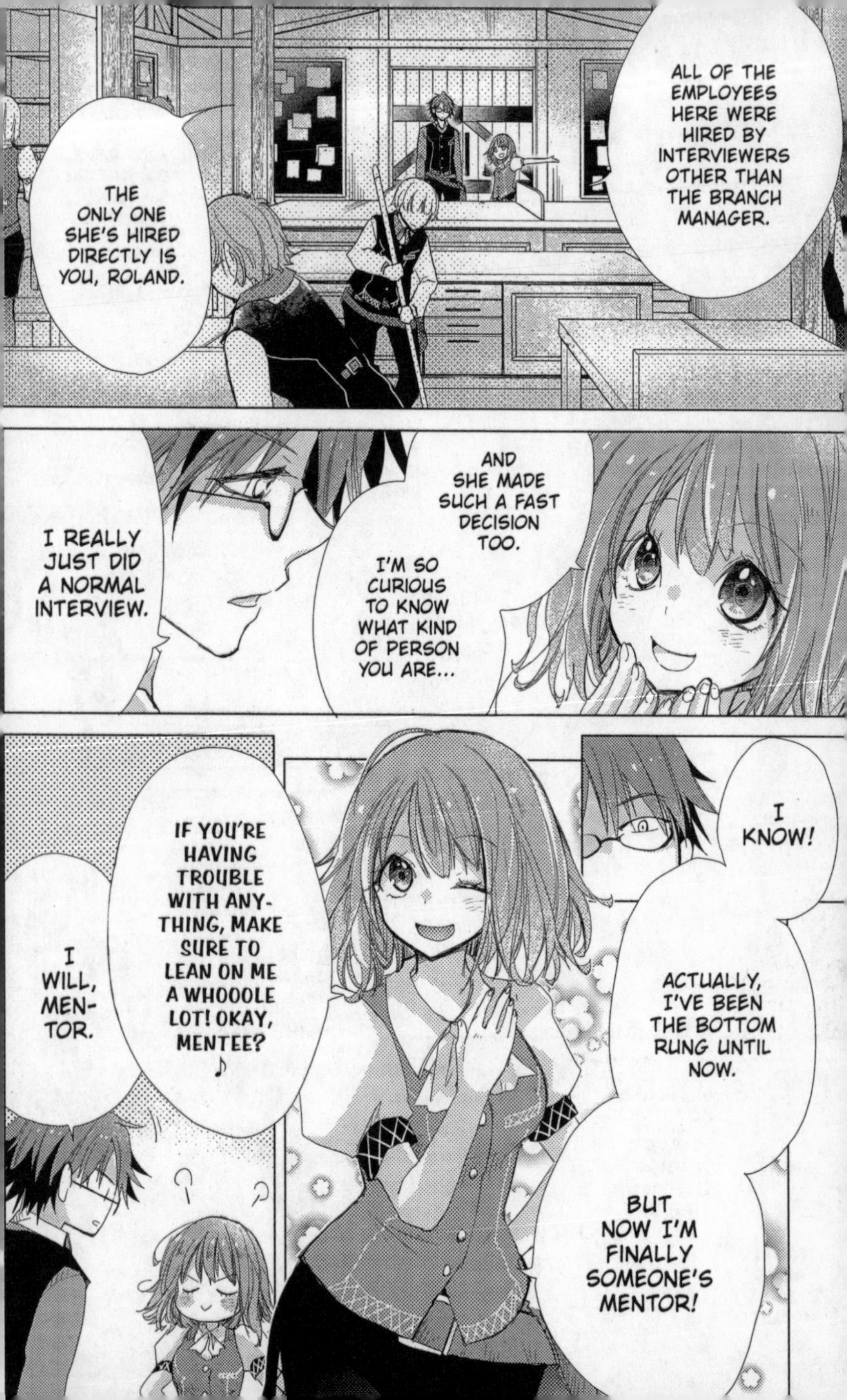
ALL OF THE EMPLOYEES HERE WERE HIRED BY INTERVIEWERS OTHER THAN THE BRANCH MANAGER.
THE ONLY ONE SHE'S HIRED DIRECTLY IS YOU, ROLAND.
AND SHE MADE SUCH A FAST DECISION TOO.
I'M SO CURIOUS TO KNOW WHAT KIND OF PERSON YOU ARE...
I REALLY JUST DID A NORMAL INTERVIEW.
I KNOW!
ACTUALLY, I'VE BEEN THE BOTTOM RUNG UNTIL NOW.
BUT NOW I'M FINALLY SOMEONE'S MENTOR!
IF YOU'RE HAVING TROUBLE WITH ANY-THING, MAKE SURE TO LEAN ON ME A WHOOOLE LOT! OKAY, MENTEE? ♪
I WILL, MEN-TOR.

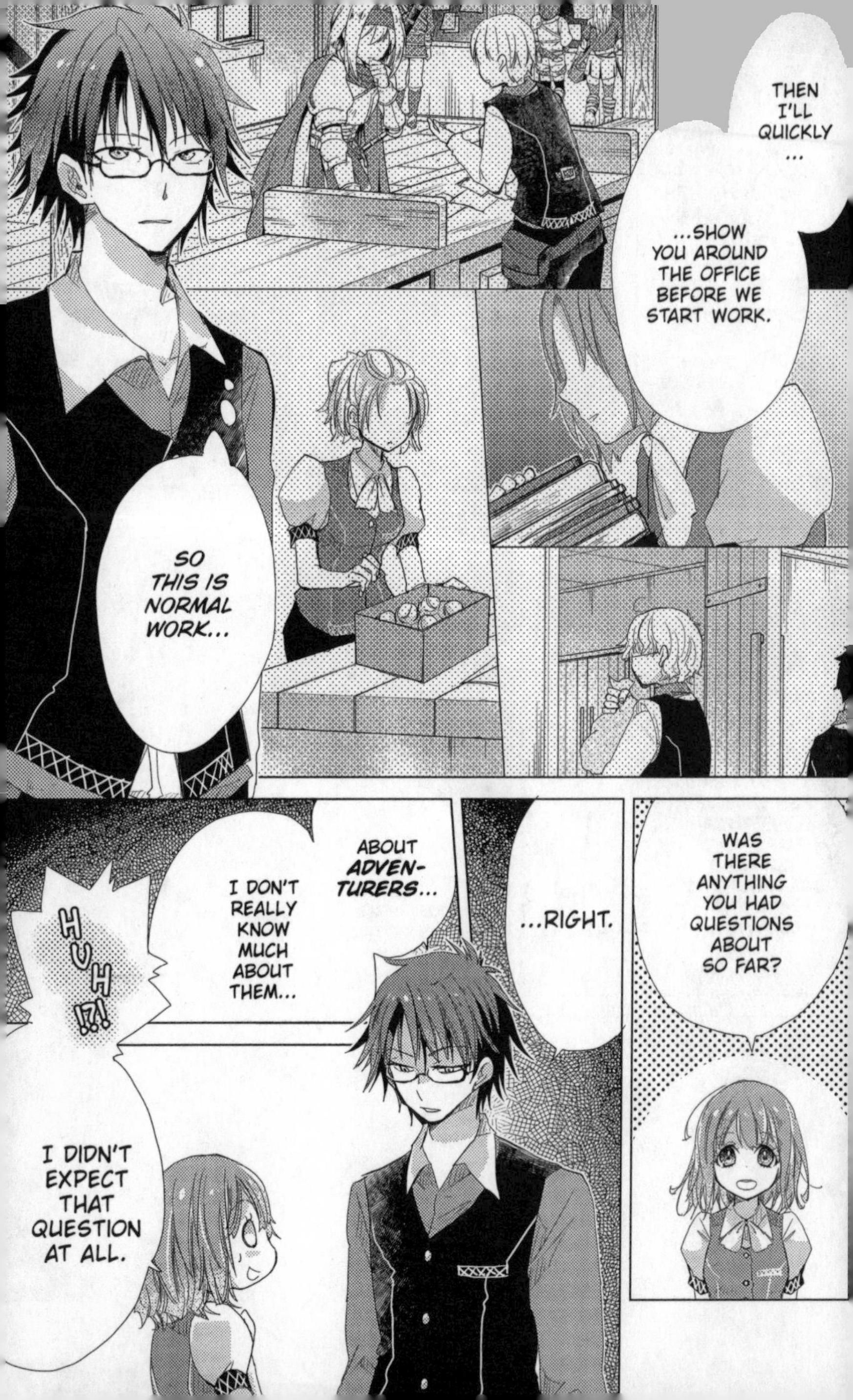
THEN I'LL QUICKLY...
...SHOW YOU AROUND THE OFFICE BEFORE WE START WORK.
SO THIS IS NORMAL WORK...
WAS THERE ANYTHING YOU HAD QUESTIONS ABOUT SO FAR?
...RIGHT.
ABOUT ADVENTURERS...
I DON'T REALLY KNOW MUCH ABOUT THEM...
HUH!?!
I DIDN'T EXPECT THAT QUESTION AT ALL.

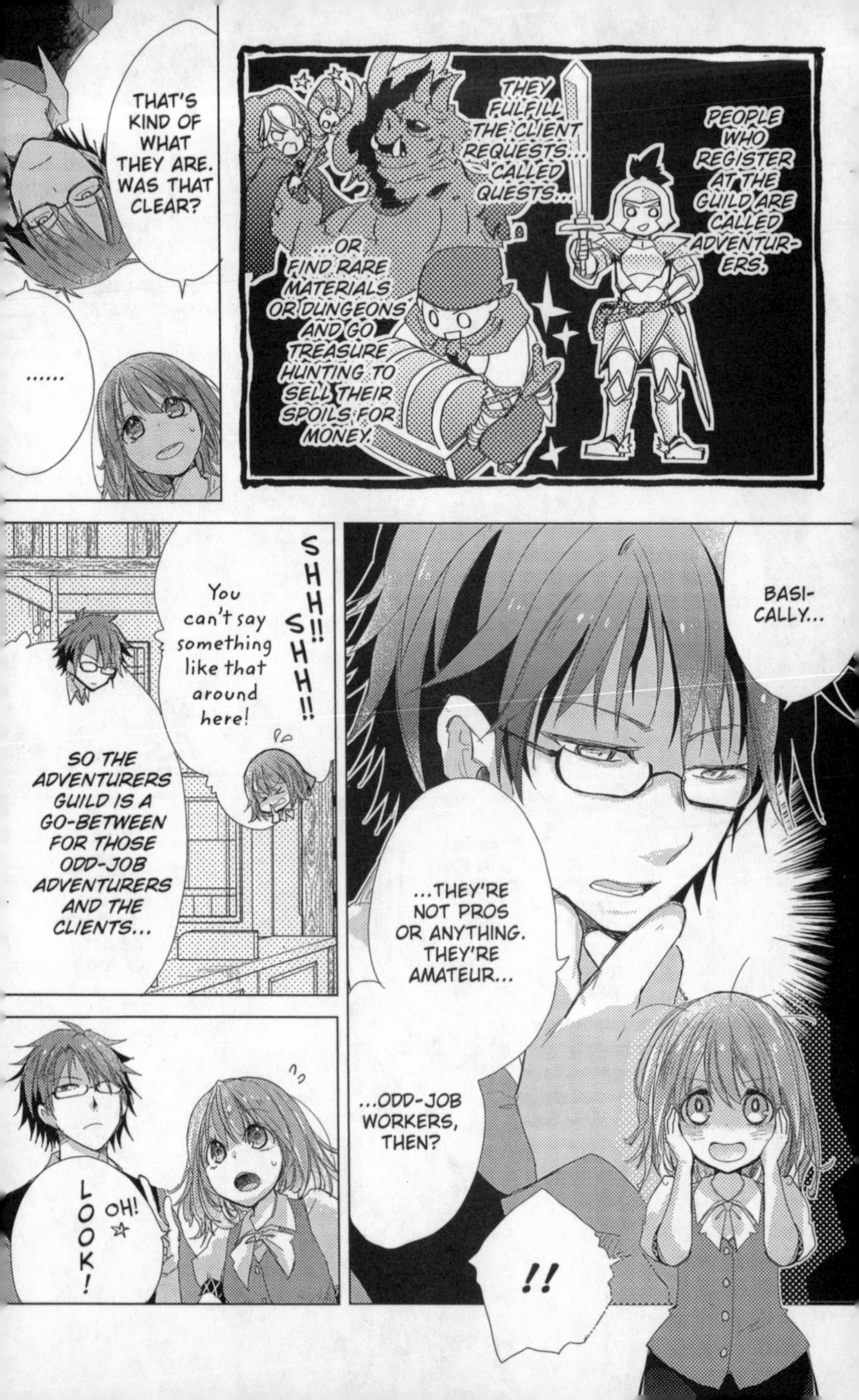
PEOPLE WHO REGISTER AT THE GUILD ARE CALLED ADVENTURERS.
THEY FULFILL THE CLIENT REQUESTS... CALLED QUESTS...
...OR FIND RARE MATERIALS OR DUNGEONS AND GO TREASURE HUNTING TO SELL THEIR SPOILS FOR MONEY.
THAT'S KIND OF WHAT THEY ARE. WAS THAT CLEAR?
......
BASICALLY...
...THEY'RE NOT PROS OR ANYTHING. THEY'RE AMATEUR...
...ODD-JOB WORKERS, THEN?
!!
SHH!! SHH!!
You can't say something like that around here!
SO THE ADVENTURERS GUILD IS A GO-BETWEEN FOR THOSE ODD-JOB ADVENTURERS AND THE CLIENTS...
OH!
LOOK!

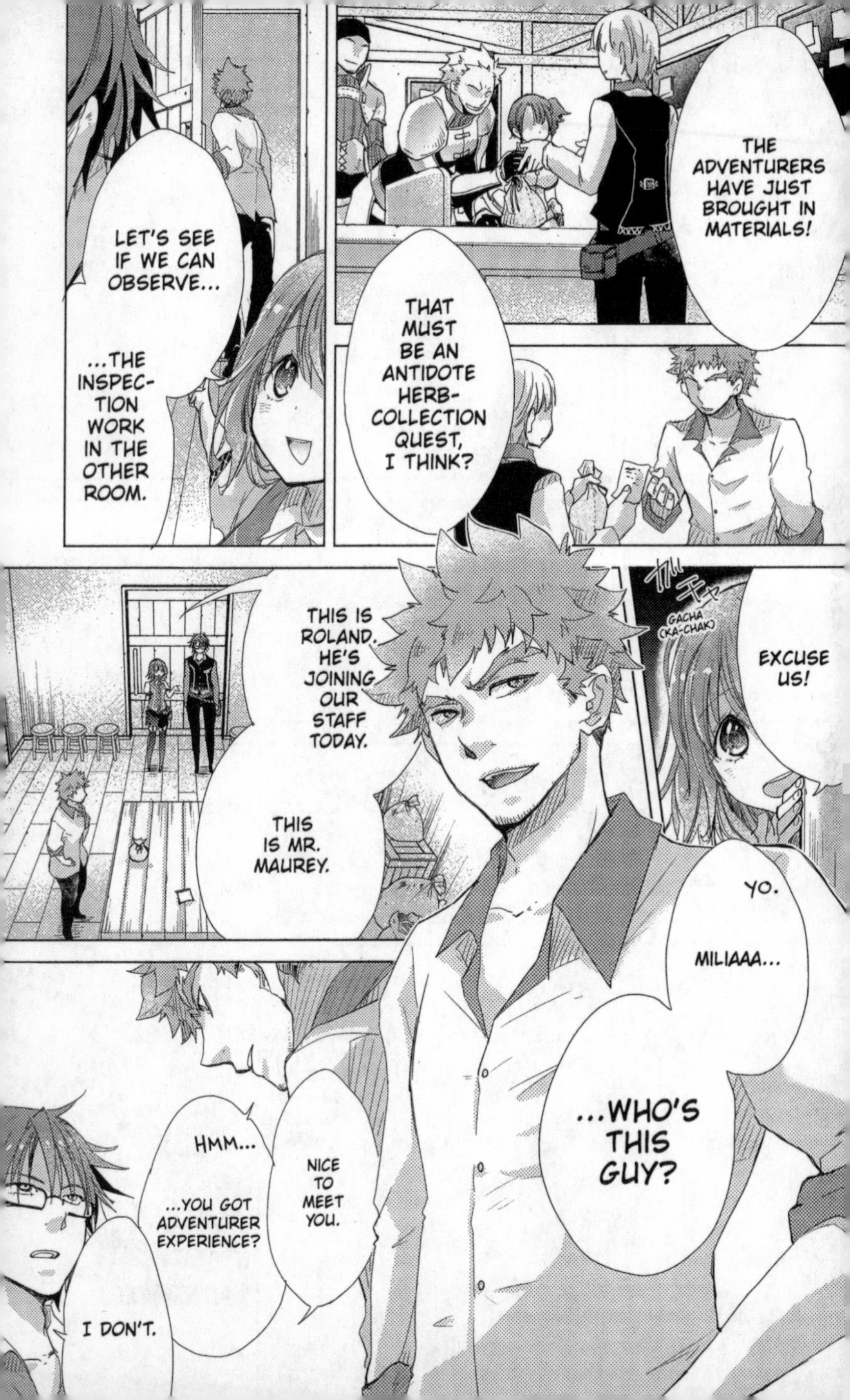
THE ADVENTURERS HAVE JUST BROUGHT IN MATERIALS!
THAT MUST BE AN ANTIDOTE HERB-COLLECTION QUEST, I THINK?
LET'S SEE IF WE CAN OBSERVE...
...THE INSPEC-TION WORK IN THE OTHER ROOM.
GACHA (KA-CHAK)
EXCUSE US!
YO.
MILIAAA...
...WHO'S THIS GUY?
THIS IS ROLAND. HE'S JOINING OUR STAFF TODAY.
THIS IS MR. MAUREY.
NICE TO MEET YOU.
HMM...
...YOU GOT ADVENTURER EXPERIENCE?
I DON'T.

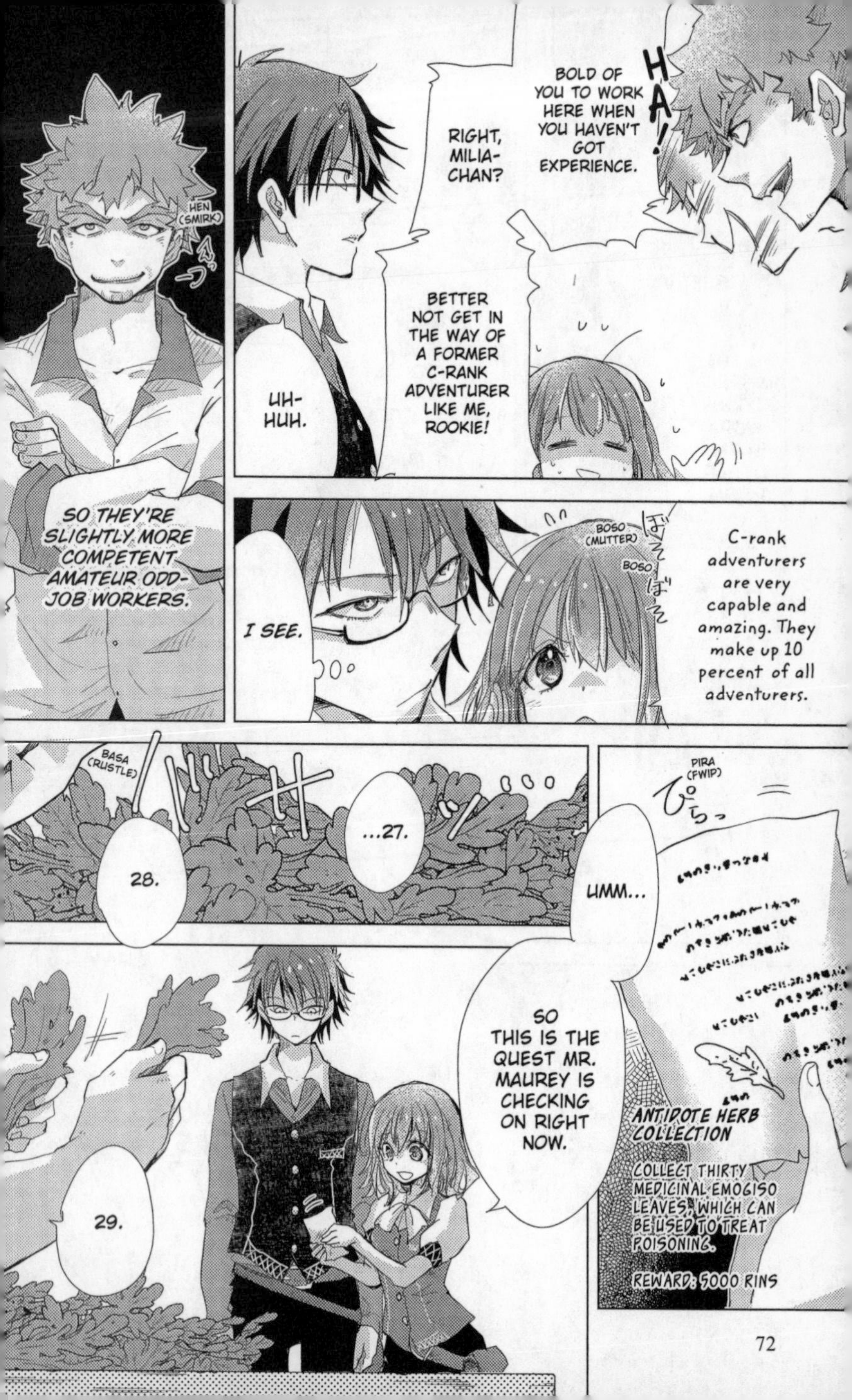
HA!
BOLD OF YOU TO WORK HERE WHEN YOU HAVEN'T GOT EXPERIENCE.
RIGHT, MILIA-CHAN?
BETTER NOT GET IN THE WAY OF A FORMER C-RANK ADVENTURER LIKE ME, ROOKIE!
UH-HUH.
C-rank adventurers are very capable and amazing. They make up 10 percent of all adventurers.
BOSO (MUTTER)
BOSO
I SEE.
HEN (SMIRK)
SO THEY'RE SLIGHTLY MORE COMPETENT AMATEUR ODD-JOB WORKERS.
PIRA (FWIP)
UMM...
ANTIDOTE HERB COLLECTION
COLLECT THIRTY MEDICINAL EMOGISO LEAVES, WHICH CAN BE USED TO TREAT POISONING.
REWARD: 5000 RINS
BASA (RUSTLE)
...27.
28.
SO THIS IS THE QUEST MR. MAUREY IS CHECKING ON RIGHT NOW.
29.

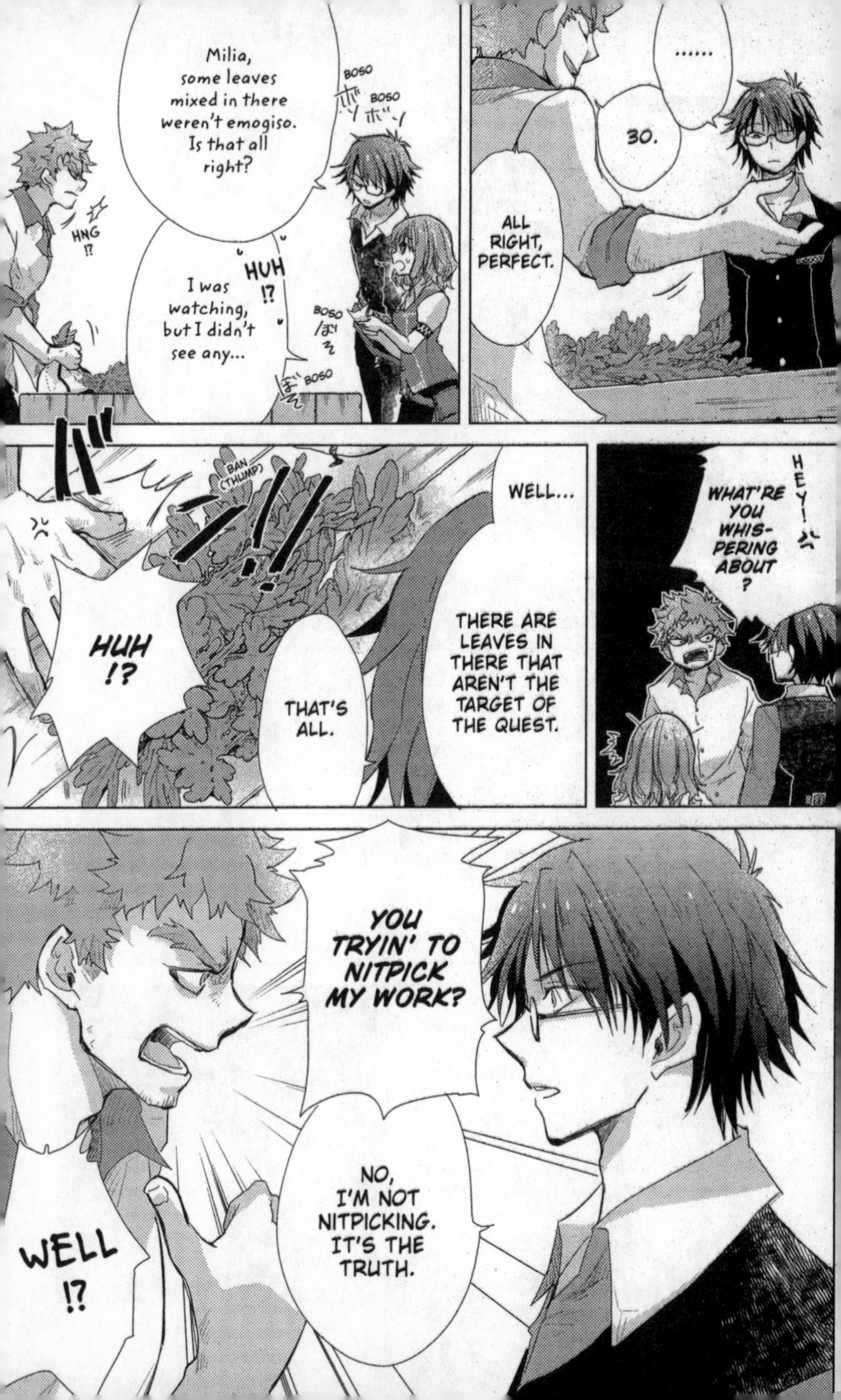
......
30.
ALL RIGHT, PERFECT.
Milia, some leaves mixed in there weren't emogiso. Is that all right?
BOSO
BOSO
HUH!?
I was watching, but I didn't see any...
BOSO
BOSO
HNG!?
HEY!
WHAT'RE YOU WHISPERING ABOUT?
WELL...
THERE ARE LEAVES IN THERE THAT AREN'T THE TARGET OF THE QUEST.
THAT'S ALL.
BAN (THUMP)
HUH!?
YOU TRYIN' TO NITPICK MY WORK?
NO, I'M NOT NITPICKING. IT'S THE TRUTH.
WELL!?

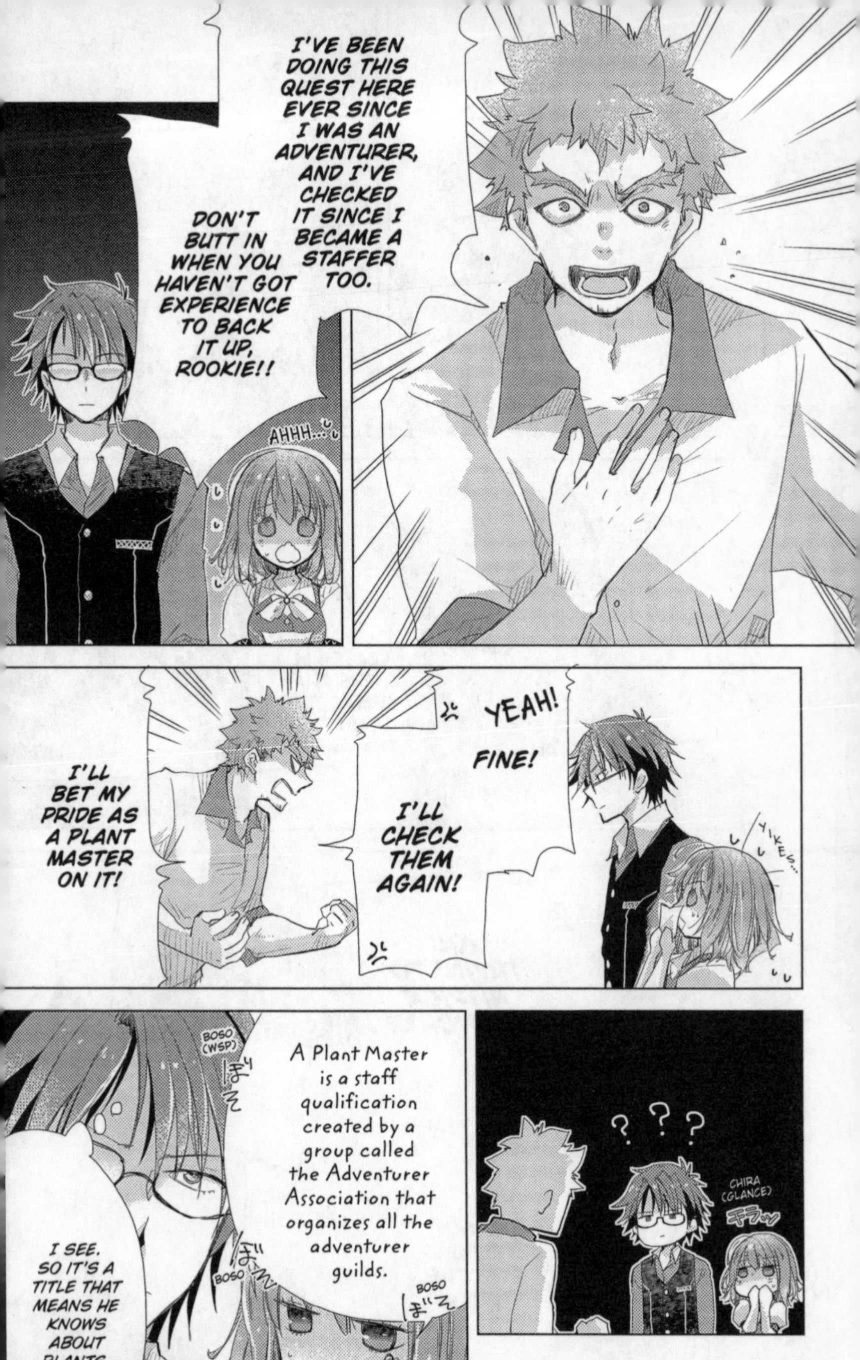
I'VE BEEN DOING THIS QUEST HERE EVER SINCE I WAS AN ADVENTURER, AND I'VE CHECKED IT SINCE I BECAME A STAFFER TOO.
DON'T BUTT IN WHEN YOU HAVEN'T GOT EXPERIENCE TO BACK IT UP, ROOKIE!!
AHHH...
YEAH!
YIKES...
FINE!
I'LL CHECK THEM AGAIN!
I'LL BET MY PRIDE AS A PLANT MASTER ON IT!
? ? ?
CHIRA (GLANCE)
BOSO (WSP)
A Plant Master is a staff qualification created by a group called the Adventurer Association that organizes all the adventurer guilds.
BOSO
BOSO
I SEE. SO IT'S A TITLE THAT MEANS HE KNOWS ABOUT PLANTS.

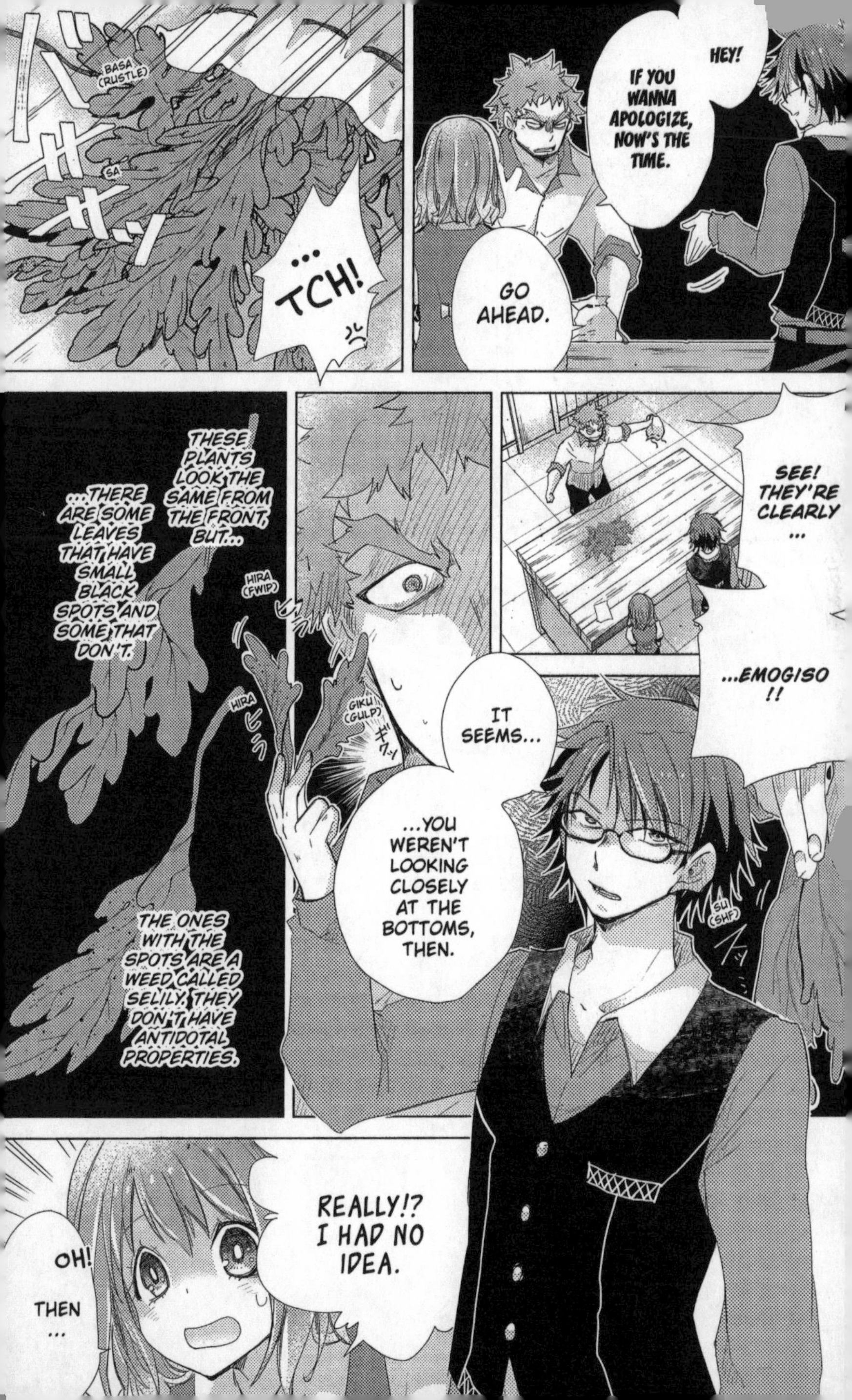
HEY!
IF YOU WANNA APOLOGIZE, NOW'S THE TIME.
GO AHEAD.
BASA (RUSTLE)
SA
...TCH!
SEE! THEY'RE CLEARLY...
...EMOGISO!!
IT SEEMS...
...YOU WEREN'T LOOKING CLOSELY AT THE BOTTOMS, THEN.
SU (SHF)
GIKU (GULP)
HIRA (FWIP)
HIRA
THESE PLANTS LOOK THE SAME FROM THE FRONT, BUT...
...THERE ARE SOME LEAVES THAT HAVE SMALL BLACK SPOTS AND SOME THAT DON'T.
THE ONES WITH THE SPOTS ARE A WEED CALLED SELILY. THEY DON'T HAVE ANTIDOTAL PROPERTIES.
REALLY!? I HAD NO IDEA.
OH!
THEN...

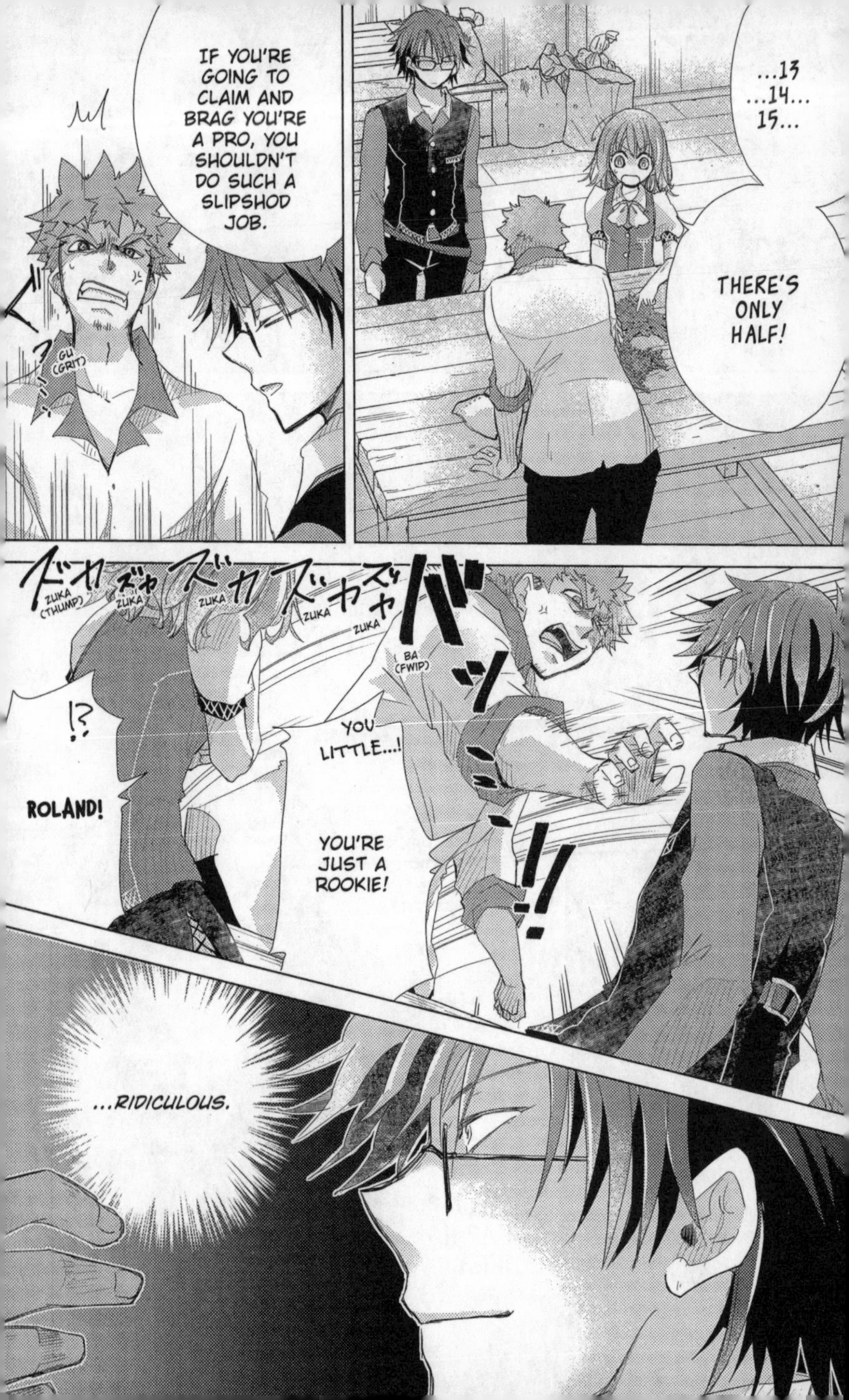
...13
...14...
15...
THERE'S ONLY HALF!
IF YOU'RE GOING TO CLAIM AND BRAG YOU'RE A PRO, YOU SHOULDN'T DO SUCH A SLIPSHOD JOB.
GU (GRIT)
ZUKA (THUMP)
ZUKA
ZUKA
ZUKA
ZUKA
BA (FWIP)
YOU LITTLE...!
YOU'RE JUST A ROOKIE!
!?
ROLAND!
...RIDICULOUS.

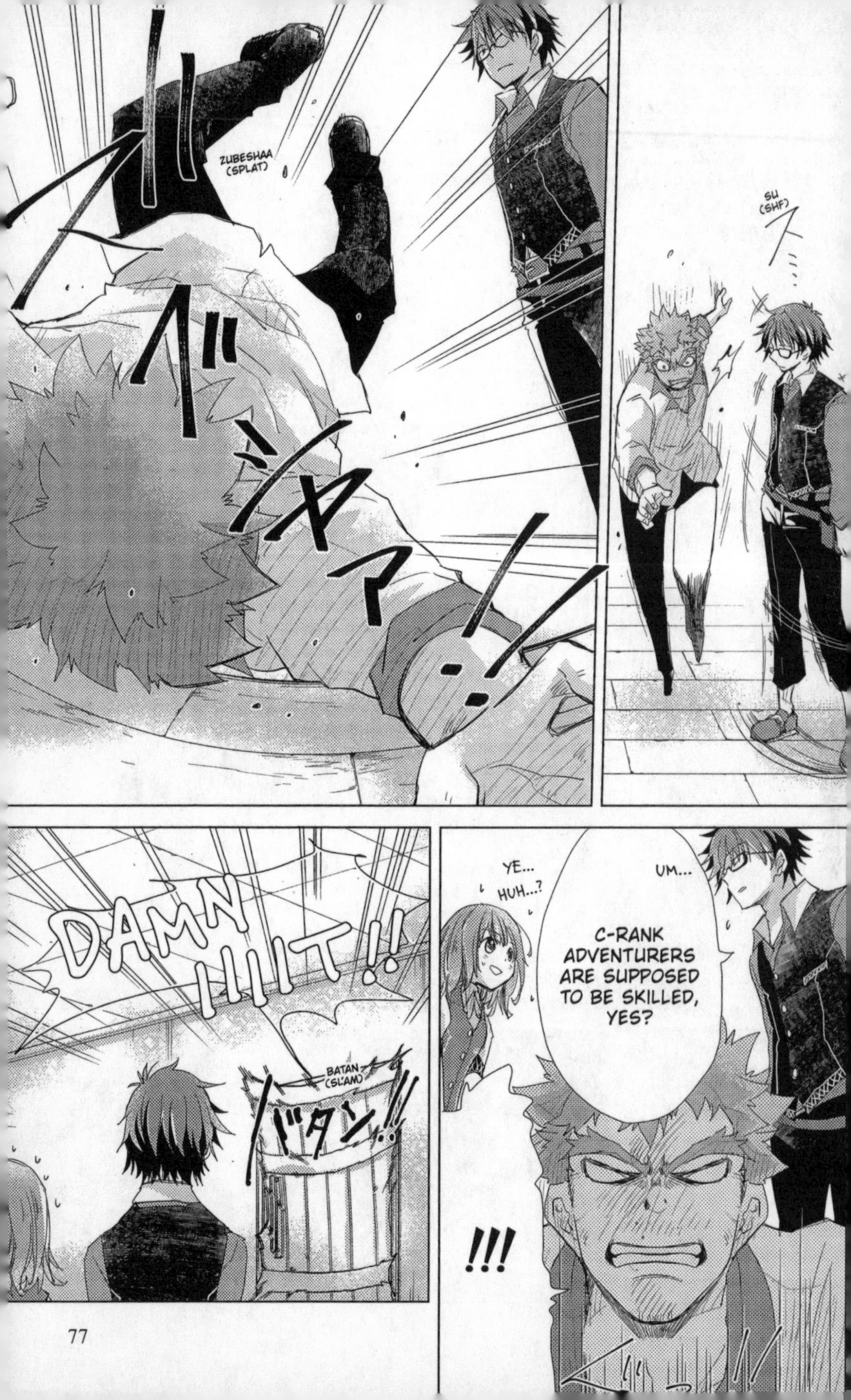
ZUBESHAA (SPLAT)
SU (SHF)
UM...
C-RANK ADVENTURERS ARE SUPPOSED TO BE SKILLED, YES?
YE... HUH...?
!!!
DAMN IIIIT!!
BATAN (SLAM)

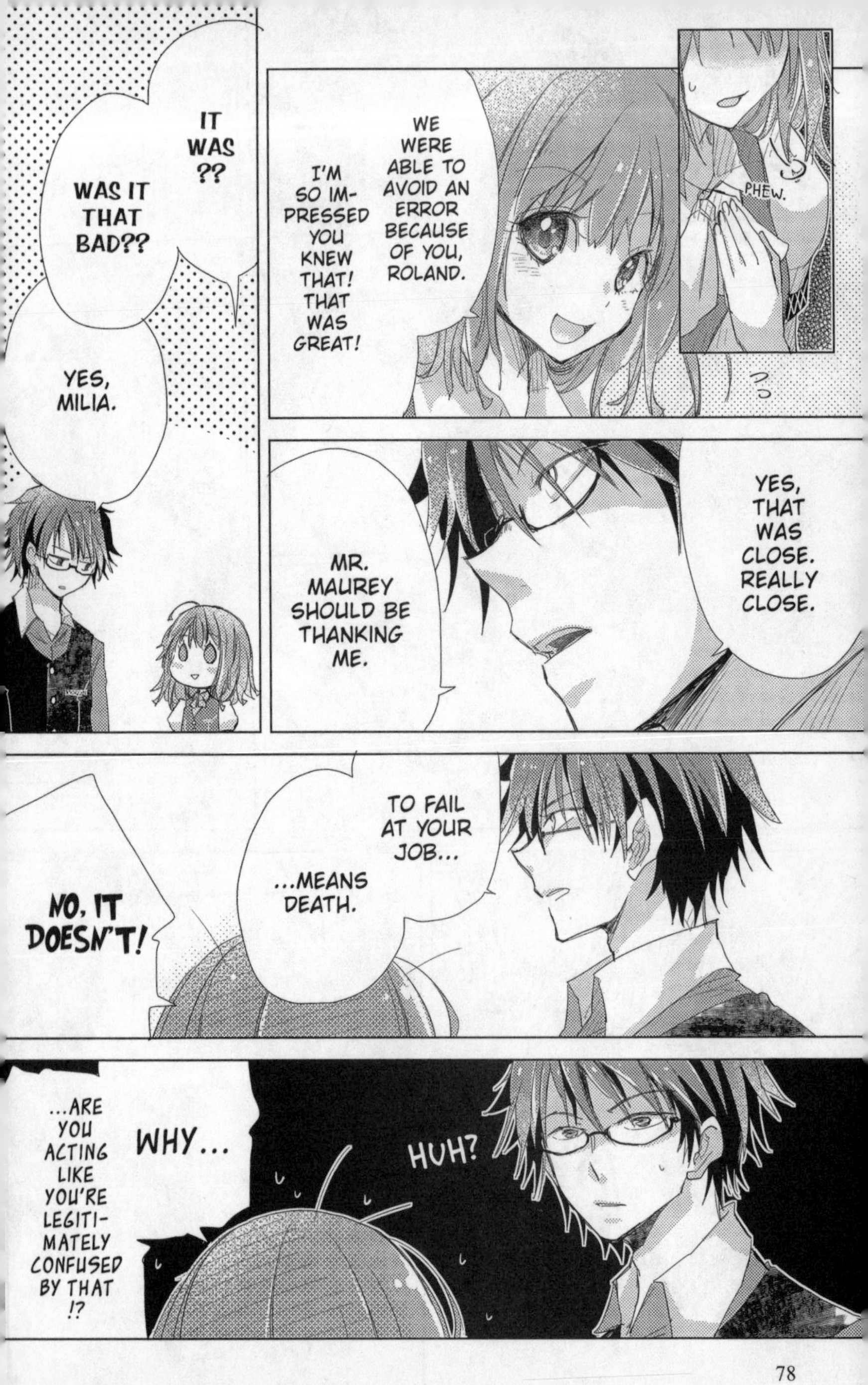
PHEW.
WE WERE ABLE TO AVOID AN ERROR BECAUSE OF YOU, ROLAND.
I'M SO IM-PRESSED YOU KNEW THAT! THAT WAS GREAT!
YES, THAT WAS CLOSE. REALLY CLOSE.
MR. MAUREY SHOULD BE THANKING ME.
IT WAS ??
WAS IT THAT BAD??
YES, MILIA.
TO FAIL AT YOUR JOB...
...MEANS DEATH.
NO, IT DOESN'T!
HUH?
WHY...
...ARE YOU ACTING LIKE YOU'RE LEGITI-MATELY CONFUSED BY THAT !?

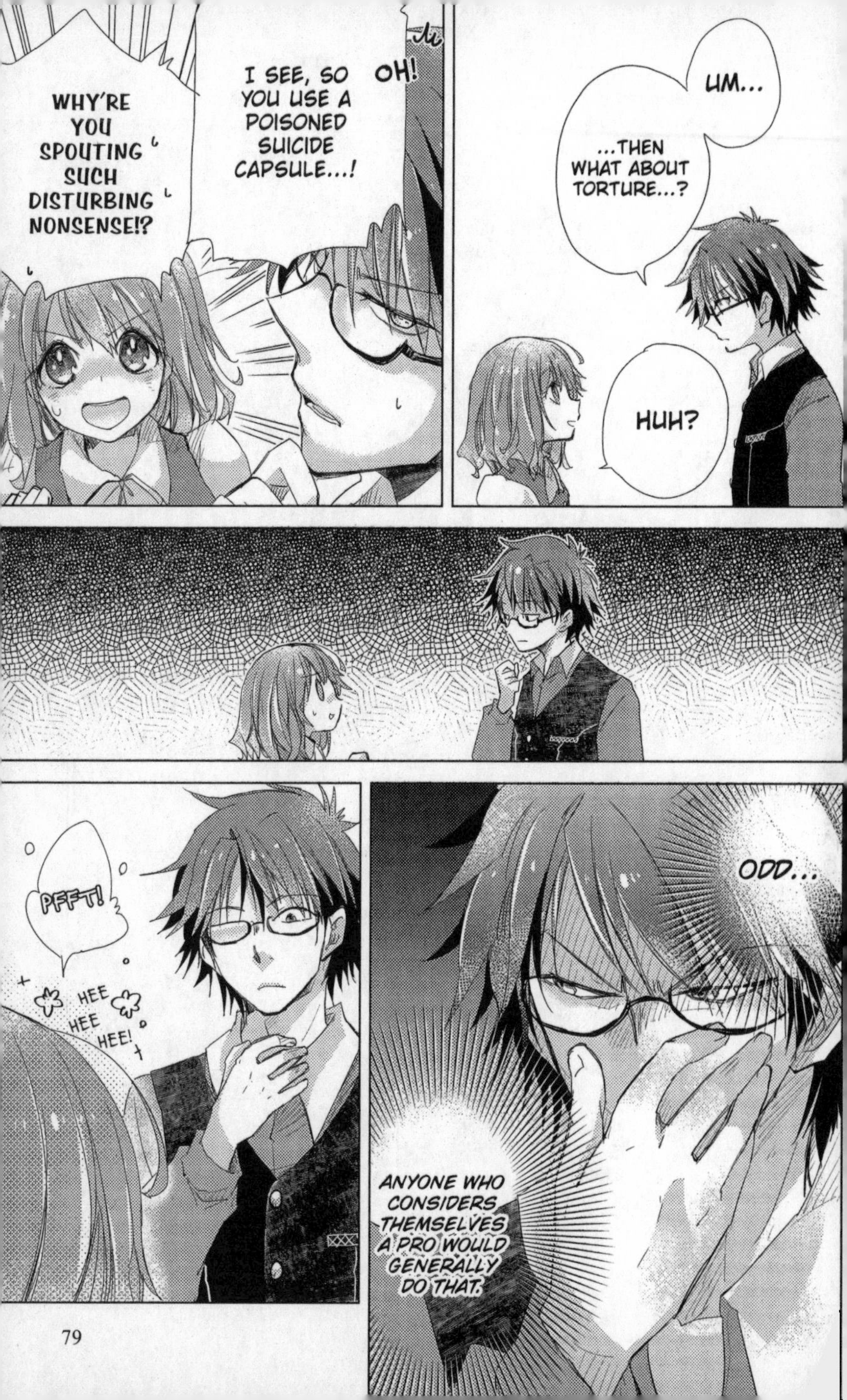
UM...
...THEN WHAT ABOUT TORTURE...?
HUH?
OH!
I SEE, SO YOU USE A POISONED SUICIDE CAPSULE...!
WHY'RE YOU SPOUTING SUCH DISTURBING NONSENSE!?
ODD...
ANYONE WHO CONSIDERS THEMSELVES A PRO WOULD GENERALLY DO THAT.
PFFT!
HEE HEE HEE!

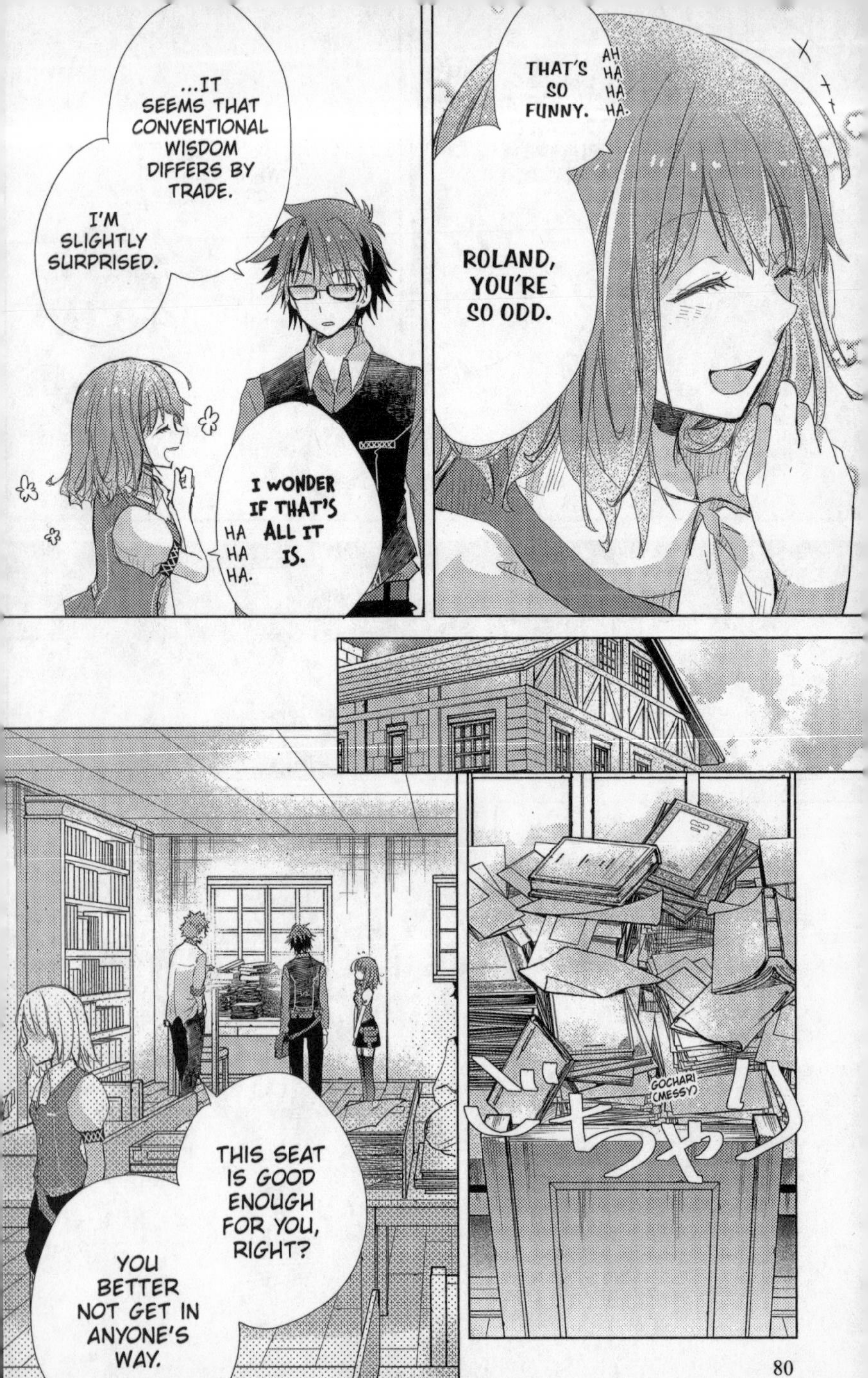
THAT'S SO FUNNY.
AH HA HA HA.
ROLAND, YOU'RE SO ODD.
...IT SEEMS THAT CONVENTIONAL WISDOM DIFFERS BY TRADE.
I'M SLIGHTLY SURPRISED.
HA HA HA.
I WONDER IF THAT'S ALL IT IS.
ごちゃり
GOCHARI (MESSY)
THIS SEAT IS GOOD ENOUGH FOR YOU, RIGHT?
YOU BETTER NOT GET IN ANYONE'S WAY.

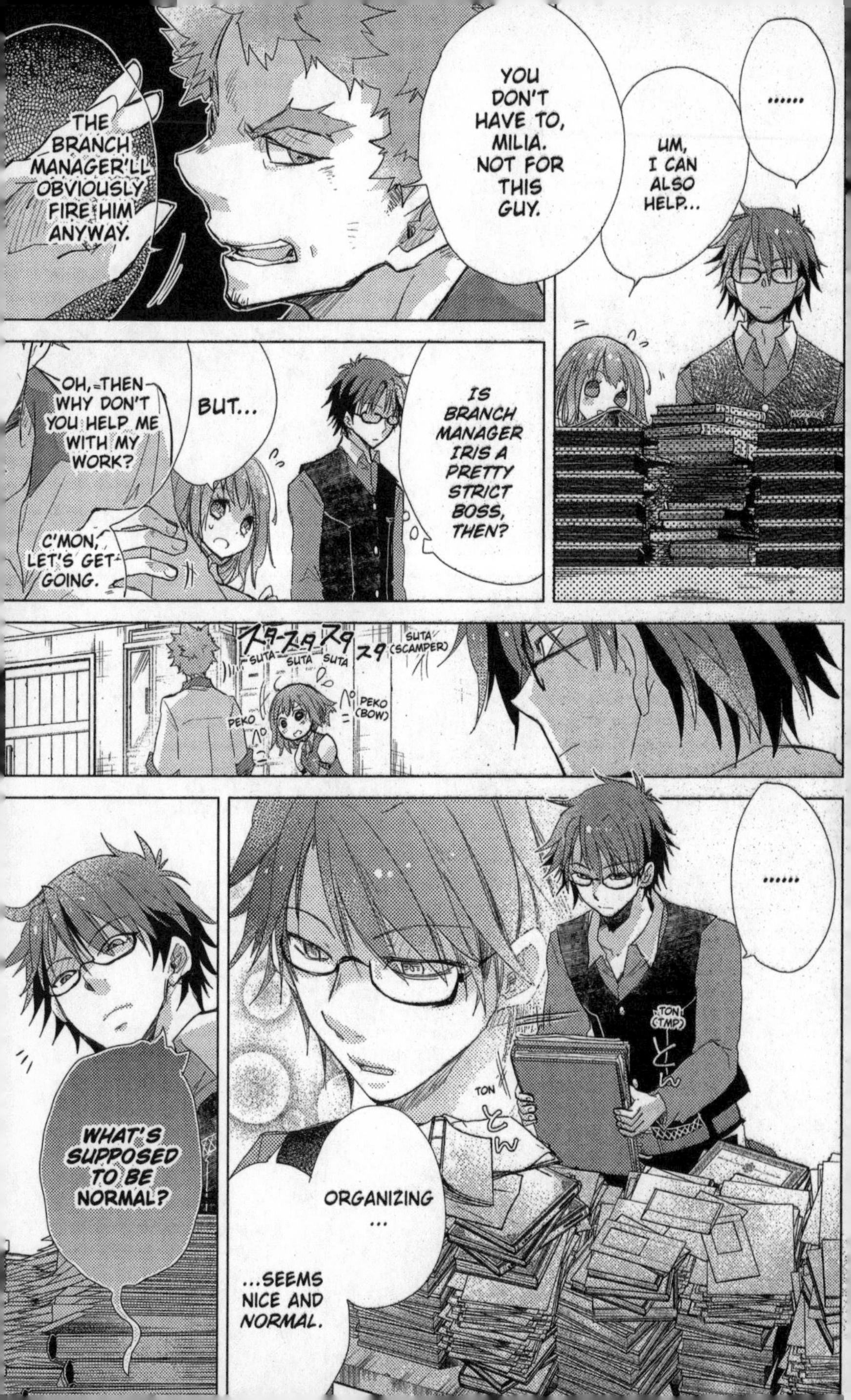
......
UM, I CAN ALSO HELP...
YOU DON'T HAVE TO, MILIA. NOT FOR THIS GUY.
THE BRANCH MANAGER'LL OBVIOUSLY FIRE HIM ANYWAY.
IS BRANCH MANAGER IRIS A PRETTY STRICT BOSS, THEN?
BUT...
OH, THEN WHY DON'T YOU HELP ME WITH MY WORK?
C'MON, LET'S GET GOING.
スタスタスタスタ
SUTA SUTA SUTA SUTA (SCAMPER)
PEKO (BOW)
PEKO
......
とん
TON (TMP)
とん
TON
ORGANIZING ...
...SEEMS NICE AND NORMAL.
WHAT'S SUPPOSED TO BE NORMAL?

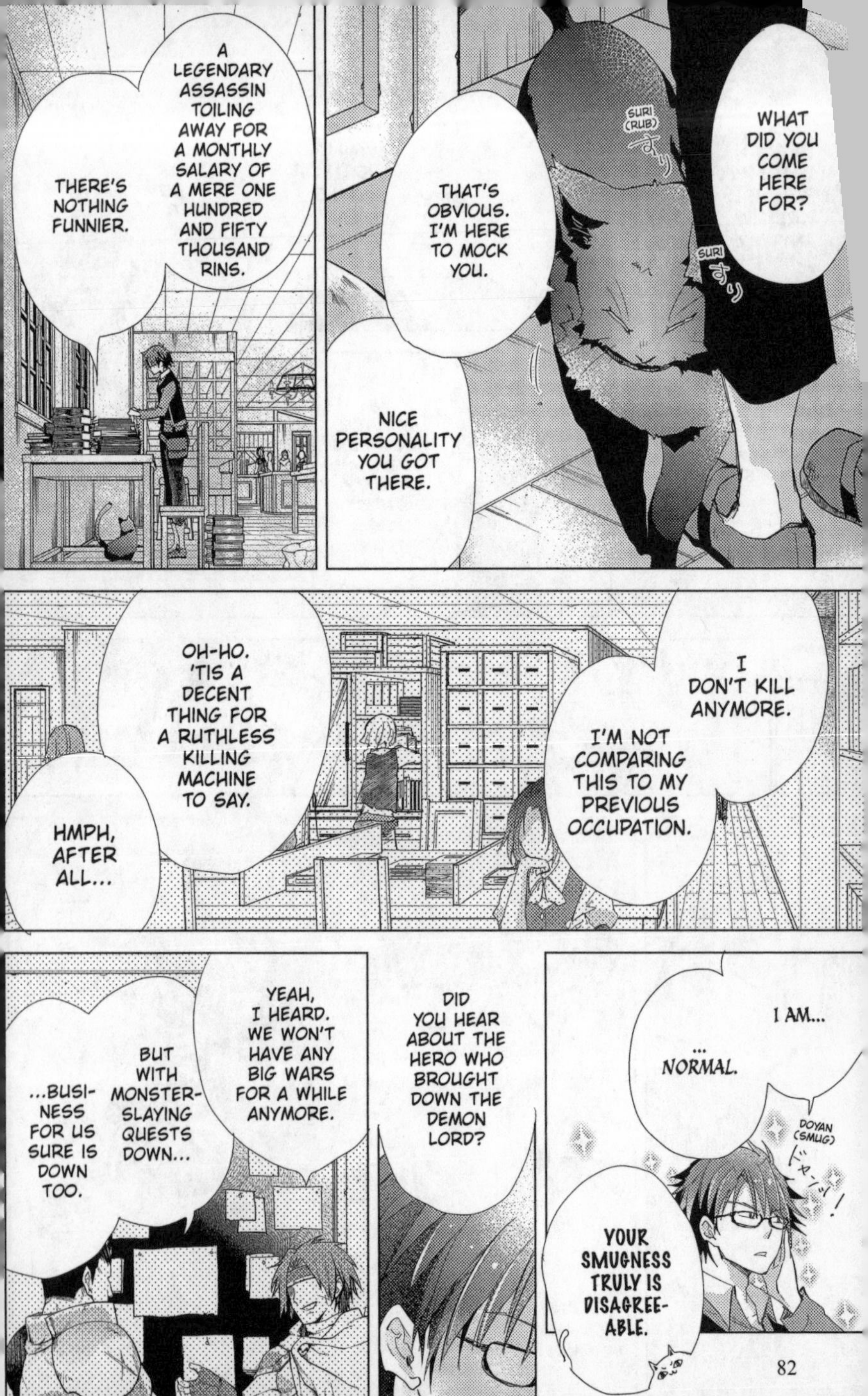
WHAT DID YOU COME HERE FOR?
SURI (RUB) すり
SURI すり
THAT'S OBVIOUS. I'M HERE TO MOCK YOU.
NICE PERSONALITY YOU GOT THERE.
A LEGENDARY ASSASSIN TOILING AWAY FOR A MONTHLY SALARY OF A MERE ONE HUNDRED AND FIFTY THOUSAND RINS.
THERE'S NOTHING FUNNIER.
I DON'T KILL ANYMORE.
I'M NOT COMPARING THIS TO MY PREVIOUS OCCUPATION.
OH-HO. 'TIS A DECENT THING FOR A RUTHLESS KILLING MACHINE TO SAY.
HMPH, AFTER ALL...
I AM...
... NORMAL.
DOYAN (SMUG) ドヤーッ!
YOUR SMUGNESS TRULY IS DISAGREEABLE.
DID YOU HEAR ABOUT THE HERO WHO BROUGHT DOWN THE DEMON LORD?
YEAH, I HEARD. WE WON'T HAVE ANY BIG WARS FOR A WHILE ANYMORE.
BUT WITH MONSTER-SLAYING QUESTS DOWN...
...BUSINESS FOR US SURE IS DOWN TOO.

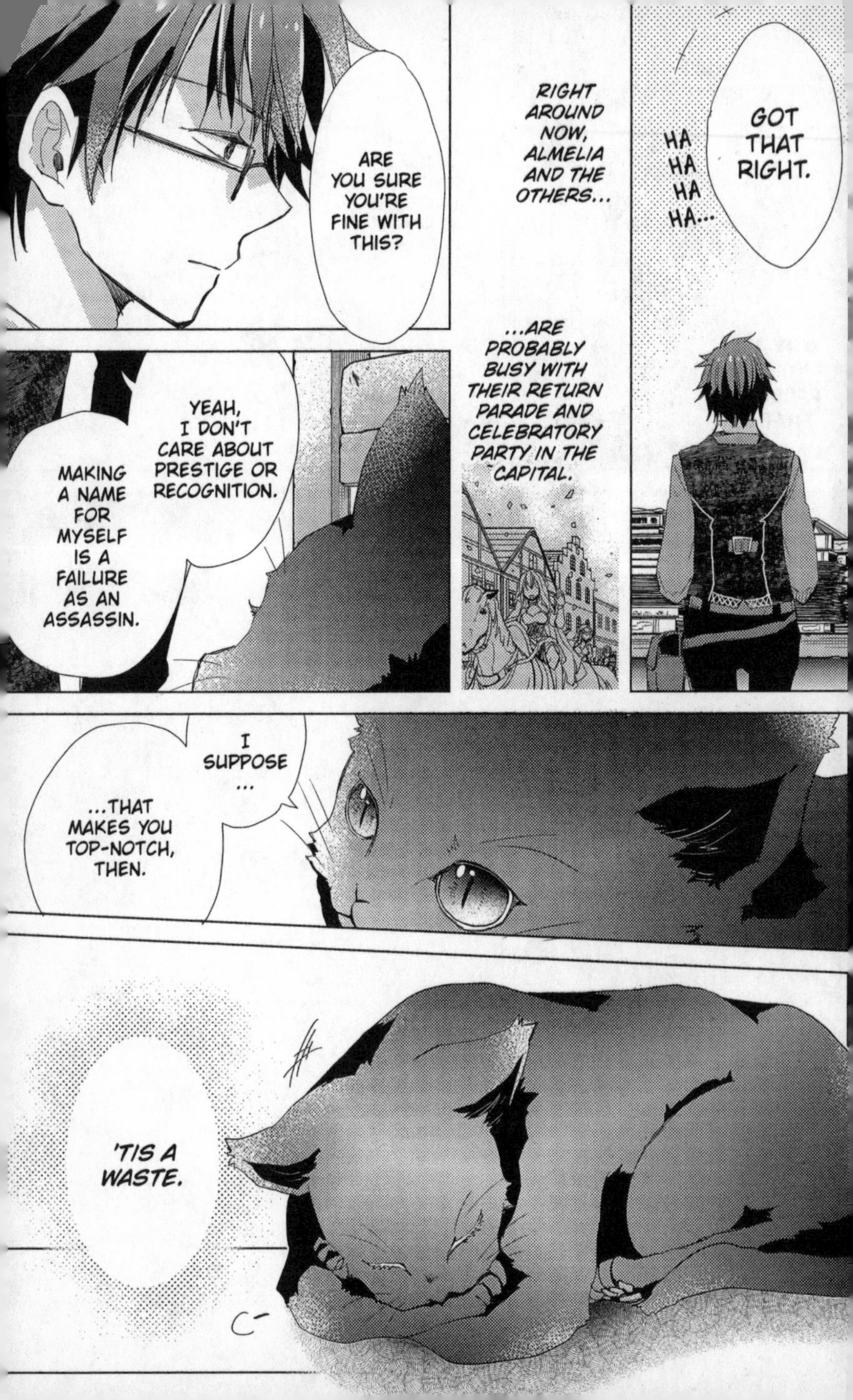
GOT THAT RIGHT.
HA HA HA HA...
RIGHT AROUND NOW, ALMELIA AND THE OTHERS...
...ARE PROBABLY BUSY WITH THEIR RETURN PARADE AND CELEBRATORY PARTY IN THE CAPITAL.
ARE YOU SURE YOU'RE FINE WITH THIS?
YEAH, I DON'T CARE ABOUT PRESTIGE OR RECOGNITION.
MAKING A NAME FOR MYSELF IS A FAILURE AS AN ASSASSIN.
I SUPPOSE...
...THAT MAKES YOU TOP-NOTCH, THEN.
'TIS A WASTE.

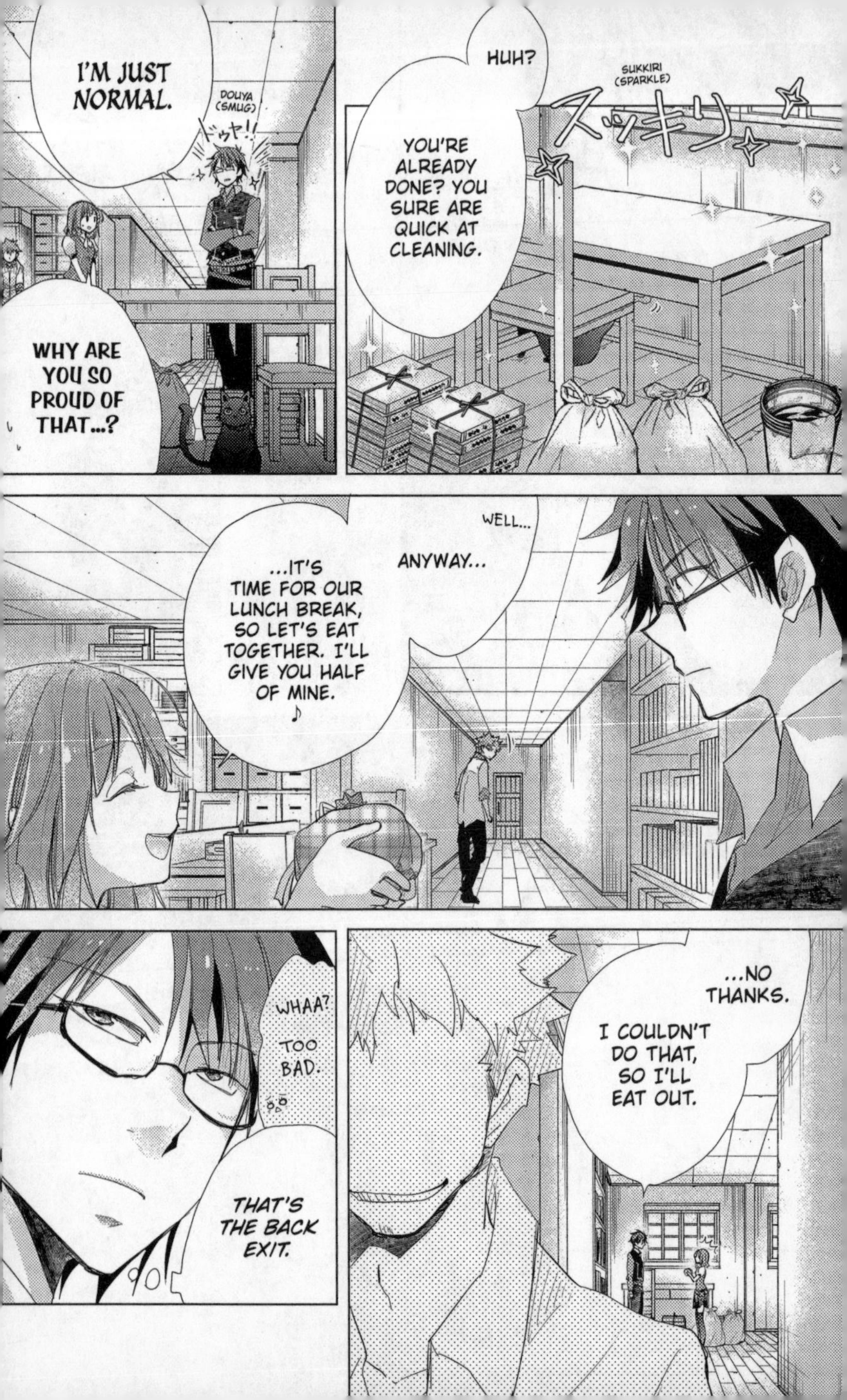
HUH?
YOU'RE ALREADY DONE? YOU SURE ARE QUICK AT CLEANING.
SUKKIRI (SPARKLE)
スッキリ
I'M JUST NORMAL.
DOUYA (SMUG)
ドゥヤ!!
WHY ARE YOU SO PROUD OF THAT...?
WELL...
ANYWAY...
...IT'S TIME FOR OUR LUNCH BREAK, SO LET'S EAT TOGETHER. I'LL GIVE YOU HALF OF MINE. ♪
...NO THANKS.
I COULDN'T DO THAT, SO I'LL EAT OUT.
WHAA? TOO BAD.
THAT'S THE BACK EXIT.

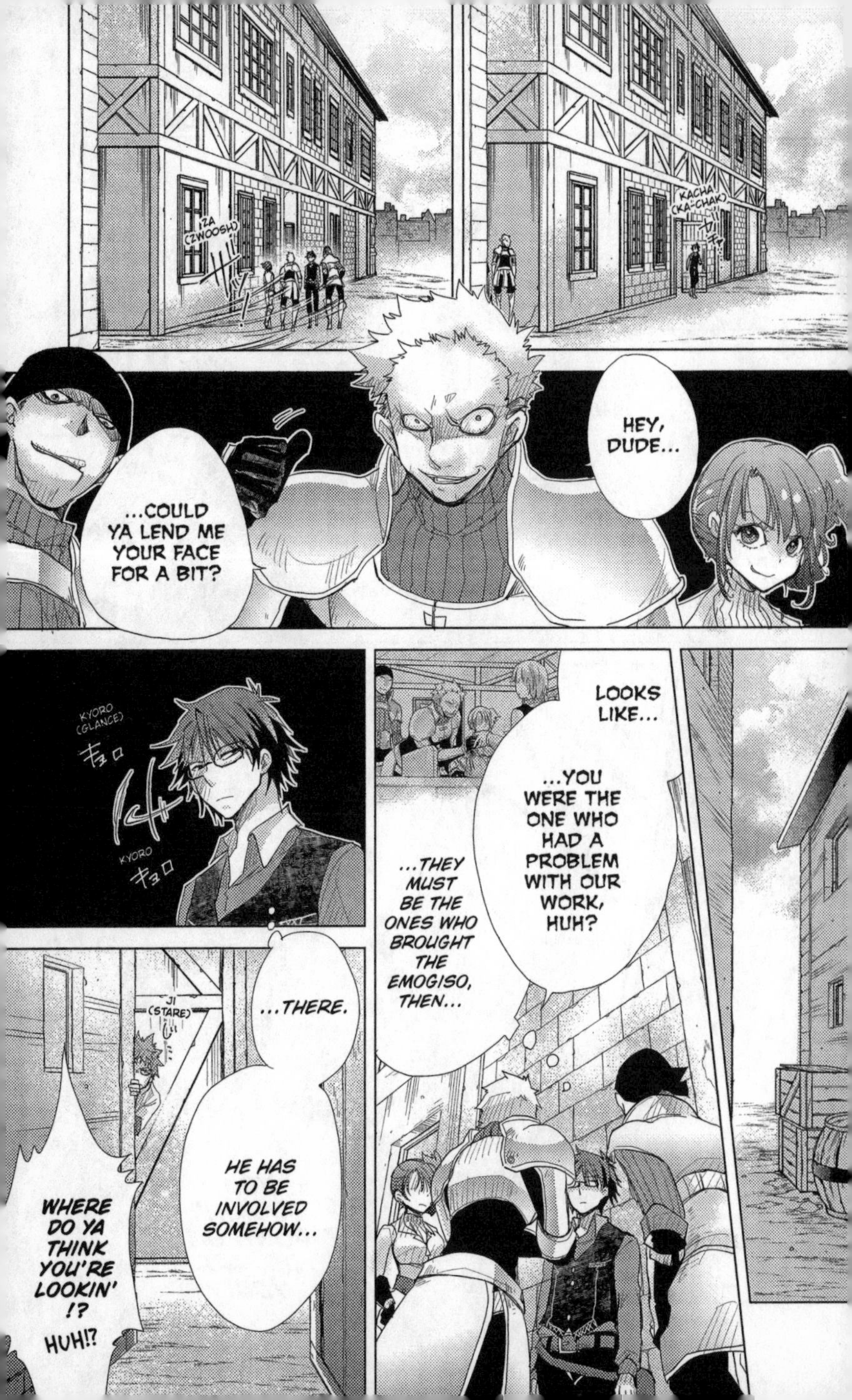
KACHA (KA-CHAK)
ZA (ZWOOSH)
HEY, DUDE...
...COULD YA LEND ME YOUR FACE FOR A BIT?
LOOKS LIKE...
...YOU WERE THE ONE WHO HAD A PROBLEM WITH OUR WORK, HUH?
...THEY MUST BE THE ONES WHO BROUGHT THE EMOGISO, THEN...
KYORO (GLANCE)
KYORO
JI (STARE)
...THERE.
HE HAS TO BE INVOLVED SOMEHOW...
WHERE DO YA THINK YOU'RE LOOKIN'!?
HUH!?

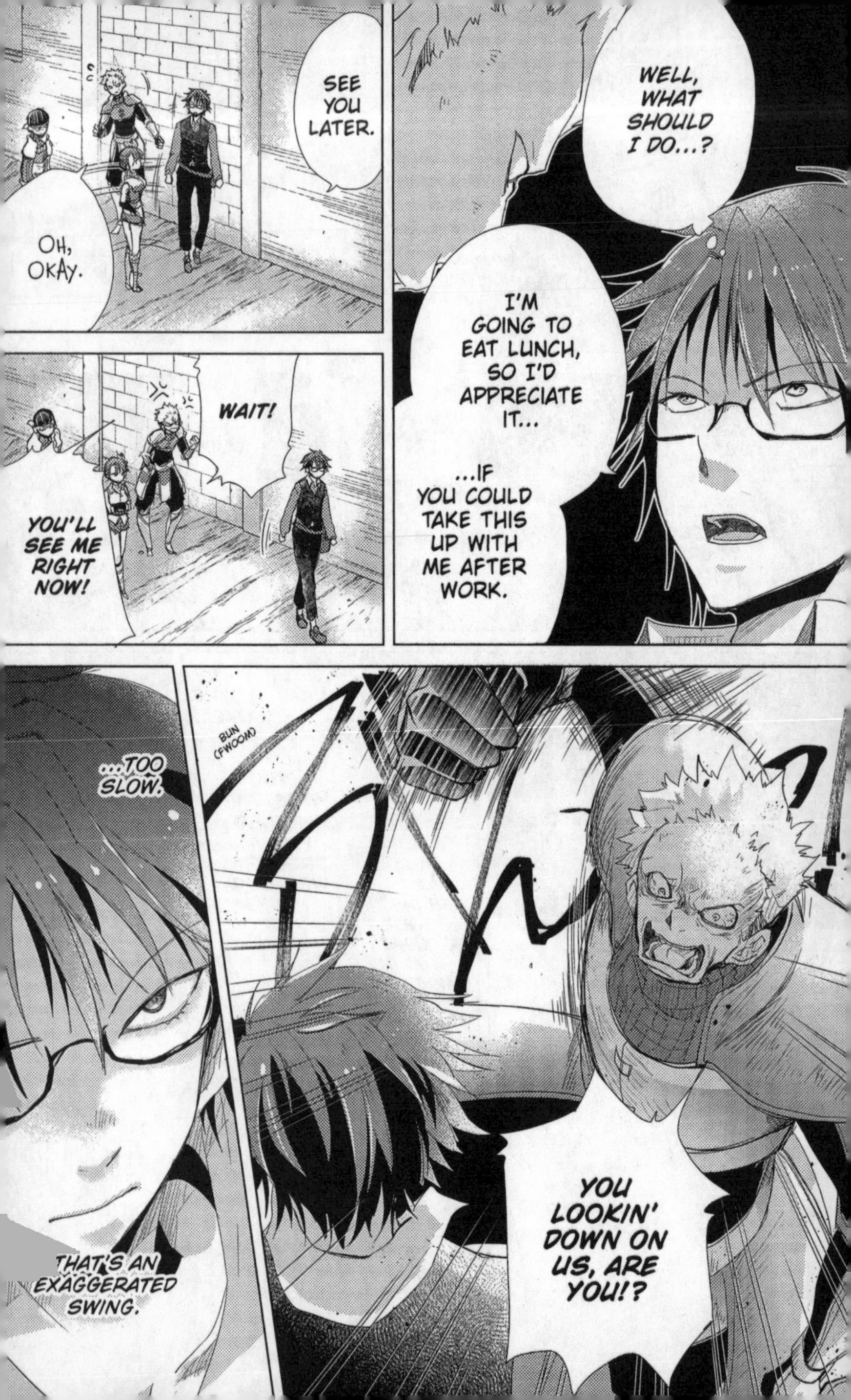
WELL, WHAT SHOULD I DO...?
I'M GOING TO EAT LUNCH, SO I'D APPRECIATE IT...
...IF YOU COULD TAKE THIS UP WITH ME AFTER WORK.
SEE YOU LATER.
OH, OKAY.
WAIT!
YOU'LL SEE ME RIGHT NOW!
BUN (FWOOM)
YOU LOOKIN' DOWN ON US, ARE YOU!?
...TOO SLOW.
THAT'S AN EXAGGERATED SWING.

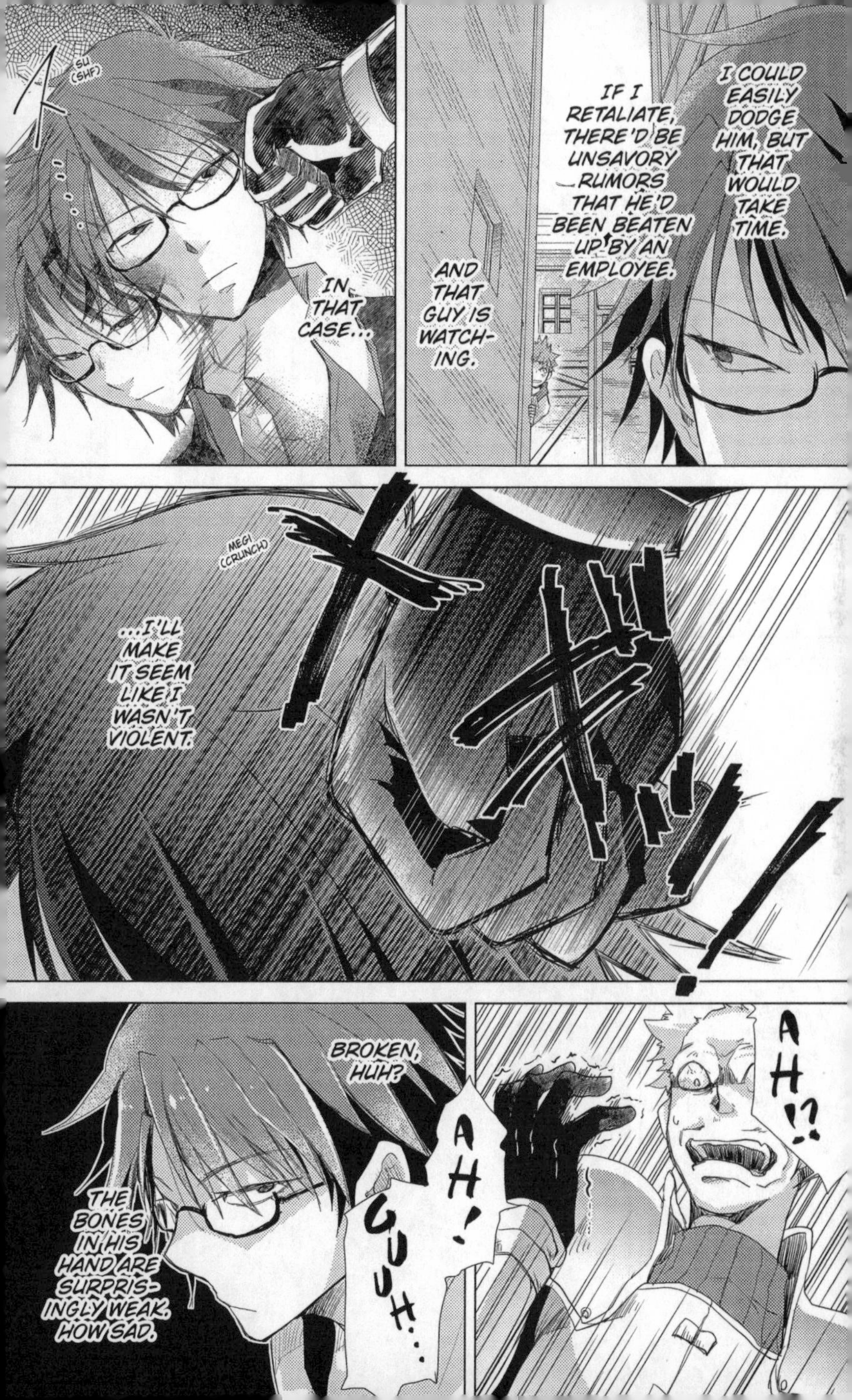
I COULD EASILY DODGE HIM, BUT THAT WOULD TAKE TIME.
IF I RETALIATE, THERE'D BE UNSAVORY RUMORS THAT HE'D BEEN BEATEN UP BY AN EMPLOYEE.
AND THAT GUY IS WATCHING.
SU (SHF)
IN THAT CASE...
MEGI (CRUNCH)
...I'LL MAKE IT SEEM LIKE I WASN'T VIOLENT.
AH!?
AH! GUUH...
BROKEN, HUH?
THE BONES IN HIS HAND ARE SURPRISINGLY WEAK. HOW SAD.

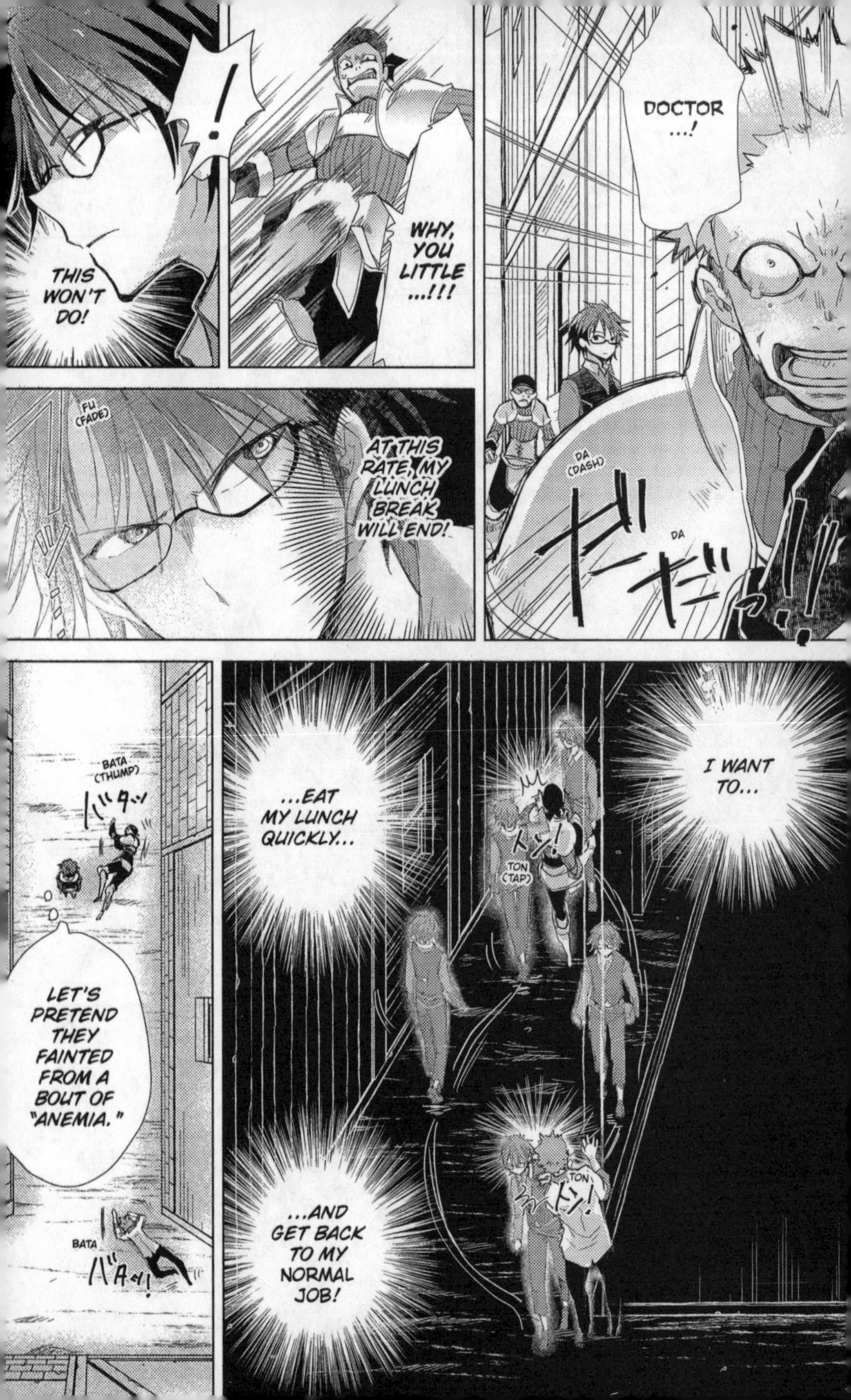
DOCTOR ...!
DA (DASH)
DA
WHY, YOU LITTLE ...!!!
!
THIS WON'T DO!
FU (FADE)
AT THIS RATE, MY LUNCH BREAK WILL END!
I WANT TO...
...EAT MY LUNCH QUICKLY...
TON (TAP)
...AND GET BACK TO MY NORMAL JOB!
TON
BATA (THUMP)
LET'S PRETEND THEY FAINTED FROM A BOUT OF "ANEMIA."
BATA

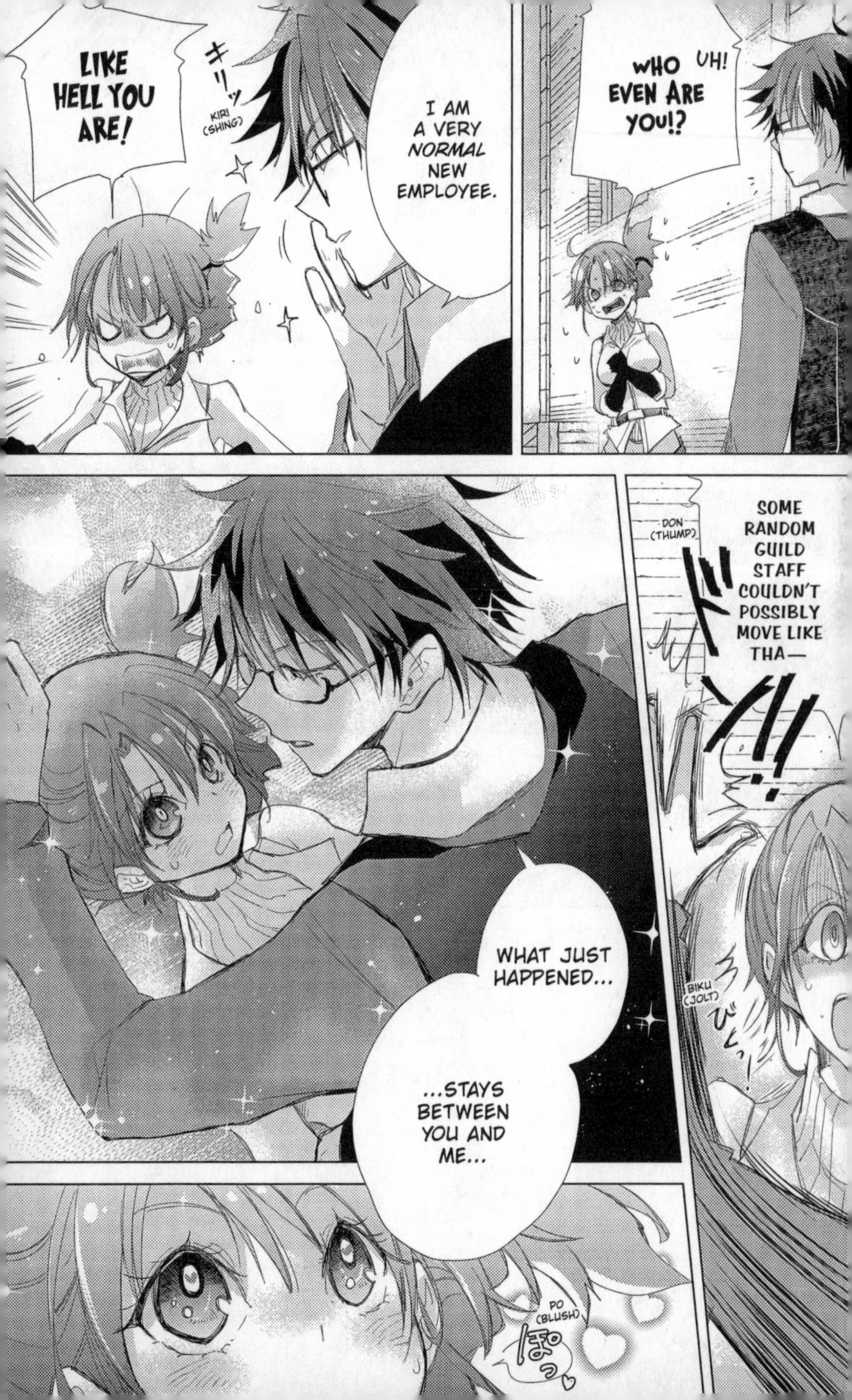

UH!
WHO EVEN ARE YOU!?
I AM A VERY *NORMAL* NEW EMPLOYEE.
KIRI (SHING)
LIKE HELL YOU ARE!
SOME RANDOM GUILD STAFF COULDN'T POSSIBLY MOVE LIKE THA—
DON (THUMP)
BIKU (JOLT)
WHAT JUST HAPPENED...
...STAYS BETWEEN YOU AND ME...
PO (BLUSH)

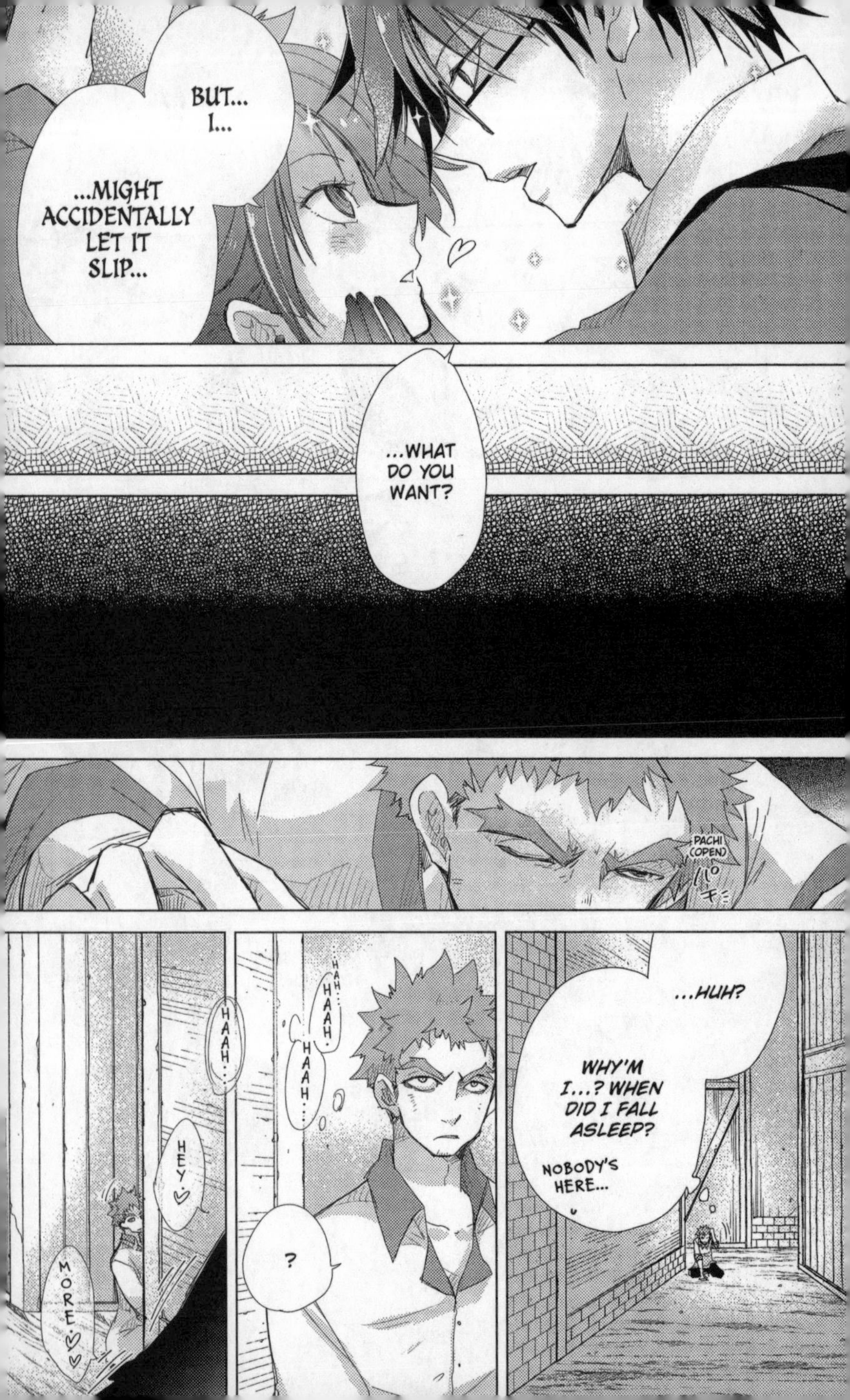
BUT... I...
...MIGHT ACCIDENTALLY LET IT SLIP...
...WHAT DO YOU WANT?
PACHI (OPEN)
パチ
...HUH?
WHY'M I...? WHEN DID I FALL ASLEEP?
NOBODY'S HERE...
HAAH...
HAAH...
?
HAAH...
HEY♡
MORE♡

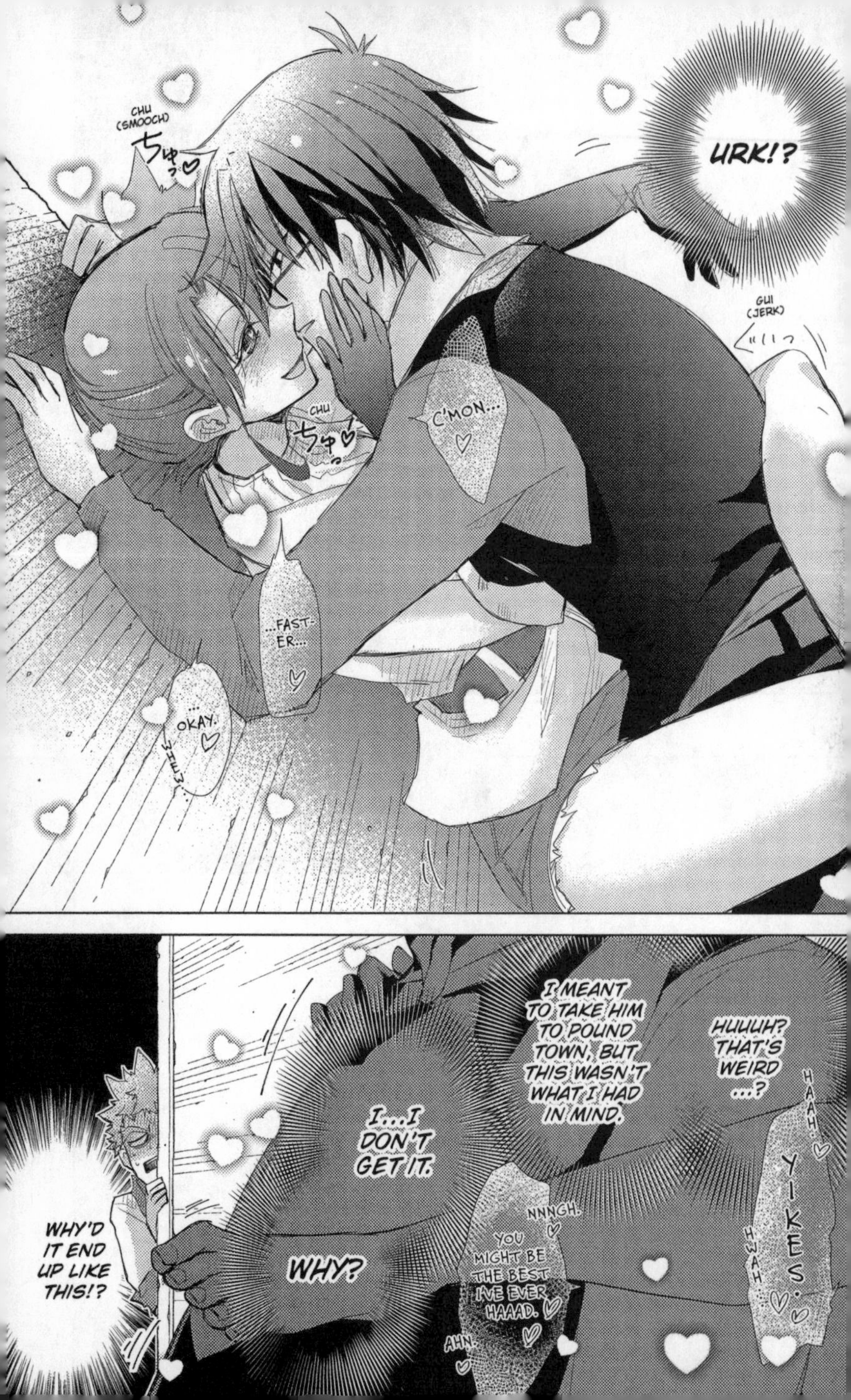
URK!?
GUI (JERK)
ぐいっ
C'MON... ♡
CHU (SMOOCH)
ちゅっ♡
CHU
ちゅ♡
...FASTER... ♡
...OKAY. ♡
WHEW...
HUUUH? THAT'S WEIRD ...?
HAAAH. ♡
YIKES. ♡
HWAH...
I MEANT TO TAKE HIM TO POUND TOWN, BUT THIS WASN'T WHAT I HAD IN MIND.
I...I DON'T GET IT.
NNNGH. ♡
YOU MIGHT BE THE BEST I'VE EVER HAAAD. ♡
WHY?
AHN. ♡
WHY'D IT END UP LIKE THIS!?

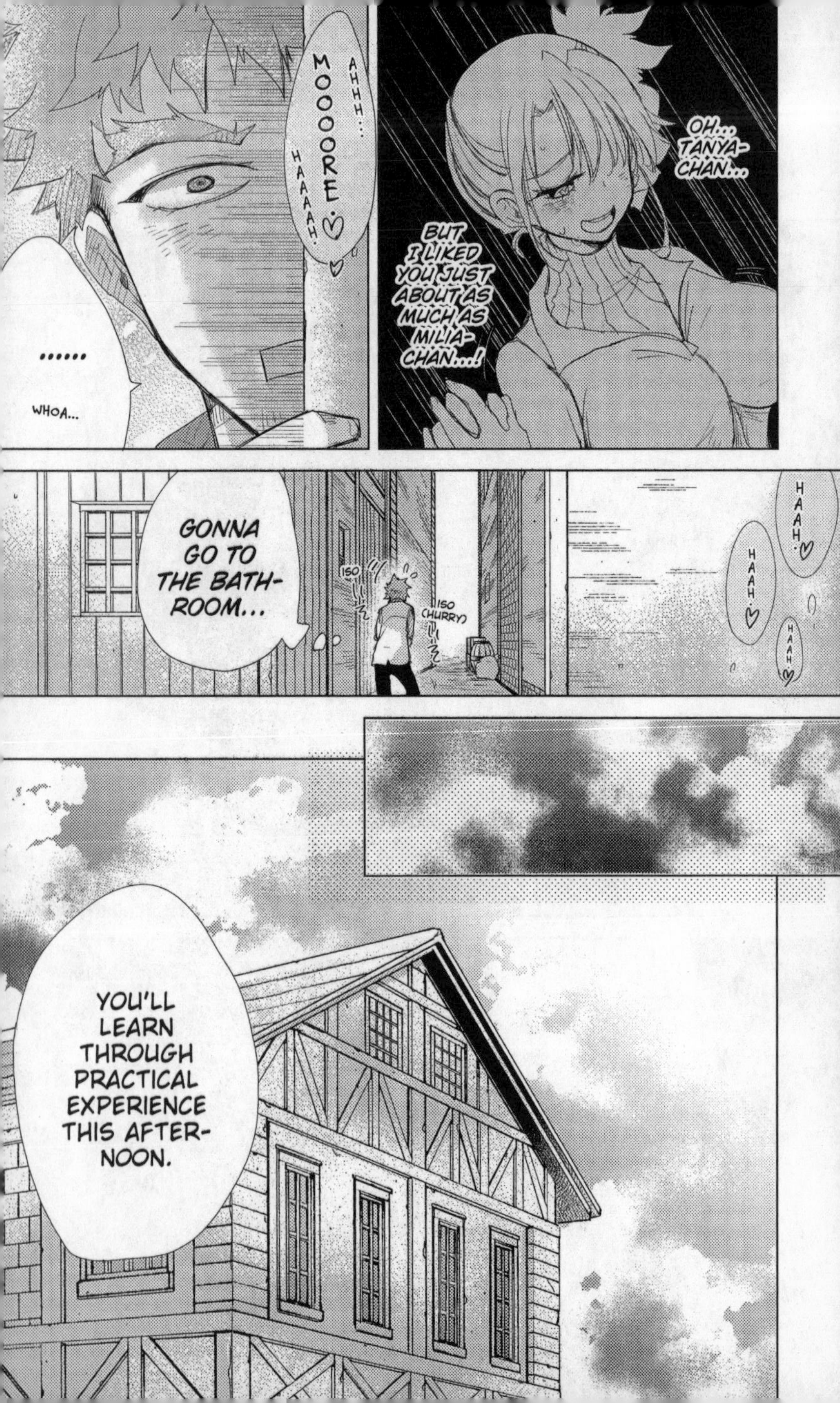
OH... TANYA-CHAN...
BUT I LIKED YOU JUST ABOUT AS MUCH AS MILIA-CHAN...!
AHHH... MOOOORE ♥
HAAAAAH!
......
WHOA...
HAAH ♥
HAAH ♥
HAAH ♥
ISO (HURRY)
ISO
GONNA GO TO THE BATH-ROOM...
YOU'LL LEARN THROUGH PRACTICAL EXPERIENCE THIS AFTER-NOON.

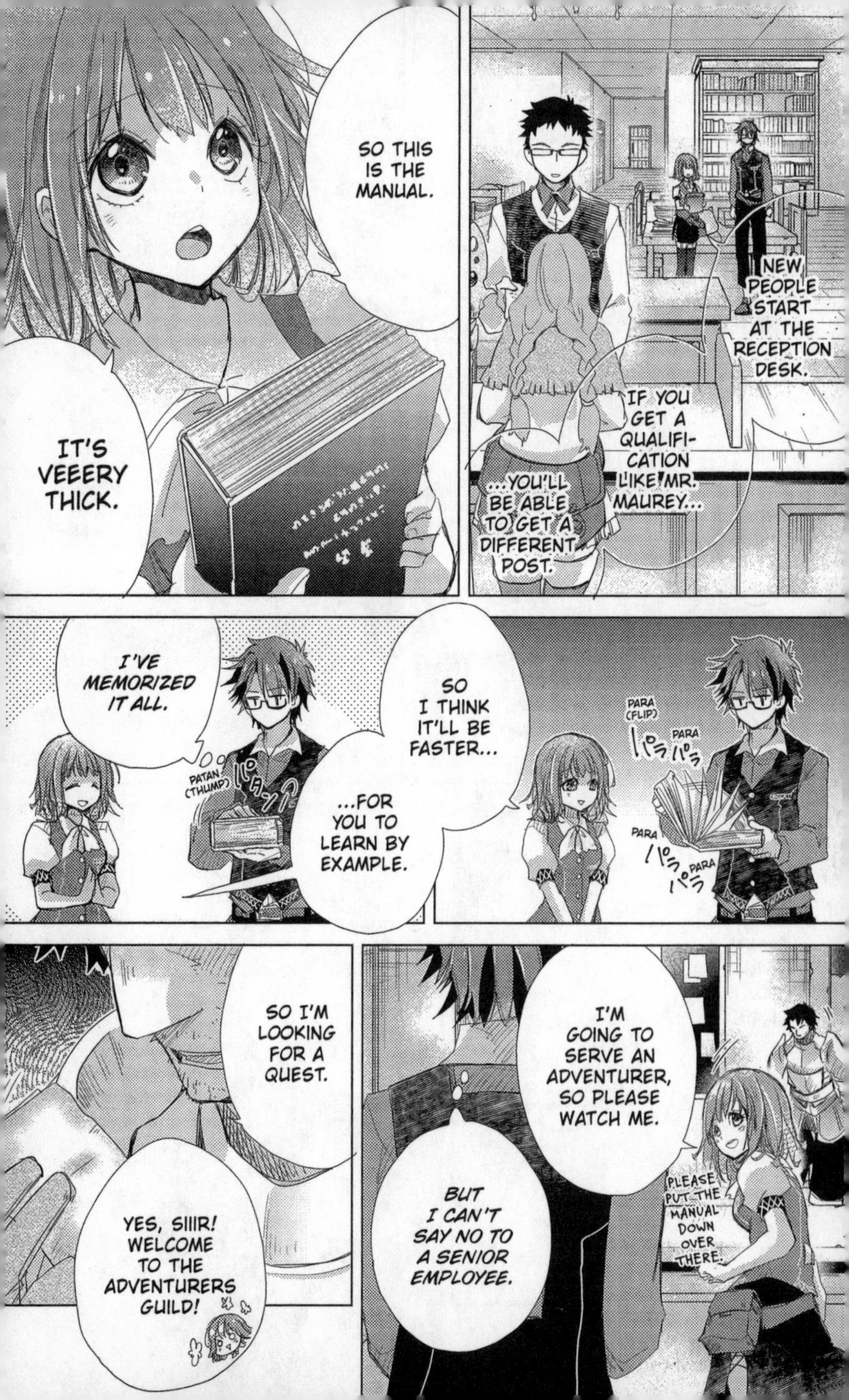
NEW PEOPLE START AT THE RECEPTION DESK.
IF YOU GET A QUALIFICATION LIKE MR. MAUREY...
...YOU'LL BE ABLE TO GET A DIFFERENT POST.
SO THIS IS THE MANUAL.
IT'S VEEERY THICK.
PARA (FLIP)
PARA
PARA
PARA
I'VE MEMORIZED IT ALL.
PATAN (THUMP)
SO I THINK IT'LL BE FASTER...
...FOR YOU TO LEARN BY EXAMPLE.
I'M GOING TO SERVE AN ADVENTURER, SO PLEASE WATCH ME.
PLEASE PUT THE MANUAL DOWN OVER THERE.
BUT I CAN'T SAY NO TO A SENIOR EMPLOYEE.
SO I'M LOOKING FOR A QUEST.
YES, SIIIR! WELCOME TO THE ADVENTURERS GUILD!

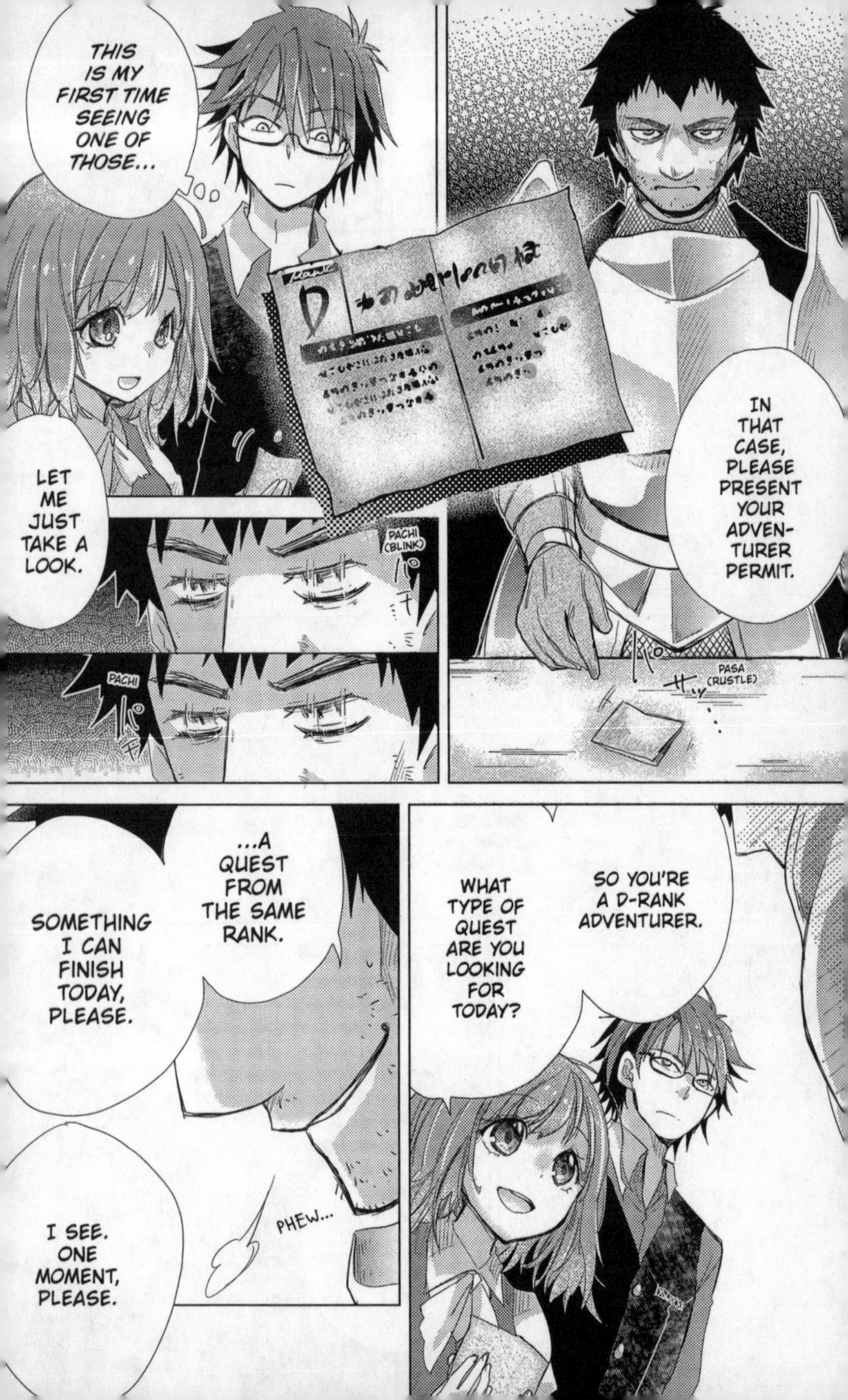
IN THAT CASE, PLEASE PRESENT YOUR ADVENTURER PERMIT.
PASA (RUSTLE)
THIS IS MY FIRST TIME SEEING ONE OF THOSE...
LET ME JUST TAKE A LOOK.
PACHI (BLINK)
PACHI
SO YOU'RE A D-RANK ADVENTURER.
WHAT TYPE OF QUEST ARE YOU LOOKING FOR TODAY?
...A QUEST FROM THE SAME RANK.
SOMETHING I CAN FINISH TODAY, PLEASE.
PHEW...
I SEE. ONE MOMENT, PLEASE.

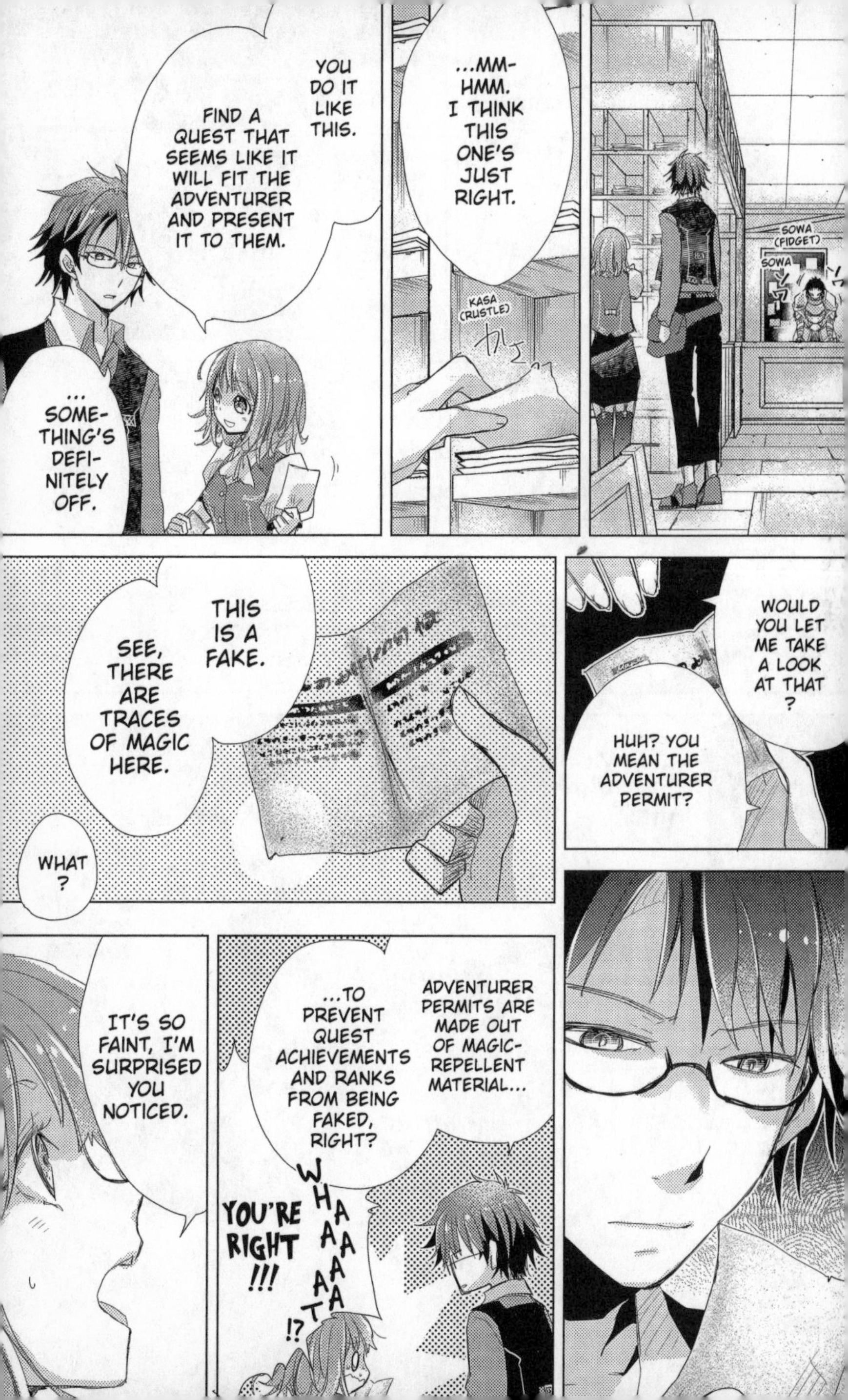
SOWA (FIDGET)
SOWA
...MM-HMM. I THINK THIS ONE'S JUST RIGHT.
KASA (RUSTLE)
YOU DO IT LIKE THIS.
FIND A QUEST THAT SEEMS LIKE IT WILL FIT THE ADVENTURER AND PRESENT IT TO THEM.
...SOMETHING'S DEFINITELY OFF.
WOULD YOU LET ME TAKE A LOOK AT THAT?
HUH? YOU MEAN THE ADVENTURER PERMIT?
THIS IS A FAKE.
SEE, THERE ARE TRACES OF MAGIC HERE.
WHAT?
ADVENTURER PERMITS ARE MADE OUT OF MAGIC-REPELLENT MATERIAL...
...TO PREVENT QUEST ACHIEVEMENTS AND RANKS FROM BEING FAKED, RIGHT?
WHAAAAAAT
YOU'RE RIGHT!!!
!?
IT'S SO FAINT, I'M SURPRISED YOU NOTICED.

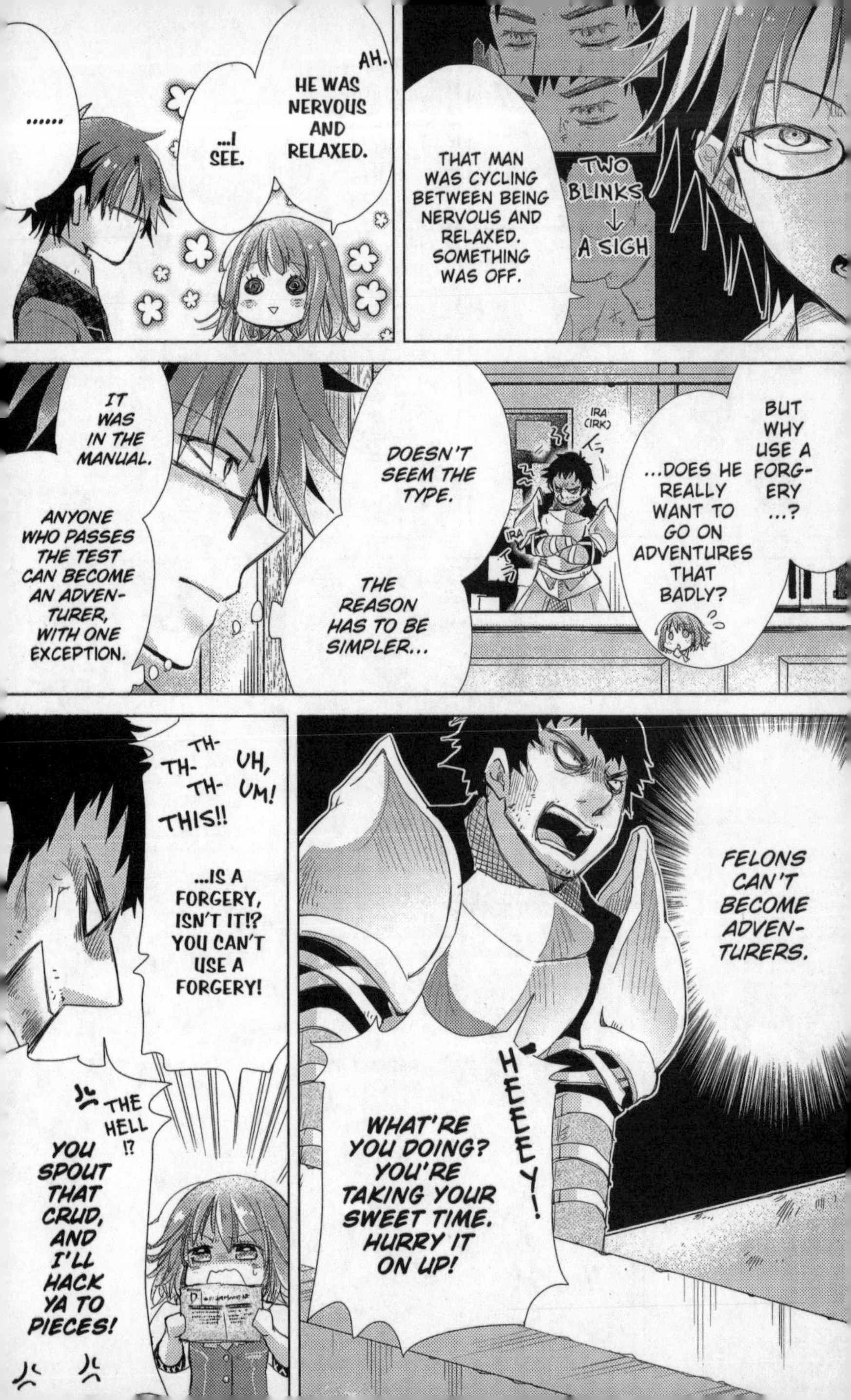
TWO BLINKS → A SIGH
THAT MAN WAS CYCLING BETWEEN BEING NERVOUS AND RELAXED. SOMETHING WAS OFF.
AH. HE WAS NERVOUS AND RELAXED.
...I SEE.
......
BUT WHY USE A FORGERY ...?
...DOES HE REALLY WANT TO GO ON ADVENTURES THAT BADLY?
IRA (IRK)
IRA
DOESN'T SEEM THE TYPE.
THE REASON HAS TO BE SIMPLER...
IT WAS IN THE MANUAL.
ANYONE WHO PASSES THE TEST CAN BECOME AN ADVENTURER, WITH ONE EXCEPTION.
FELONS CAN'T BECOME ADVENTURERS.
HEEEY!
WHAT'RE YOU DOING? YOU'RE TAKING YOUR SWEET TIME. HURRY IT ON UP!
UH, UM!
TH- TH- TH- THIS!!
...IS A FORGERY, ISN'T IT!? YOU CAN'T USE A FORGERY!
THE HELL!?
YOU SPOUT THAT CRUD, AND I'LL HACK YA TO PIECES!

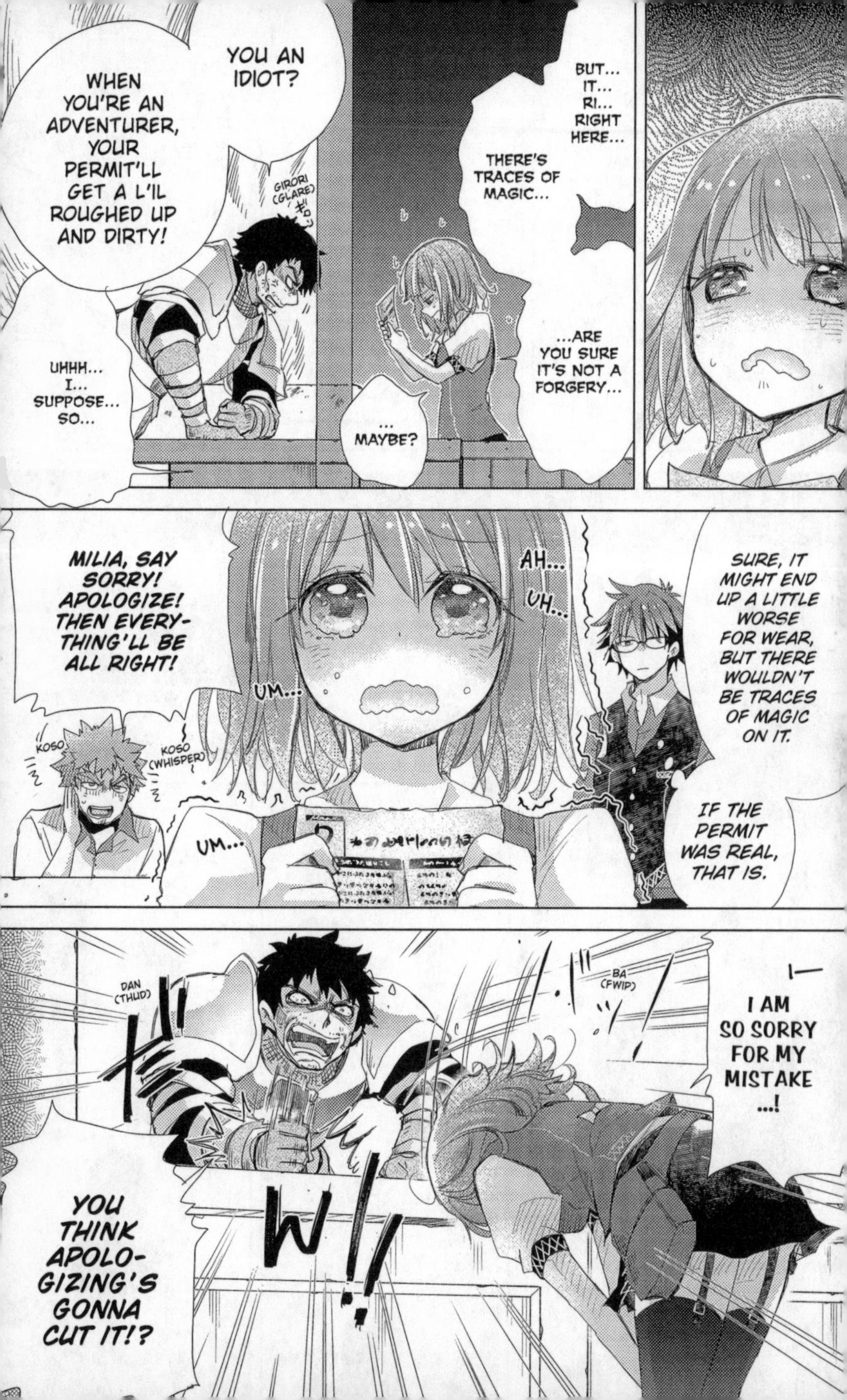

BUT... IT... RI... RIGHT HERE...
THERE'S TRACES OF MAGIC...
...ARE YOU SURE IT'S NOT A FORGERY...
... MAYBE?
YOU AN IDIOT?
WHEN YOU'RE AN ADVENTURER, YOUR PERMIT'LL GET A L'IL ROUGHED UP AND DIRTY!
GIRORI (GLARE)
UHHH... I... SUPPOSE... SO...
SURE, IT MIGHT END UP A LITTLE WORSE FOR WEAR, BUT THERE WOULDN'T BE TRACES OF MAGIC ON IT.
IF THE PERMIT WAS REAL, THAT IS.
AH... UH...
UM...
MILIA, SAY SORRY! APOLOGIZE! THEN EVERYTHING'LL BE ALL RIGHT!
KOSO
KOSO (WHISPER)
UM...
I AM SO SORRY FOR MY MISTAKE ...!
BA (FWIP)
DAN (THUD)
YOU THINK APOLOGIZING'S GONNA CUT IT!?

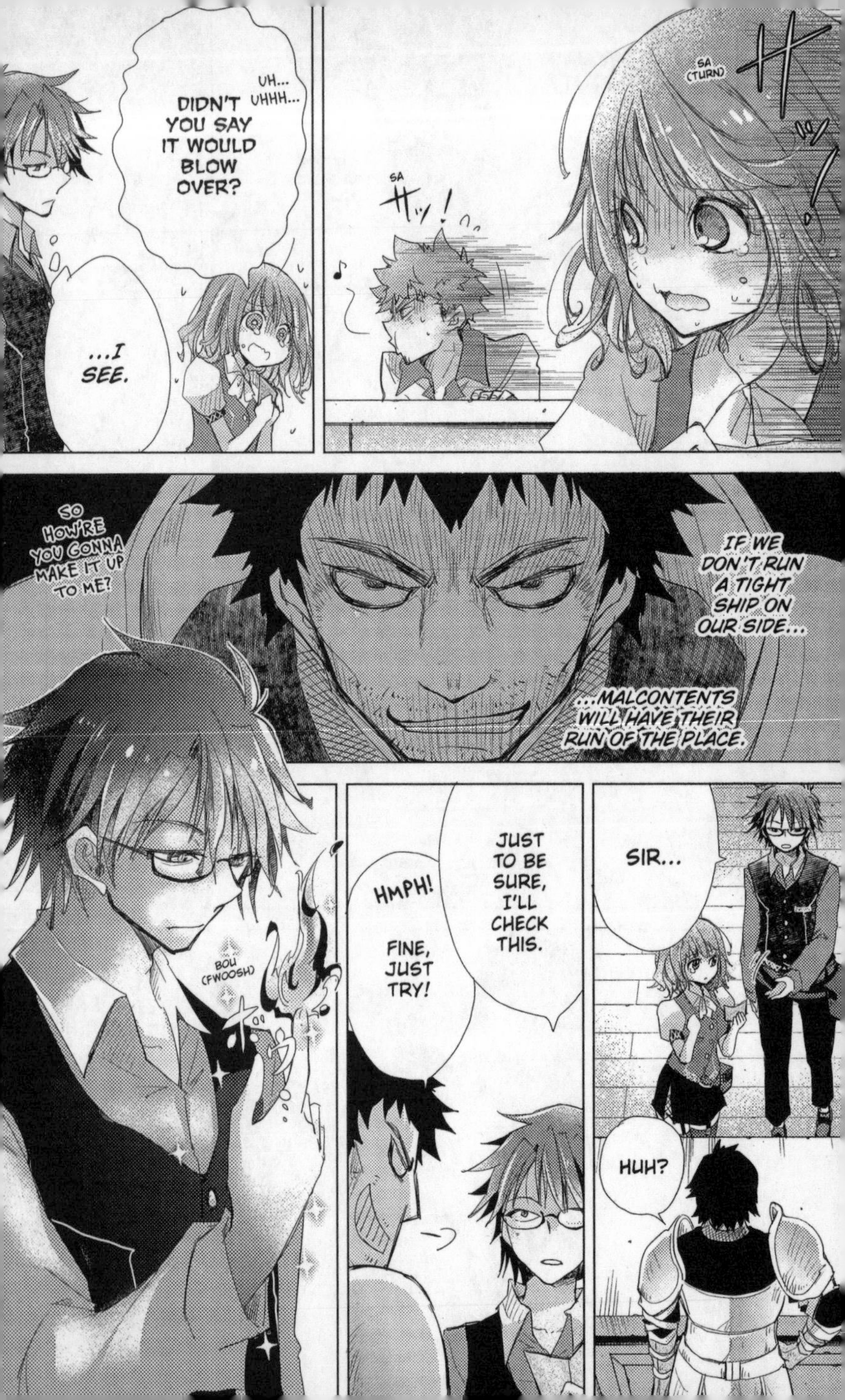
SA (TURN)
SA
UH... UHHH...
DIDN'T YOU SAY IT WOULD BLOW OVER?
...I SEE.
IF WE DON'T RUN A TIGHT SHIP ON OUR SIDE...
...MALCONTENTS WILL HAVE THEIR RUN OF THE PLACE.
SO HOW'RE YOU GONNA MAKE IT UP TO ME?
SIR...
HUH?
JUST TO BE SURE, I'LL CHECK THIS.
HMPH!
FINE, JUST TRY!
BOU (FWOOSH)

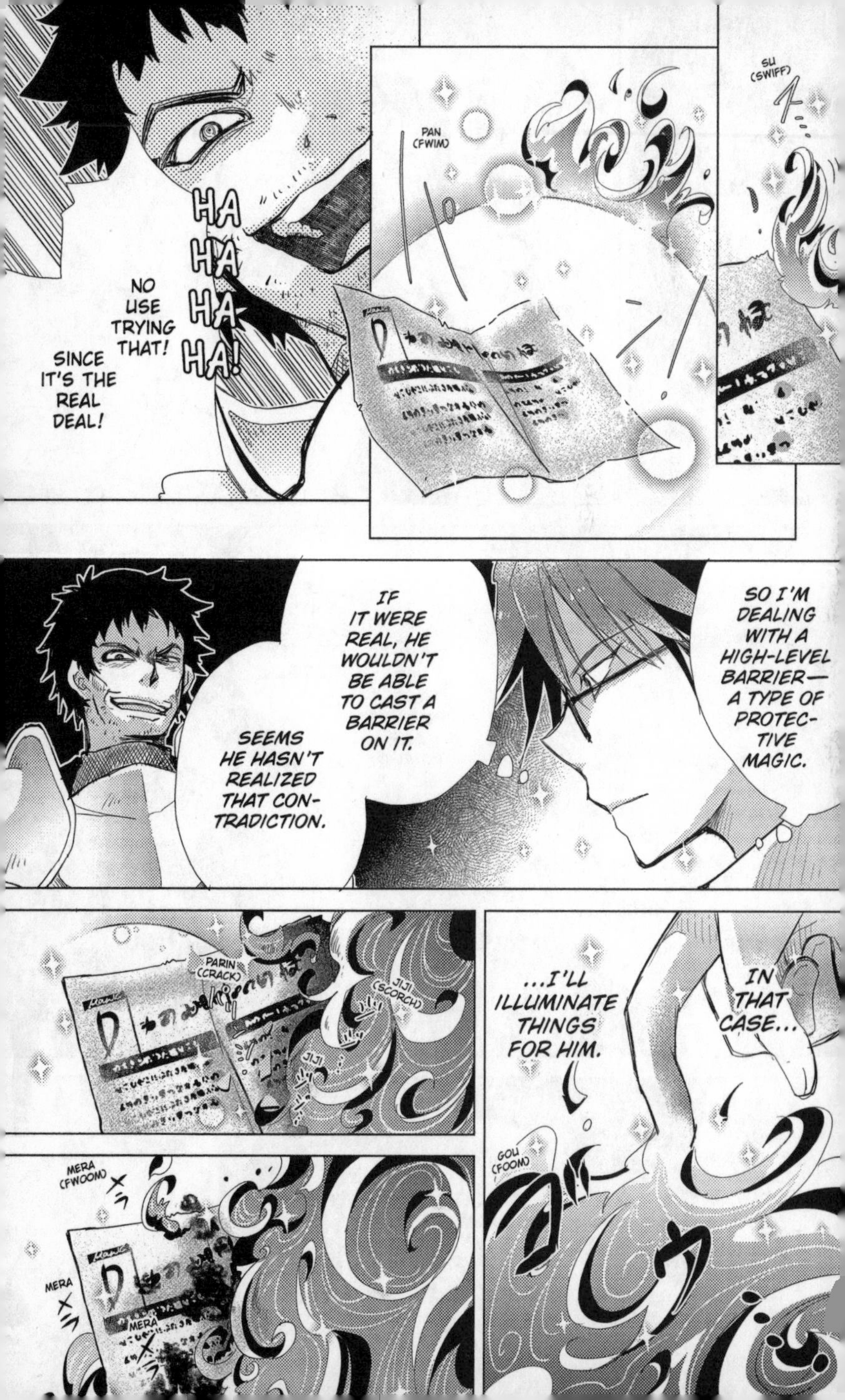
SU (SWIFF)
PAN (FWIM)
HA HA HA HA!
NO USE TRYING THAT!
SINCE IT'S THE REAL DEAL!
SO I'M DEALING WITH A HIGH-LEVEL BARRIER— A TYPE OF PROTECTIVE MAGIC.
IF IT WERE REAL, HE WOULDN'T BE ABLE TO CAST A BARRIER ON IT.
SEEMS HE HASN'T REALIZED THAT CONTRADICTION.
IN THAT CASE...
...I'LL ILLUMINATE THINGS FOR HIM.
GOU (FOOM)
PARIN (CRACK)
JIJI (SCORCH)
JIJI
MERA (FWOOM)
MERA
MERA

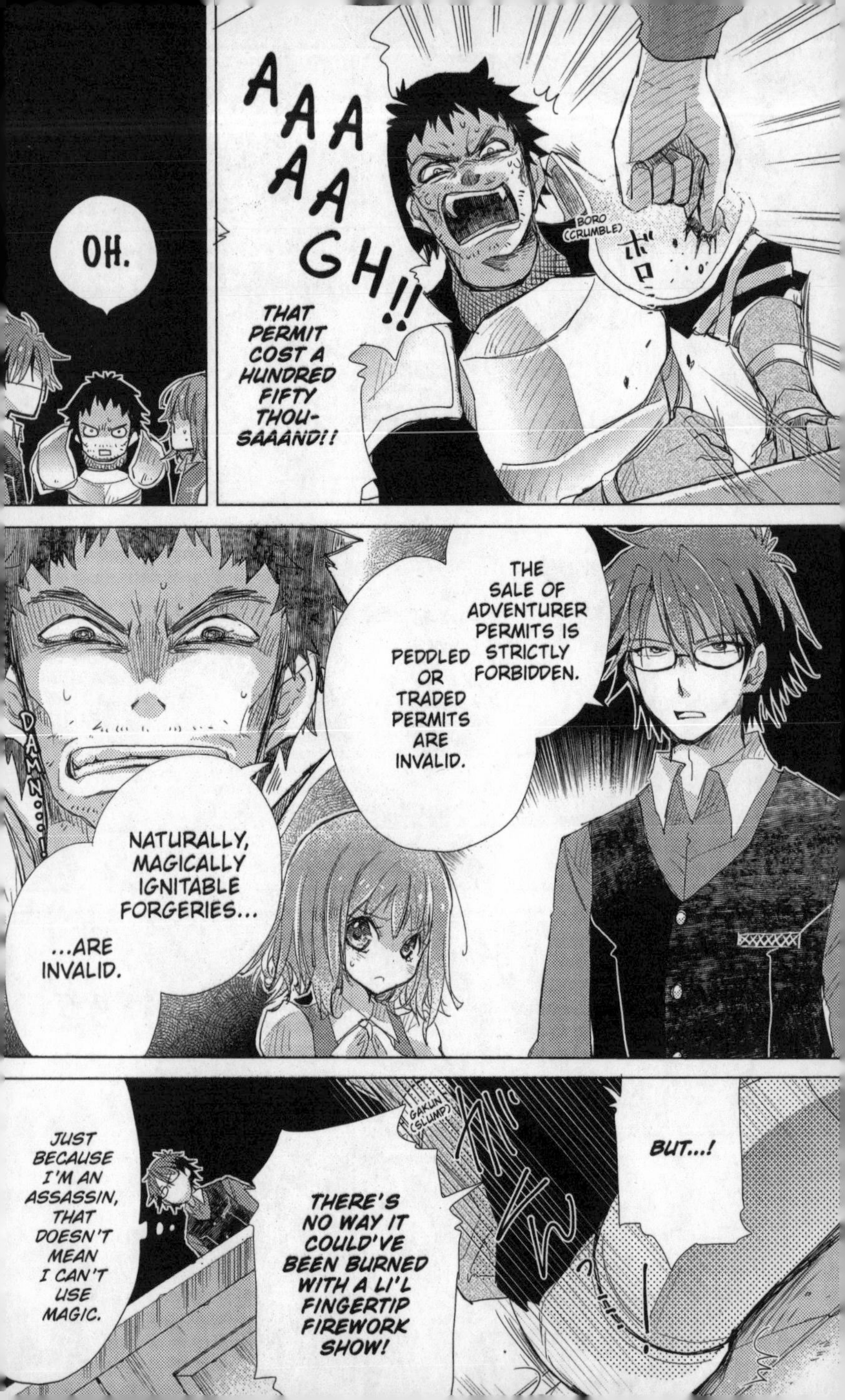
AAAAAGH!!
BORO (CRUMBLE)
THAT PERMIT COST A HUNDRED FIFTY THOU-SAAAND!!
OH.
THE SALE OF ADVENTURER PERMITS IS STRICTLY FORBIDDEN.
PEDDLED OR TRADED PERMITS ARE INVALID.
DAMNooo!
NATURALLY, MAGICALLY IGNITABLE FORGERIES...
...ARE INVALID.
BUT...!
GAKUN (SLUMP)
THERE'S NO WAY IT COULD'VE BEEN BURNED WITH A LI'L FINGERTIP FIREWORK SHOW!
JUST BECAUSE I'M AN ASSASSIN, THAT DOESN'T MEAN I CAN'T USE MAGIC.

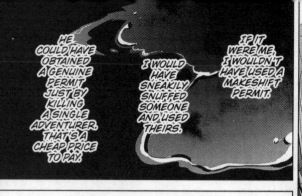

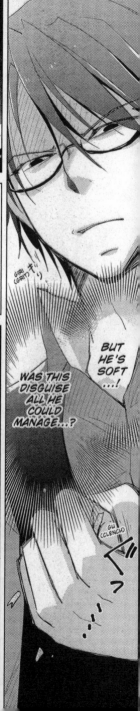

GIRI (GRIT)
BUT HE'S SOFT ...!
WAS THIS DISGUISE ALL HE COULD MANAGE...?
GU (CLENCH)
IF IT WERE ME, I WOULDN'T HAVE USED A MAKESHIFT PERMIT.
I WOULD HAVE SNEAKILY SNUFFED SOMEONE AND USED THEIRS.
HE COULD HAVE OBTAINED A GENUINE PERMIT JUST BY KILLING A SINGLE ADVENTURER. THAT'S A CHEAP PRICE TO PAY.
ADVENTURER PERMITS DON'T CONTAIN INFO ABOUT A PERSON'S APPEARANCE.
NAME
RANK
D
AS LONG AS THE GUILD STAFF DOESN'T KNOW THE PERSON, YOU WON'T GET FIGURED OUT.
ACCEPTED QUESTS AND SUCCESSES
WORK IS IN THE DETAILS.
IT'S HIS OWN FAULT FOR DOING A HALF-ASSED JOB.
YOU'RE LUCKY...
...YOU'RE AN ADVENTURER.

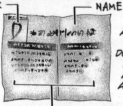

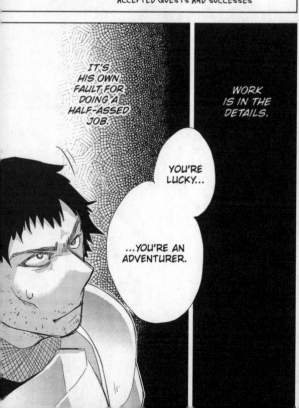

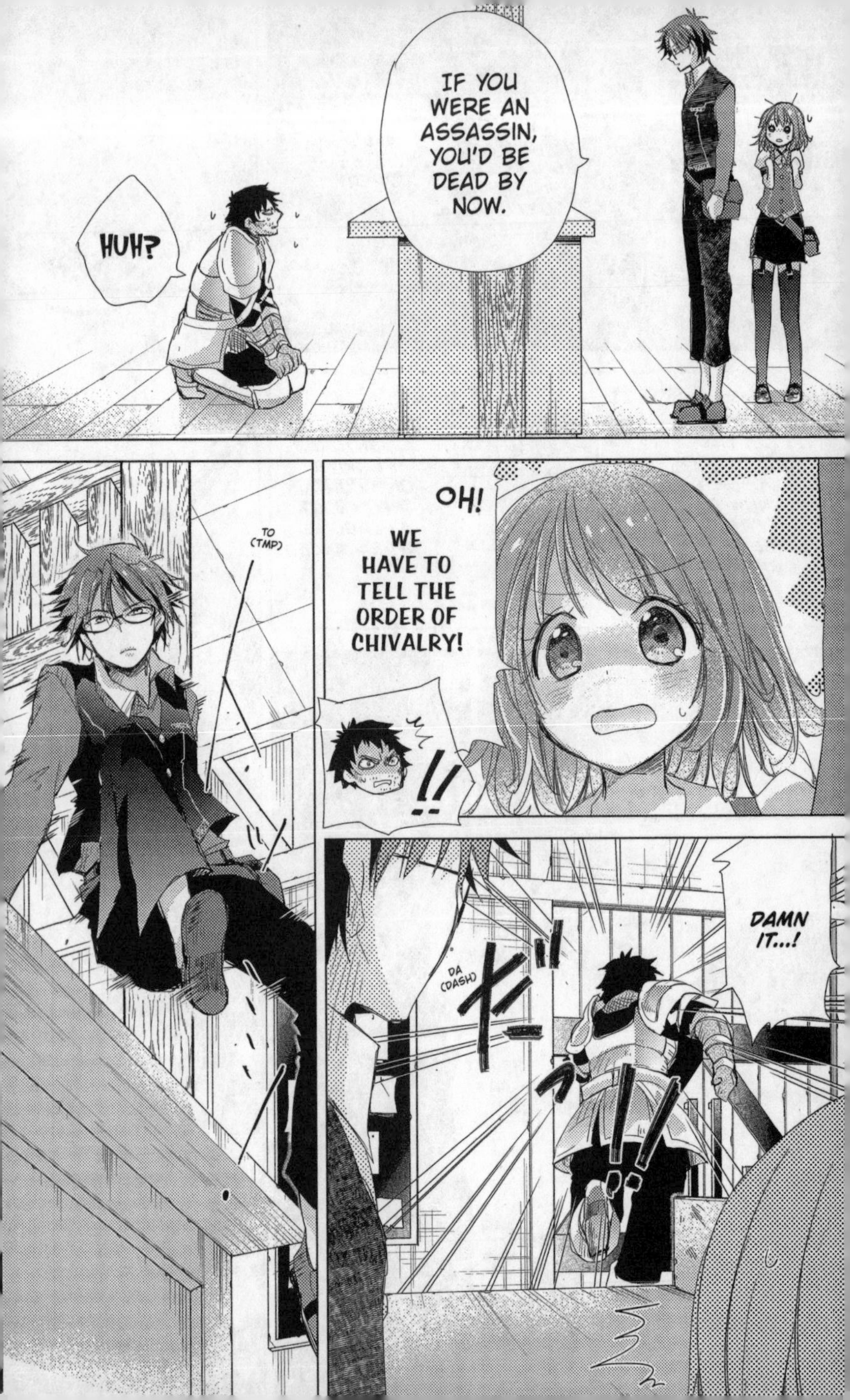
IF YOU WERE AN ASSASSIN, YOU'D BE DEAD BY NOW.
HUH?
OH!
WE HAVE TO TELL THE ORDER OF CHIVALRY!
!!
DAMN IT...!
DA (DASH)
TO (TMP)

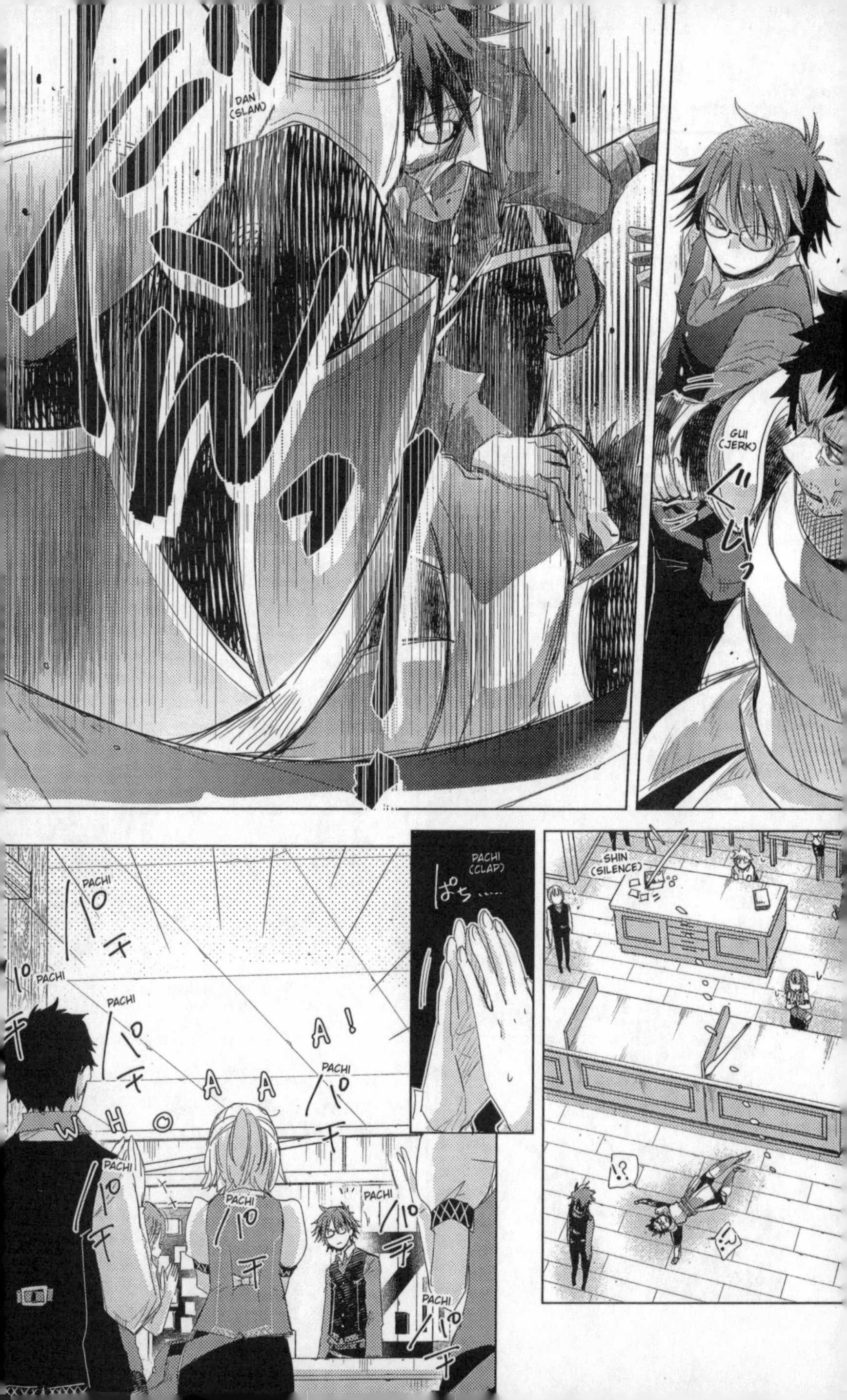
GUI
(JERK)
DAN
(SLAM)
SHIN
(SILENCE)
!?
!?
PACHI
(CLAP)
ぱち……
PACHI
PACHI
PACHI
WHOAAA!
PACHI
PACHI
PACHI
PACHI
PACHI

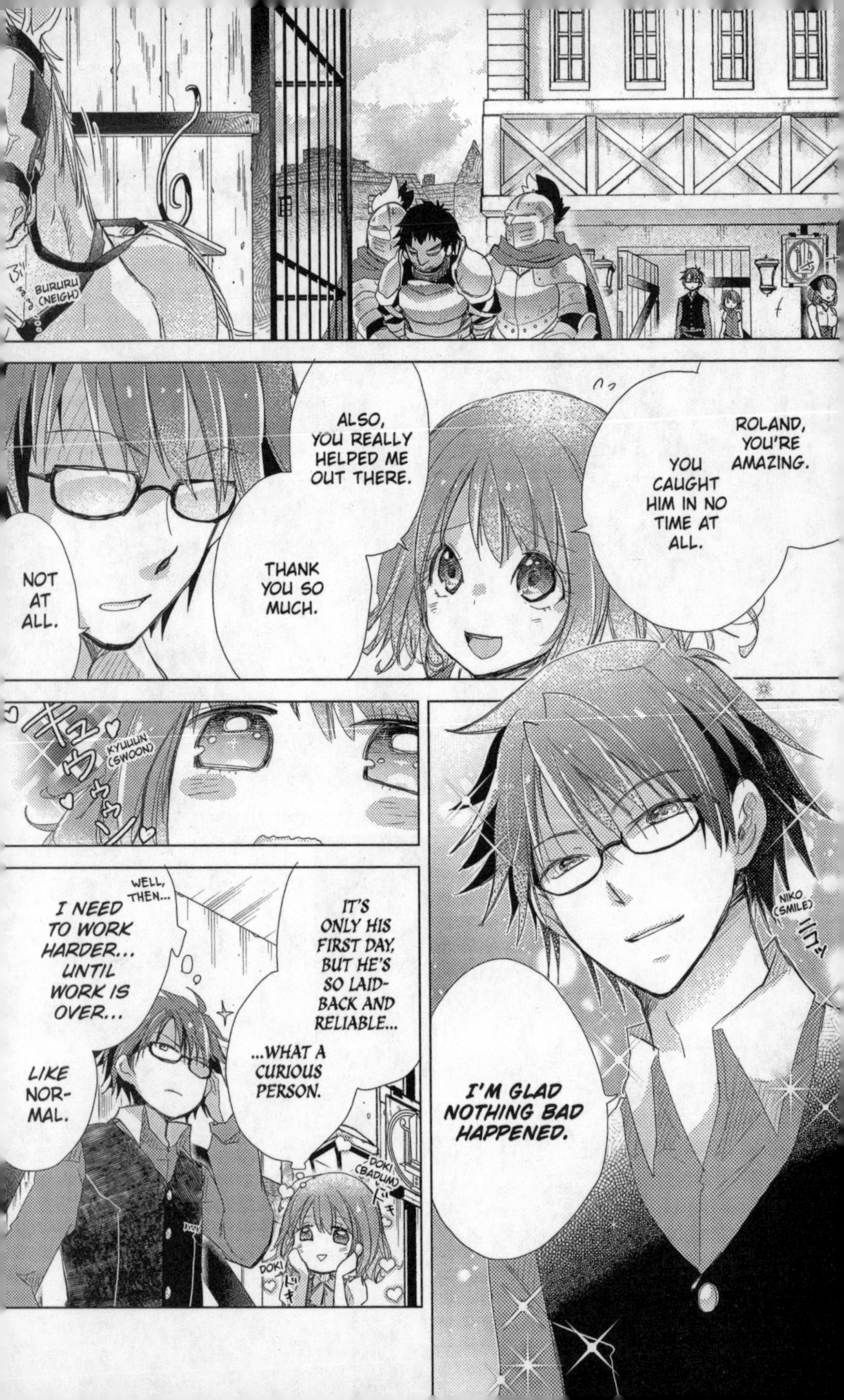
BURURU (NEIGH)
ROLAND, YOU'RE AMAZING.
YOU CAUGHT HIM IN NO TIME AT ALL.
ALSO, YOU REALLY HELPED ME OUT THERE.
THANK YOU SO MUCH.
NOT AT ALL.
NIKO (SMILE)
I'M GLAD NOTHING BAD HAPPENED.
KYUUUN (SWOON)
IT'S ONLY HIS FIRST DAY, BUT HE'S SO LAID-BACK AND RELIABLE...
...WHAT A CURIOUS PERSON.
DOKI (BADUM)
DOKI
WELL, THEN...
I NEED TO WORK HARDER... UNTIL WORK IS OVER...
LIKE NORMAL.

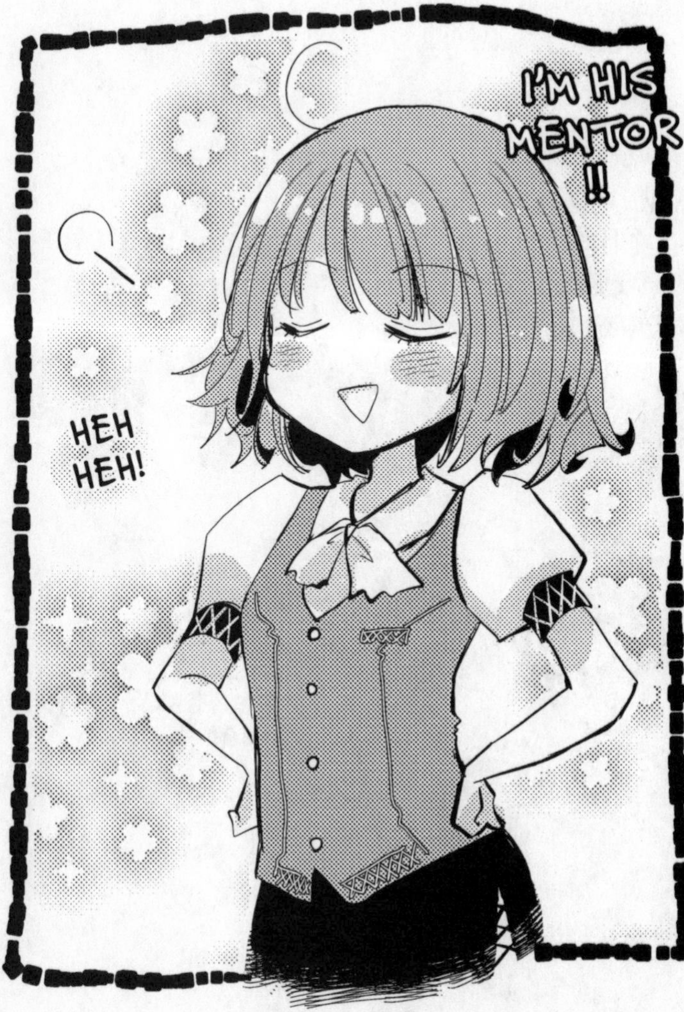
I'M HIS MENTOR !!
HEH HEH!

AFTER HIS LUNCH BREAK, MAUREY CAME BACK LOOKING KIND OF REFRESHED.

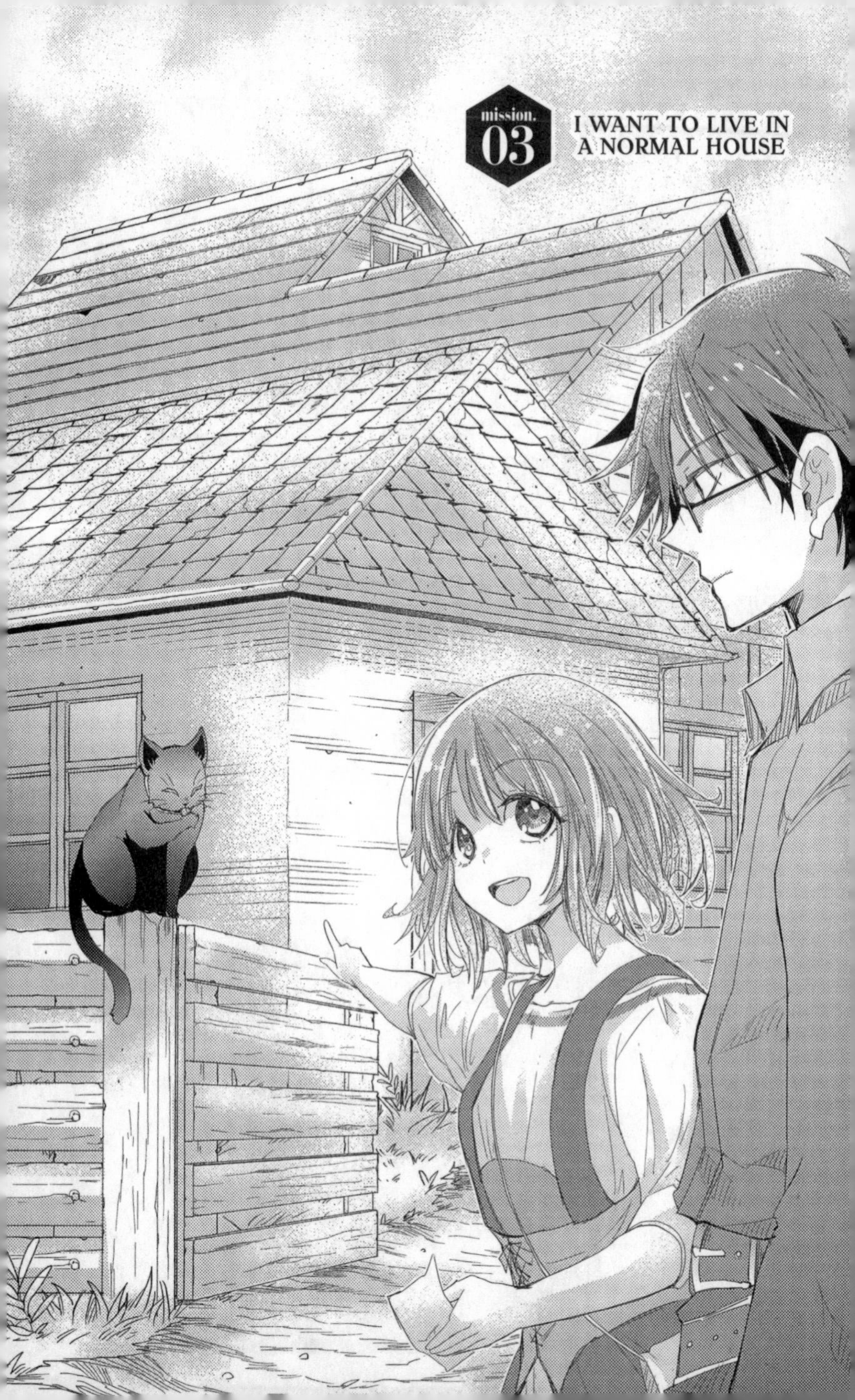
mission.
03
I WANT TO LIVE IN
A NORMAL HOUSE

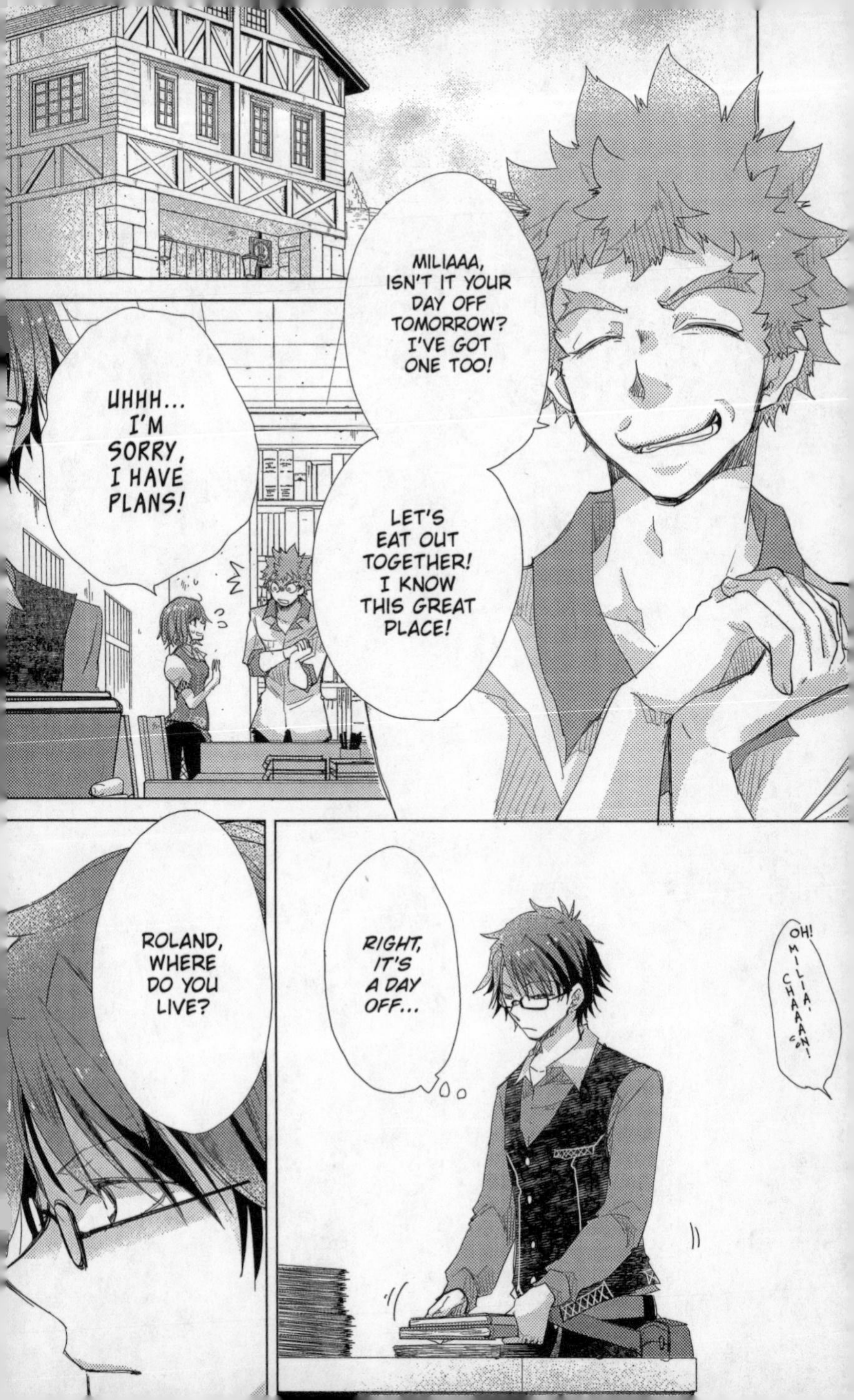
MILIAAA, ISN'T IT YOUR DAY OFF TOMORROW? I'VE GOT ONE TOO!
LET'S EAT OUT TOGETHER! I KNOW THIS GREAT PLACE!
UHHH... I'M SORRY, I HAVE PLANS!
OH! MILIA-CHAAAAN!
RIGHT, IT'S A DAY OFF...
ROLAND, WHERE DO YOU LIVE?

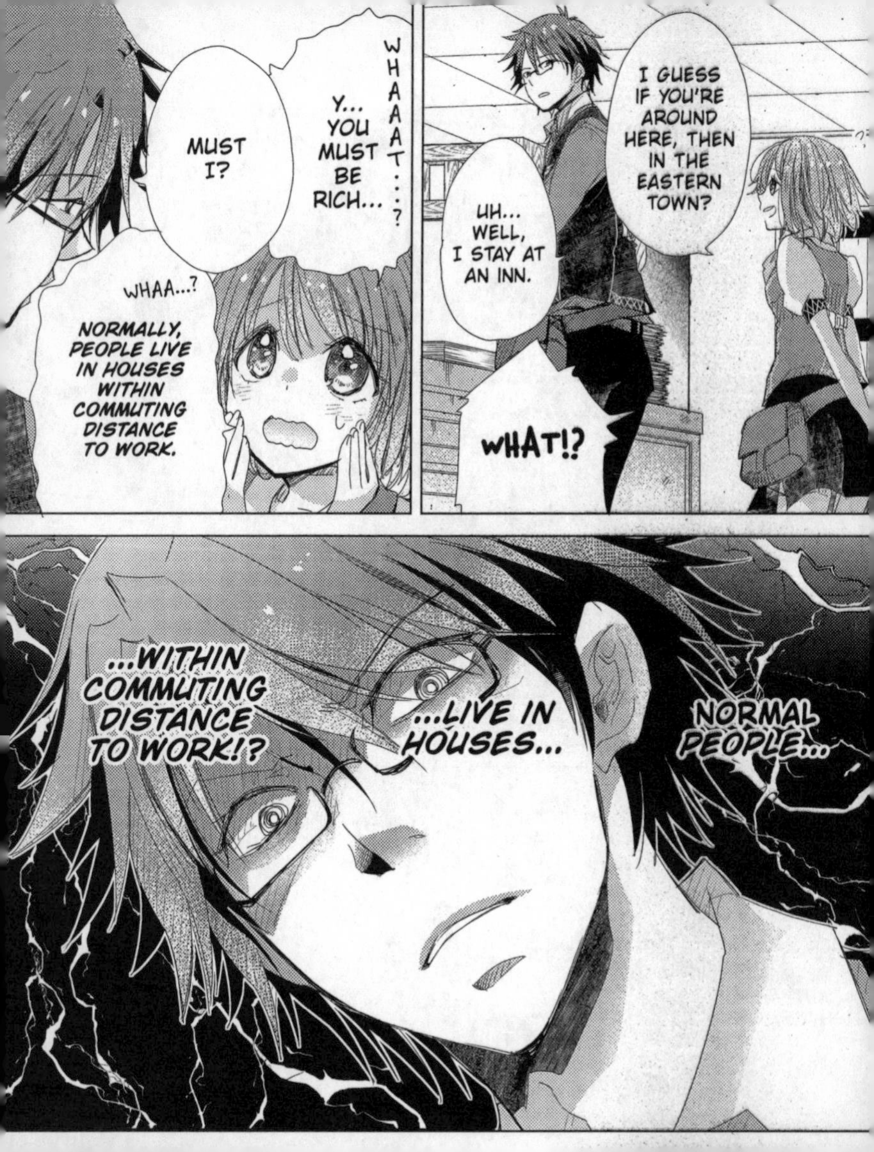
I GUESS IF YOU'RE AROUND HERE, THEN IN THE EASTERN TOWN?
UH... WELL, I STAY AT AN INN.
WHAT!?
WHAAAAT...?
Y... YOU MUST BE RICH...
MUST I?
WHAA...?
NORMALLY, PEOPLE LIVE IN HOUSES WITHIN COMMUTING DISTANCE TO WORK.
NORMAL PEOPLE...
...LIVE IN HOUSES...
...WITHIN COMMUTING DISTANCE TO WORK!?

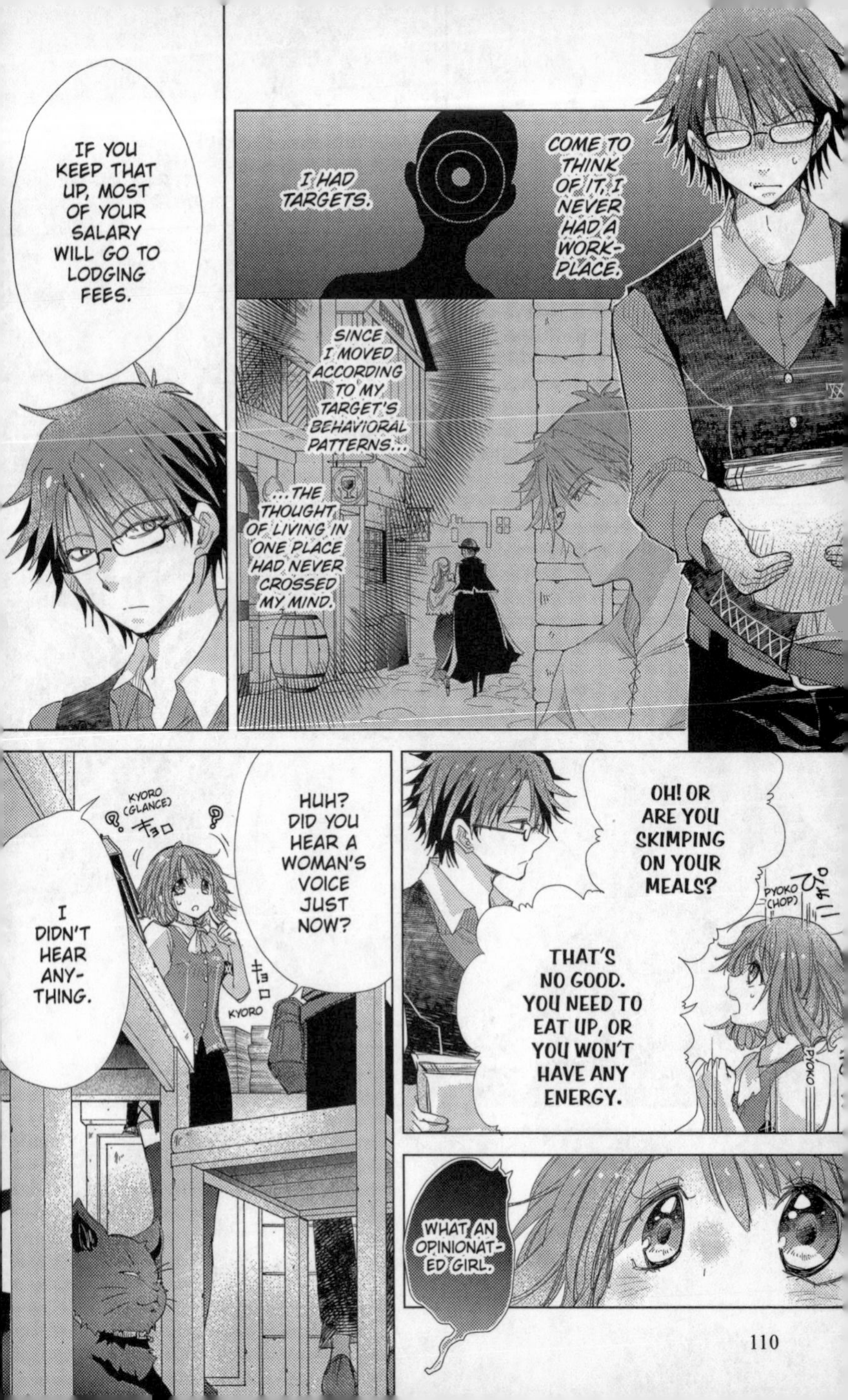
COME TO THINK OF IT, I NEVER HAD A WORK-PLACE.
I HAD TARGETS.
SINCE I MOVED ACCORDING TO MY TARGET'S BEHAVIORAL PATTERNS...
...THE THOUGHT OF LIVING IN ONE PLACE HAD NEVER CROSSED MY MIND.
IF YOU KEEP THAT UP, MOST OF YOUR SALARY WILL GO TO LODGING FEES.
OH! OR ARE YOU SKIMPING ON YOUR MEALS?
PYOKO (HOP)
PYOKO
THAT'S NO GOOD. YOU NEED TO EAT UP, OR YOU WON'T HAVE ANY ENERGY.
WHAT AN OPINIONAT-ED GIRL.
HUH? DID YOU HEAR A WOMAN'S VOICE JUST NOW?
KYORO (GLANCE)
KYORO
I DIDN'T HEAR ANY-THING.

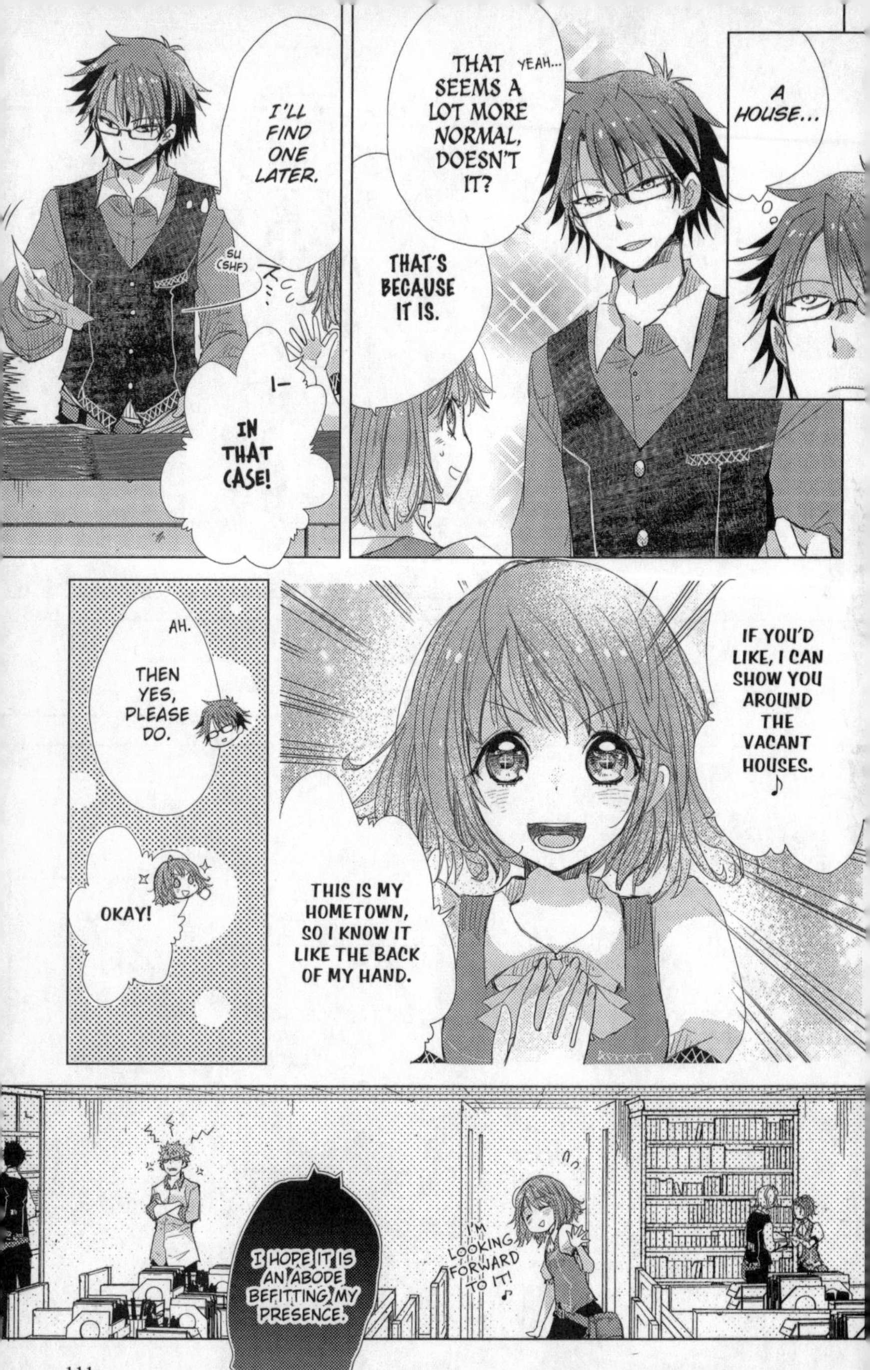
A HOUSE...
THAT SEEMS A LOT MORE NORMAL, DOESN'T IT?
YEAH...
THAT'S BECAUSE IT IS.
I'LL FIND ONE LATER.
SU (SHF)
I—
IN THAT CASE!
IF YOU'D LIKE, I CAN SHOW YOU AROUND THE VACANT HOUSES. ♪
THIS IS MY HOMETOWN, SO I KNOW IT LIKE THE BACK OF MY HAND.
AH.
THEN YES, PLEASE DO.
OKAY!
I'M LOOKING FORWARD TO IT! ♪
I HOPE IT IS AN ABODE BEFITTING MY PRESENCE.

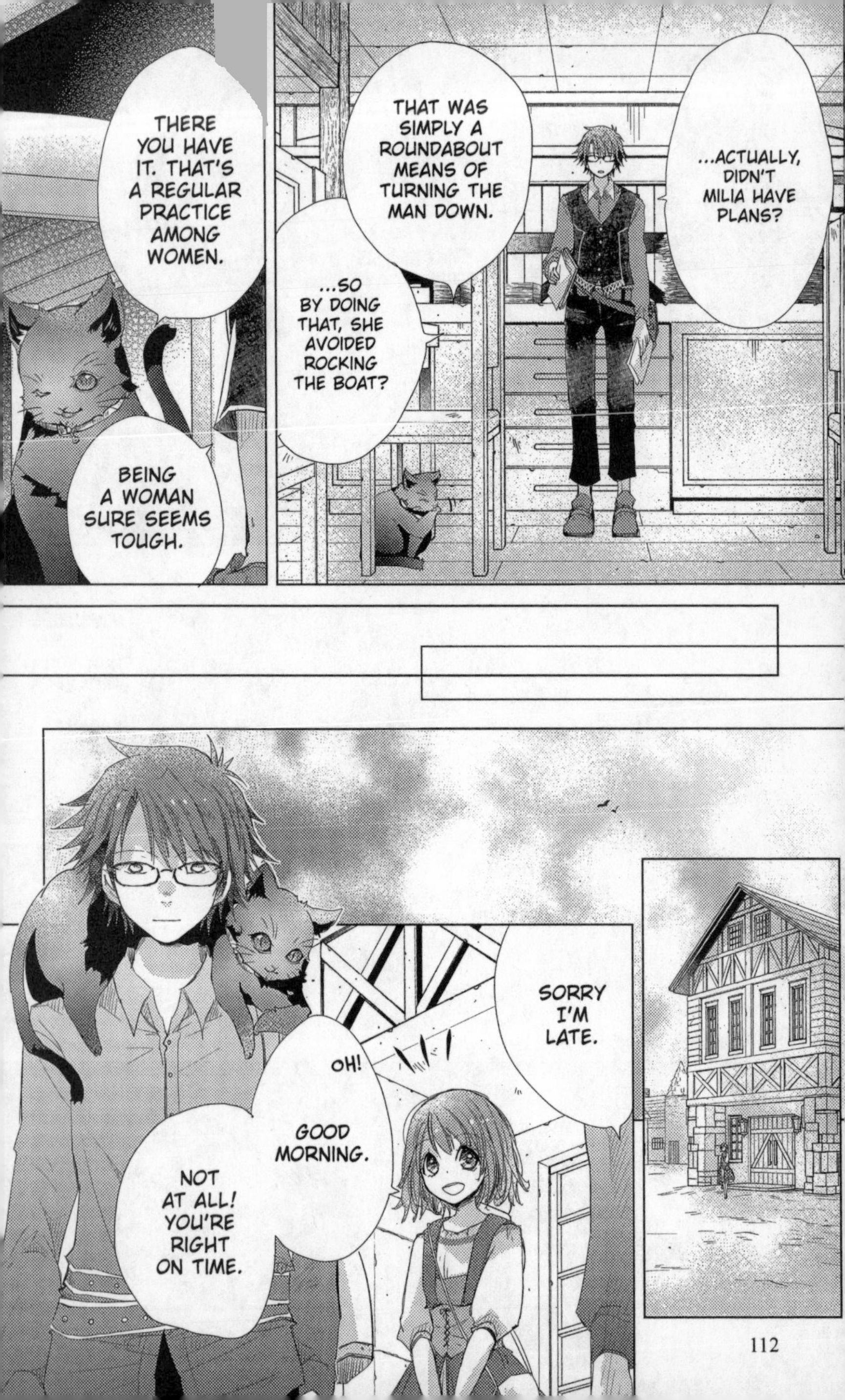
...ACTUALLY, DIDN'T MILIA HAVE PLANS?
THAT WAS SIMPLY A ROUNDABOUT MEANS OF TURNING THE MAN DOWN.
...SO BY DOING THAT, SHE AVOIDED ROCKING THE BOAT?
THERE YOU HAVE IT. THAT'S A REGULAR PRACTICE AMONG WOMEN.
BEING A WOMAN SURE SEEMS TOUGH.
SORRY I'M LATE.
OH!
GOOD MORNING.
NOT AT ALL! YOU'RE RIGHT ON TIME.

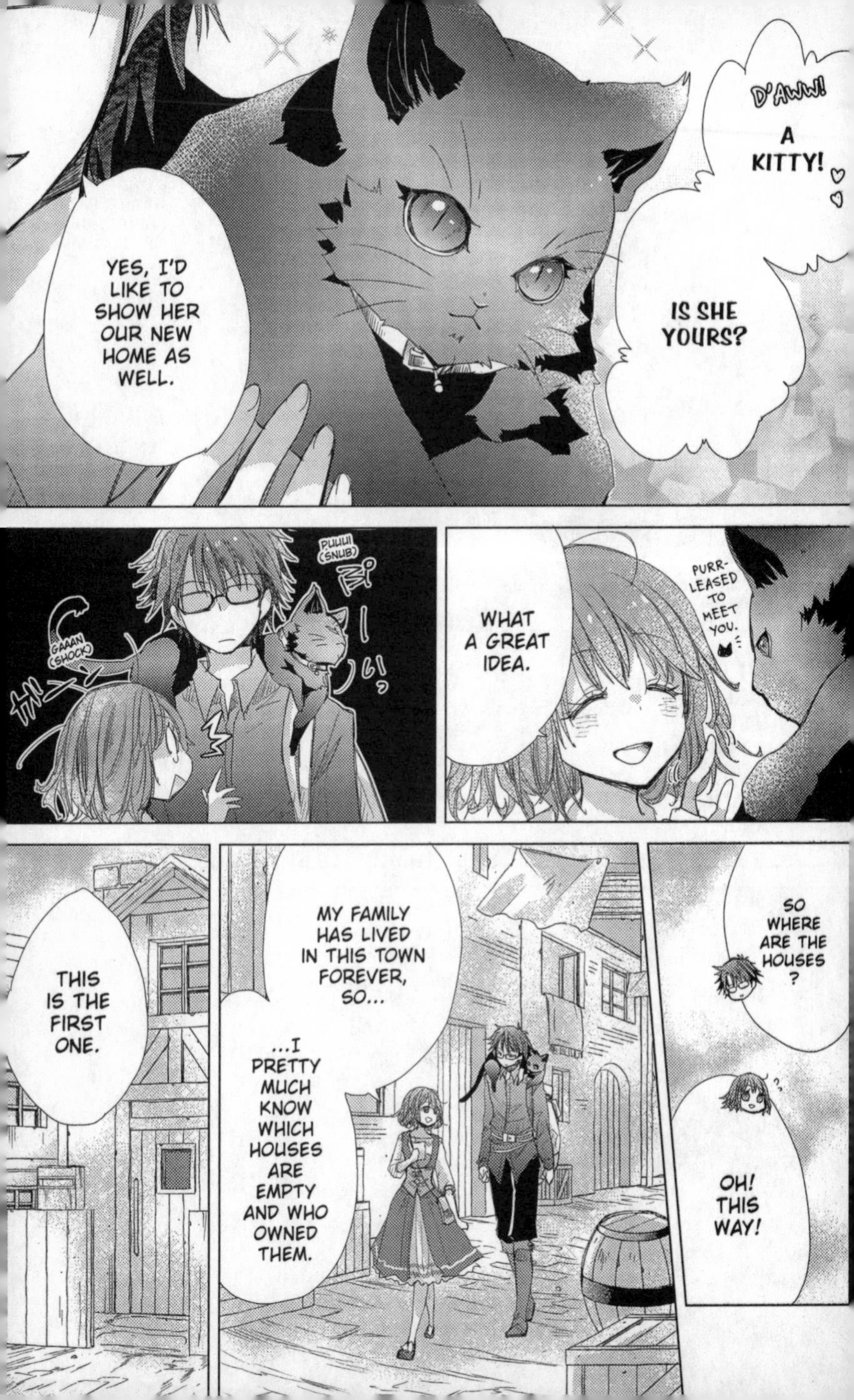
D'AWW!
A KITTY!
IS SHE YOURS?
YES, I'D LIKE TO SHOW HER OUR NEW HOME AS WELL.
PURR-LEASED TO MEET YOU.
WHAT A GREAT IDEA.
PUUUI (SNUB)
GAAAN (SHOCK)
SO WHERE ARE THE HOUSES?
OH! THIS WAY!
MY FAMILY HAS LIVED IN THIS TOWN FOREVER, SO...
...I PRETTY MUCH KNOW WHICH HOUSES ARE EMPTY AND WHO OWNED THEM.
THIS IS THE FIRST ONE.

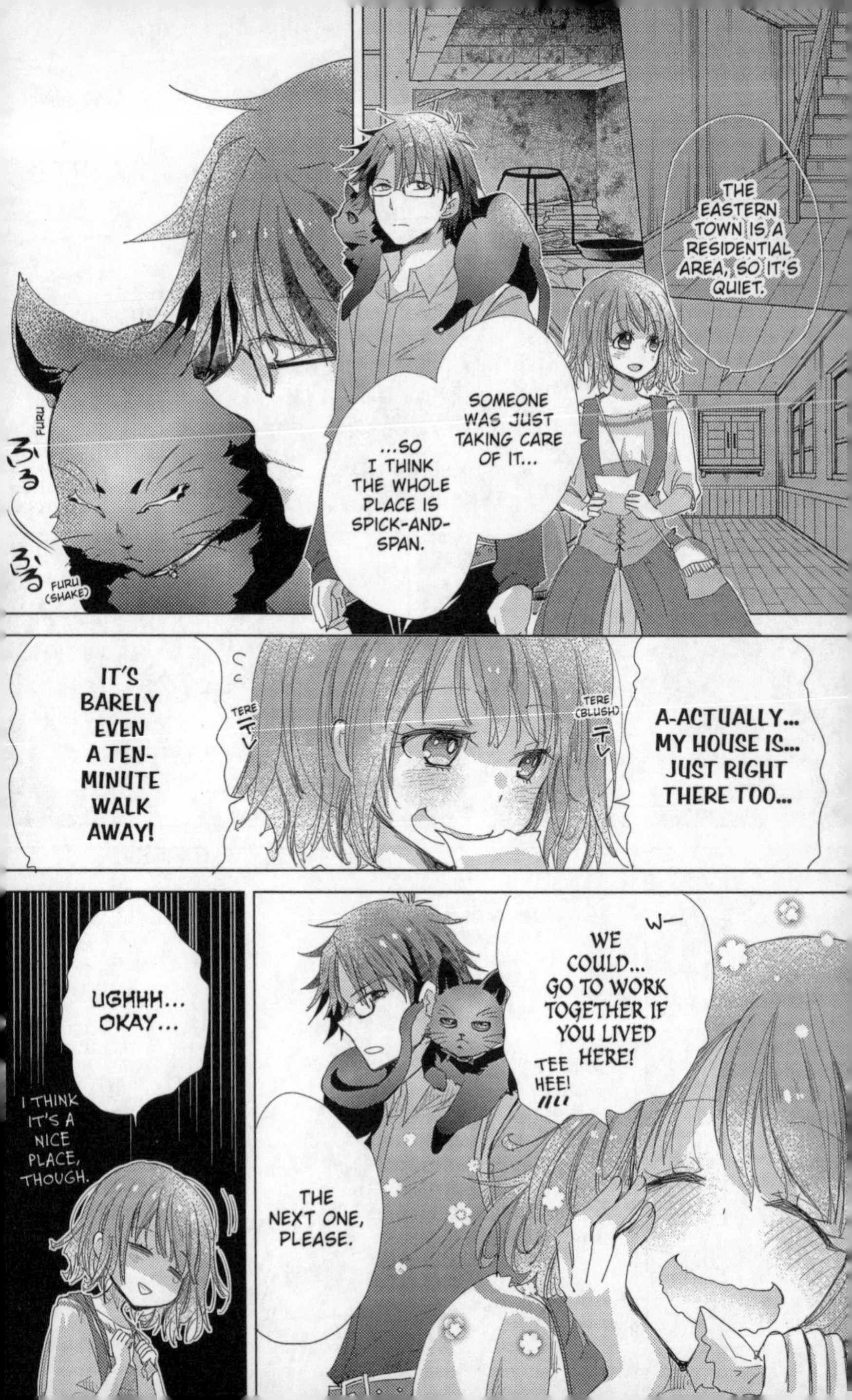
THE EASTERN TOWN IS A RESIDENTIAL AREA, SO IT'S QUIET.
SOMEONE WAS JUST TAKING CARE OF IT...
...SO I THINK THE WHOLE PLACE IS SPICK-AND-SPAN.
ふる FURU
ふる FURU (SHAKE)
A-ACTUALLY... MY HOUSE IS... JUST RIGHT THERE TOO...
テレ TERE (BLUSH)
テレ TERE
IT'S BARELY EVEN A TEN-MINUTE WALK AWAY!
W— WE COULD... GO TO WORK TOGETHER IF YOU LIVED HERE!
TEE HEE!
THE NEXT ONE, PLEASE.
UGHHH... OKAY...
I THINK IT'S A NICE PLACE, THOUGH.

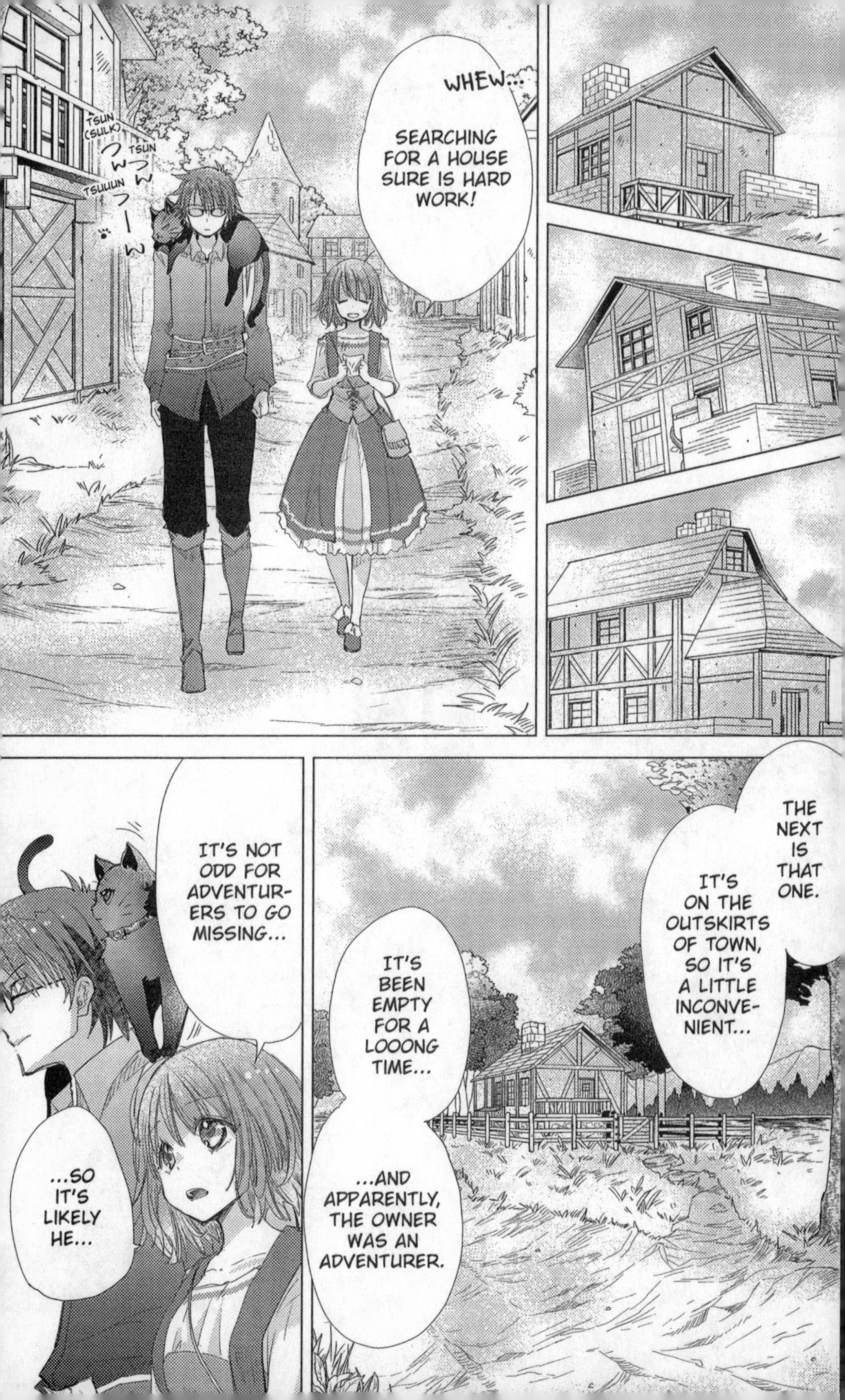
WHEW...
SEARCHING FOR A HOUSE SURE IS HARD WORK!
TSUN (SULK)
TSUN
TSUUUN
THE NEXT IS THAT ONE.
IT'S ON THE OUTSKIRTS OF TOWN, SO IT'S A LITTLE INCONVE-NIENT...
IT'S BEEN EMPTY FOR A LOOONG TIME...
...AND APPARENTLY, THE OWNER WAS AN ADVENTURER.
IT'S NOT ODD FOR ADVENTUR-ERS TO GO MISSING...
...SO IT'S LIKELY HE...

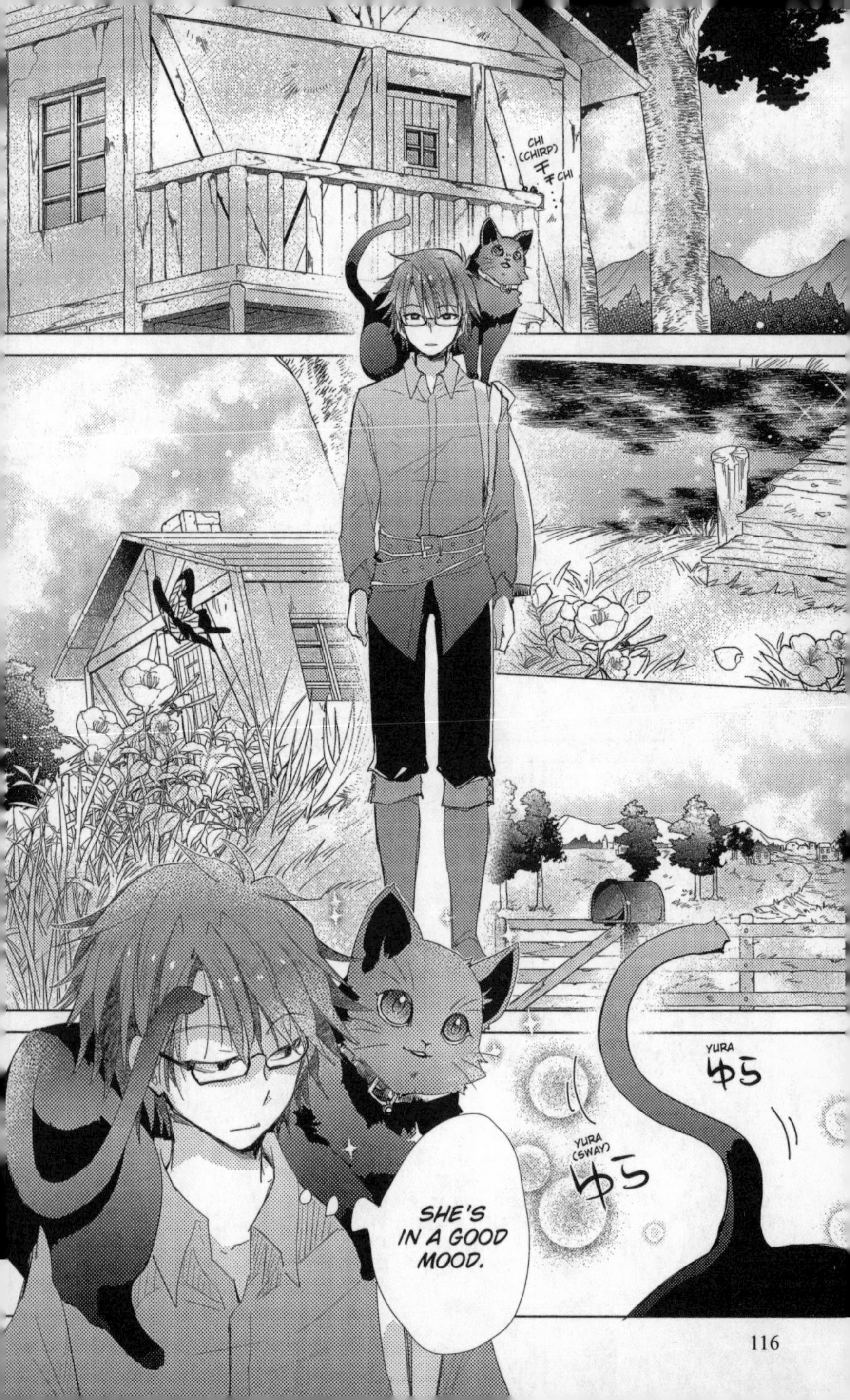
CHI (CHIRP)
チ
チ CHI
YURA
ゆら
YURA (SWAY)
ゆら
SHE'S IN A GOOD MOOD.

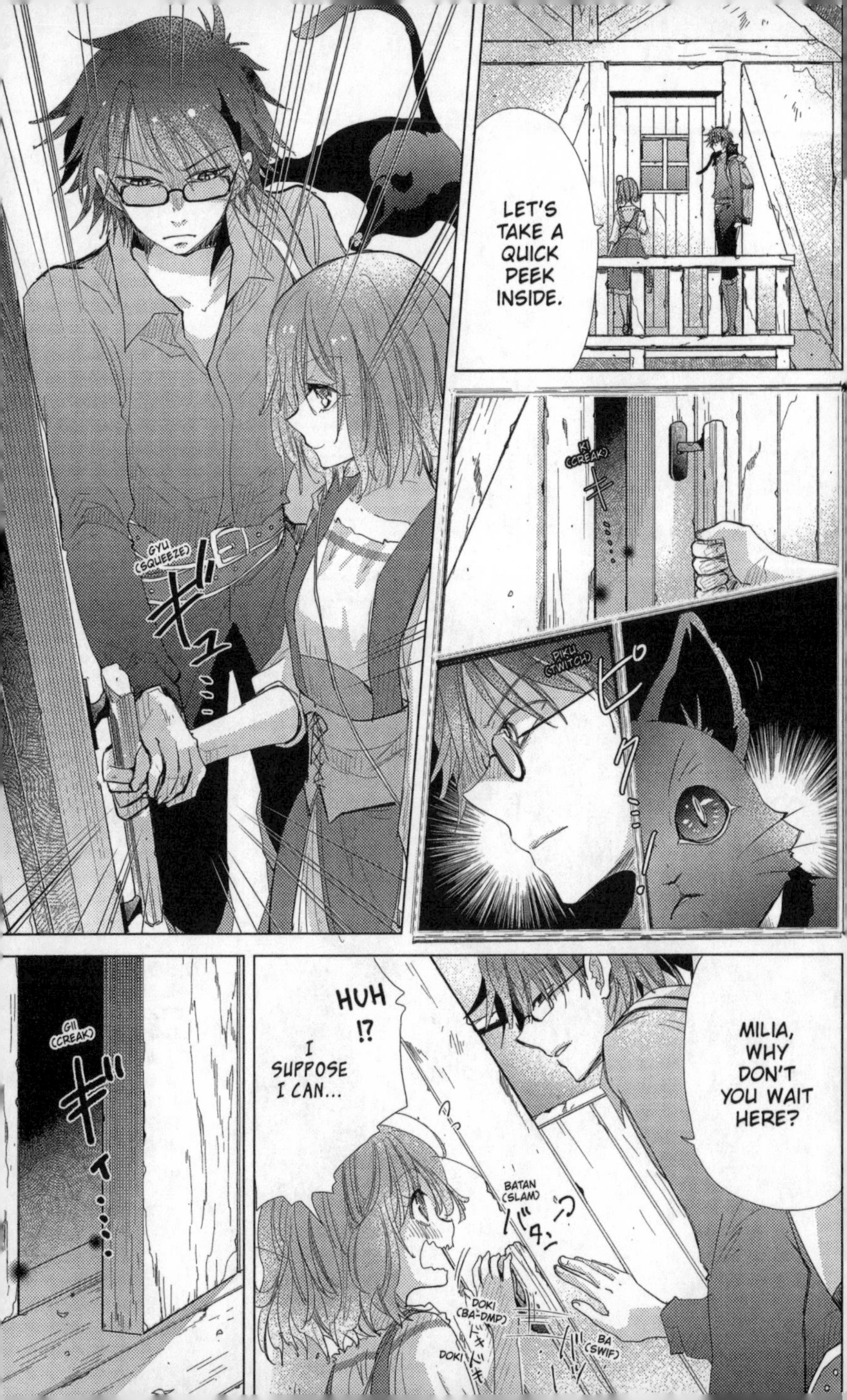
LET'S TAKE A QUICK PEEK INSIDE.
KI (CREAK)
PIKU (TWITCH)
GYU (SQUEEZE)
MILIA, WHY DON'T YOU WAIT HERE?
HUH !?
I SUPPOSE I CAN...
BATAN (SLAM)
DOKI (BA-DMP)
DOKI
BA (SWIF)
GII (CREAK)

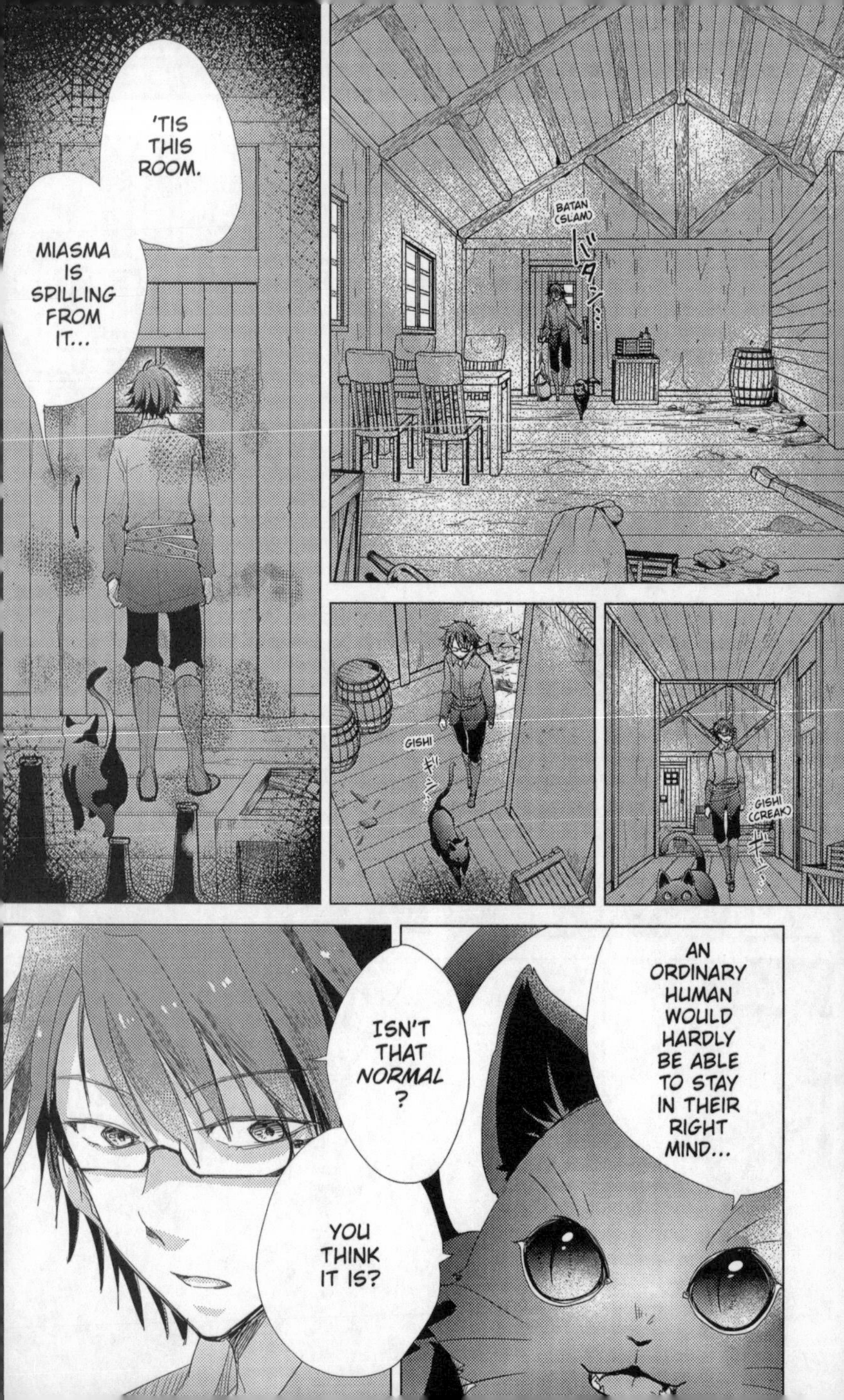

BATAN (SLAM)
GISHI (CREAK)
GISHI
'TIS THIS ROOM.
MIASMA IS SPILLING FROM IT...
AN ORDINARY HUMAN WOULD HARDLY BE ABLE TO STAY IN THEIR RIGHT MIND...
ISN'T THAT *NORMAL*?
YOU THINK IT IS?

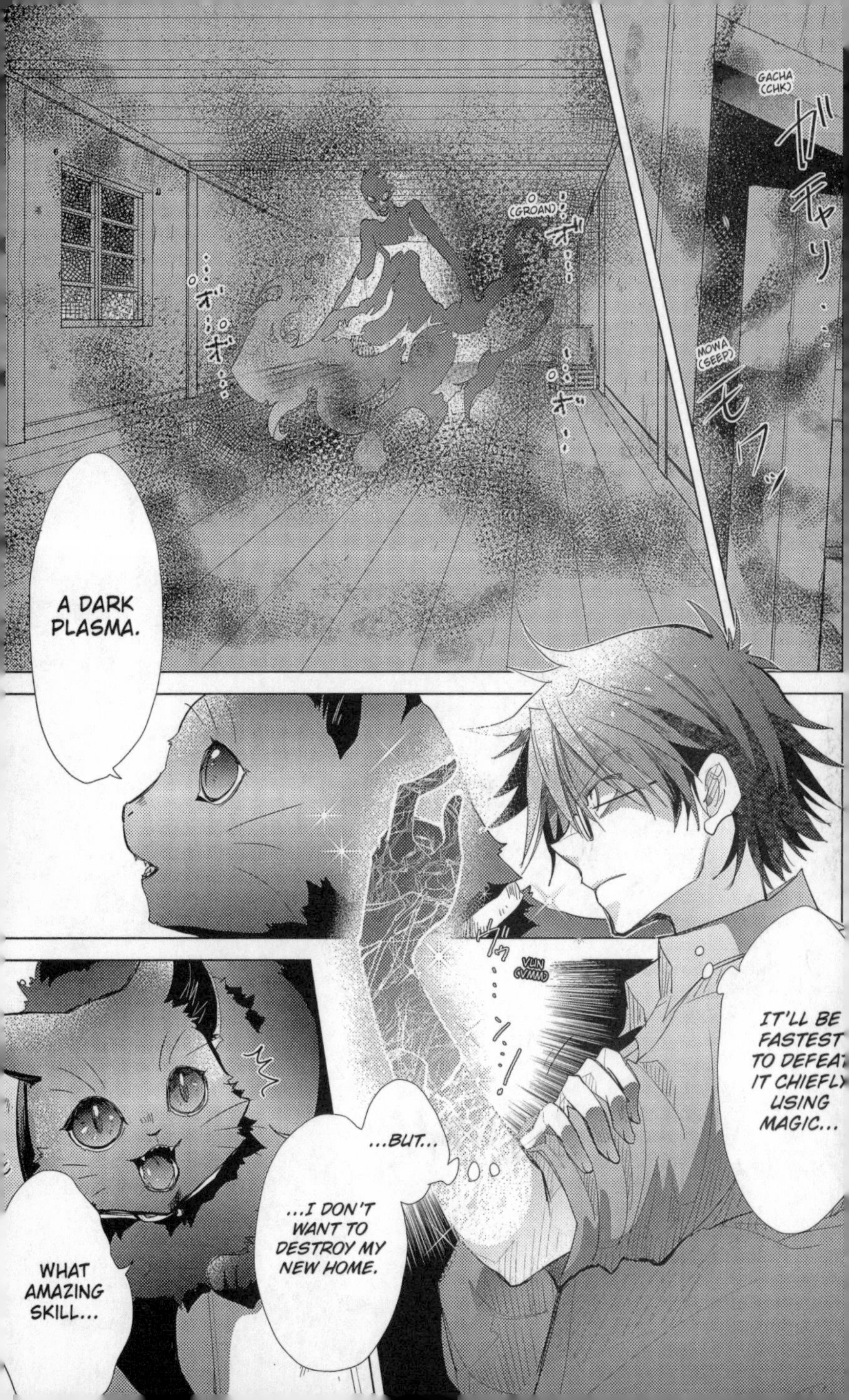
GACHA (CHK)
ガチャリ…
MOWA (SEEP)
モワッ
O (GROAN)
A DARK PLASMA.
IT'LL BE FASTEST TO DEFEAT IT CHIEFLY USING MAGIC...
VUN (VMM)
...BUT...
...I DON'T WANT TO DESTROY MY NEW HOME.
WHAT AMAZING SKILL...

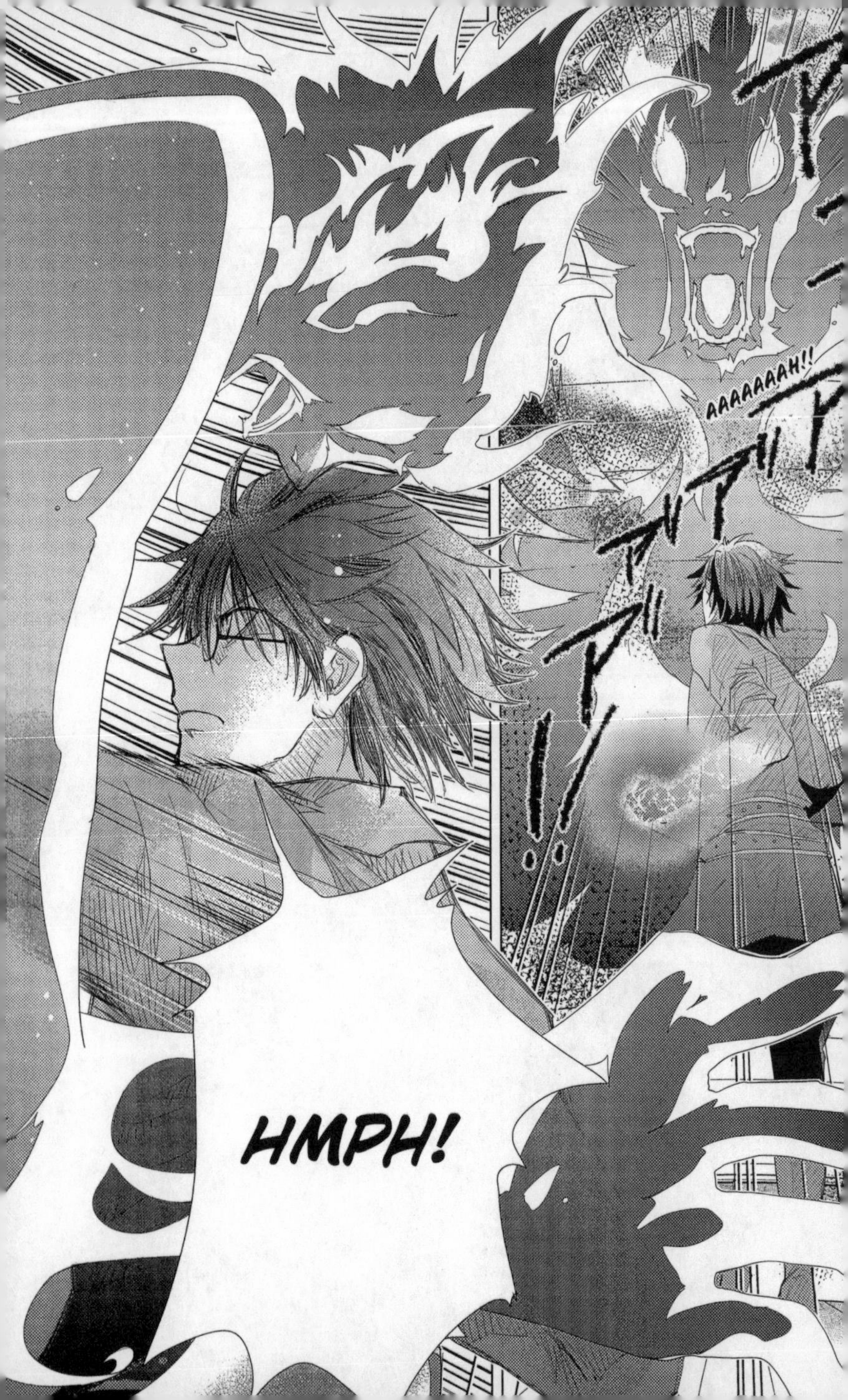
AAAAAAAH!!
HMPH!

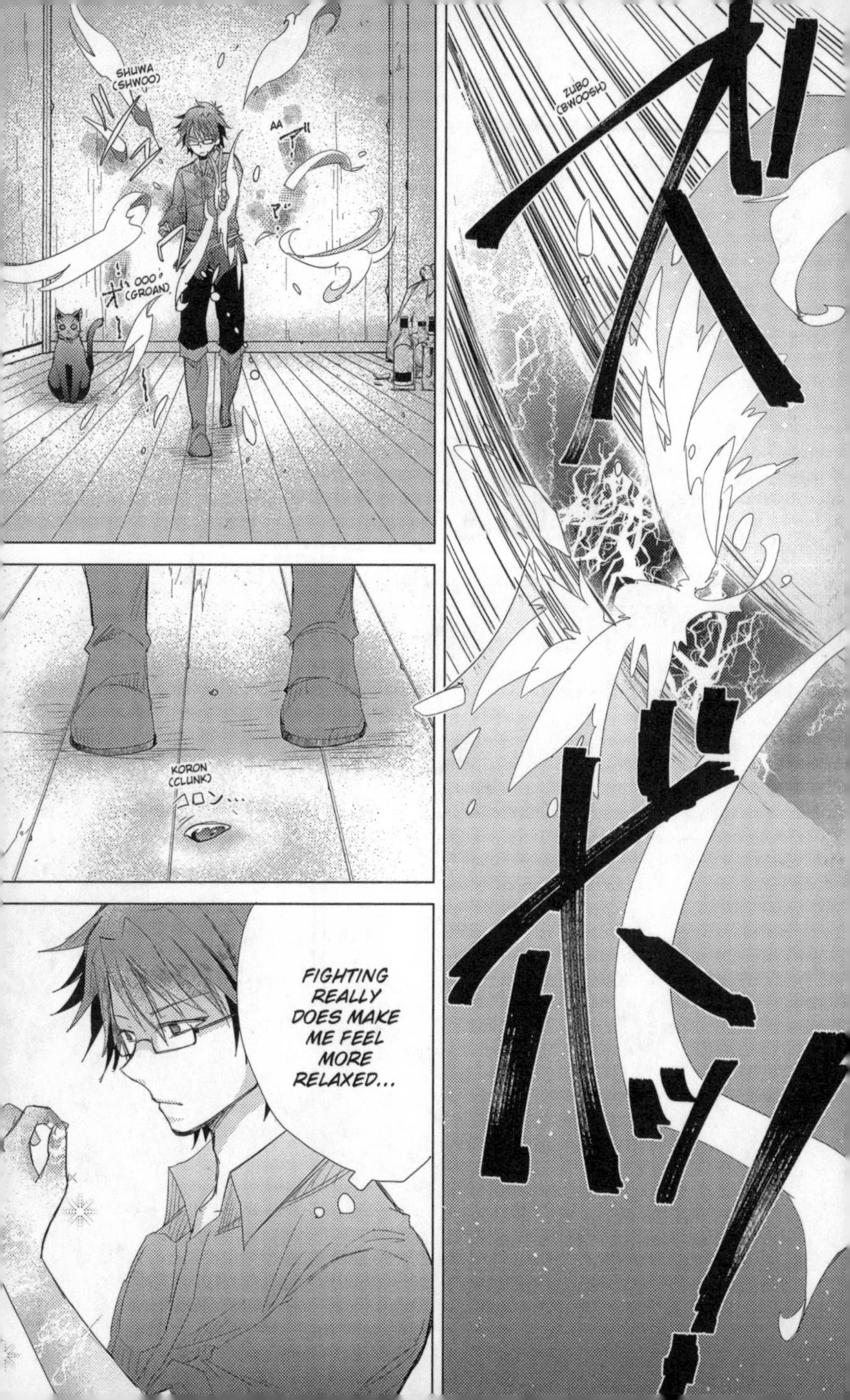

ZUBO (BWOOSH)
SHUWA (SHWOO)
AA
OOO (GROAN)
KORON (CLUNK)
コロン…
FIGHTING REALLY DOES MAKE ME FEEL MORE RELAXED...

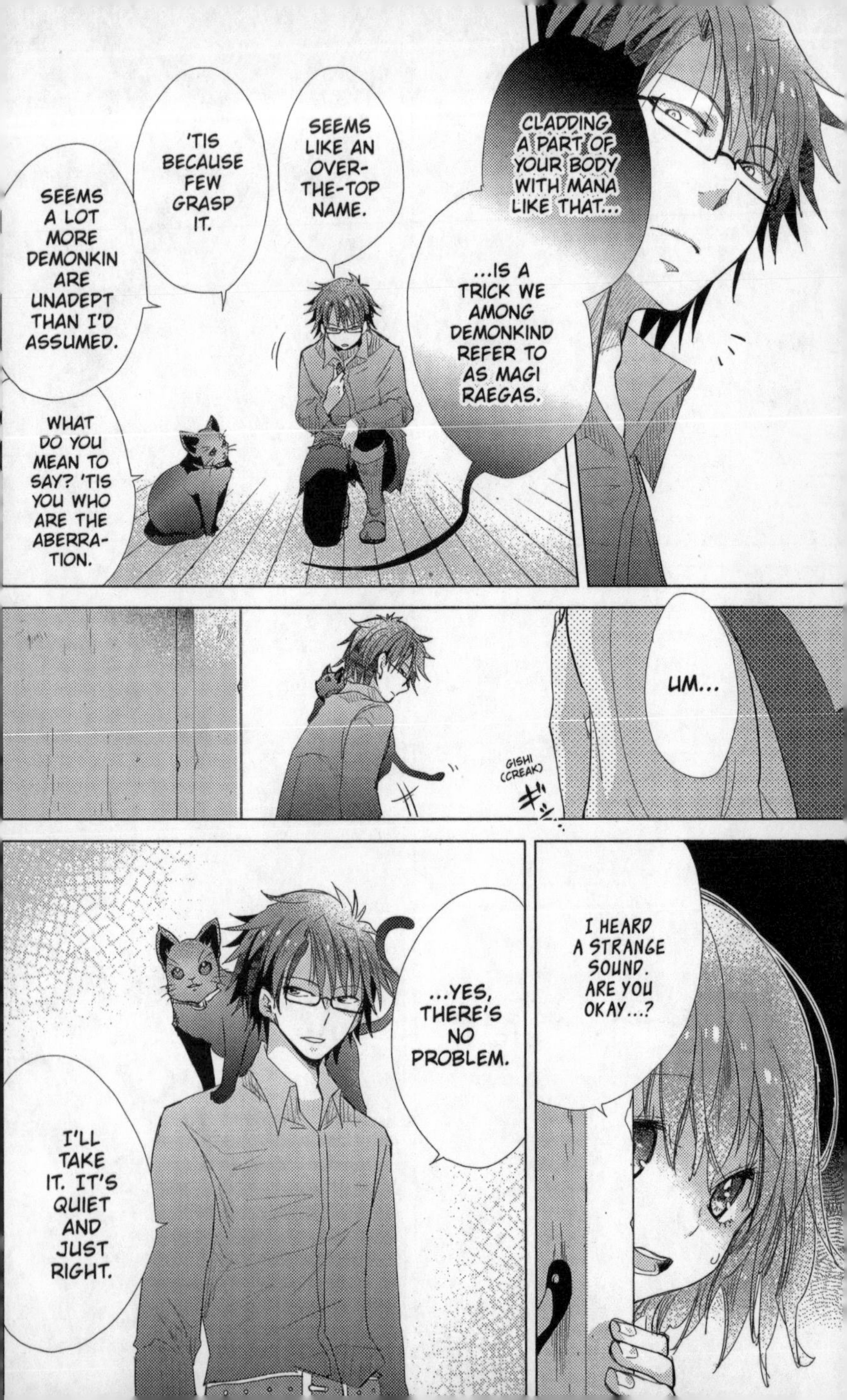
CLADDING A PART OF YOUR BODY WITH MANA LIKE THAT...
...IS A TRICK WE AMONG DEMONKIND REFER TO AS MAGI RAEGAS.
SEEMS LIKE AN OVER-THE-TOP NAME.
'TIS BECAUSE FEW GRASP IT.
SEEMS A LOT MORE DEMONKIN ARE UNADEPT THAN I'D ASSUMED.
WHAT DO YOU MEAN TO SAY? 'TIS YOU WHO ARE THE ABERRATION.
UM...
GISHI (CREAK)
I HEARD A STRANGE SOUND. ARE YOU OKAY...?
...YES, THERE'S NO PROBLEM.
I'LL TAKE IT. IT'S QUIET AND JUST RIGHT.

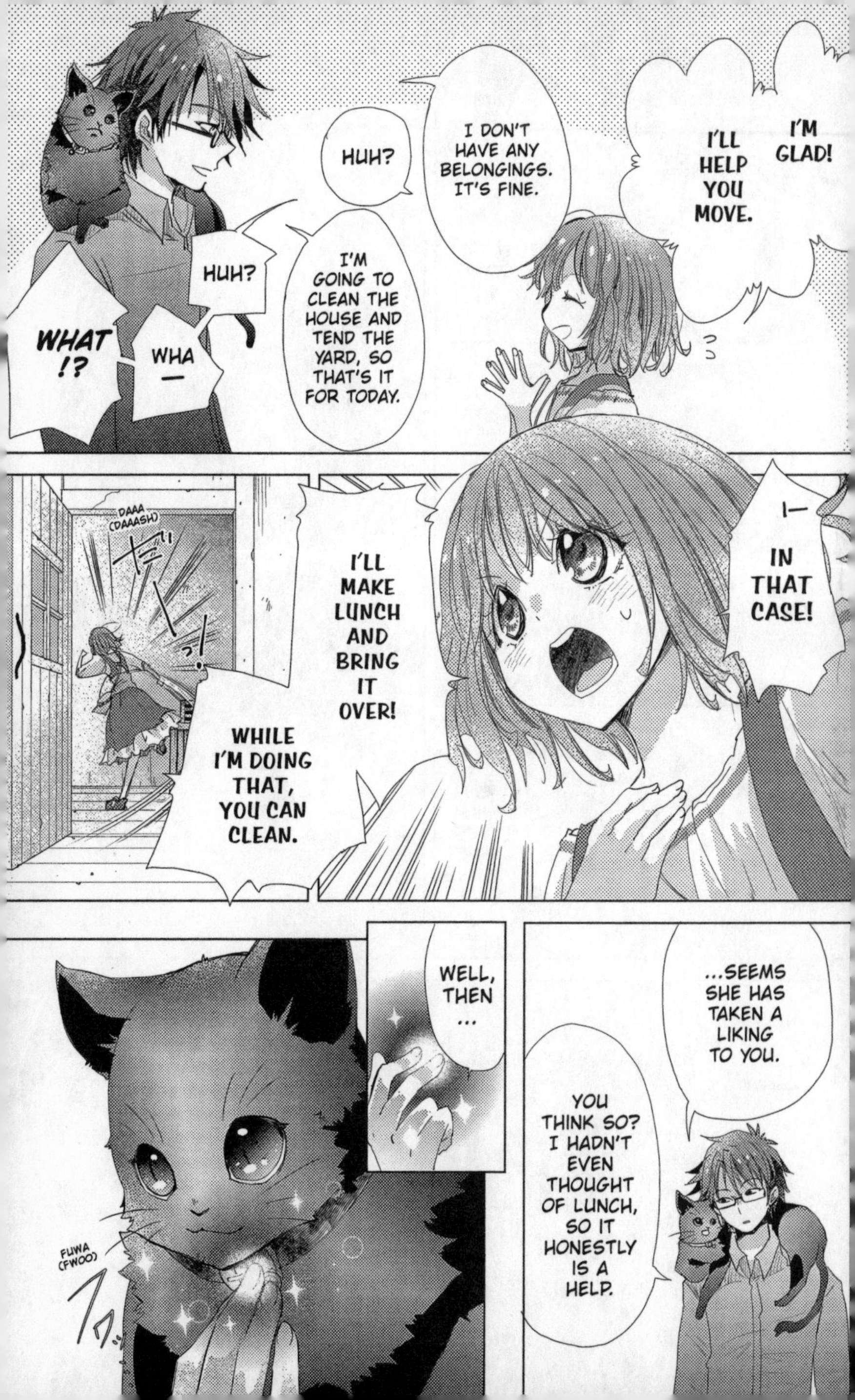
I'M GLAD!
I'LL HELP YOU MOVE.
I DON'T HAVE ANY BELONGINGS. IT'S FINE.
HUH?
I'M GOING TO CLEAN THE HOUSE AND TEND THE YARD, SO THAT'S IT FOR TODAY.
HUH?
WHA—
WHAT!?
I— IN THAT CASE!
I'LL MAKE LUNCH AND BRING IT OVER!
WHILE I'M DOING THAT, YOU CAN CLEAN.
DAAA (DAAASH)
...SEEMS SHE HAS TAKEN A LIKING TO YOU.
YOU THINK SO? I HADN'T EVEN THOUGHT OF LUNCH, SO IT HONESTLY IS A HELP.
WELL, THEN ...
FUWA (FWOO)

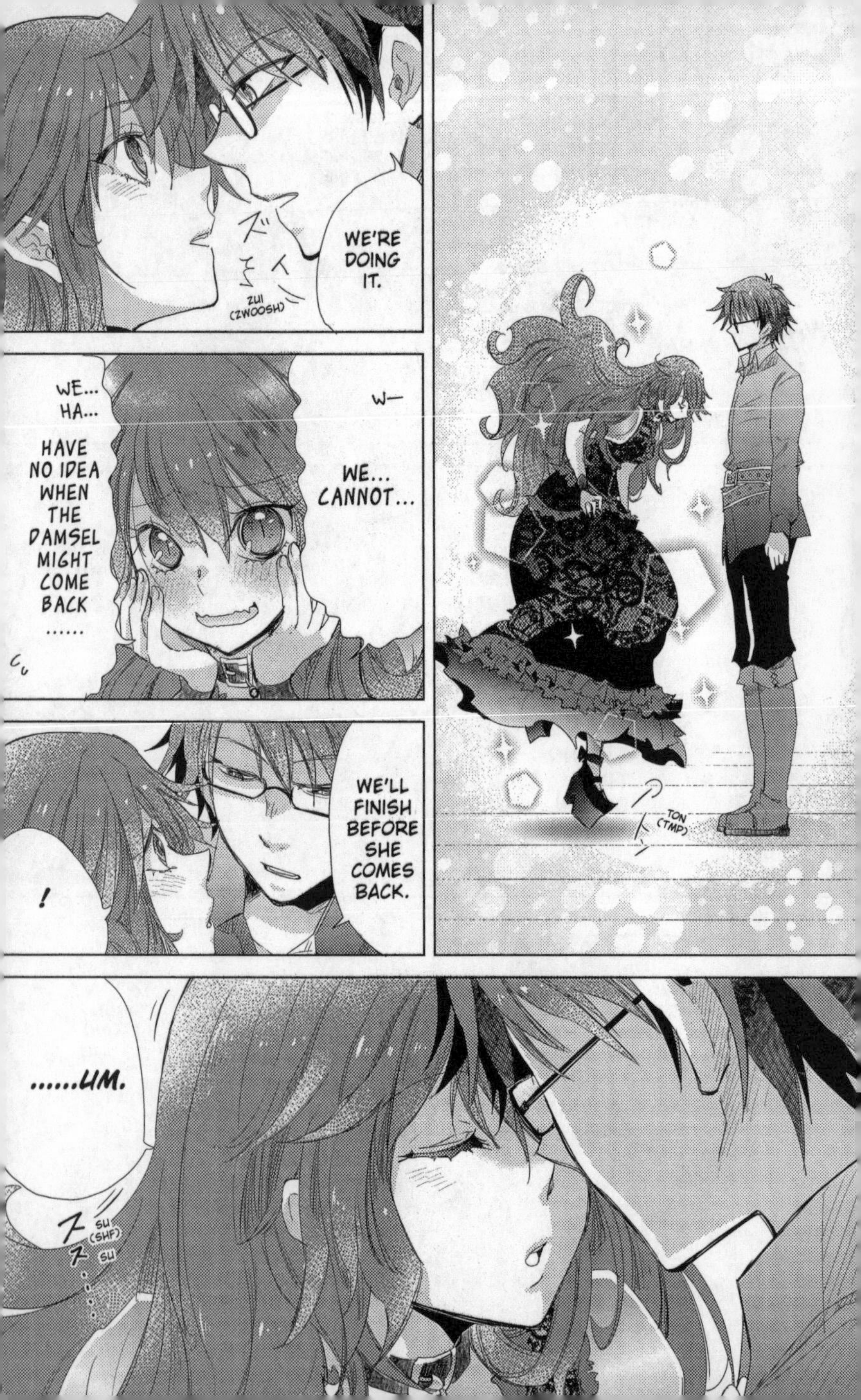
TON (TMP)
WE'RE DOING IT.
ZUI (ZWOOSH)
W—
WE... CANNOT...
WE... HA... HAVE NO IDEA WHEN THE DAMSEL MIGHT COME BACK ......
WE'LL FINISH BEFORE SHE COMES BACK.
!
......UM.
SU (SHF) SU

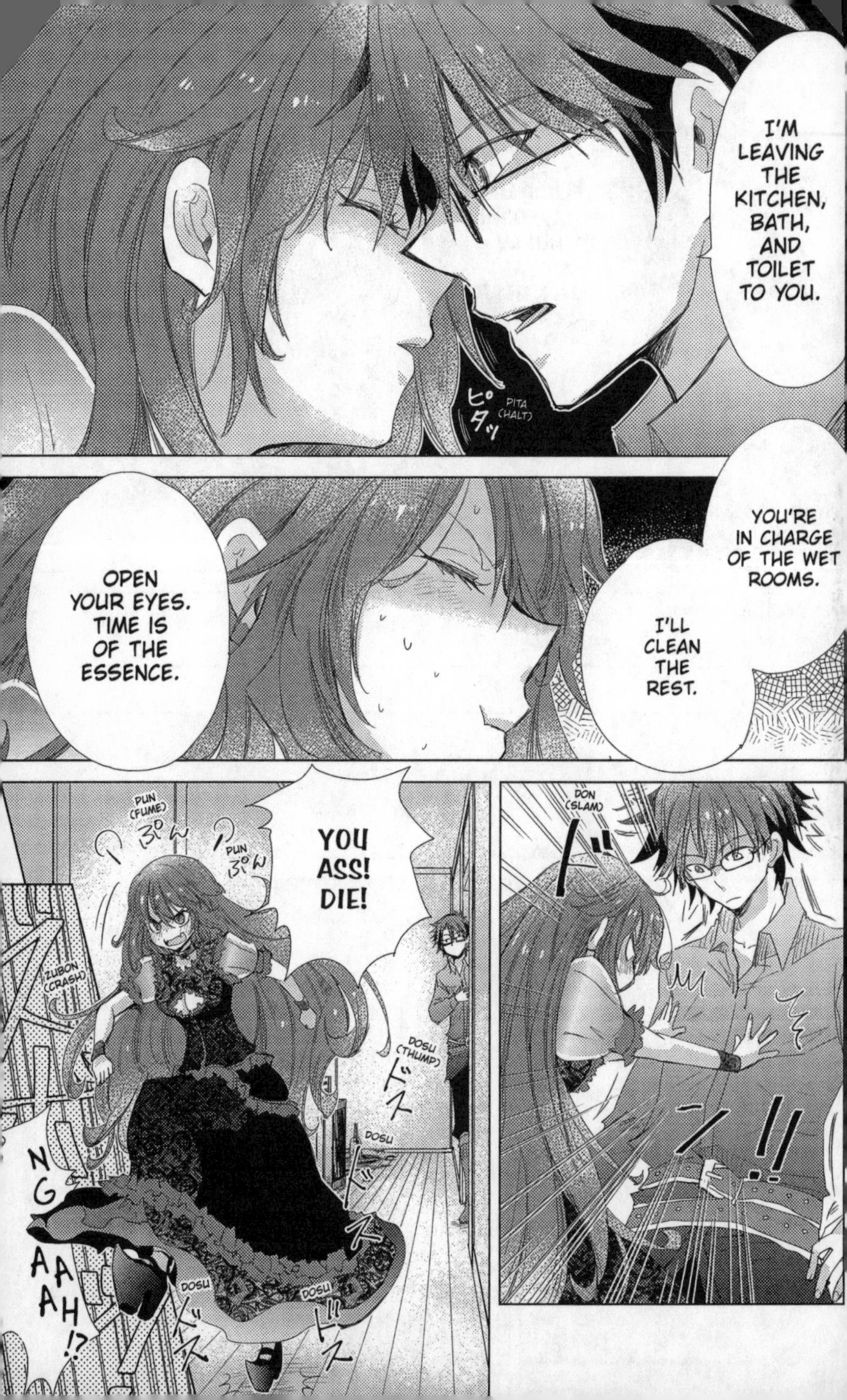
I'M LEAVING THE KITCHEN, BATH, AND TOILET TO YOU.
ピタッ
PITA (HALT)
YOU'RE IN CHARGE OF THE WET ROOMS.
I'LL CLEAN THE REST.
OPEN YOUR EYES. TIME IS OF THE ESSENCE.
DON (SLAM)
YOU ASS! DIE!
PUN (FUME)
ぷん
PUN
ぷん
DOSU (THUMP)
ドス
DOSU
ZUBON (CRASH)
DOSU
DOSU
NGAAAH!?

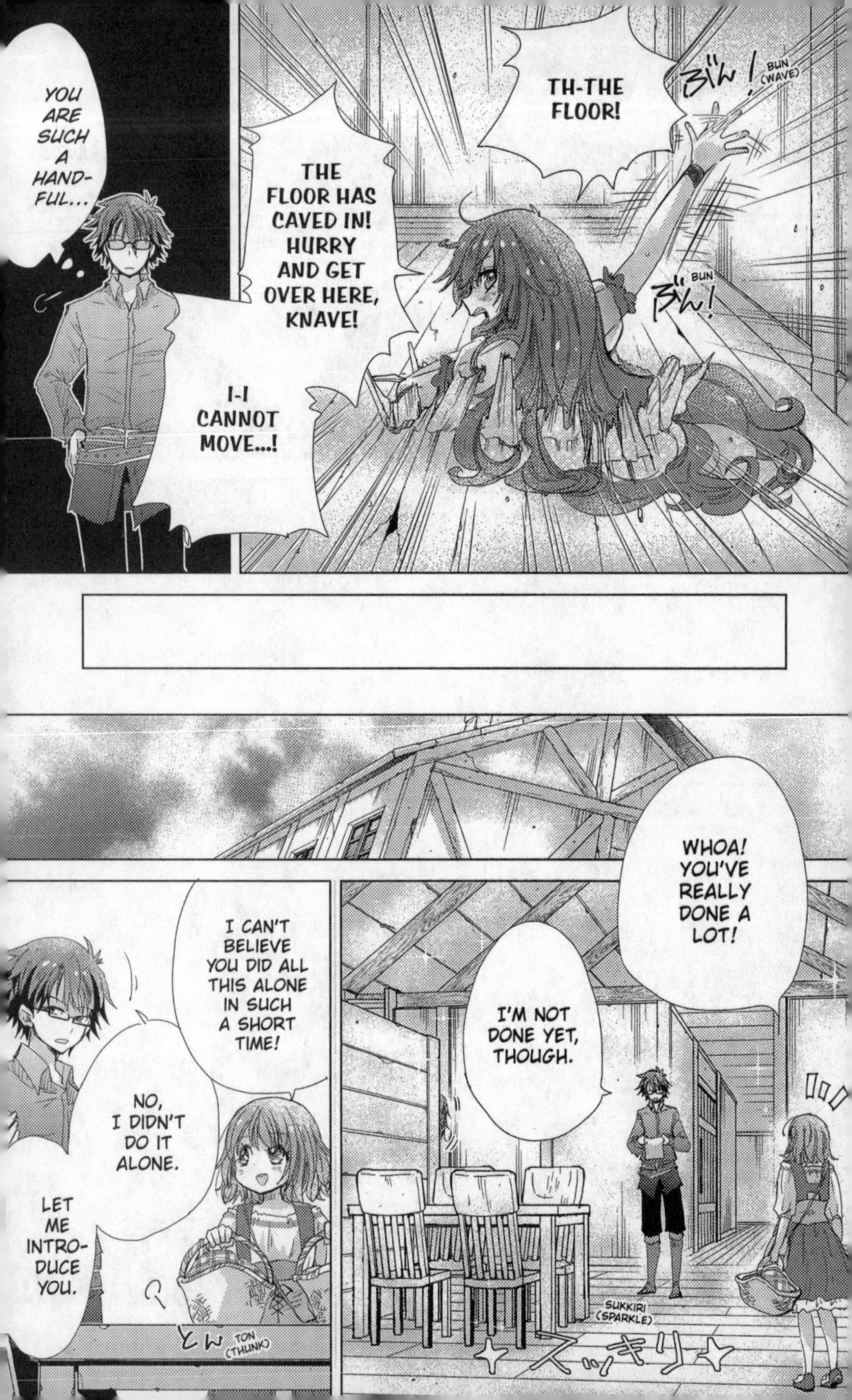

TH-THE FLOOR!
ぶん! BUN (WAVE)
ぶん! BUN
THE FLOOR HAS CAVED IN! HURRY AND GET OVER HERE, KNAVE!
I-I CANNOT MOVE...!
YOU ARE SUCH A HANDFUL...
WHOA! YOU'VE REALLY DONE A LOT!
I'M NOT DONE YET, THOUGH.
SUKKIRI (SPARKLE)
スッキリ
I CAN'T BELIEVE YOU DID ALL THIS ALONE IN SUCH A SHORT TIME!
NO, I DIDN'T DO IT ALONE.
LET ME INTRODUCE YOU.
とん TON (THUNK)

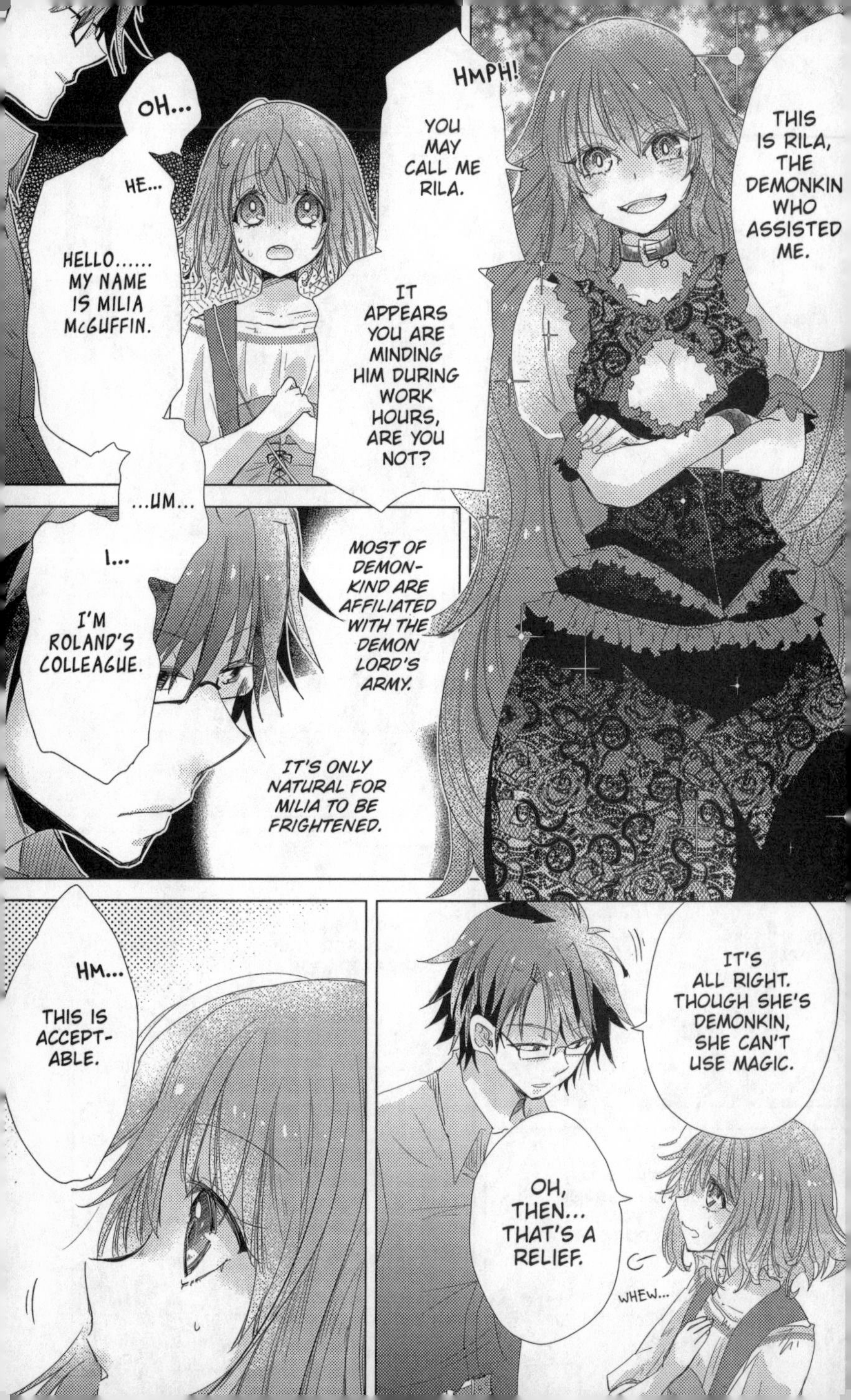
THIS IS RILA, THE DEMONKIN WHO ASSISTED ME.
HMPH!
YOU MAY CALL ME RILA.
OH...
HE...
HELLO...... MY NAME IS MILIA McGUFFIN.
IT APPEARS YOU ARE MINDING HIM DURING WORK HOURS, ARE YOU NOT?
...UM...
I...
I'M ROLAND'S COLLEAGUE.
MOST OF DEMON-KIND ARE AFFILIATED WITH THE DEMON LORD'S ARMY.
IT'S ONLY NATURAL FOR MILIA TO BE FRIGHTENED.
IT'S ALL RIGHT. THOUGH SHE'S DEMONKIN, SHE CAN'T USE MAGIC.
OH, THEN... THAT'S A RELIEF.
WHEW...
HM...
THIS IS ACCEPT-ABLE.

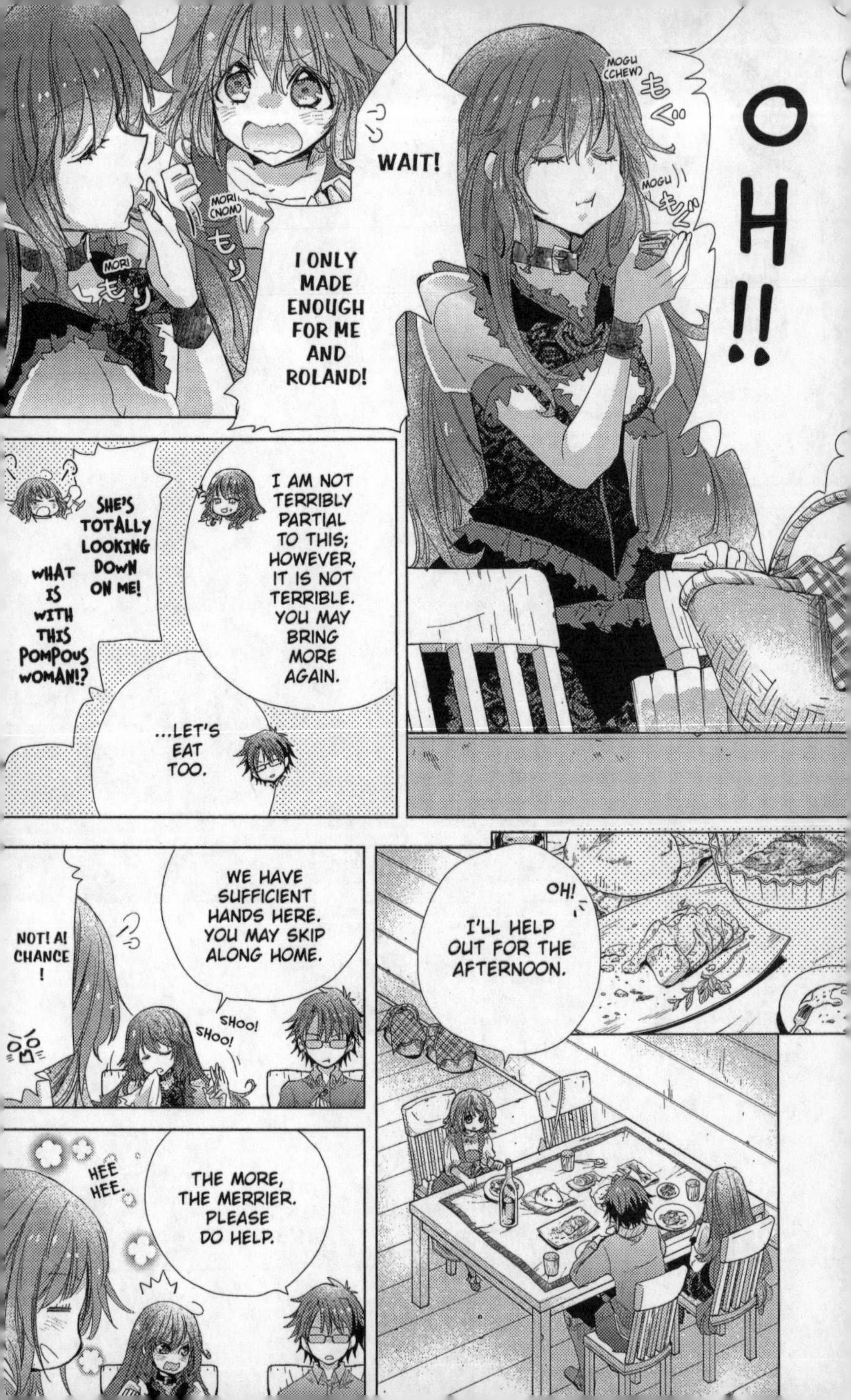
OH!!
MOGU (CHEW)
もぐ
MOGU
もぐ
WAIT!
I ONLY MADE ENOUGH FOR ME AND ROLAND!
MORI (NOM)
もり
MORI
もり
I AM NOT TERRIBLY PARTIAL TO THIS; HOWEVER, IT IS NOT TERRIBLE. YOU MAY BRING MORE AGAIN.
SHE'S TOTALLY LOOKING DOWN ON ME!
WHAT IS WITH THIS POMPOUS WOMAN!?
...LET'S EAT TOO.
OH!
I'LL HELP OUT FOR THE AFTERNOON.
WE HAVE SUFFICIENT HANDS HERE. YOU MAY SKIP ALONG HOME.
SHOO! SHOO!
NOT! A! CHANCE!
THE MORE, THE MERRIER. PLEASE DO HELP.
HEE HEE.

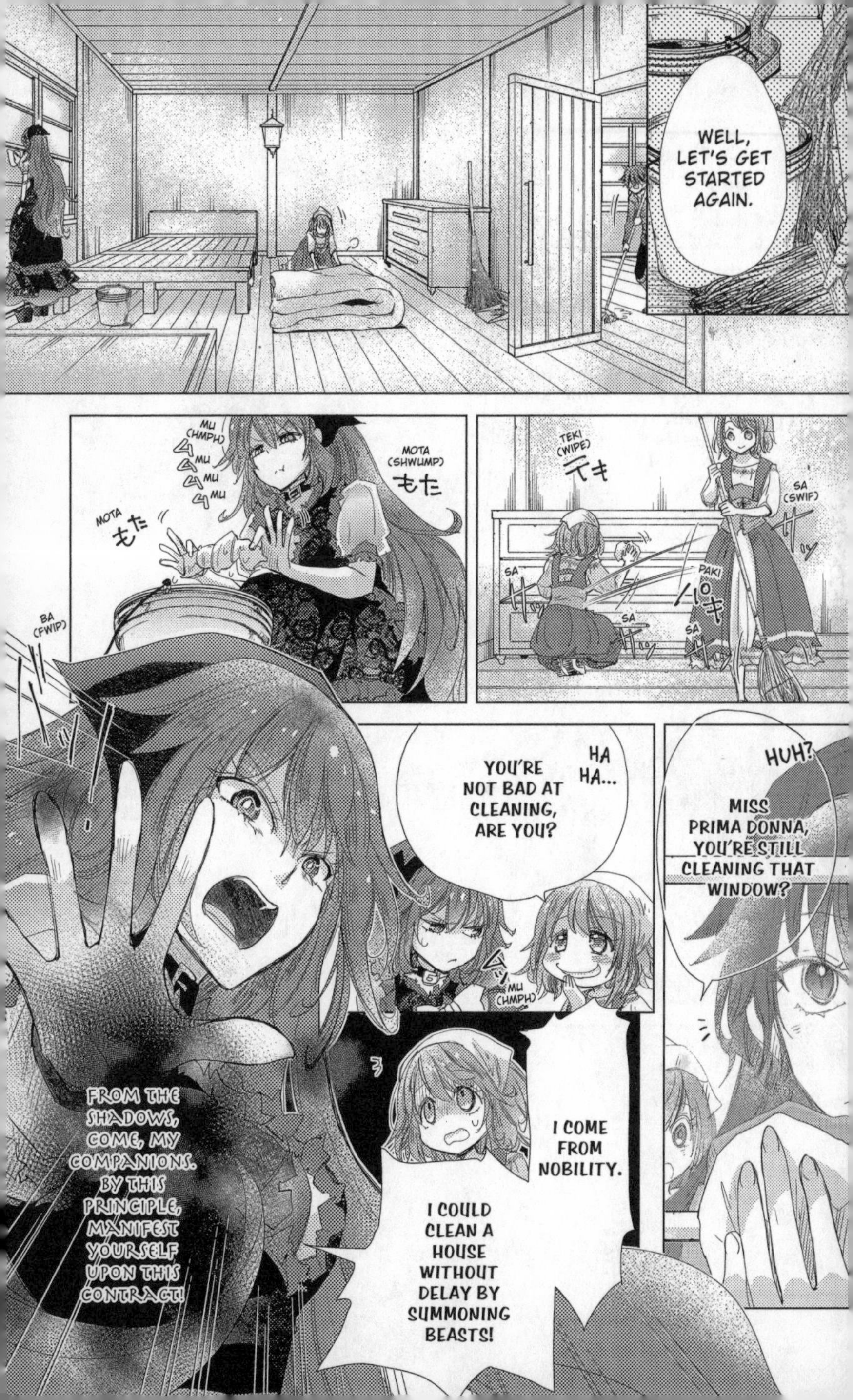
WELL, LET'S GET STARTED AGAIN.
TEKI (WIPE) テキ
SA (SWIF)
SA
PAKI
SA
SA
MU (HMPH)
MU MU MU
MOTA (SHWUMP) もた
MOTA もた
HUH?
MISS PRIMA DONNA, YOU'RE STILL CLEANING THAT WINDOW?
YOU'RE NOT BAD AT CLEANING, ARE YOU?
HA HA...
MU (HMPH)
I COME FROM NOBILITY.
I COULD CLEAN A HOUSE WITHOUT DELAY BY SUMMONING BEASTS!
BA (FWIP)
FROM THE SHADOWS, COME, MY COMPANIONS. BY THIS PRINCIPLE, MANIFEST YOURSELF UPON THIS CONTRACT!

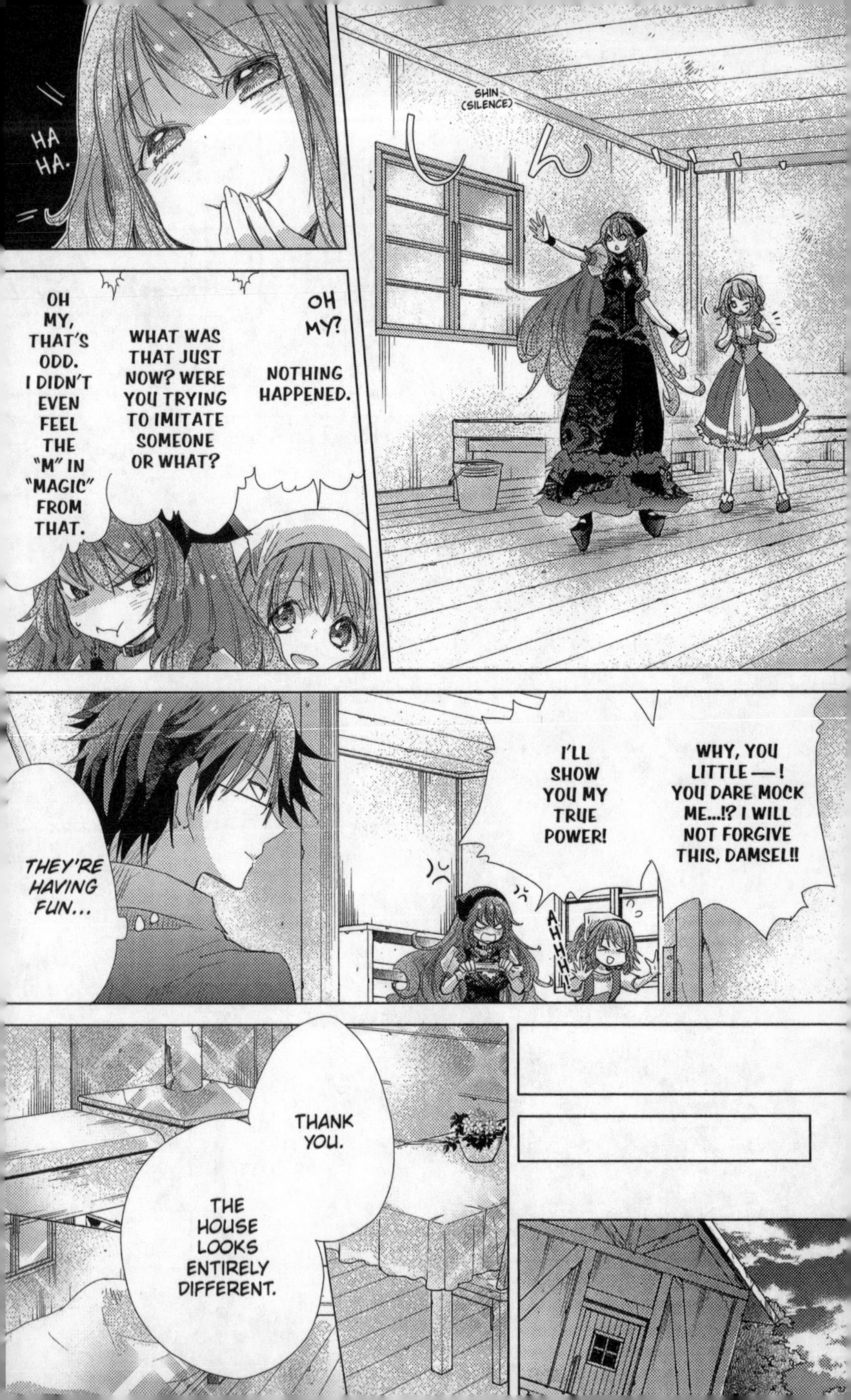
SHIN (SILENCE)
HA HA.
OH MY?
NOTHING HAPPENED.
WHAT WAS THAT JUST NOW? WERE YOU TRYING TO IMITATE SOMEONE OR WHAT?
OH MY, THAT'S ODD. I DIDN'T EVEN FEEL THE "M" IN "MAGIC" FROM THAT.
WHY, YOU LITTLE—! YOU DARE MOCK ME...!? I WILL NOT FORGIVE THIS, DAMSEL!!
I'LL SHOW YOU MY TRUE POWER!
AHHHH!
THEY'RE HAVING FUN...
THANK YOU.
THE HOUSE LOOKS ENTIRELY DIFFERENT.

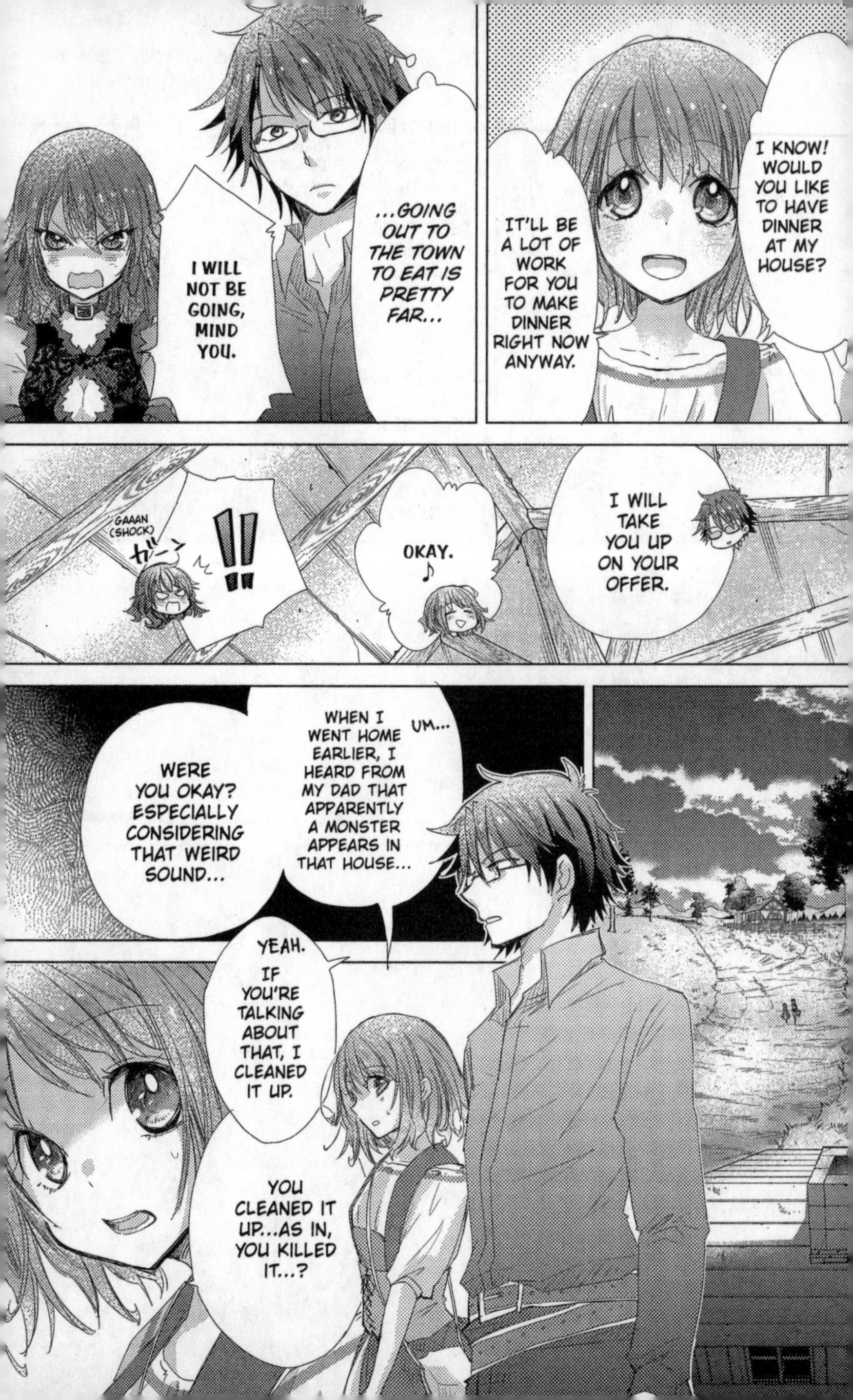
I KNOW! WOULD YOU LIKE TO HAVE DINNER AT MY HOUSE?
IT'LL BE A LOT OF WORK FOR YOU TO MAKE DINNER RIGHT NOW ANYWAY.
...GOING OUT TO THE TOWN TO EAT IS PRETTY FAR...
I WILL NOT BE GOING, MIND YOU.
I WILL TAKE YOU UP ON YOUR OFFER.
OKAY. ♪
!!
GAAAN (SHOCK)
ガーン
UM...
WHEN I WENT HOME EARLIER, I HEARD FROM MY DAD THAT APPARENTLY A MONSTER APPEARS IN THAT HOUSE...
WERE YOU OKAY? ESPECIALLY CONSIDERING THAT WEIRD SOUND...
YEAH. IF YOU'RE TALKING ABOUT THAT, I CLEANED IT UP.
YOU CLEANED IT UP...AS IN, YOU KILLED IT...?

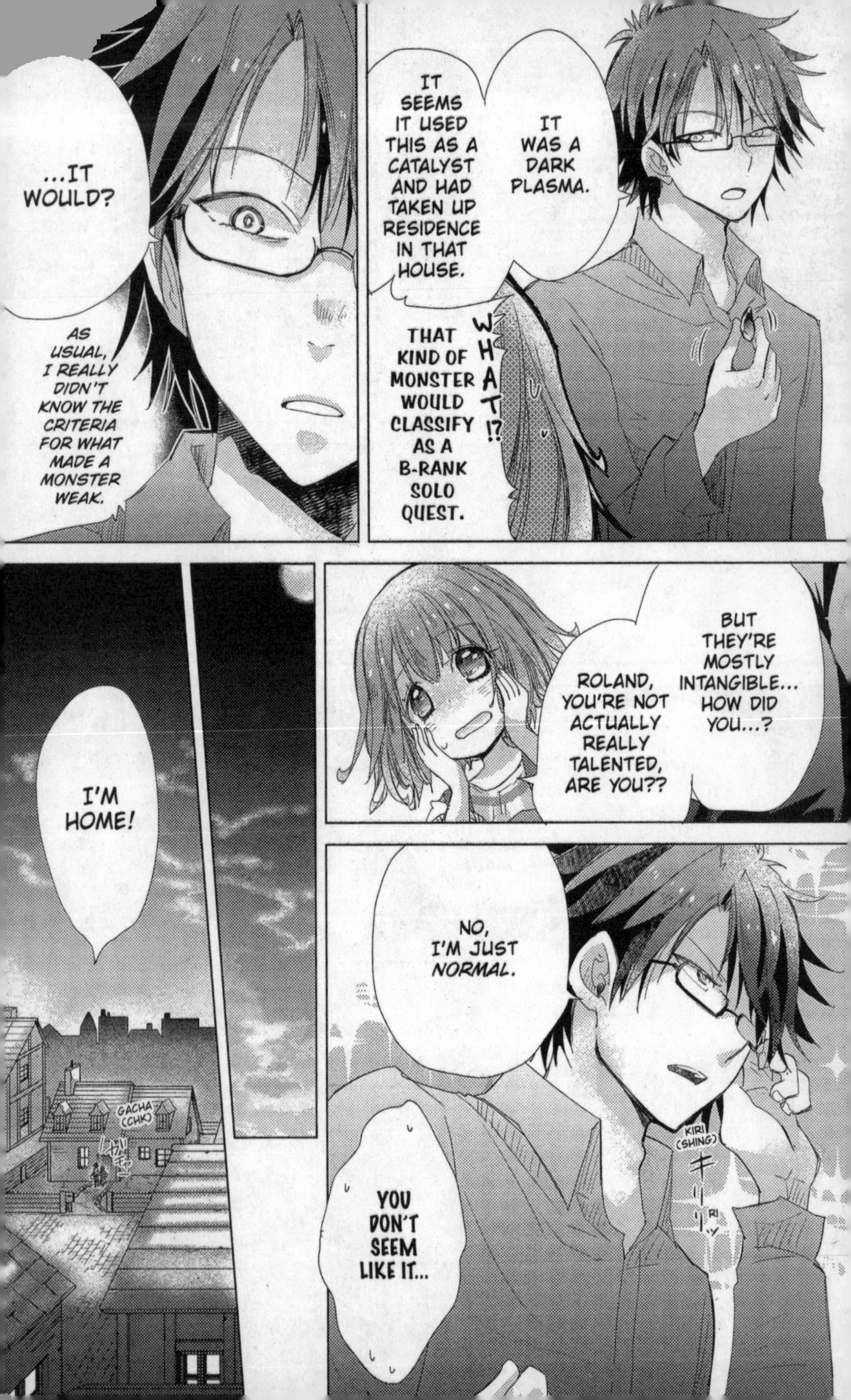
IT WAS A DARK PLASMA.
IT SEEMS IT USED THIS AS A CATALYST AND HAD TAKEN UP RESIDENCE IN THAT HOUSE.
THAT KIND OF MONSTER WOULD CLASSIFY AS A B-RANK SOLO QUEST.
WHAT!?
...IT WOULD?
AS USUAL, I REALLY DIDN'T KNOW THE CRITERIA FOR WHAT MADE A MONSTER WEAK.
BUT THEY'RE MOSTLY INTANGIBLE... HOW DID YOU...?
ROLAND, YOU'RE NOT ACTUALLY REALLY TALENTED, ARE YOU??
NO, I'M JUST *NORMAL*.
KIRI (SHING)
YOU DON'T SEEM LIKE IT...
I'M HOME!
GACHA (CHK)

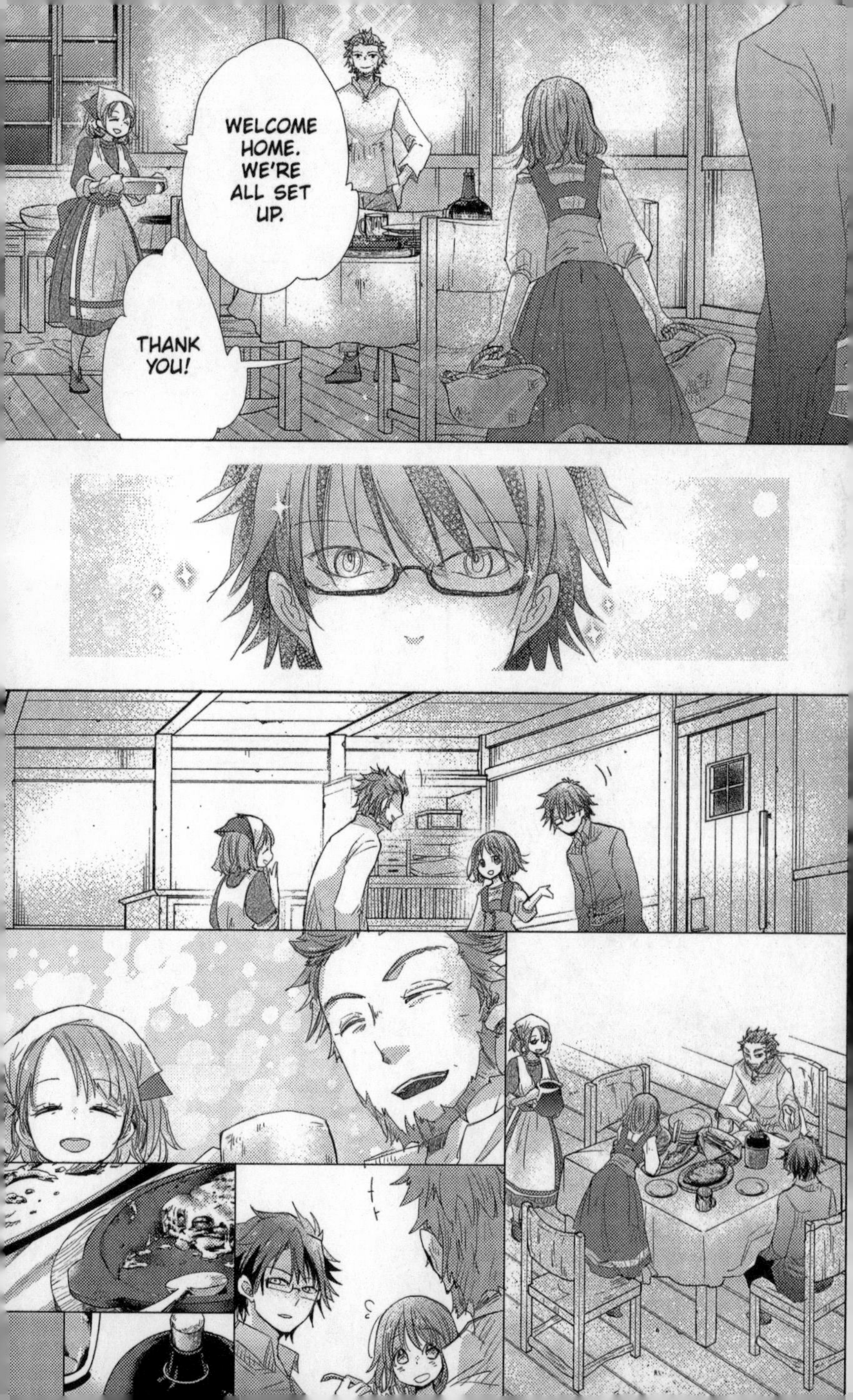
WELCOME HOME. WE'RE ALL SET UP.
THANK YOU!

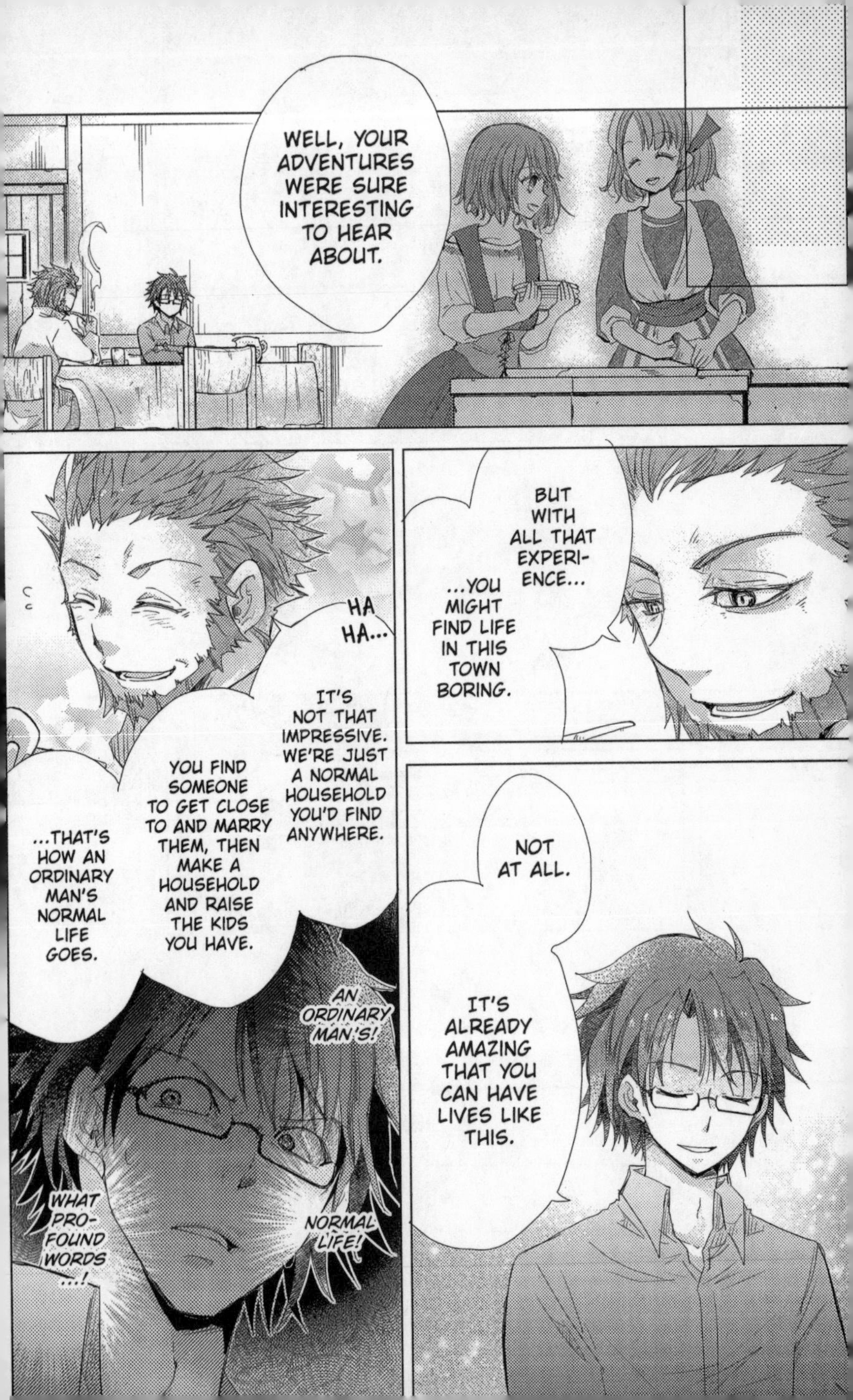
WELL, YOUR ADVENTURES WERE SURE INTERESTING TO HEAR ABOUT.
BUT WITH ALL THAT EXPERIENCE...
...YOU MIGHT FIND LIFE IN THIS TOWN BORING.
NOT AT ALL.
IT'S ALREADY AMAZING THAT YOU CAN HAVE LIVES LIKE THIS.
HA HA...
IT'S NOT THAT IMPRESSIVE. WE'RE JUST A NORMAL HOUSEHOLD YOU'D FIND ANYWHERE.
YOU FIND SOMEONE TO GET CLOSE TO AND MARRY THEM, THEN MAKE A HOUSEHOLD AND RAISE THE KIDS YOU HAVE.
...THAT'S HOW AN ORDINARY MAN'S NORMAL LIFE GOES.
AN ORDINARY MAN'S!
NORMAL LIFE!
WHAT PRO-FOUND WORDS ...!

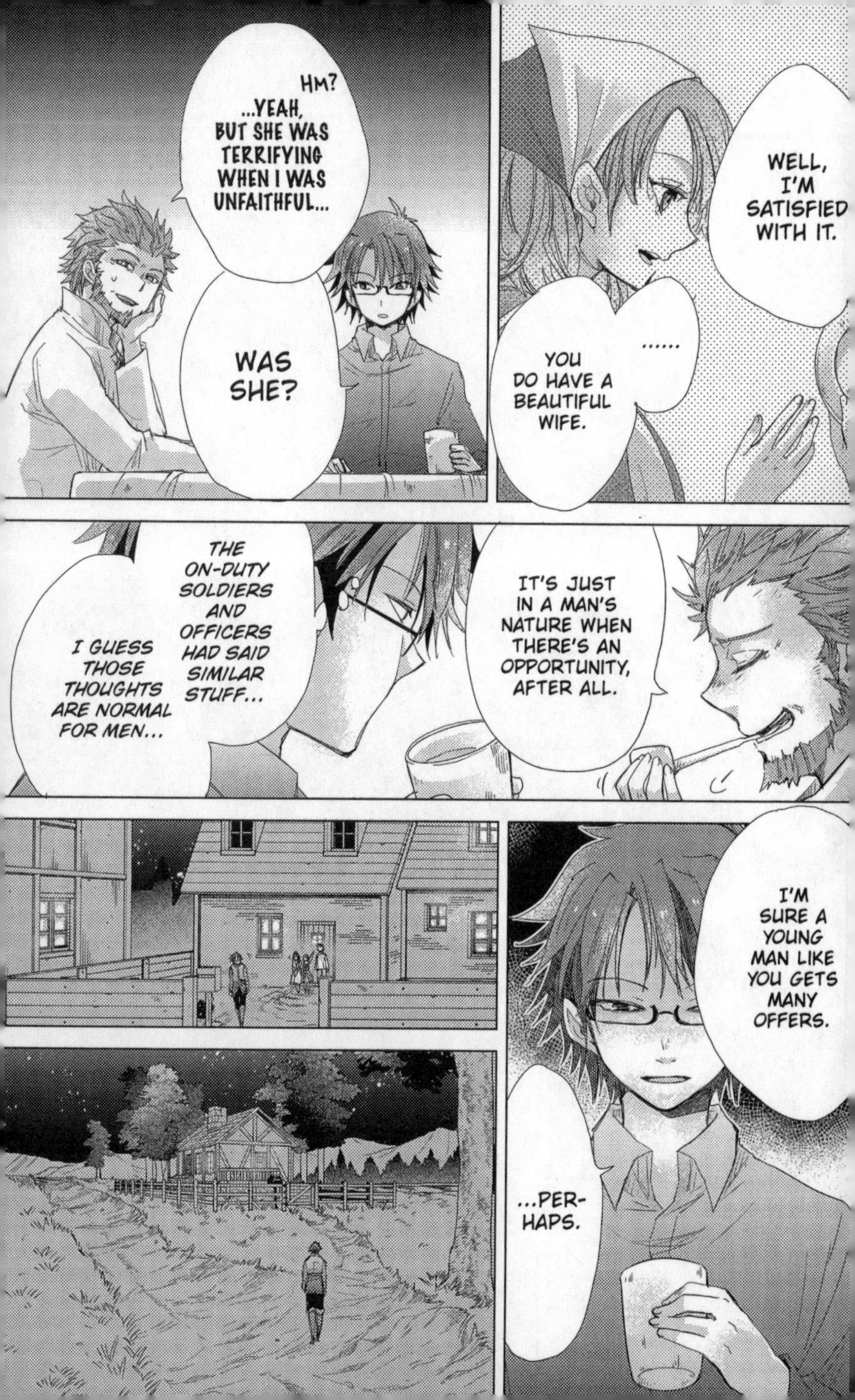
WELL, I'M SATISFIED WITH IT.
......
YOU DO HAVE A BEAUTIFUL WIFE.
HM? ...YEAH, BUT SHE WAS TERRIFYING WHEN I WAS UNFAITHFUL...
WAS SHE?
IT'S JUST IN A MAN'S NATURE WHEN THERE'S AN OPPORTUNITY, AFTER ALL.
THE ON-DUTY SOLDIERS AND OFFICERS HAD SAID SIMILAR STUFF...
I GUESS THOSE THOUGHTS ARE NORMAL FOR MEN...
I'M SURE A YOUNG MAN LIKE YOU GETS MANY OFFERS.
...PER-HAPS.

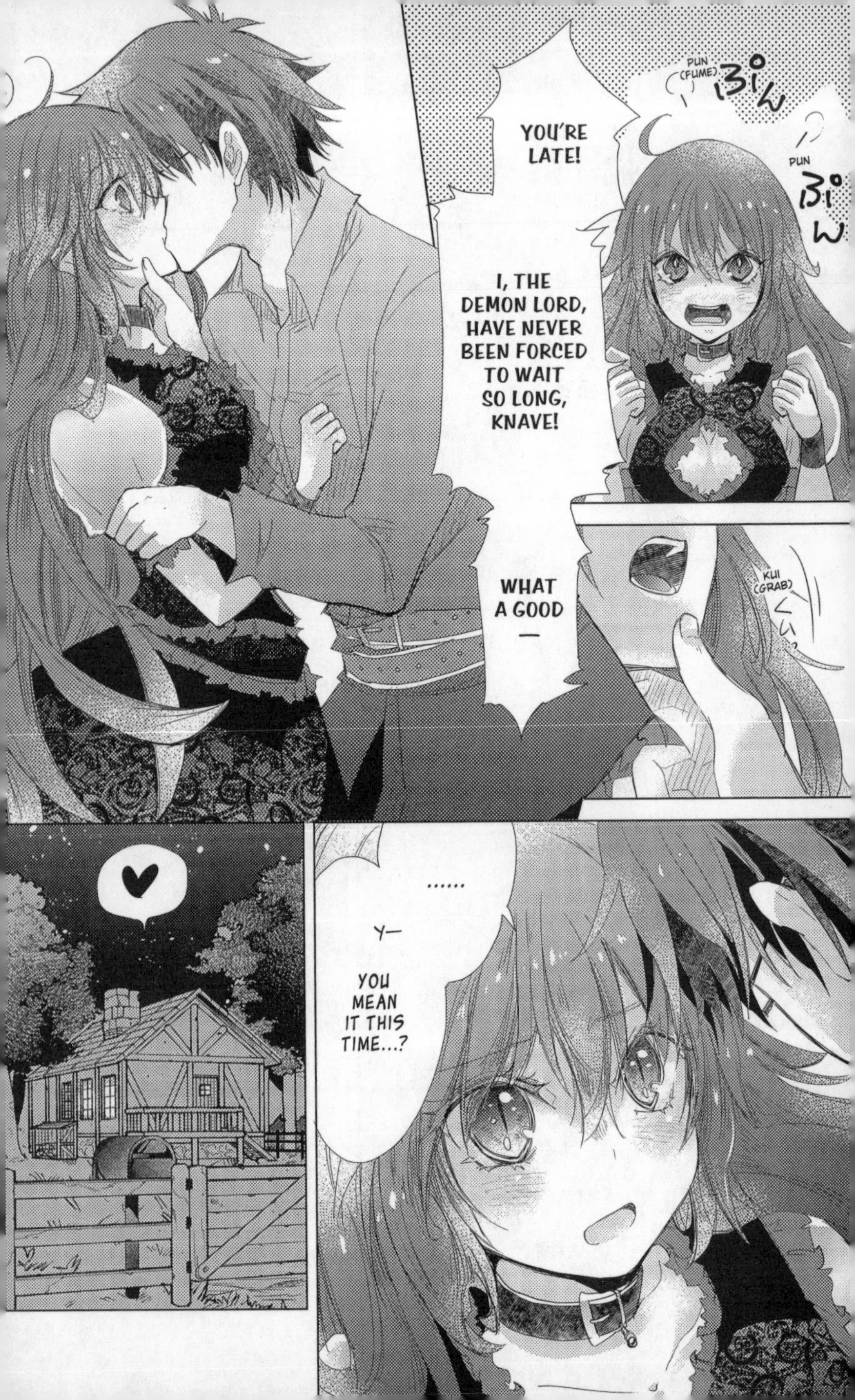
PUN (FUME) ぷん
PUN ぷん
YOU'RE LATE!
I, THE DEMON LORD, HAVE NEVER BEEN FORCED TO WAIT SO LONG, KNAVE!
KUI (GRAB) くいっ
WHAT A GOOD —
......
Y—
YOU MEAN IT THIS TIME...?
♥

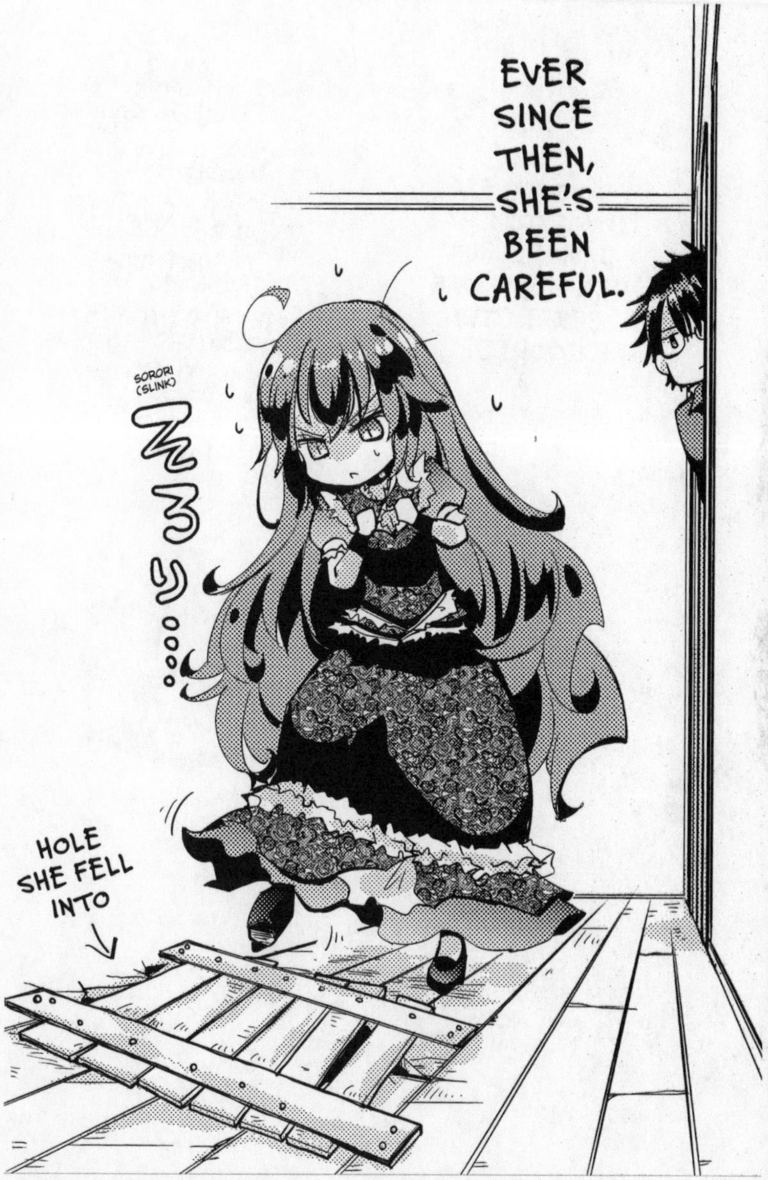
EVER SINCE THEN, SHE'S BEEN CAREFUL.
SORORI (SLINK)
そろり…
HOLE SHE FELL INTO

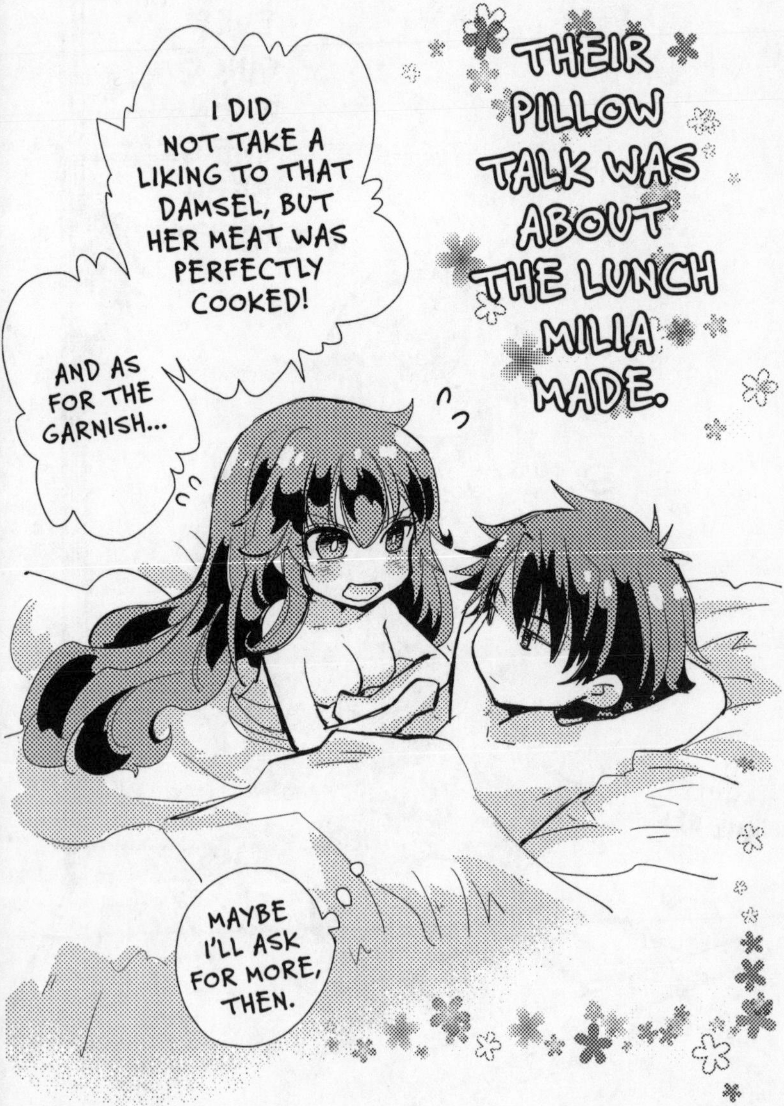
THEIR PILLOW TALK WAS ABOUT THE LUNCH MILIA MADE.
I DID NOT TAKE A LIKING TO THAT DAMSEL, BUT HER MEAT WAS PERFECTLY COOKED!
AND AS FOR THE GARNISH...
MAYBE I'LL ASK FOR MORE, THEN.

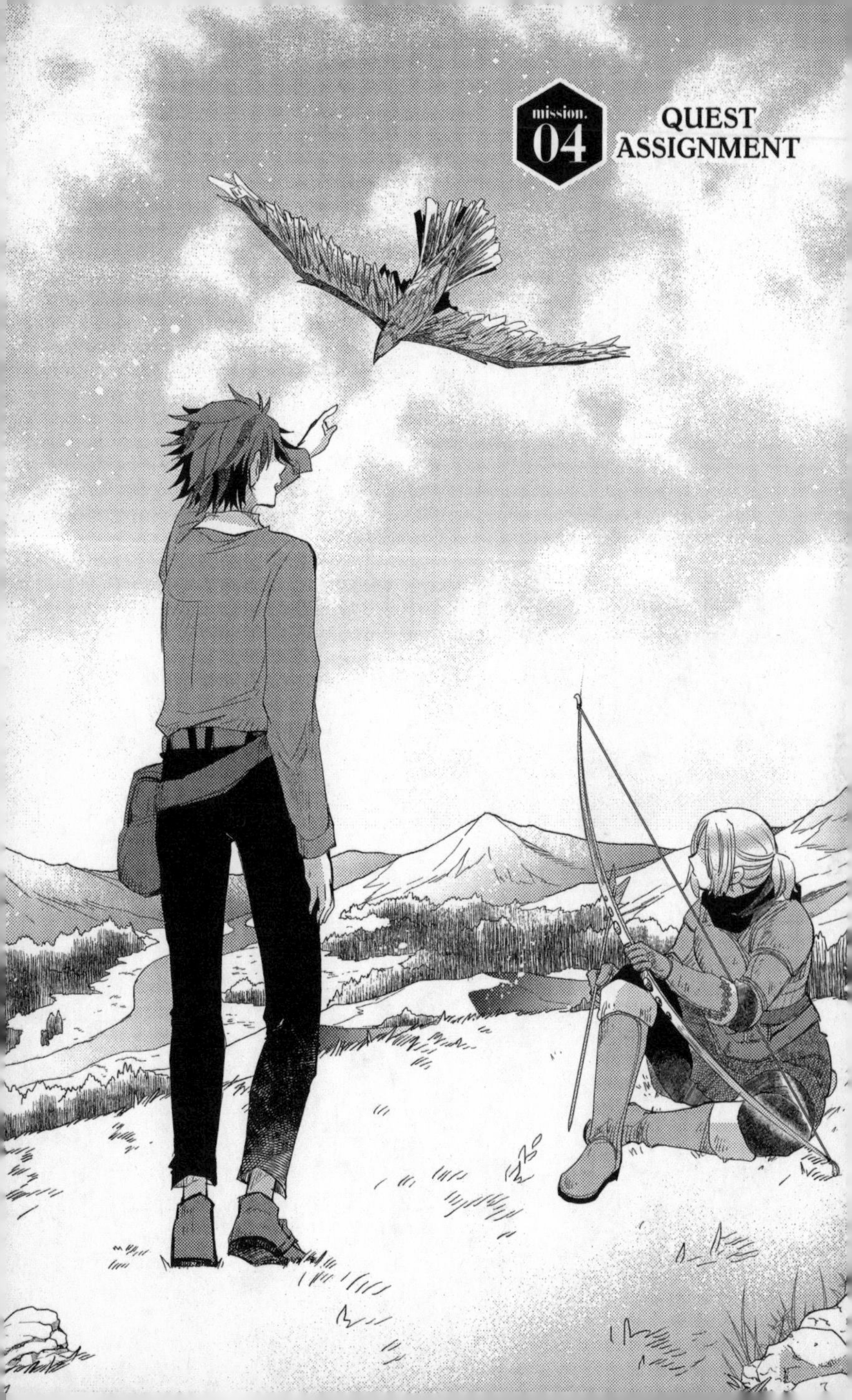
mission.
04
QUEST ASSIGNMENT

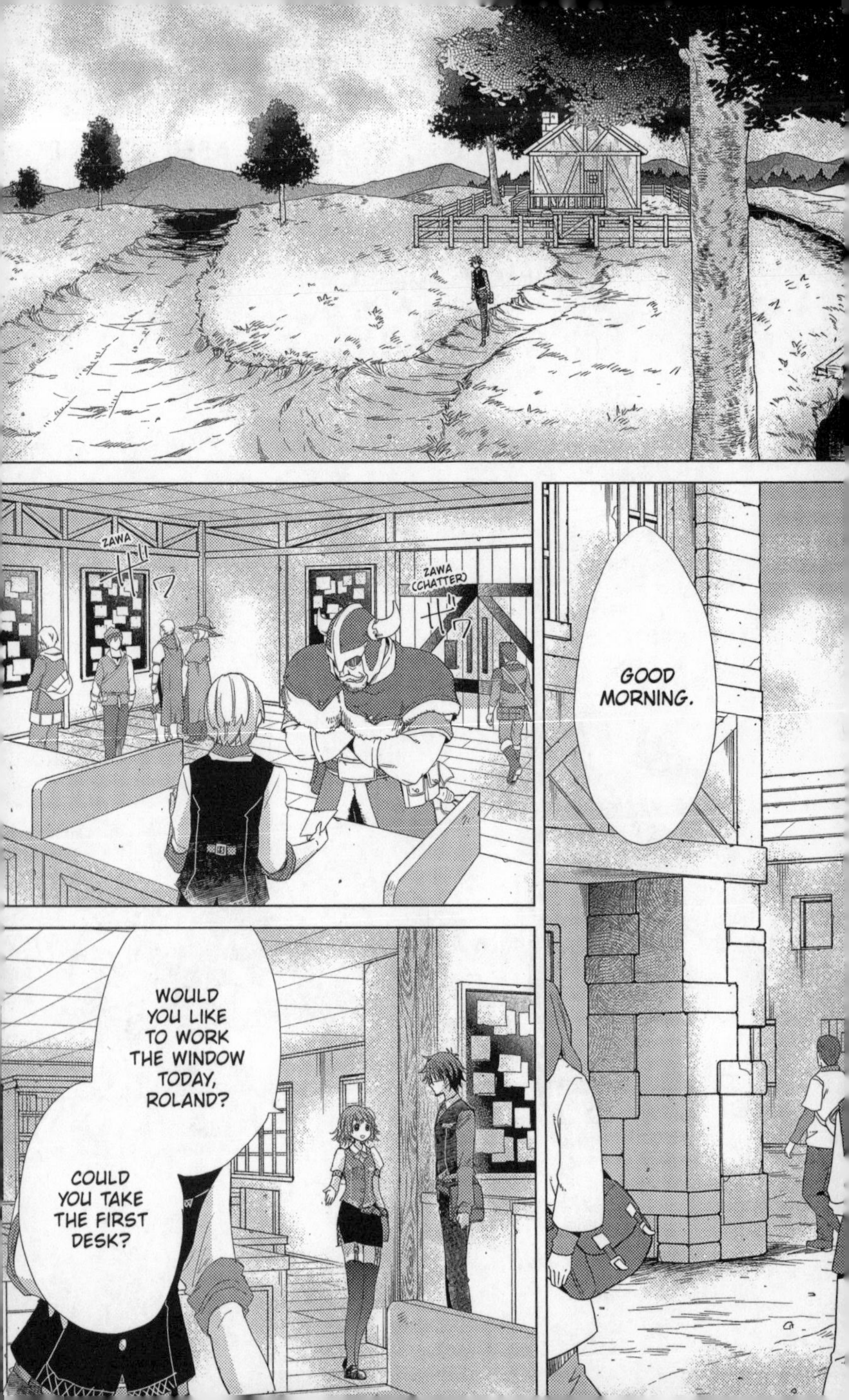
GOOD MORNING.
ZAWA (CHATTER)
ZAWA
WOULD YOU LIKE TO WORK THE WINDOW TODAY, ROLAND?
COULD YOU TAKE THE FIRST DESK?

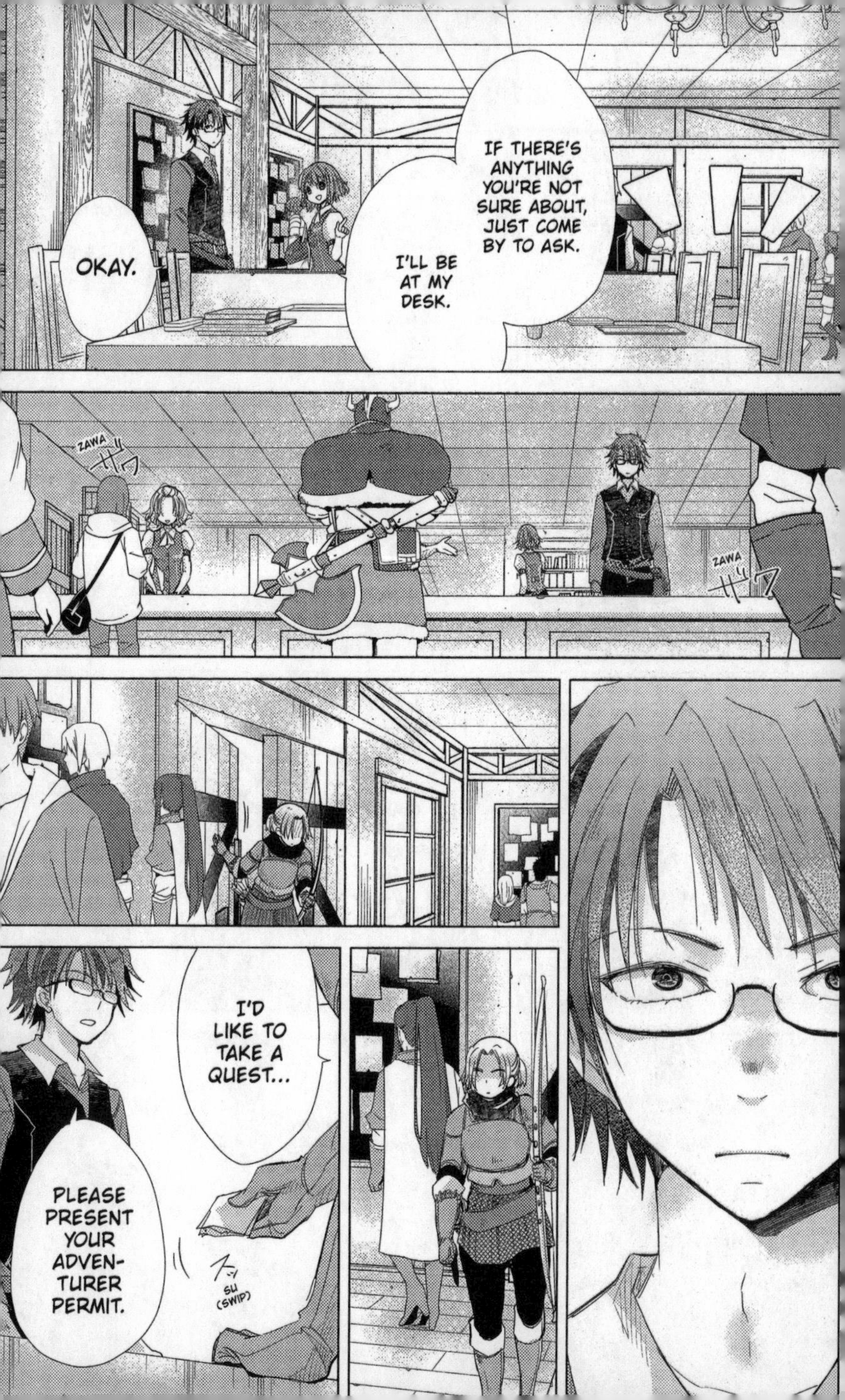
IF THERE'S ANYTHING YOU'RE NOT SURE ABOUT, JUST COME BY TO ASK.
I'LL BE AT MY DESK.
OKAY.
ZAWA
ZAWA
I'D LIKE TO TAKE A QUEST...
SU (SWIP)
PLEASE PRESENT YOUR ADVEN-TURER PERMIT.

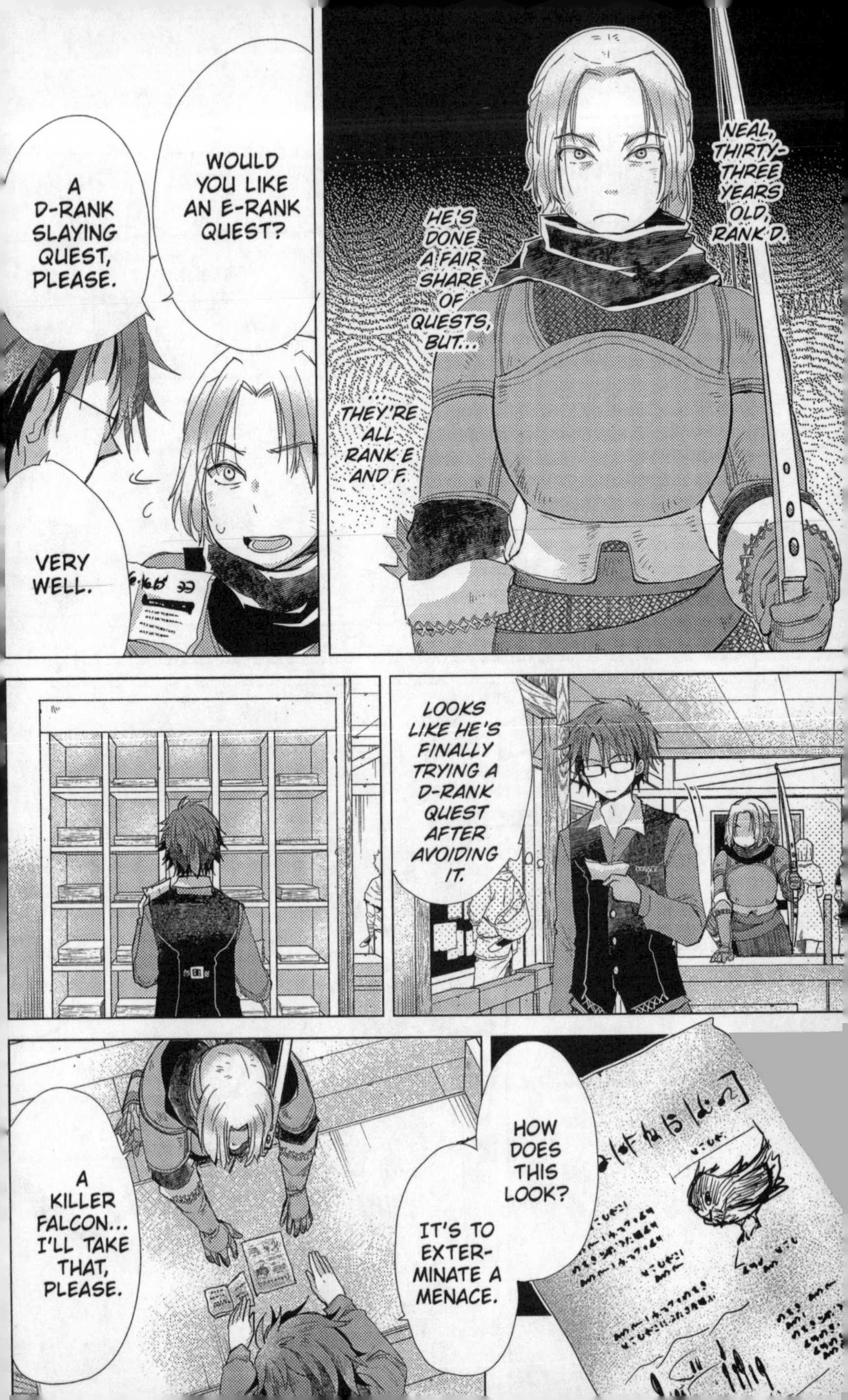
NEAL, THIRTY-THREE YEARS OLD, RANK D.
HE'S DONE A FAIR SHARE OF QUESTS, BUT...
...THEY'RE ALL RANK E AND F.
WOULD YOU LIKE AN E-RANK QUEST?
A D-RANK SLAYING QUEST, PLEASE.
VERY WELL.
LOOKS LIKE HE'S FINALLY TRYING A D-RANK QUEST AFTER AVOIDING IT.
HOW DOES THIS LOOK?
IT'S TO EXTERMINATE A MENACE.
A KILLER FALCON... I'LL TAKE THAT, PLEASE.

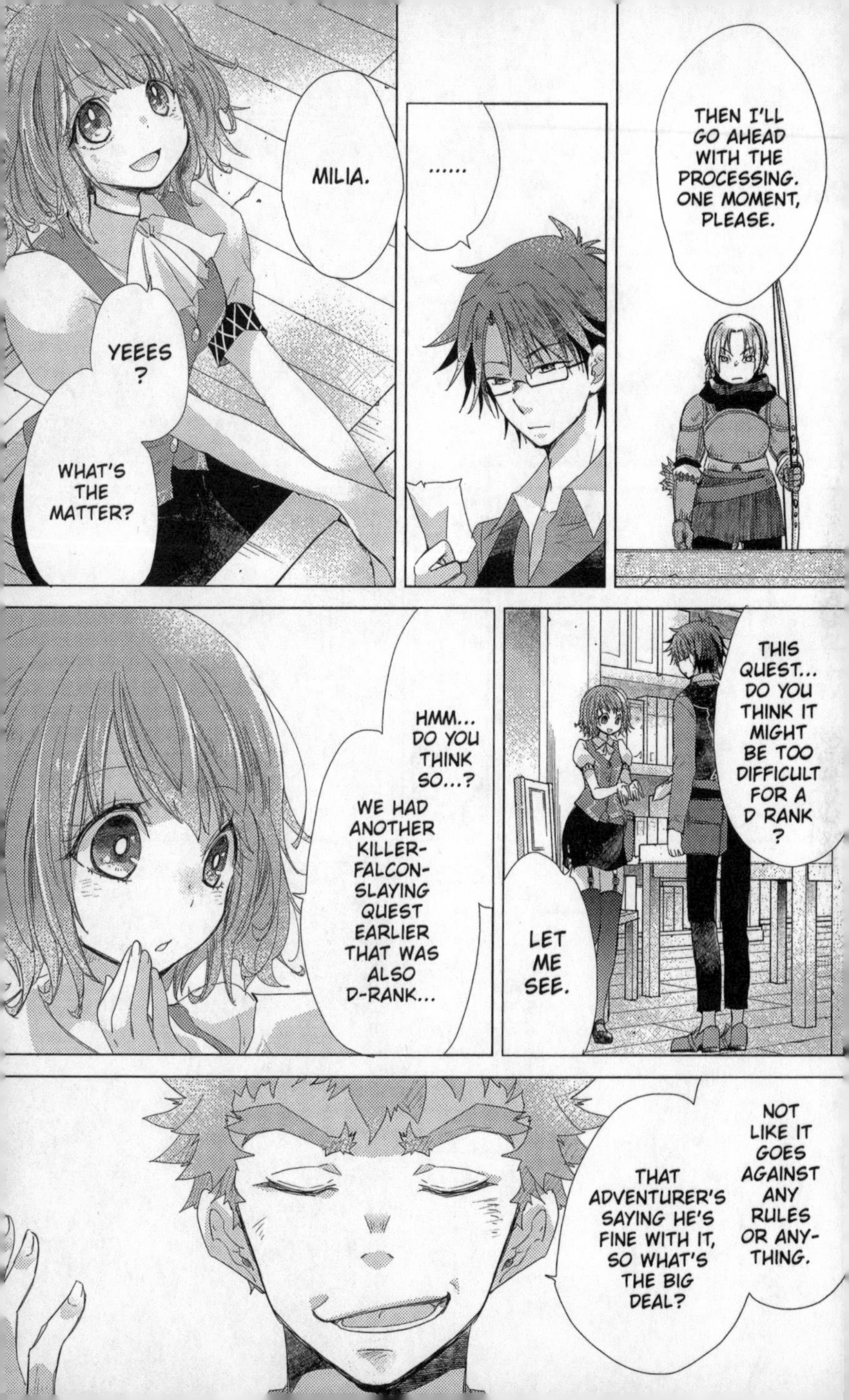
THEN I'LL GO AHEAD WITH THE PROCESSING. ONE MOMENT, PLEASE.
......
MILIA.
YEEES?
WHAT'S THE MATTER?
THIS QUEST... DO YOU THINK IT MIGHT BE TOO DIFFICULT FOR A D RANK?
LET ME SEE.
HMM... DO YOU THINK SO...?
WE HAD ANOTHER KILLER-FALCON-SLAYING QUEST EARLIER THAT WAS ALSO D-RANK...
NOT LIKE IT GOES AGAINST ANY RULES OR ANY-THING.
THAT ADVENTURER'S SAYING HE'S FINE WITH IT, SO WHAT'S THE BIG DEAL?

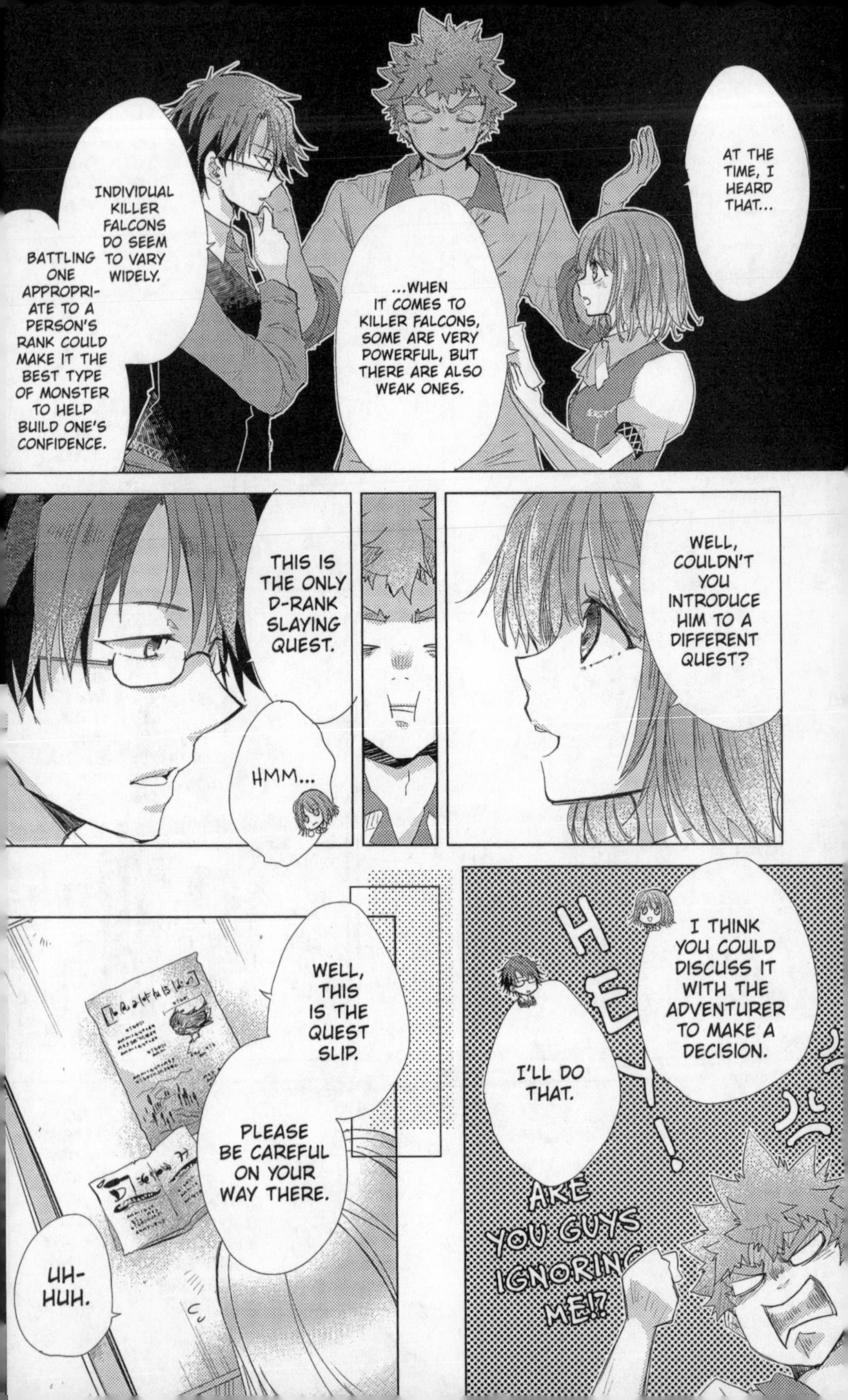
AT THE TIME, I HEARD THAT...
...WHEN IT COMES TO KILLER FALCONS, SOME ARE VERY POWERFUL, BUT THERE ARE ALSO WEAK ONES.
INDIVIDUAL KILLER FALCONS DO SEEM TO VARY WIDELY.
BATTLING ONE APPROPRIATE TO A PERSON'S RANK COULD MAKE IT THE BEST TYPE OF MONSTER TO HELP BUILD ONE'S CONFIDENCE.
WELL, COULDN'T YOU INTRODUCE HIM TO A DIFFERENT QUEST?
THIS IS THE ONLY D-RANK SLAYING QUEST.
HMM...
I THINK YOU COULD DISCUSS IT WITH THE ADVENTURER TO MAKE A DECISION.
I'LL DO THAT.
HEY!
ARE YOU GUYS IGNORING ME!?
WELL, THIS IS THE QUEST SLIP.
PLEASE BE CAREFUL ON YOUR WAY THERE.
UH-HUH.

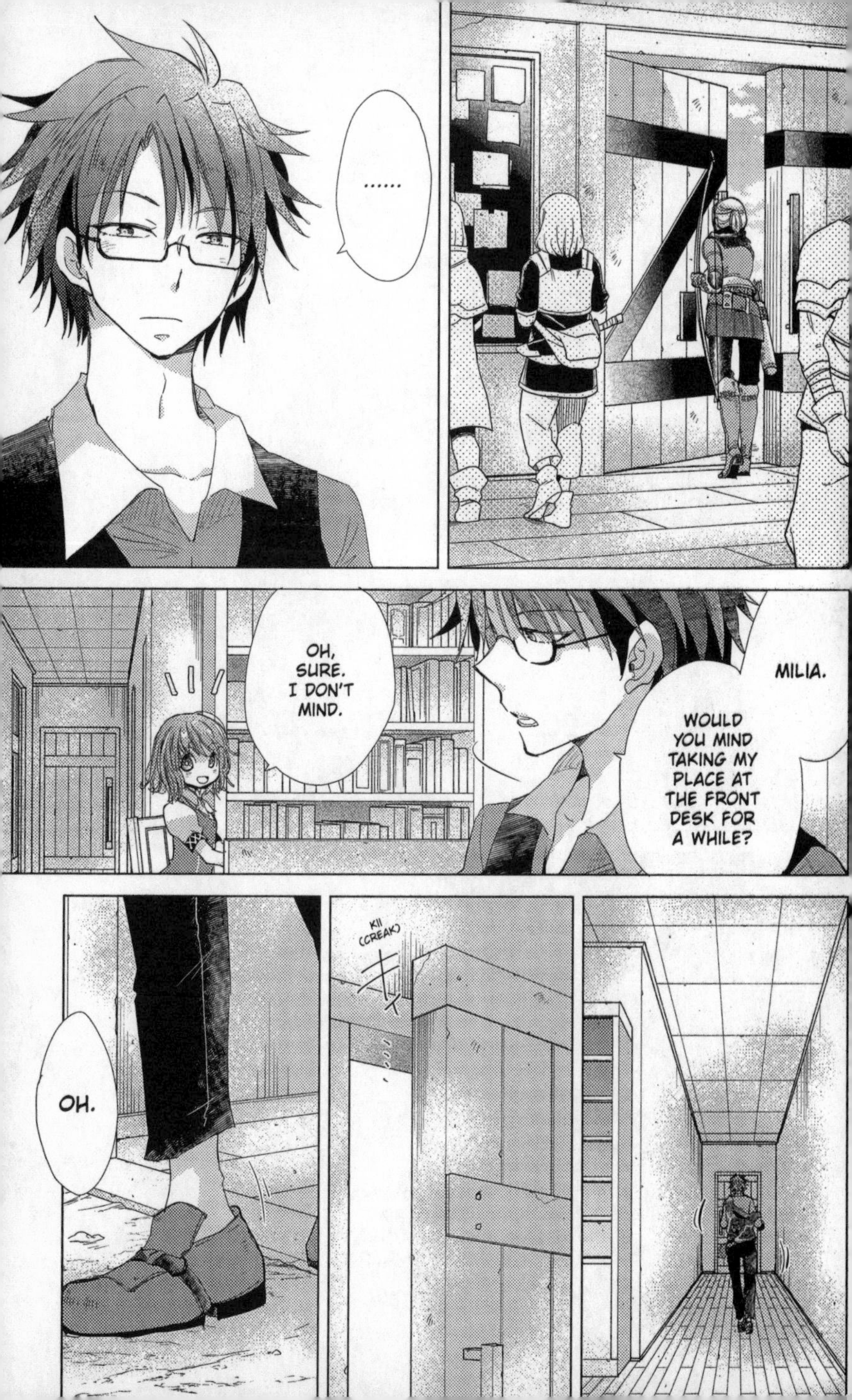
......
MILIA.
WOULD YOU MIND TAKING MY PLACE AT THE FRONT DESK FOR A WHILE?
OH, SURE. I DON'T MIND.
KII (CREAK)
OH.

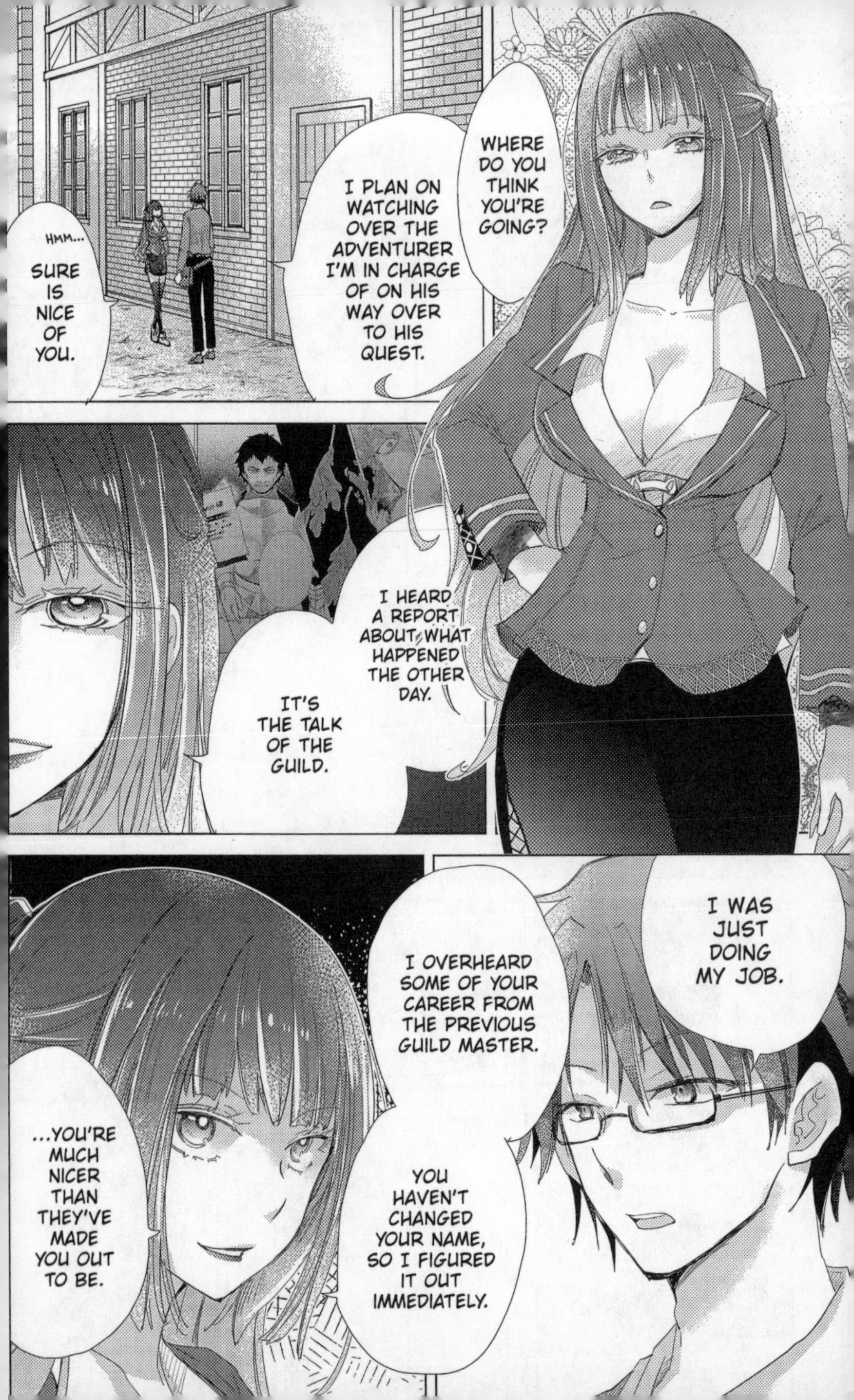
WHERE DO YOU THINK YOU'RE GOING?
I PLAN ON WATCHING OVER THE ADVENTURER I'M IN CHARGE OF ON HIS WAY OVER TO HIS QUEST.
HMM...
SURE IS NICE OF YOU.
I HEARD A REPORT ABOUT WHAT HAPPENED THE OTHER DAY.
IT'S THE TALK OF THE GUILD.
I WAS JUST DOING MY JOB.
I OVERHEARD SOME OF YOUR CAREER FROM THE PREVIOUS GUILD MASTER.
YOU HAVEN'T CHANGED YOUR NAME, SO I FIGURED IT OUT IMMEDIATELY.
...YOU'RE MUCH NICER THAN THEY'VE MADE YOU OUT TO BE.

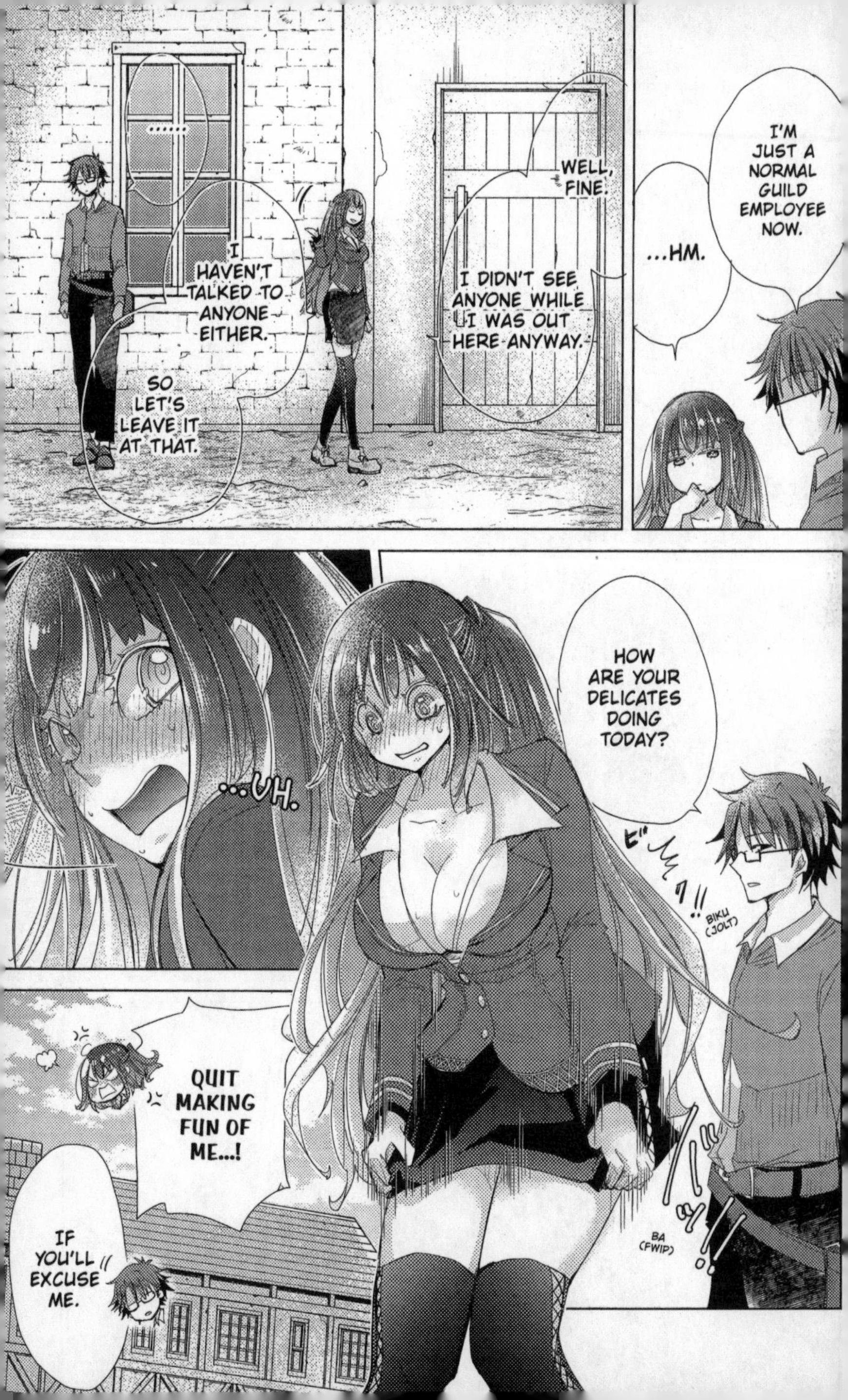
I'M JUST A NORMAL GUILD EMPLOYEE NOW.
...HM.
WELL, FINE.
I DIDN'T SEE ANYONE WHILE I WAS OUT HERE ANYWAY.
......
I HAVEN'T TALKED TO ANYONE EITHER.
SO LET'S LEAVE IT AT THAT.
HOW ARE YOUR DELICATES DOING TODAY?
BIKU (JOLT)
BA (FWIP)
...UH.
QUIT MAKING FUN OF ME...!
IF YOU'LL EXCUSE ME.

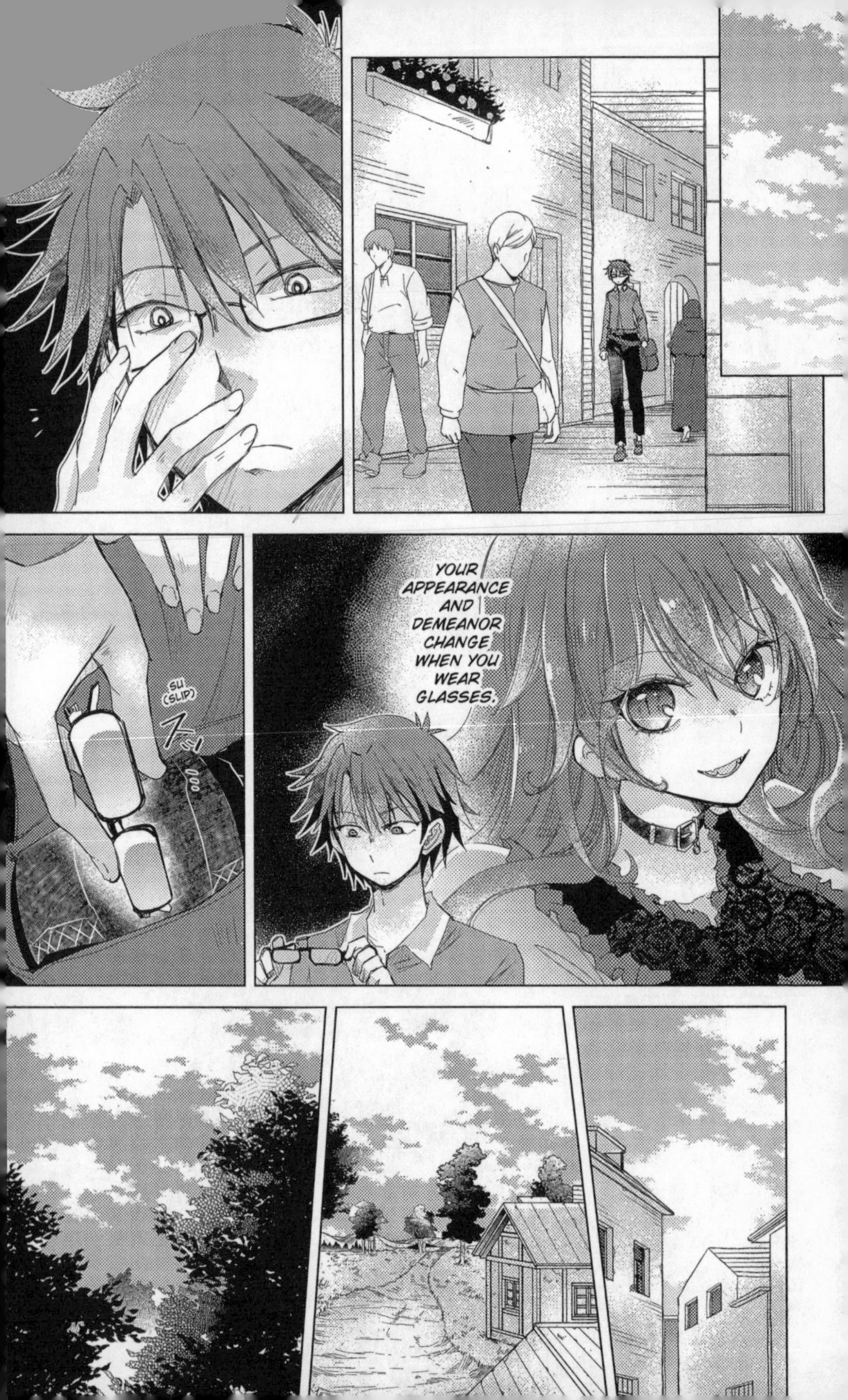
YOUR APPEARANCE AND DEMEANOR CHANGE WHEN YOU WEAR GLASSES.
SU (SLIP)

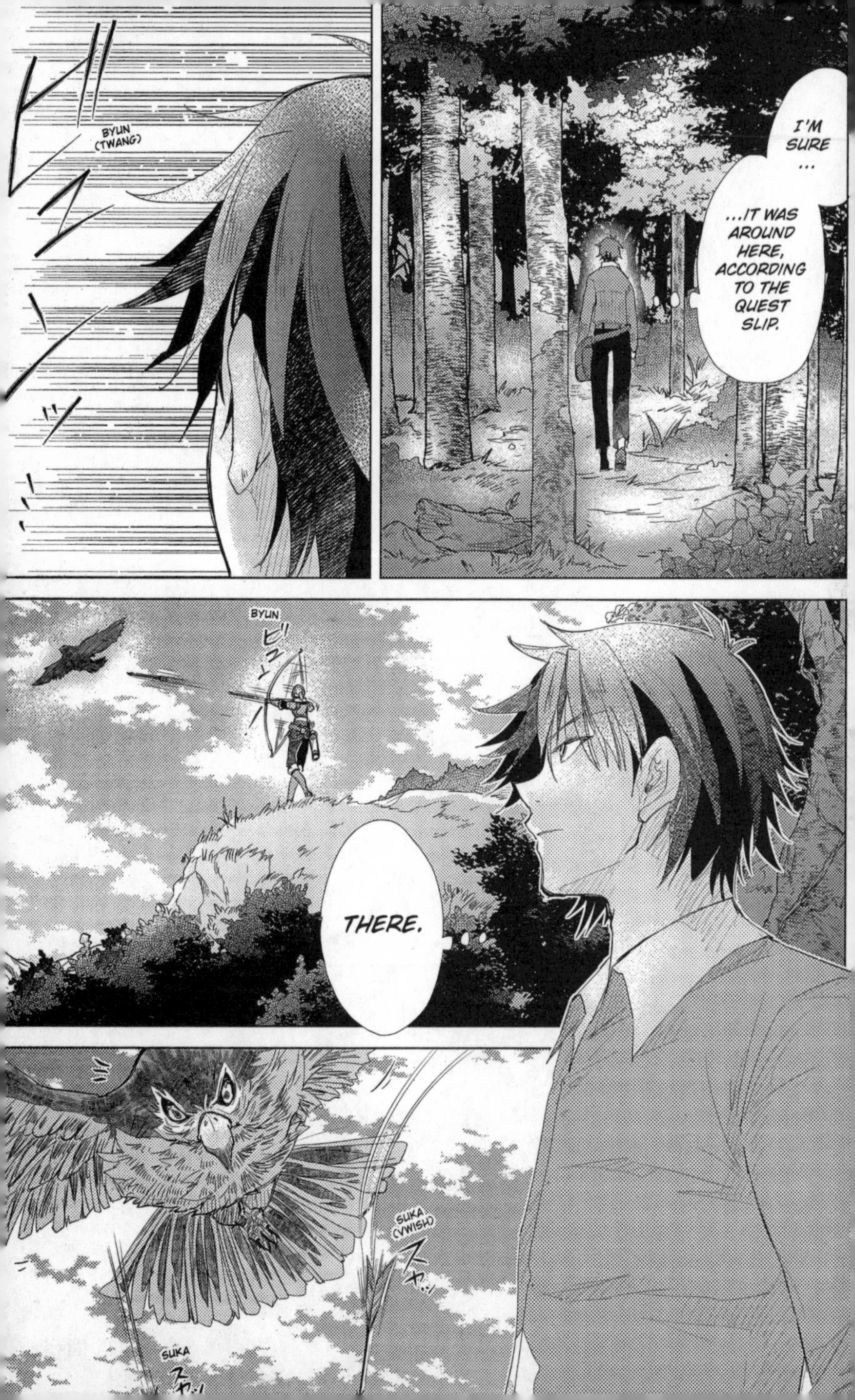
I'M SURE...
...IT WAS AROUND HERE, ACCORDING TO THE QUEST SLIP.
BYUN (TWANG)
BYUN
THERE.
SUKA (VWISH)
SUKA

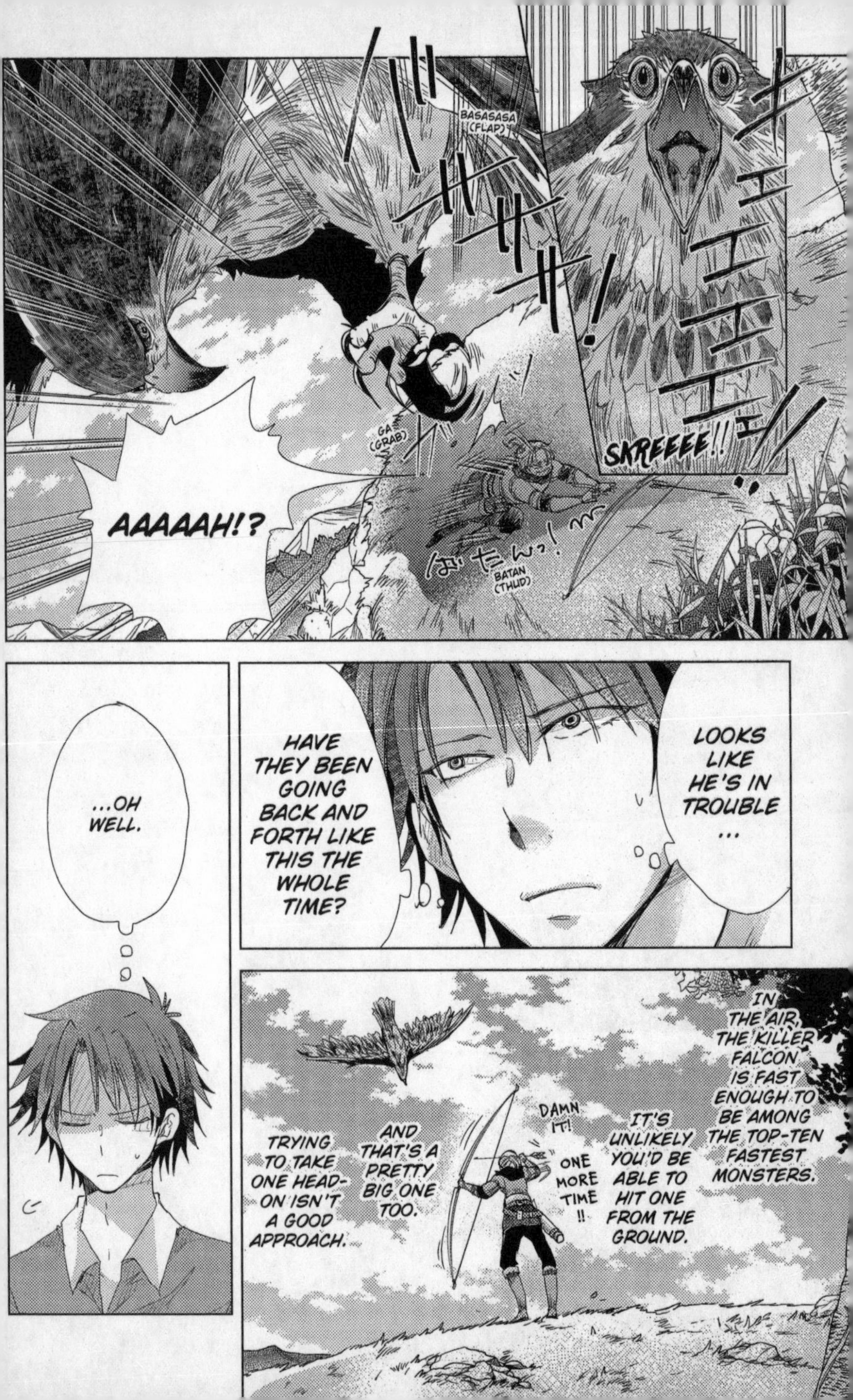
SKREEEE!!
BASASASA (FLAP)
GA (GRAB)
BATAN (THUD)
AAAAAH!?
LOOKS LIKE HE'S IN TROUBLE...
HAVE THEY BEEN GOING BACK AND FORTH LIKE THIS THE WHOLE TIME?
IN THE AIR, THE KILLER FALCON IS FAST ENOUGH TO BE AMONG THE TOP-TEN FASTEST MONSTERS.
IT'S UNLIKELY YOU'D BE ABLE TO HIT ONE FROM THE GROUND.
DAMN IT!
ONE MORE TIME!!
AND THAT'S A PRETTY BIG ONE TOO.
TRYING TO TAKE ONE HEAD-ON ISN'T A GOOD APPROACH.
...OH WELL.

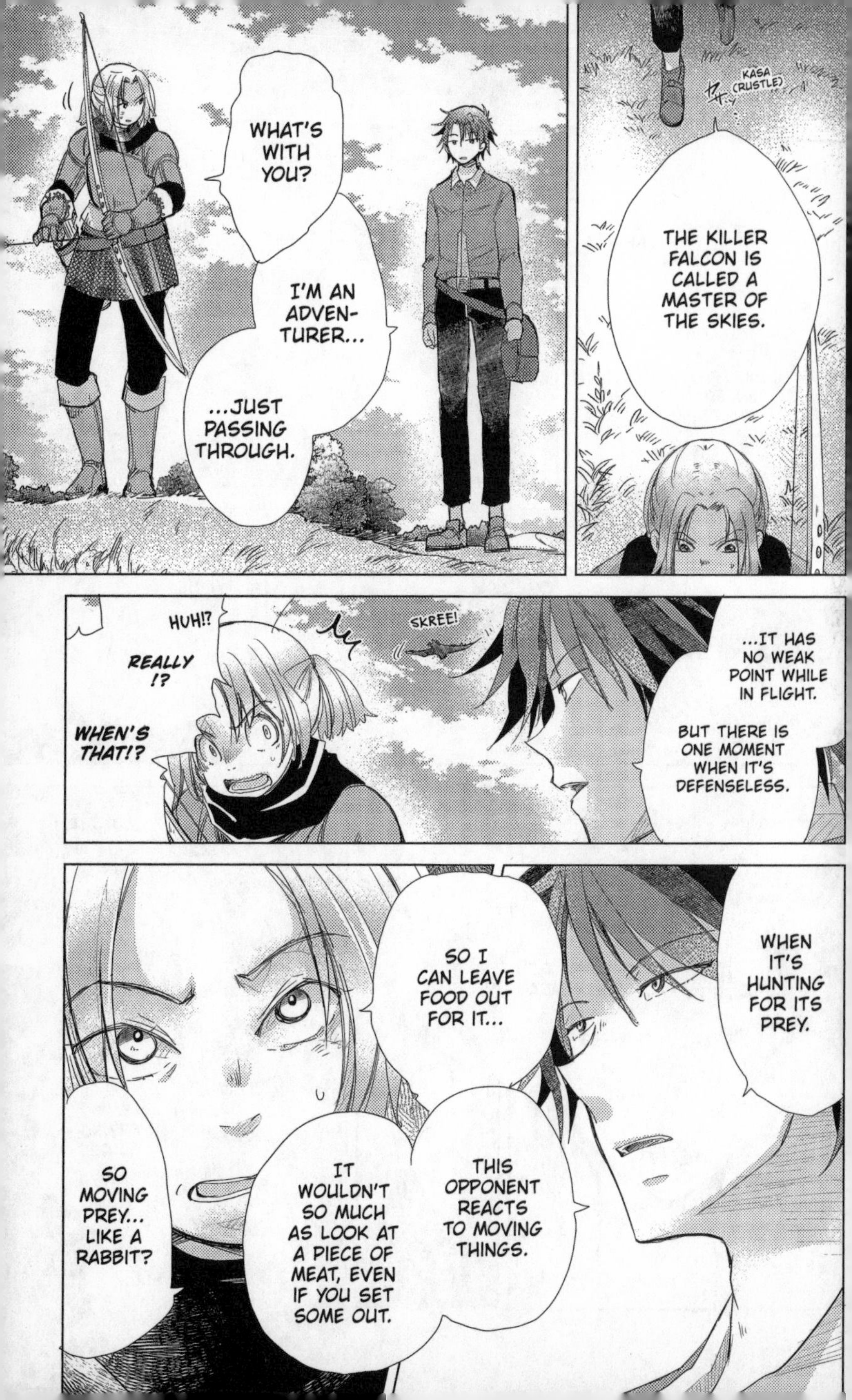
KASA (RUSTLE)
THE KILLER FALCON IS CALLED A MASTER OF THE SKIES.
WHAT'S WITH YOU?
I'M AN ADVENTURER...
...JUST PASSING THROUGH.
...IT HAS NO WEAK POINT WHILE IN FLIGHT.
BUT THERE IS ONE MOMENT WHEN IT'S DEFENSELESS.
SKREE!
HUH!?
REALLY!?
WHEN'S THAT!?
WHEN IT'S HUNTING FOR ITS PREY.
SO I CAN LEAVE FOOD OUT FOR IT...
THIS OPPONENT REACTS TO MOVING THINGS.
IT WOULDN'T SO MUCH AS LOOK AT A PIECE OF MEAT, EVEN IF YOU SET SOME OUT.
SO MOVING PREY... LIKE A RABBIT?

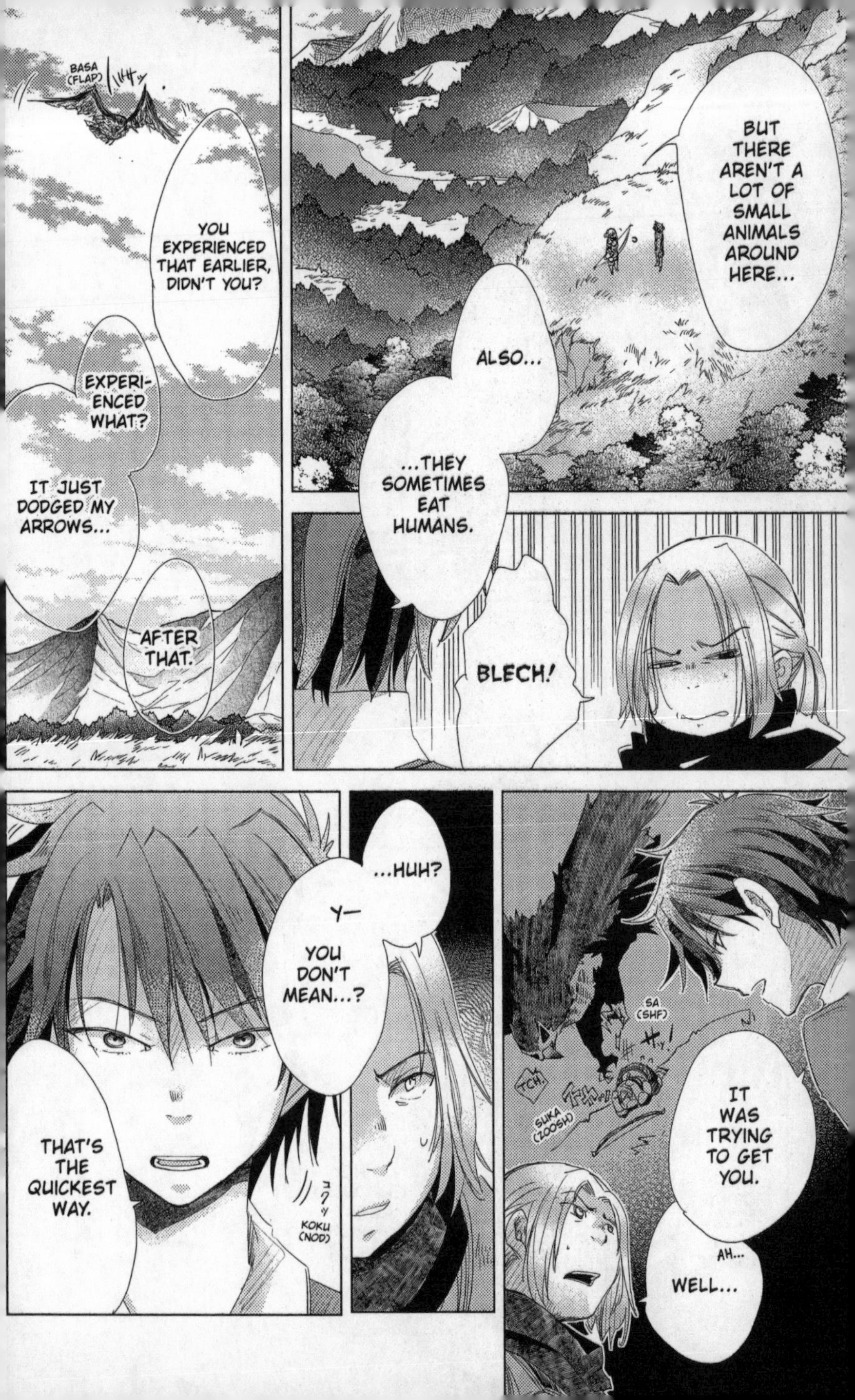
BUT THERE AREN'T A LOT OF SMALL ANIMALS AROUND HERE...
ALSO...
...THEY SOMETIMES EAT HUMANS.
BLECH!
BASA (FLAP)
YOU EXPERIENCED THAT EARLIER, DIDN'T YOU?
EXPERIENCED WHAT?
IT JUST DODGED MY ARROWS...
AFTER THAT.
SA (SHF)
TCH.
SUKA (ZOOSH)
IT WAS TRYING TO GET YOU.
AH...
WELL...
...HUH?
Y—
YOU DON'T MEAN...?
KOKU (NOD)
THAT'S THE QUICKEST WAY.

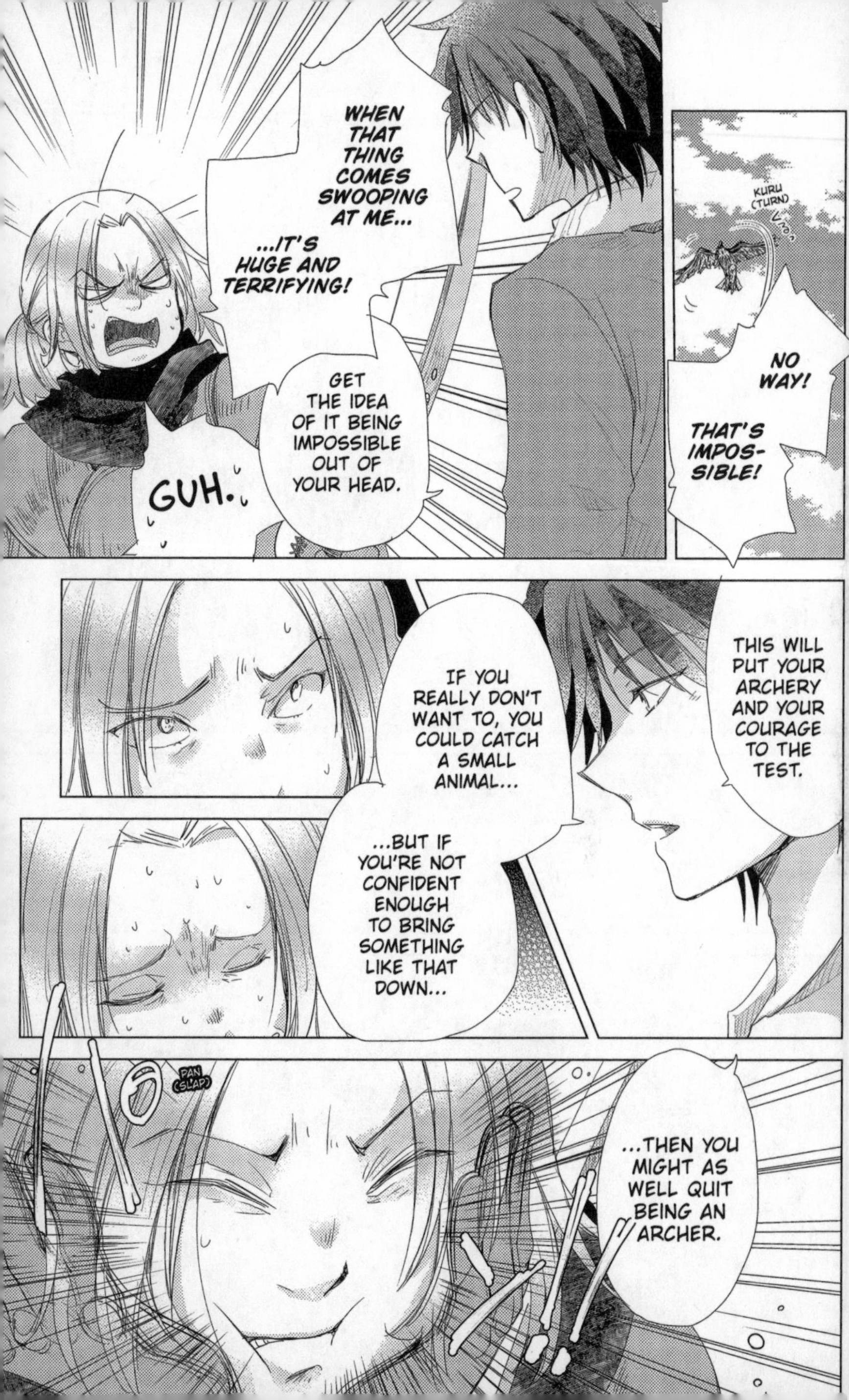
KURU (TURN)
NO WAY!
THAT'S IMPOSSIBLE!
WHEN THAT THING COMES SWOOPING AT ME...
...IT'S HUGE AND TERRIFYING!
GET THE IDEA OF IT BEING IMPOSSIBLE OUT OF YOUR HEAD.
GUH.
THIS WILL PUT YOUR ARCHERY AND YOUR COURAGE TO THE TEST.
IF YOU REALLY DON'T WANT TO, YOU COULD CATCH A SMALL ANIMAL...
...BUT IF YOU'RE NOT CONFIDENT ENOUGH TO BRING SOMETHING LIKE THAT DOWN...
PAN (SLAP)
...THEN YOU MIGHT AS WELL QUIT BEING AN ARCHER.

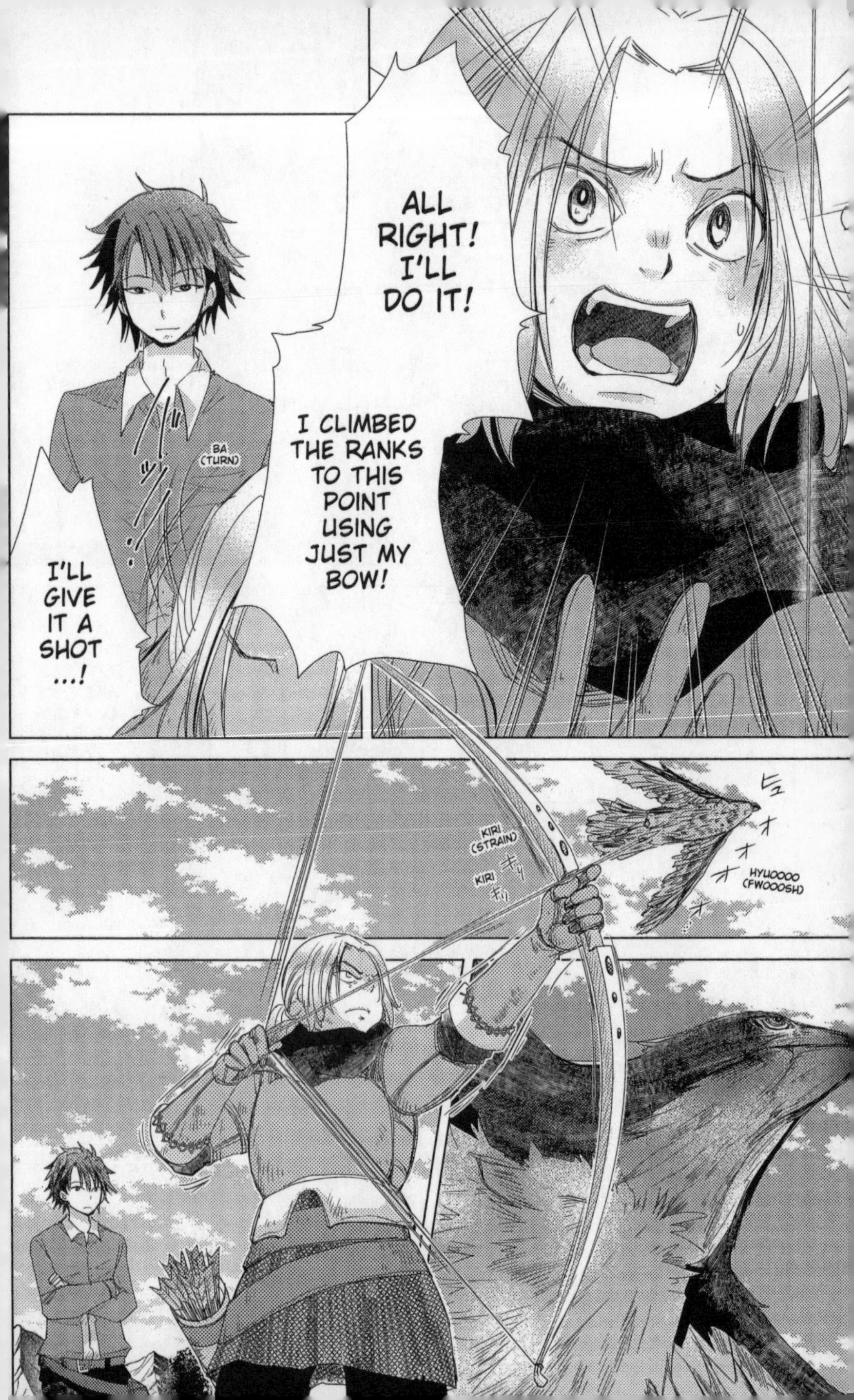
ALL RIGHT! I'LL DO IT!
I CLIMBED THE RANKS TO THIS POINT USING JUST MY BOW!
BA (TURN)
I'LL GIVE IT A SHOT ...!
ヒュオオオオ
HYUOOOO (FWOOOSH)
KIRI (STRAIN)
キリ
KIRI
キリ

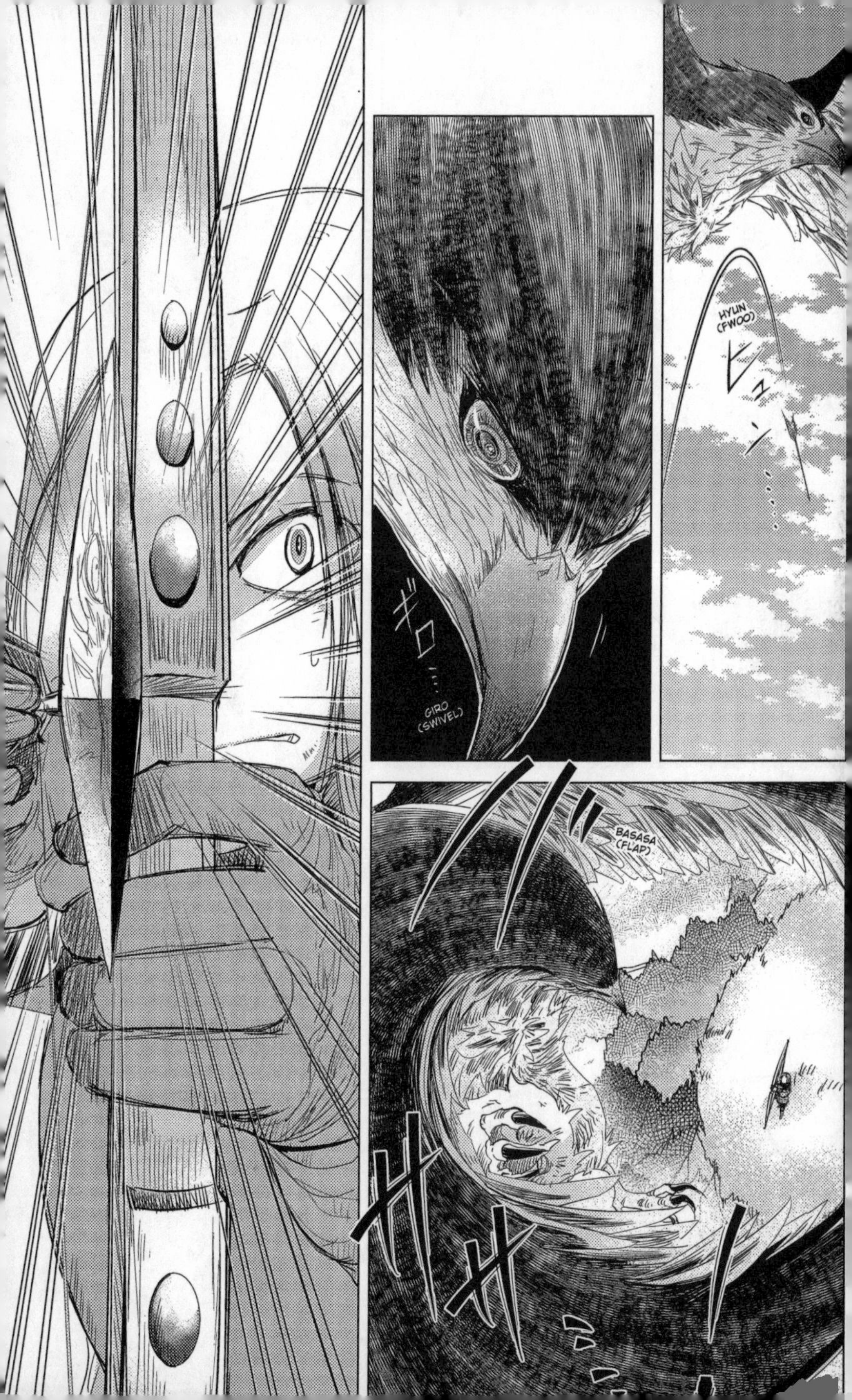
ヒュン
HYUN (FWOO)
ギロ…
GIRO (SWIVEL)
BASASA (FLAP)

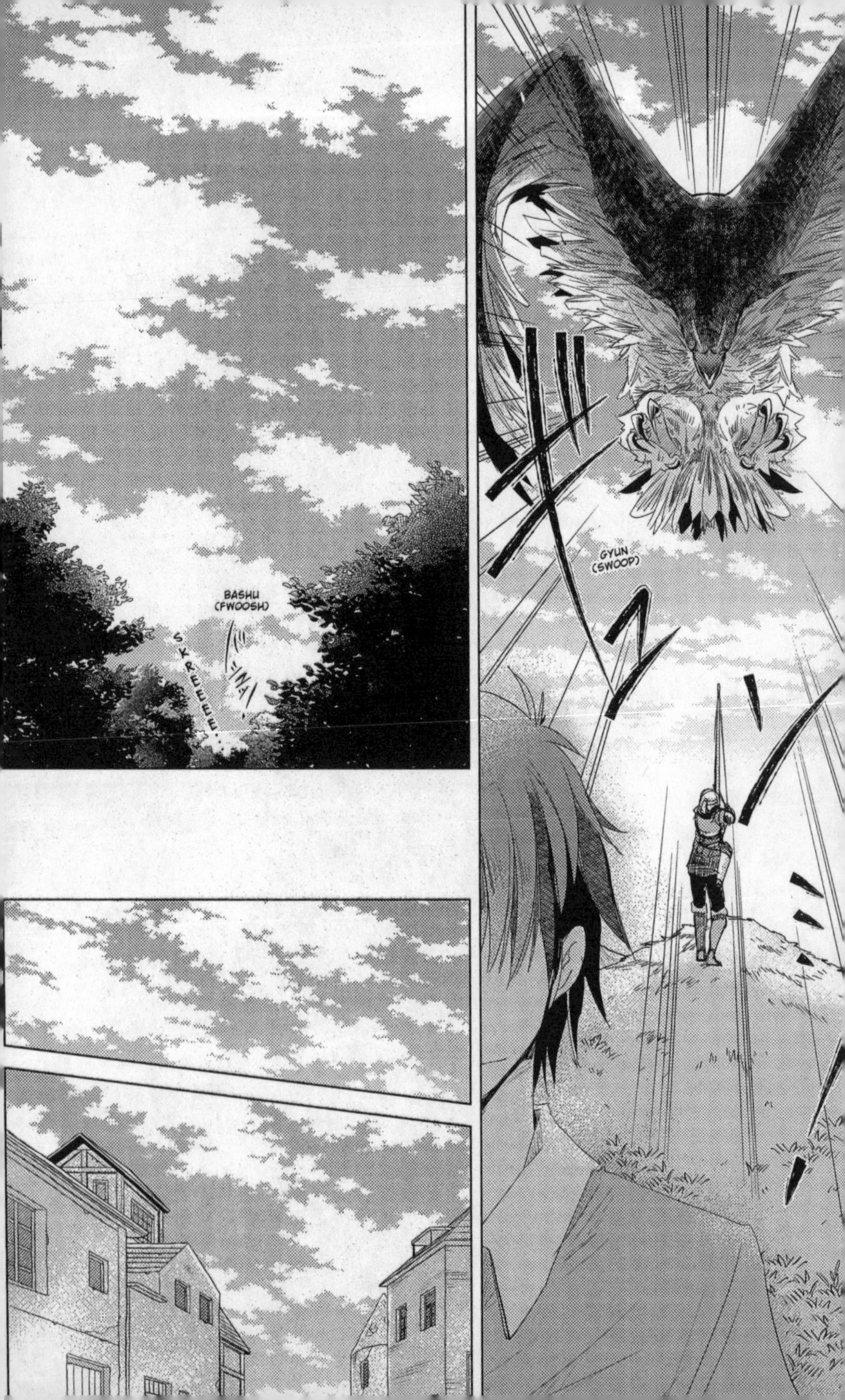
GYUN (SWOOP)
BASHU (FWOOSH)
SKREEEEE...

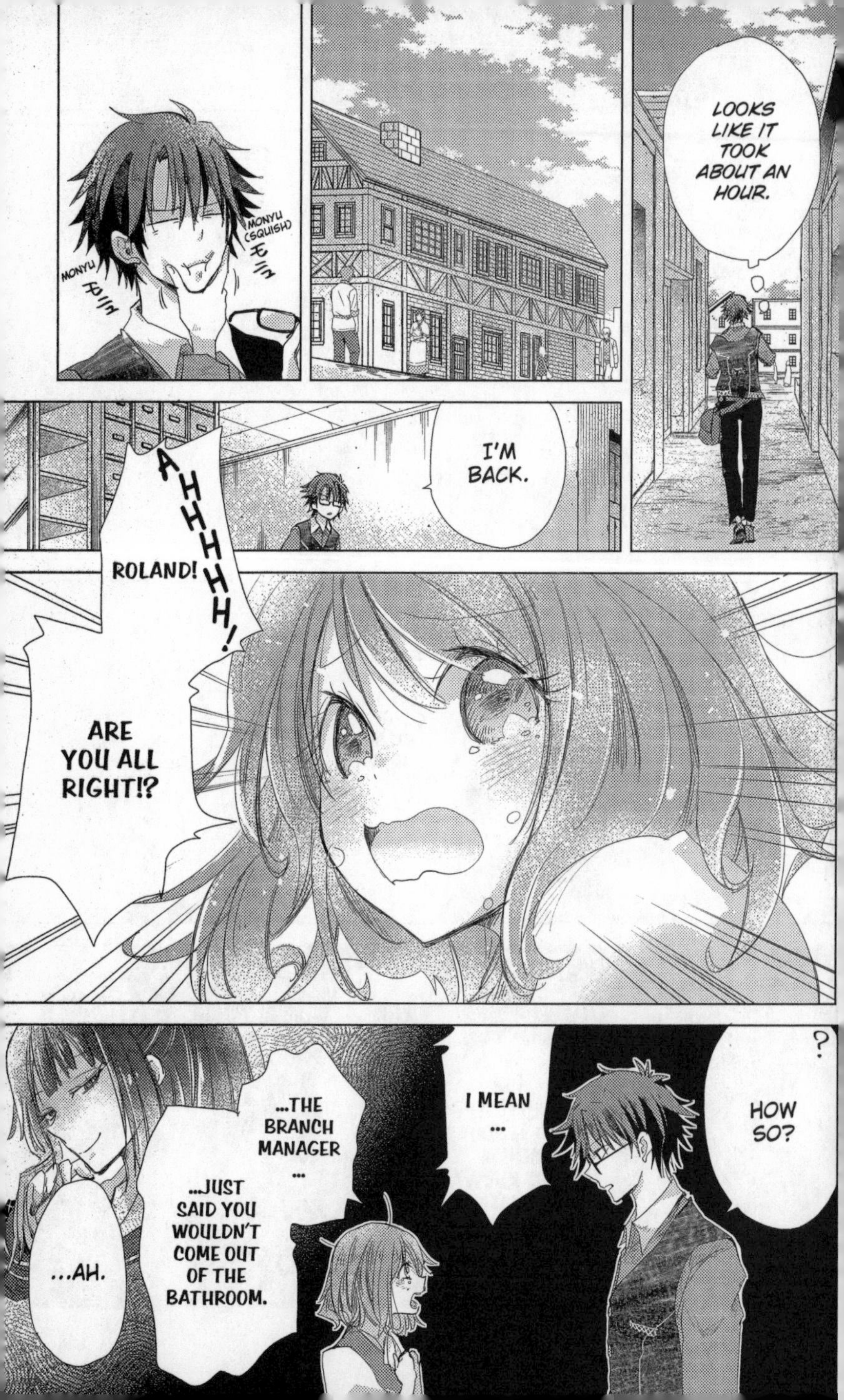

LOOKS LIKE IT TOOK ABOUT AN HOUR.
MONYU (SQUISH)
モニュ
MONYU
モニュ
I'M BACK.
AHHHHHH! ROLAND!
ARE YOU ALL RIGHT!?
?
HOW SO?
I MEAN ...
...THE BRANCH MANAGER ...
...JUST SAID YOU WOULDN'T COME OUT OF THE BATHROOM.
...AH.

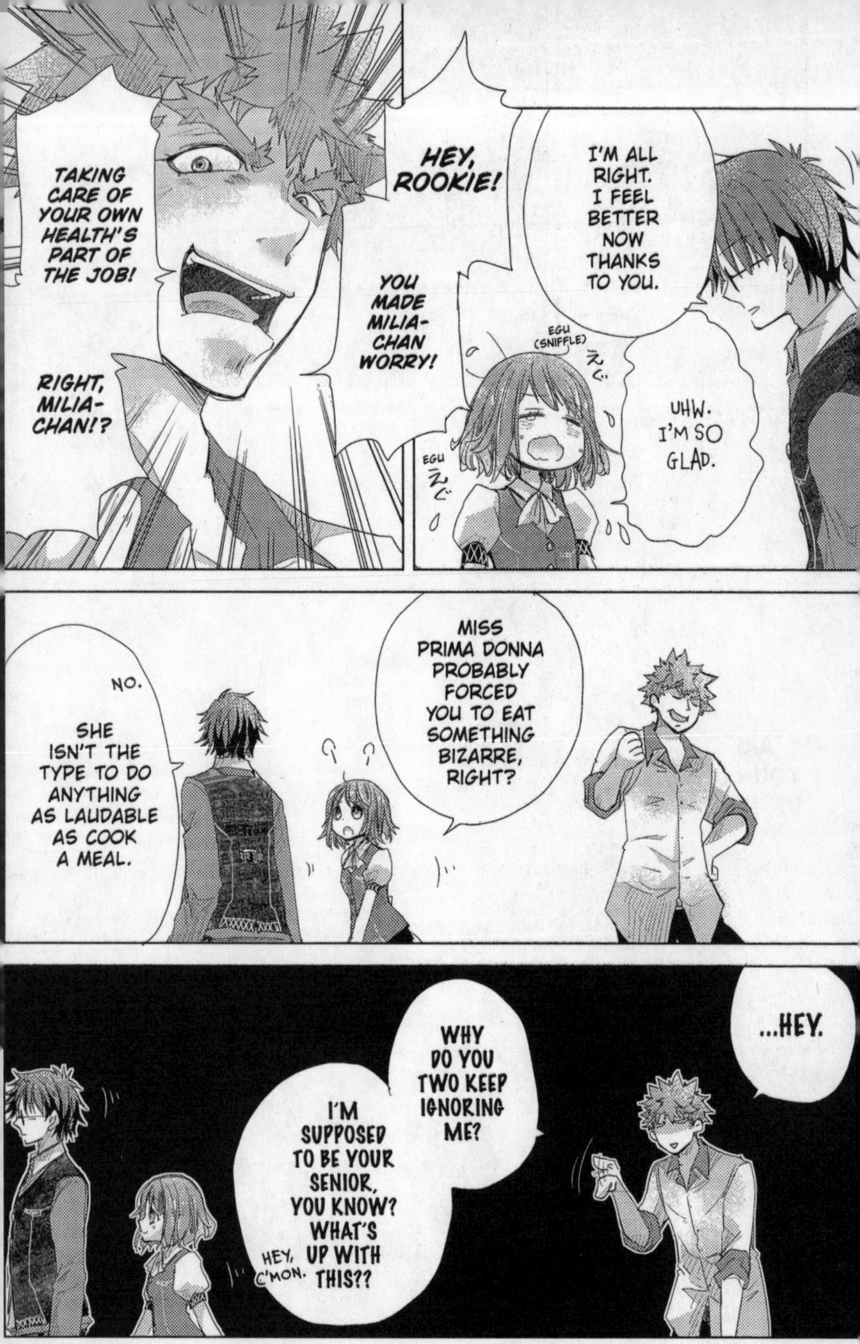
I'M ALL RIGHT. I FEEL BETTER NOW THANKS TO YOU.
EGU (SNIFFLE) えぐ
UHW. I'M SO GLAD.
EGU えぐ
HEY, ROOKIE!
YOU MADE MILIA-CHAN WORRY!
TAKING CARE OF YOUR OWN HEALTH'S PART OF THE JOB!
RIGHT, MILIA-CHAN!?
MISS PRIMA DONNA PROBABLY FORCED YOU TO EAT SOMETHING BIZARRE, RIGHT?
NO.
SHE ISN'T THE TYPE TO DO ANYTHING AS LAUDABLE AS COOK A MEAL.
...HEY.
WHY DO YOU TWO KEEP IGNORING ME?
I'M SUPPOSED TO BE YOUR SENIOR, YOU KNOW? WHAT'S UP WITH THIS??
HEY, C'MON.

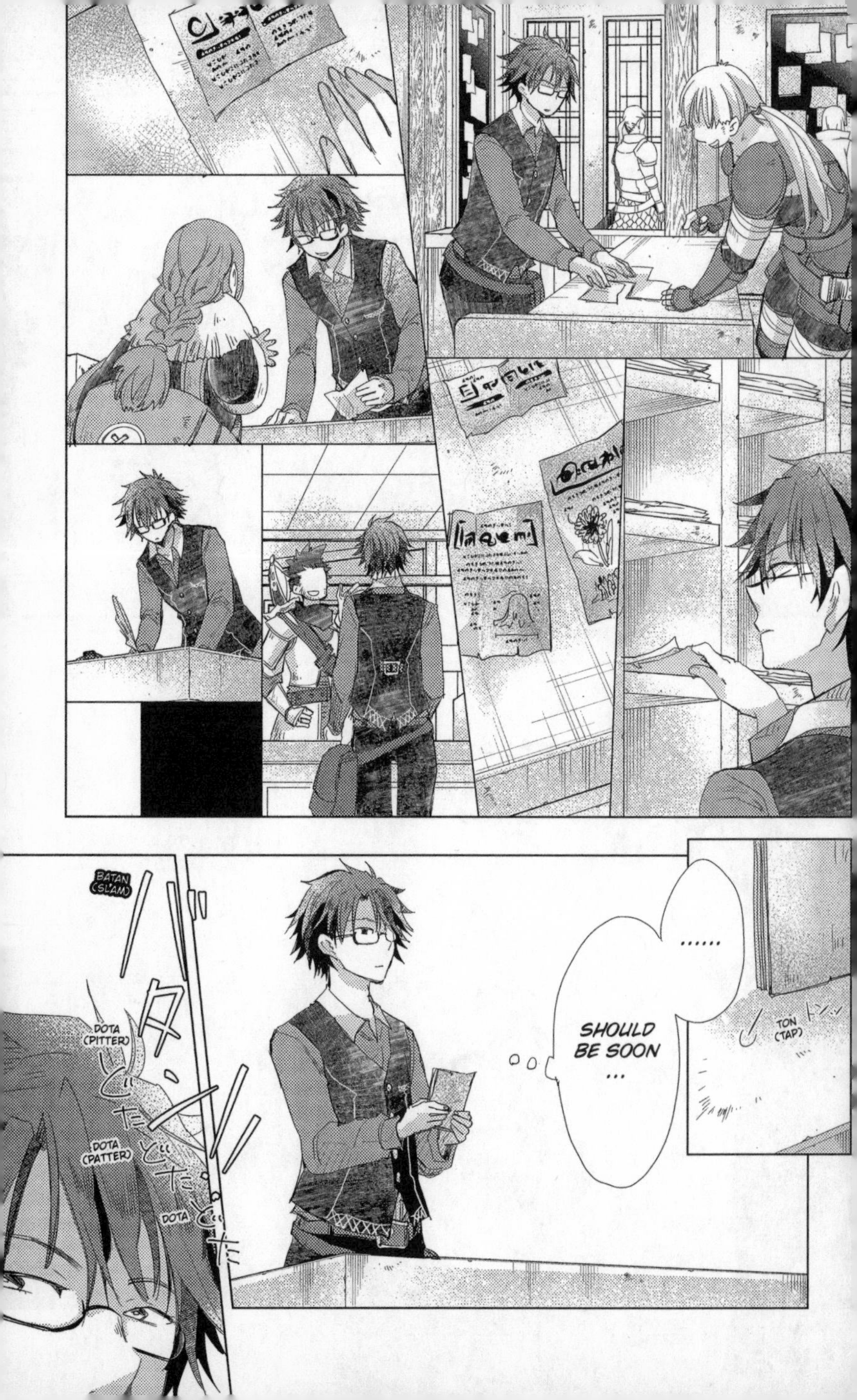
TON (TAP)
......
SHOULD BE SOON ...
BATAN (SLAM)
DOTA (PITTER)
DOTA (PATTER)
DOTA

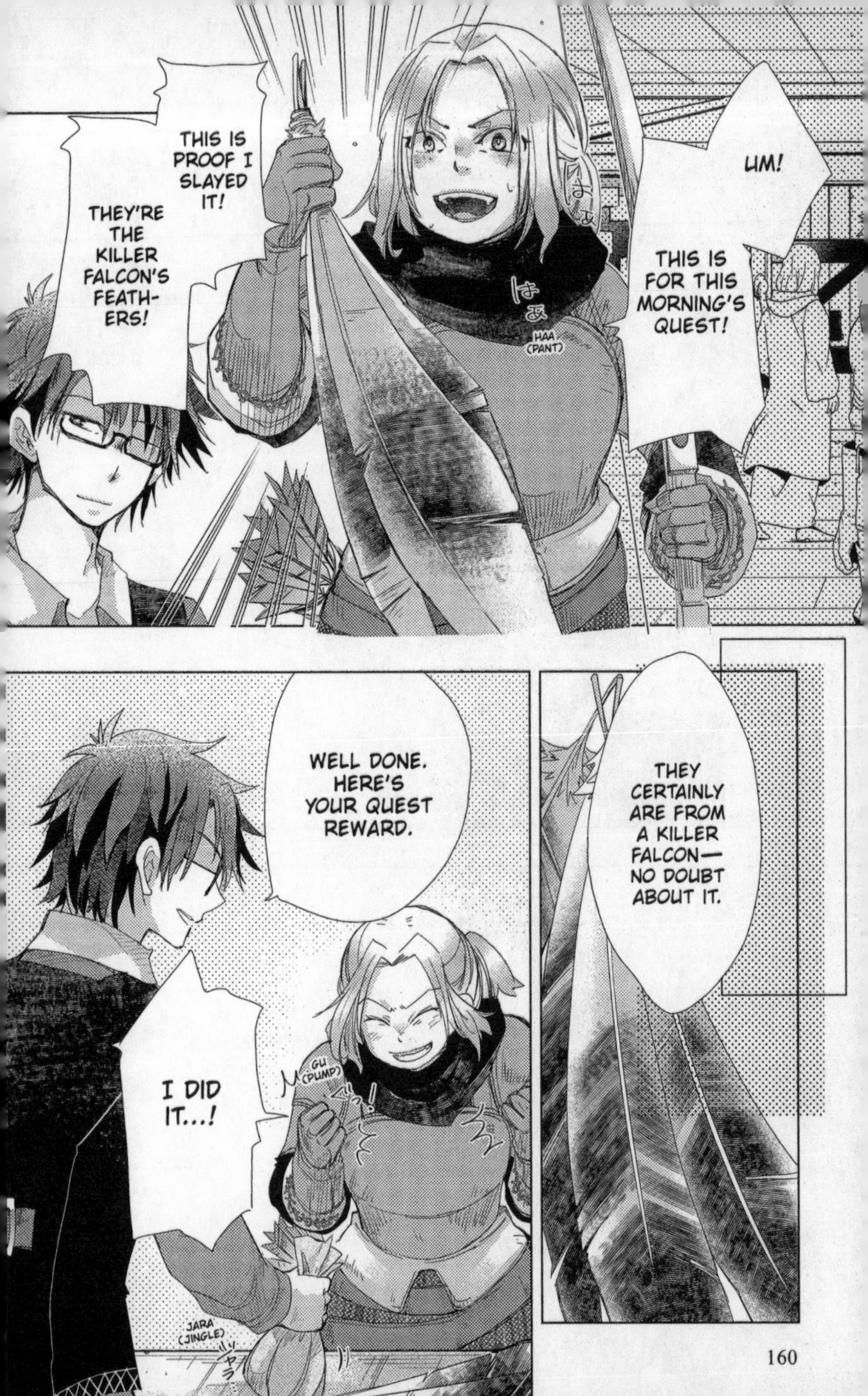
UM!
THIS IS FOR THIS MORNING'S QUEST!
HAA (PANT)
THIS IS PROOF I SLAYED IT!
THEY'RE THE KILLER FALCON'S FEATH-ERS!
THEY CERTAINLY ARE FROM A KILLER FALCON— NO DOUBT ABOUT IT.
WELL DONE. HERE'S YOUR QUEST REWARD.
GU (PUMP)
I DID IT...!
JARA (JINGLE)

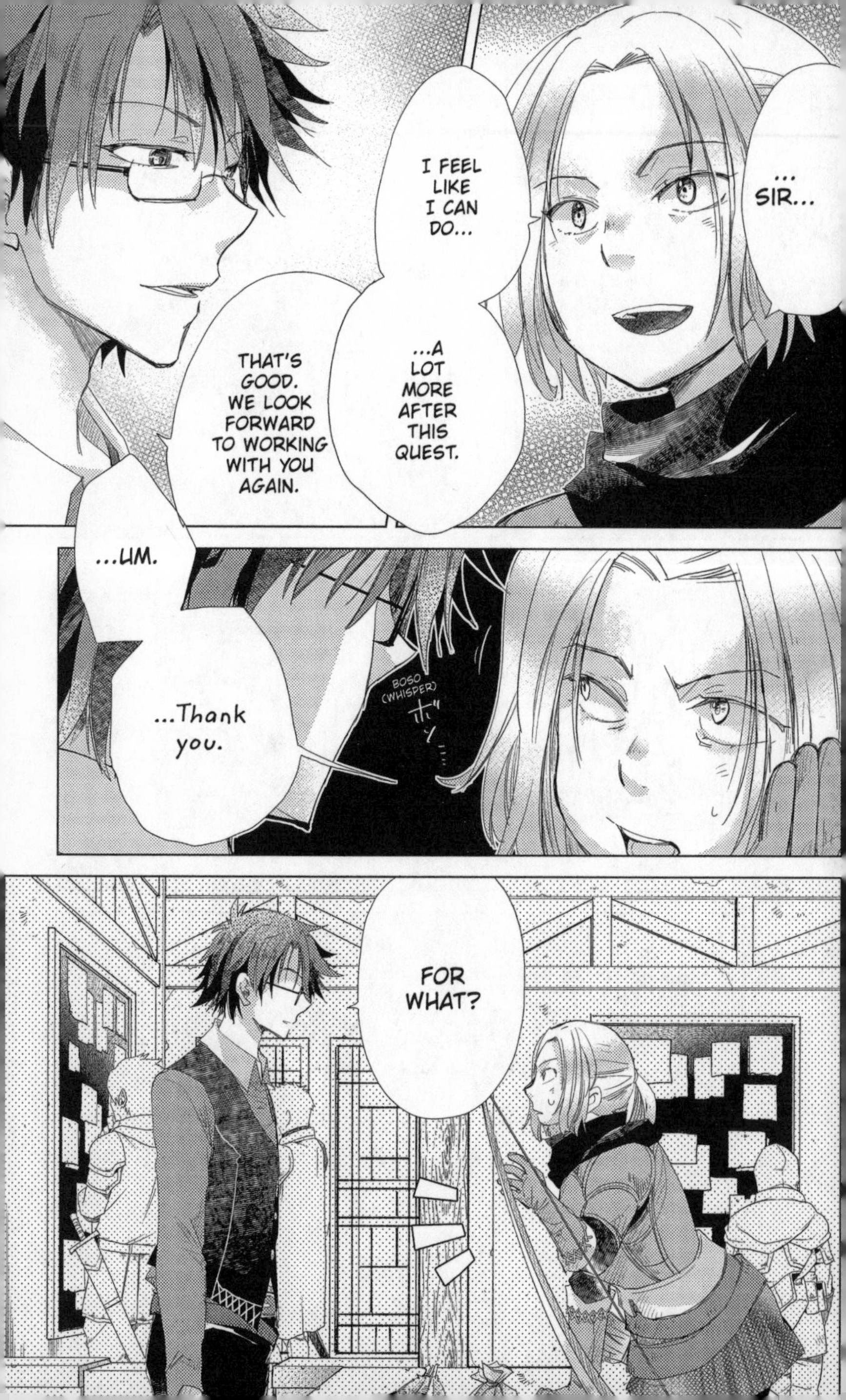
... SIR...
I FEEL LIKE I CAN DO...
...A LOT MORE AFTER THIS QUEST.
THAT'S GOOD. WE LOOK FORWARD TO WORKING WITH YOU AGAIN.
...UM.
BOSO (WHISPER)
...Thank you.
FOR WHAT?

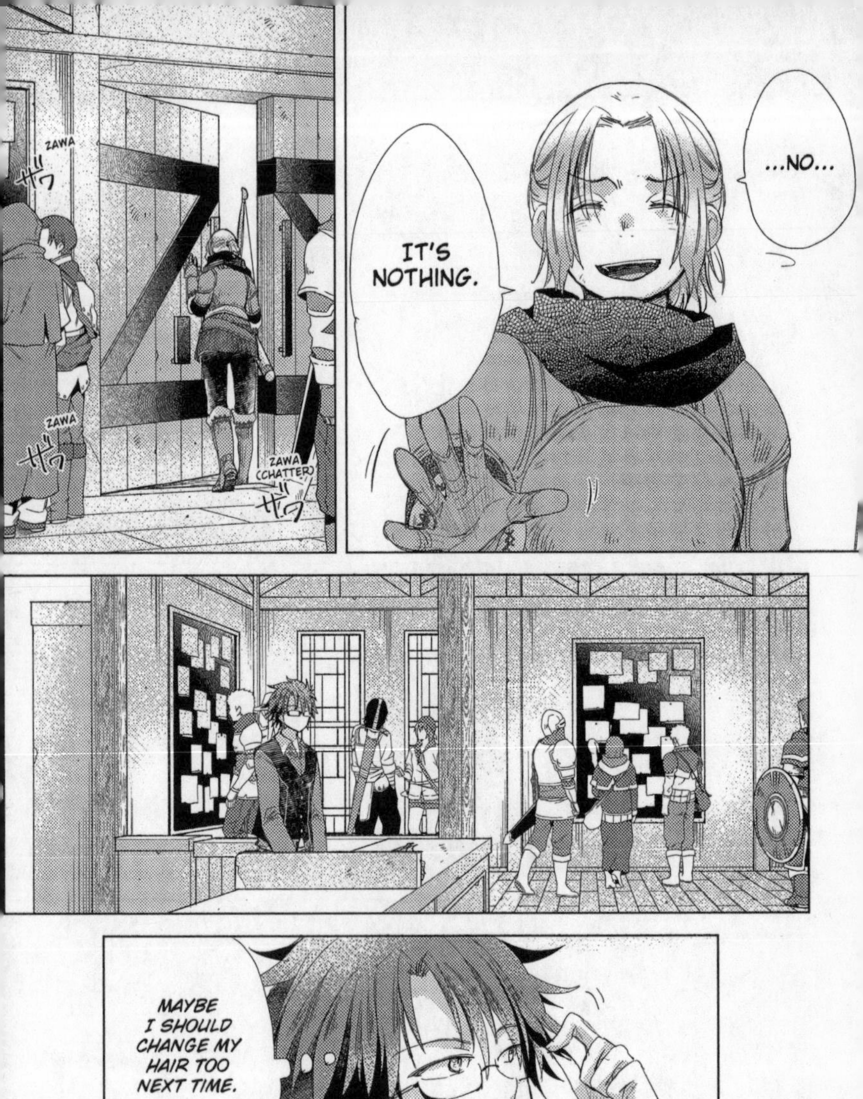
...NO...
IT'S NOTHING.
ZAWA
ZAWA
ZAWA (CHATTER)
MAYBE I SHOULD CHANGE MY HAIR TOO NEXT TIME.

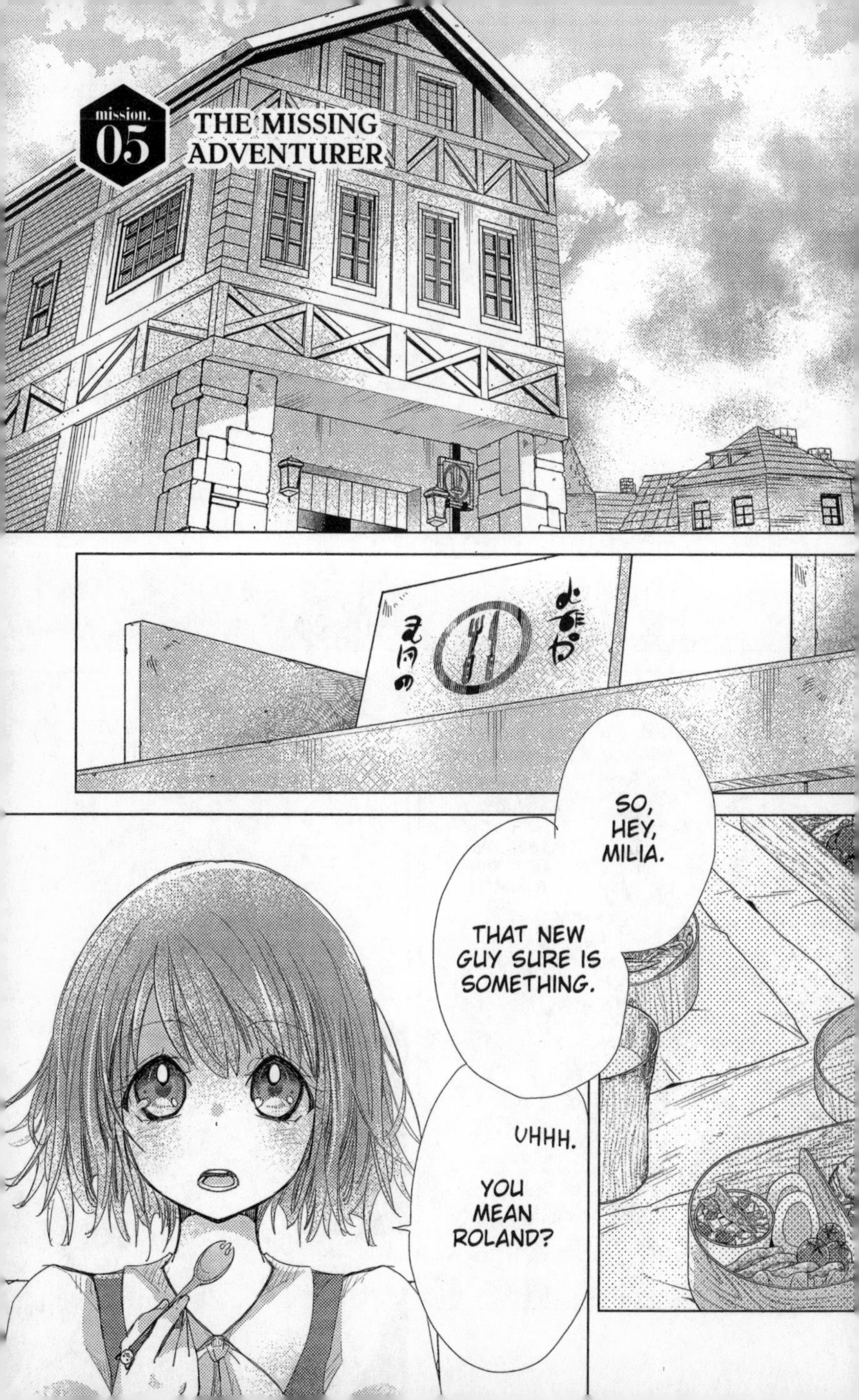
mission. 05
THE MISSING ADVENTURER
SO, HEY, MILIA.
THAT NEW GUY SURE IS SOMETHING.
UHHH.
YOU MEAN ROLAND?

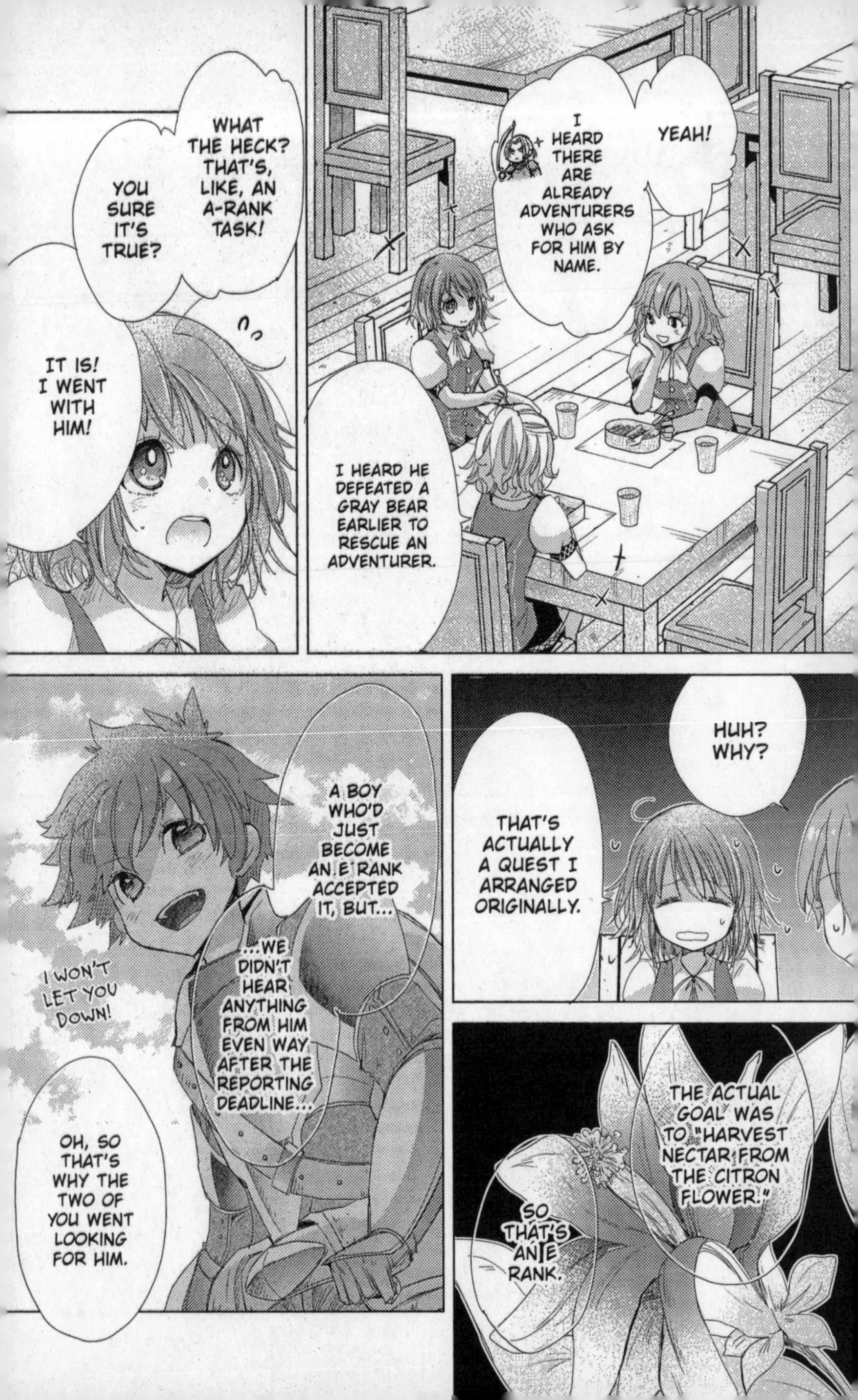
YEAH!
I HEARD THERE ARE ALREADY ADVENTURERS WHO ASK FOR HIM BY NAME.
I HEARD HE DEFEATED A GRAY BEAR EARLIER TO RESCUE AN ADVENTURER.
WHAT THE HECK? THAT'S, LIKE, AN A-RANK TASK!
YOU SURE IT'S TRUE?
IT IS! I WENT WITH HIM!
HUH? WHY?
THAT'S ACTUALLY A QUEST I ARRANGED ORIGINALLY.
THE ACTUAL GOAL WAS TO "HARVEST NECTAR FROM THE CITRON FLOWER."
SO THAT'S AN E RANK.
A BOY WHO'D JUST BECOME AN E RANK ACCEPTED IT, BUT...
...WE DIDN'T HEAR ANYTHING FROM HIM EVEN WAY AFTER THE REPORTING DEADLINE...
I WON'T LET YOU DOWN!
OH, SO THAT'S WHY THE TWO OF YOU WENT LOOKING FOR HIM.

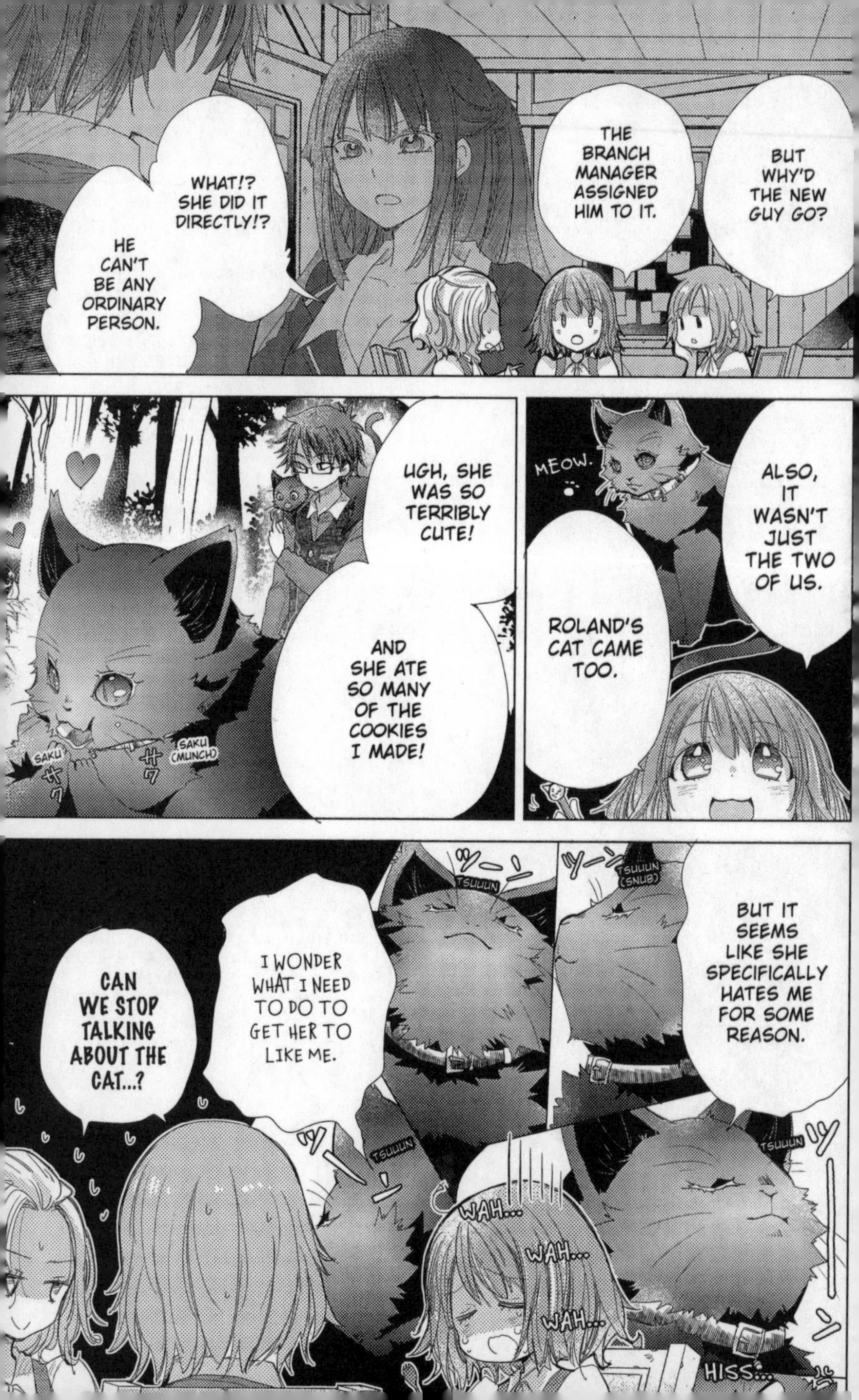
BUT WHY'D THE NEW GUY GO?
THE BRANCH MANAGER ASSIGNED HIM TO IT.
WHAT!? SHE DID IT DIRECTLY!?
HE CAN'T BE ANY ORDINARY PERSON.
ALSO, IT WASN'T JUST THE TWO OF US.
MEOW.
ROLAND'S CAT CAME TOO.
UGH, SHE WAS SO TERRIBLY CUTE!
AND SHE ATE SO MANY OF THE COOKIES I MADE!
SAKU (MUNCH)
SAKU
TSUUUN (SNUB)
BUT IT SEEMS LIKE SHE SPECIFICALLY HATES ME FOR SOME REASON.
TSUUUN
I WONDER WHAT I NEED TO DO TO GET HER TO LIKE ME.
CAN WE STOP TALKING ABOUT THE CAT...?
TSUUUN
TSUUUN
WAH...
WAH...
WAH...
HISS...

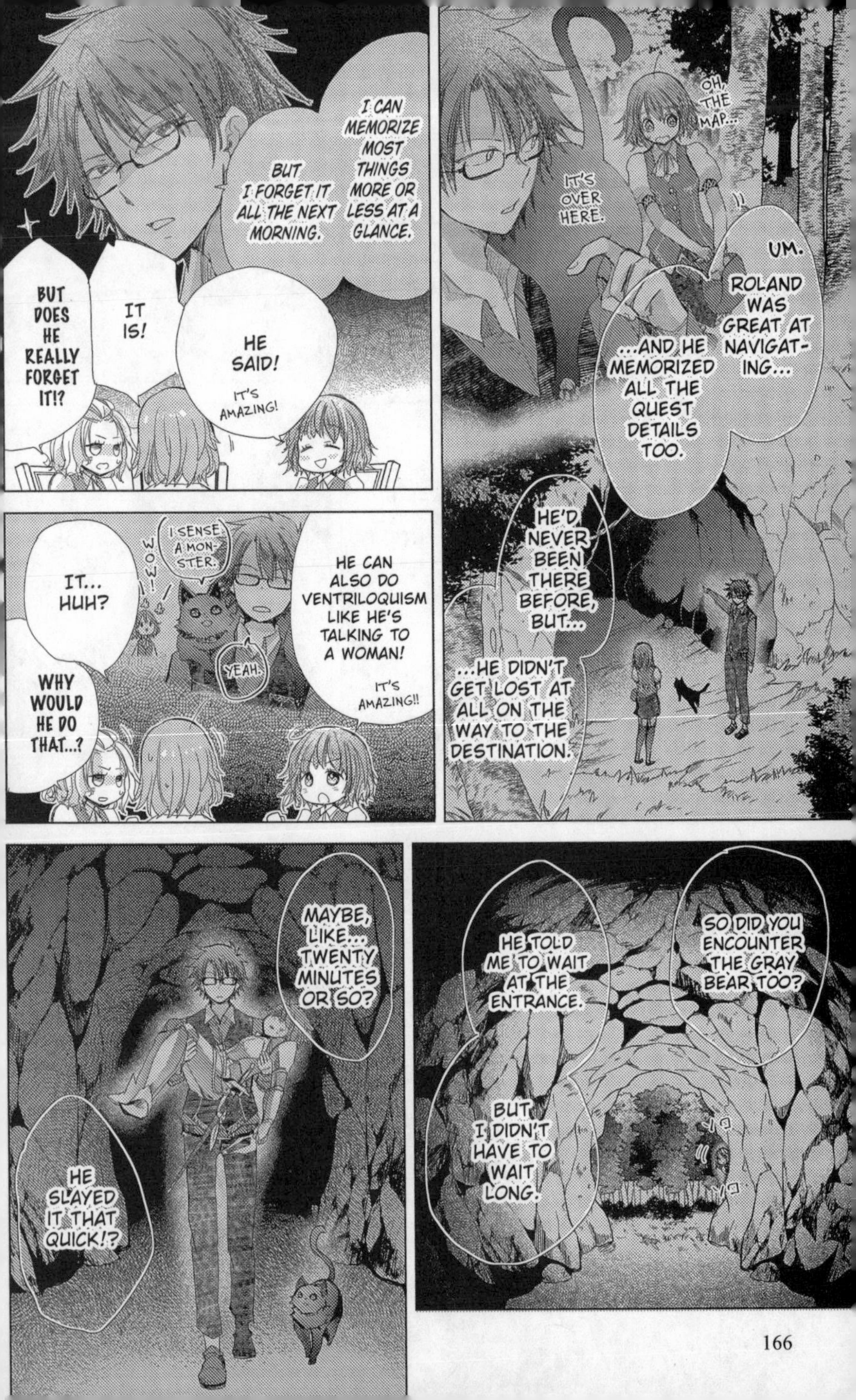
OH, THE MAP...
IT'S OVER HERE.
UM.
ROLAND WAS GREAT AT NAVIGATING...
...AND HE MEMORIZED ALL THE QUEST DETAILS TOO.
HE'D NEVER BEEN THERE BEFORE, BUT...
...HE DIDN'T GET LOST AT ALL ON THE WAY TO THE DESTINATION.
I CAN MEMORIZE MOST THINGS MORE OR LESS AT A GLANCE.
BUT I FORGET IT ALL THE NEXT MORNING.
HE SAID!
IT'S AMAZING!
IT IS!
BUT DOES HE REALLY FORGET IT!?
HE CAN ALSO DO VENTRILOQUISM LIKE HE'S TALKING TO A WOMAN!
IT'S AMAZING!!
YEAH.
I SENSE A MONSTER.
WOW!
IT... HUH?
WHY WOULD HE DO THAT...?
SO DID YOU ENCOUNTER THE GRAY BEAR TOO?
HE TOLD ME TO WAIT AT THE ENTRANCE.
BUT I DIDN'T HAVE TO WAIT LONG.
MAYBE, LIKE... TWENTY MINUTES OR SO?
HE SLAYED IT THAT QUICK!?

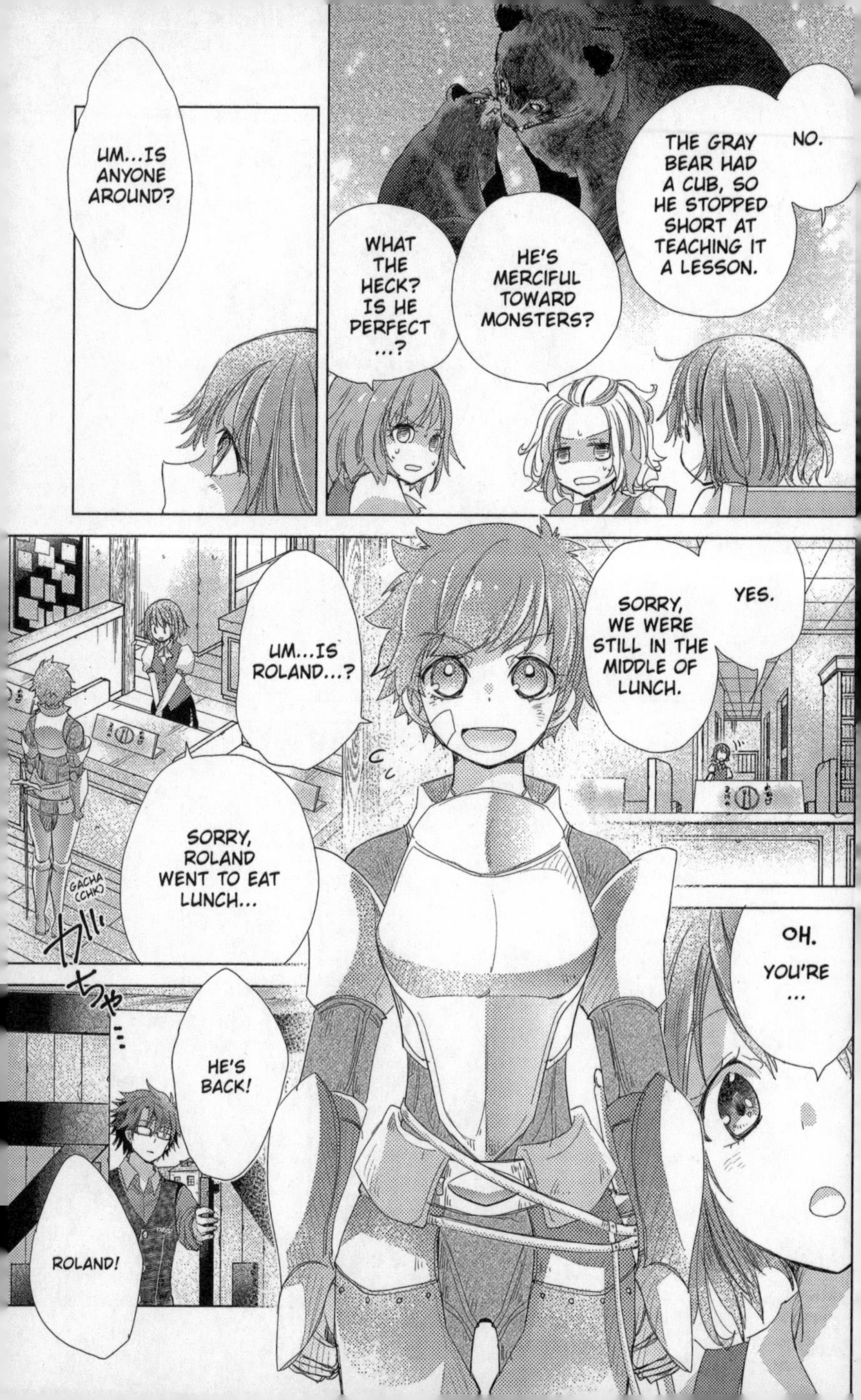
NO.
THE GRAY BEAR HAD A CUB, SO HE STOPPED SHORT AT TEACHING IT A LESSON.
HE'S MERCIFUL TOWARD MONSTERS?
WHAT THE HECK? IS HE PERFECT ...?
UM...IS ANYONE AROUND?
YES.
SORRY, WE WERE STILL IN THE MIDDLE OF LUNCH.
UM...IS ROLAND...?
SORRY, ROLAND WENT TO EAT LUNCH...
OH.
YOU'RE ...
GACHA (CHK)
HE'S BACK!
ROLAND!

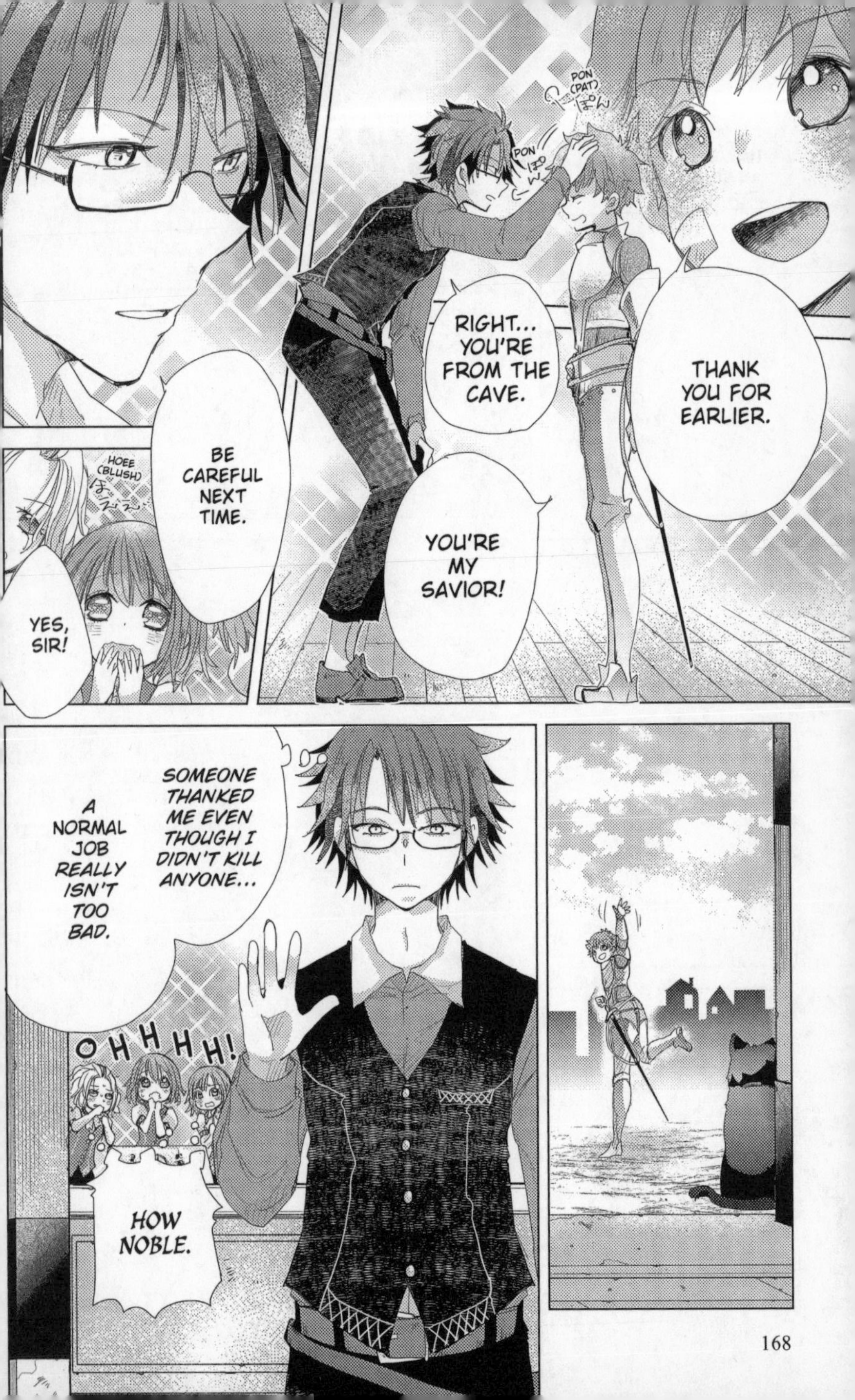
PON (PAT) ぽん
PON ぽん
THANK YOU FOR EARLIER.
RIGHT... YOU'RE FROM THE CAVE.
YOU'RE MY SAVIOR!
BE CAREFUL NEXT TIME.
HOEE (BLUSH)
YES, SIR!
SOMEONE THANKED ME EVEN THOUGH I DIDN'T KILL ANYONE...
A NORMAL JOB REALLY ISN'T TOO BAD.
OHHHH!
HOW NOBLE.

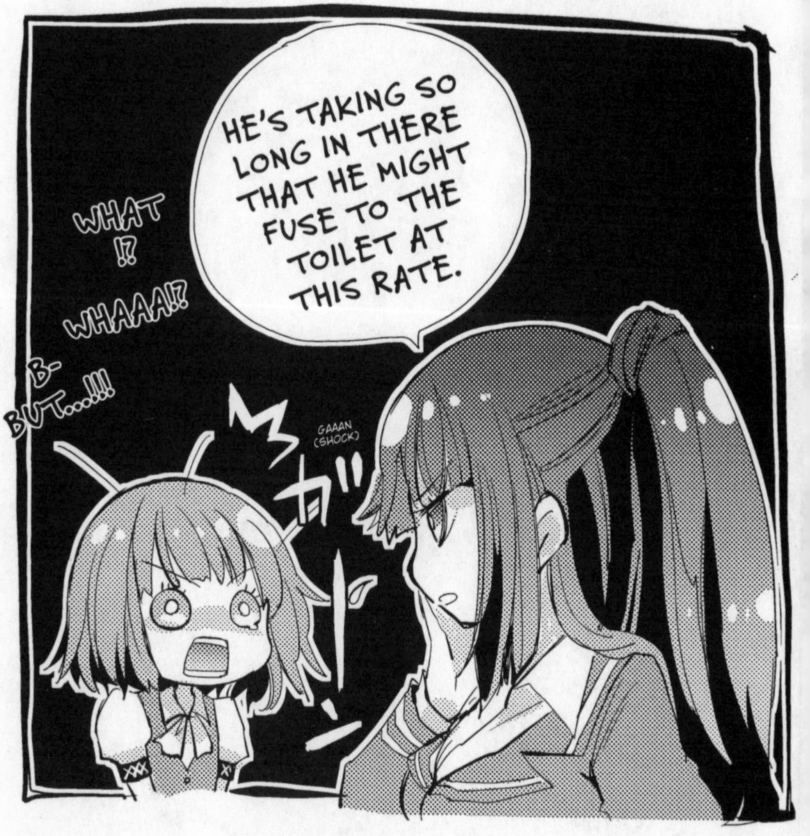
HE'S TAKING SO LONG IN THERE THAT HE MIGHT FUSE TO THE TOILET AT THIS RATE.
GAAAN (SHOCK)
WHAT!?
WHAAAA!?
B-BUT...!!!

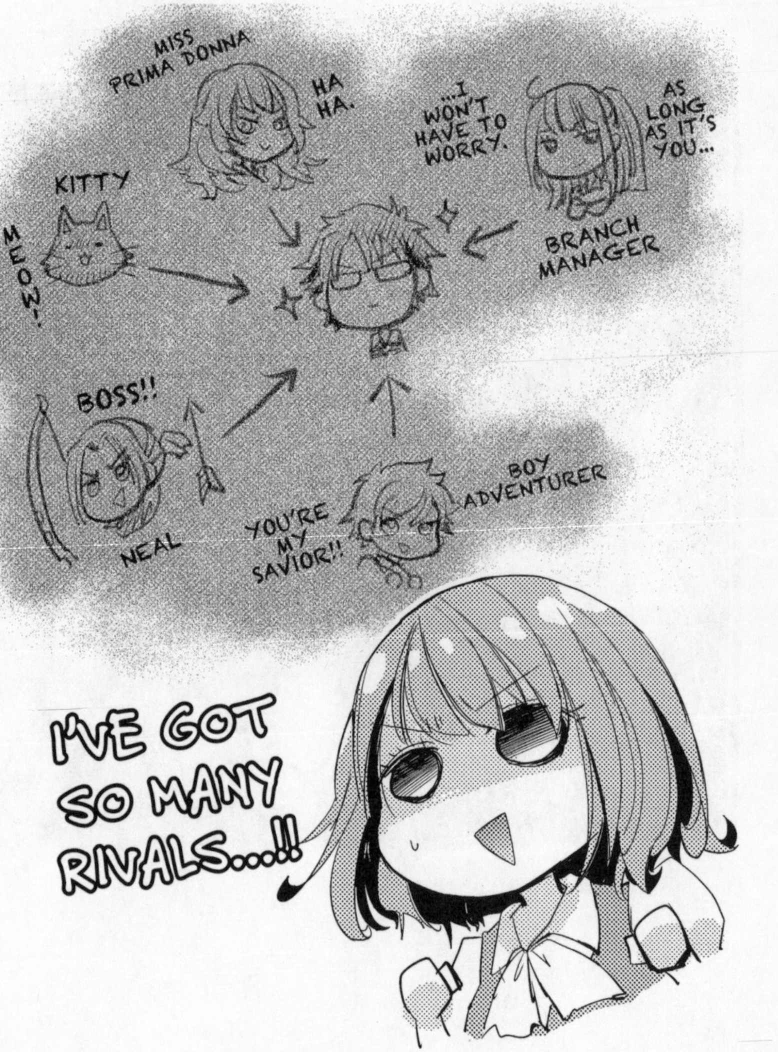
AS LONG AS IT'S YOU...
...I WON'T HAVE TO WORRY.
BRANCH MANAGER
HA HA.
MISS PRIMA DONNA
KITTY
MEOW!
BOY ADVENTURER
YOU'RE MY SAVIOR!!
BOSS!!
NEAL
I'VE GOT SO MANY RIVALS...!!

mission. 06 WE NEED ONE MORE!

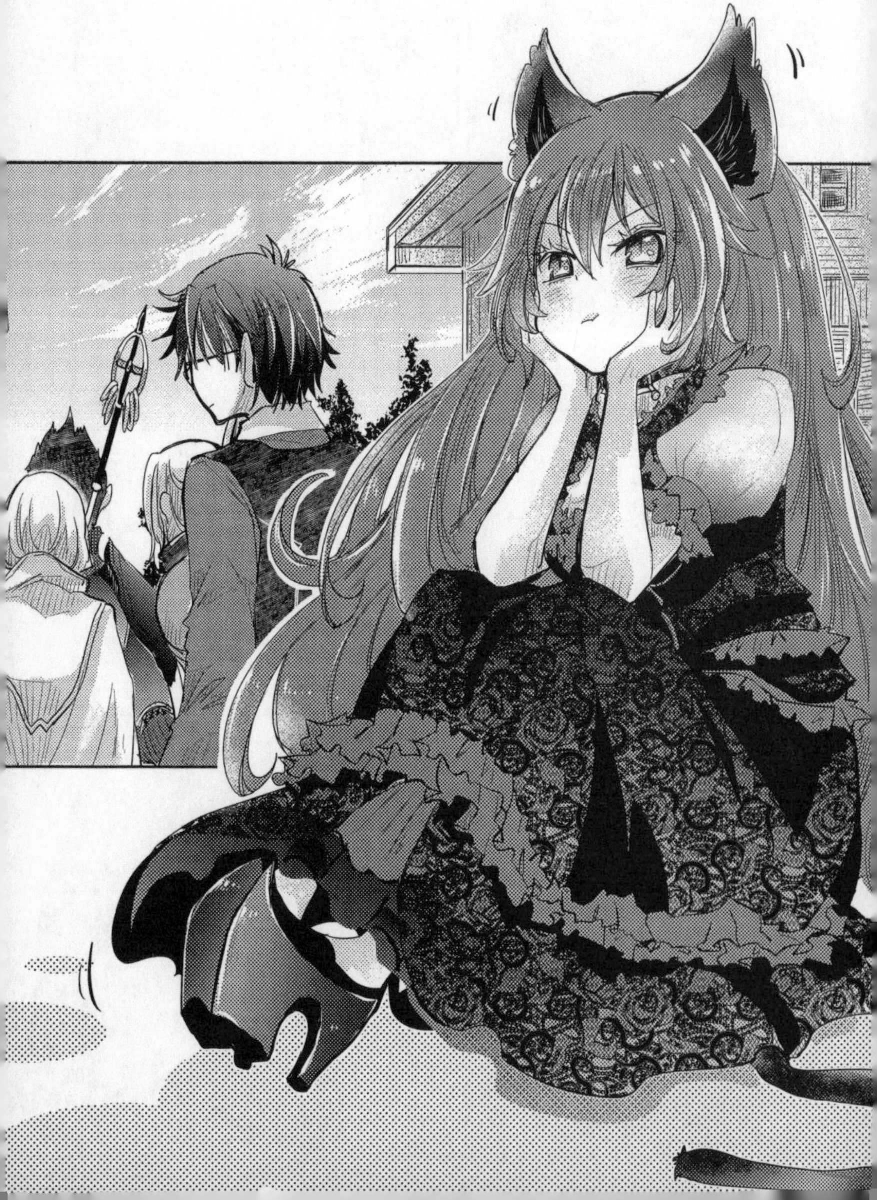

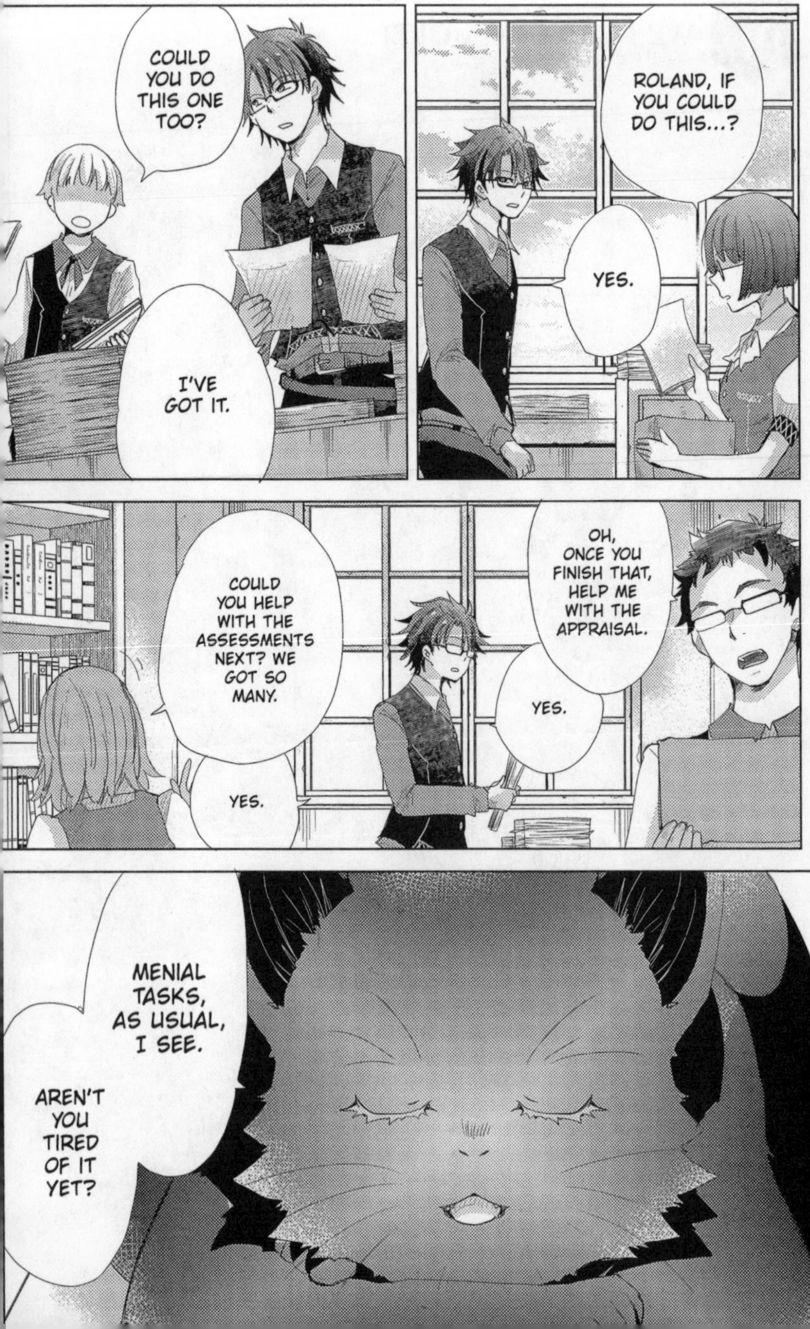
ROLAND, IF YOU COULD DO THIS...?
YES.
COULD YOU DO THIS ONE TOO?
I'VE GOT IT.
OH, ONCE YOU FINISH THAT, HELP ME WITH THE APPRAISAL.
YES.
COULD YOU HELP WITH THE ASSESSMENTS NEXT? WE GOT SO MANY.
YES.
MENIAL TASKS, AS USUAL, I SEE.
AREN'T YOU TIRED OF IT YET?

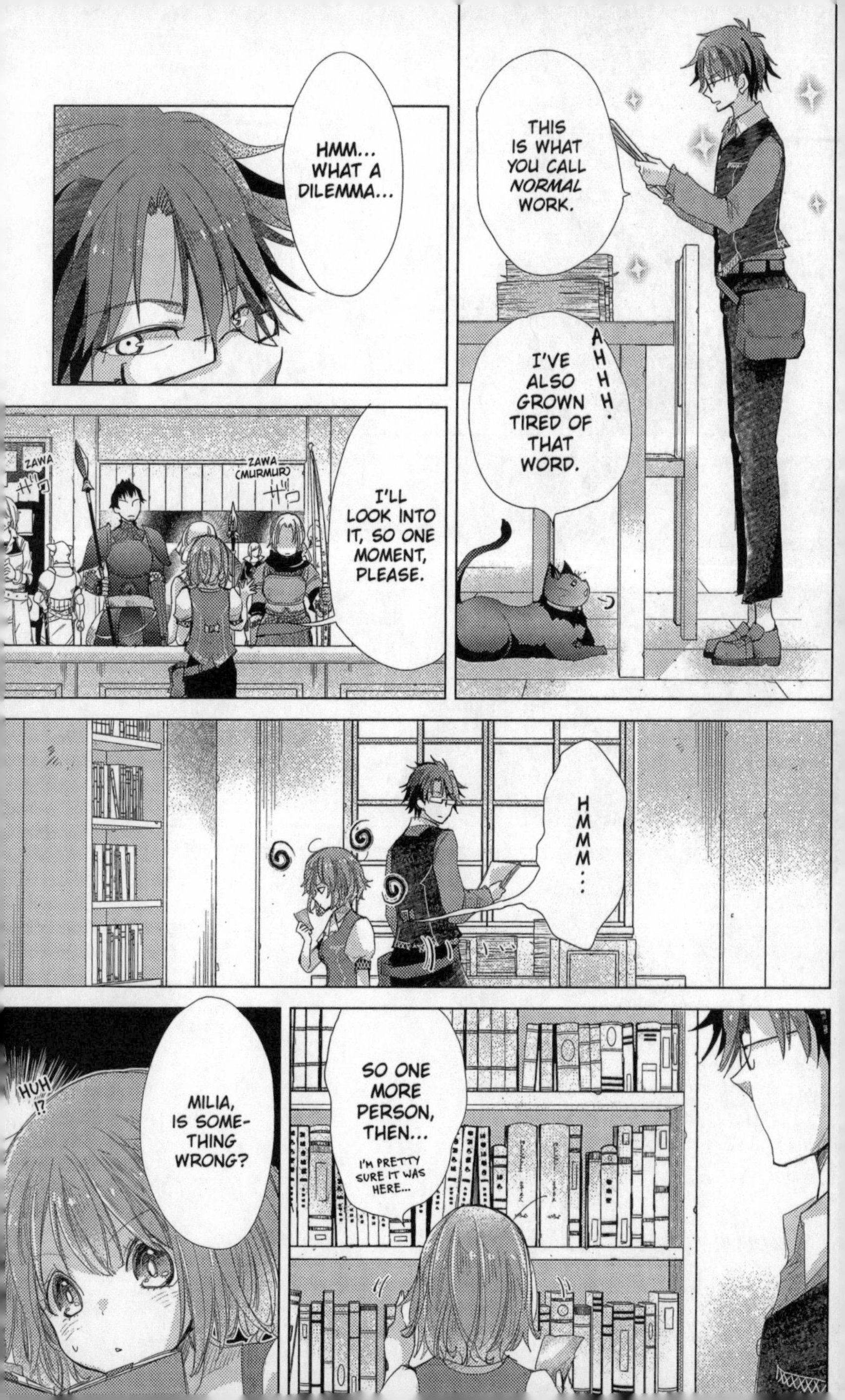
THIS IS WHAT YOU CALL *NORMAL* WORK.
I'VE ALSO GROWN TIRED OF THAT WORD.
AHHH.
HMM... WHAT A DILEMMA...
ZAWA
ZAWA (MURMUR)
I'LL LOOK INTO IT, SO ONE MOMENT, PLEASE.
HMMM...
SO ONE MORE PERSON, THEN...
I'M PRETTY SURE IT WAS HERE...
MILIA, IS SOME-THING WRONG?
HUH!?

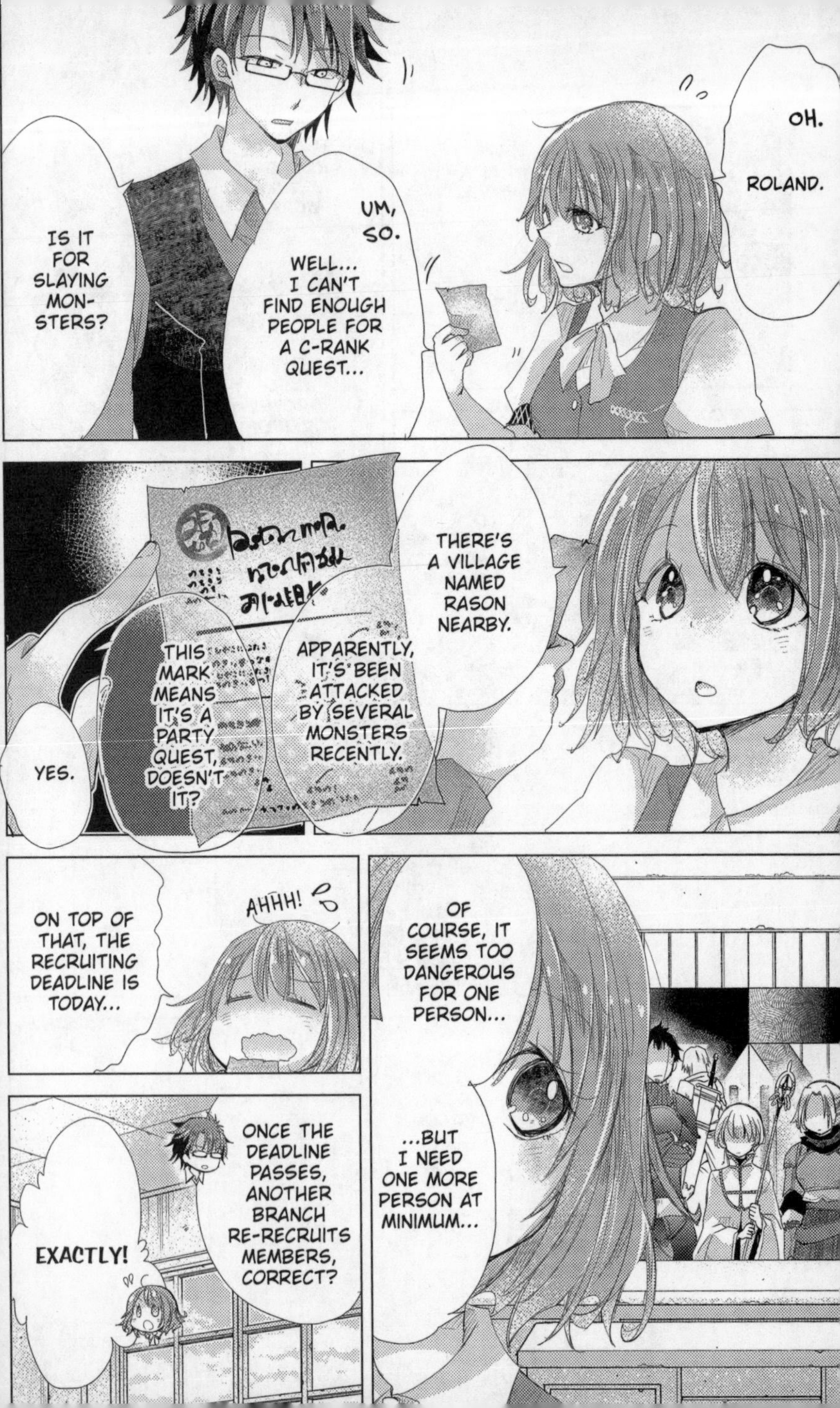
OH.
ROLAND.
UM, SO.
WELL... I CAN'T FIND ENOUGH PEOPLE FOR A C-RANK QUEST...
IS IT FOR SLAYING MON-STERS?
THERE'S A VILLAGE NAMED RASON NEARBY.
APPARENTLY, IT'S BEEN ATTACKED BY SEVERAL MONSTERS RECENTLY.
THIS MARK MEANS IT'S A PARTY QUEST, DOESN'T IT?
YES.
OF COURSE, IT SEEMS TOO DANGEROUS FOR ONE PERSON...
...BUT I NEED ONE MORE PERSON AT MINIMUM...
AHHH!
ON TOP OF THAT, THE RECRUITING DEADLINE IS TODAY...
ONCE THE DEADLINE PASSES, ANOTHER BRANCH RE-RECRUITS MEMBERS, CORRECT?
EXACTLY!

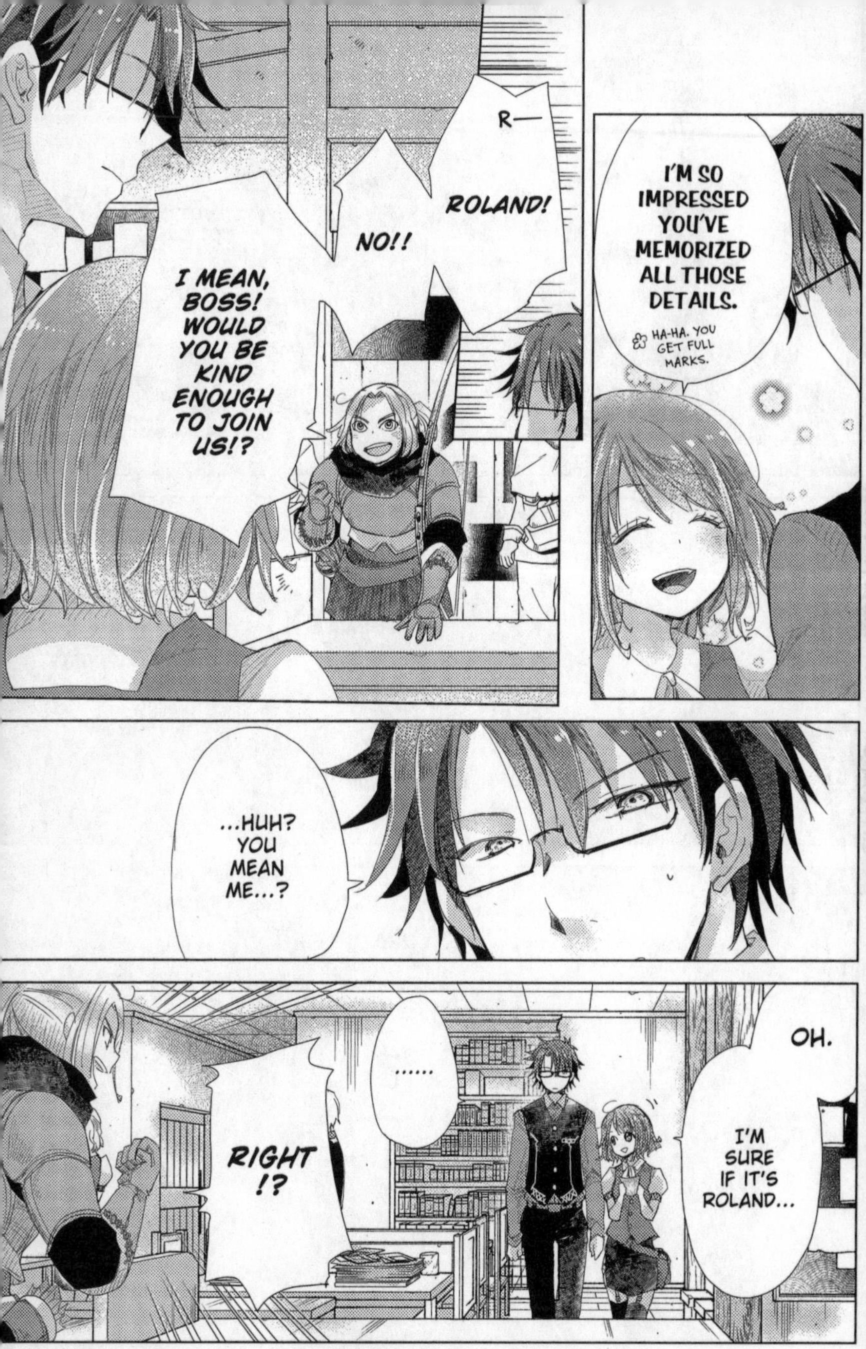
I'M SO IMPRESSED YOU'VE MEMORIZED ALL THOSE DETAILS.
HA-HA. YOU GET FULL MARKS.
R—
ROLAND!
NO!!
I MEAN, BOSS! WOULD YOU BE KIND ENOUGH TO JOIN US!?
...HUH? YOU MEAN ME...?
OH.
I'M SURE IF IT'S ROLAND...
......
RIGHT!?

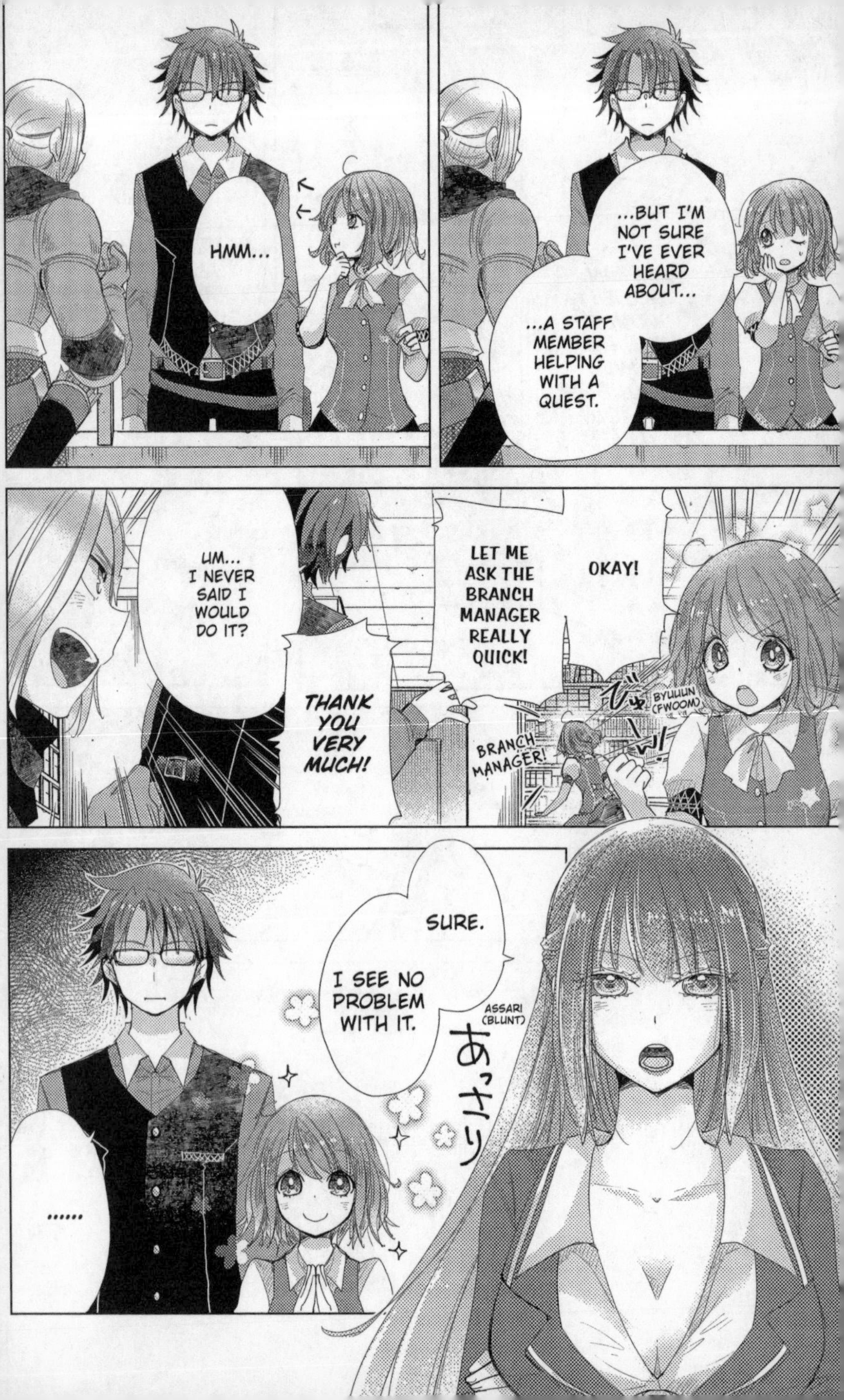
...BUT I'M NOT SURE I'VE EVER HEARD ABOUT...
...A STAFF MEMBER HELPING WITH A QUEST.
HMM...
OKAY!
BYUUUN (FWOOM)
BRANCH MANAGER!
LET ME ASK THE BRANCH MANAGER REALLY QUICK!
THANK YOU VERY MUCH!
UM... I NEVER SAID I WOULD DO IT?
SURE.
I SEE NO PROBLEM WITH IT.
ASSARI (BLUNT)
あっさり
......

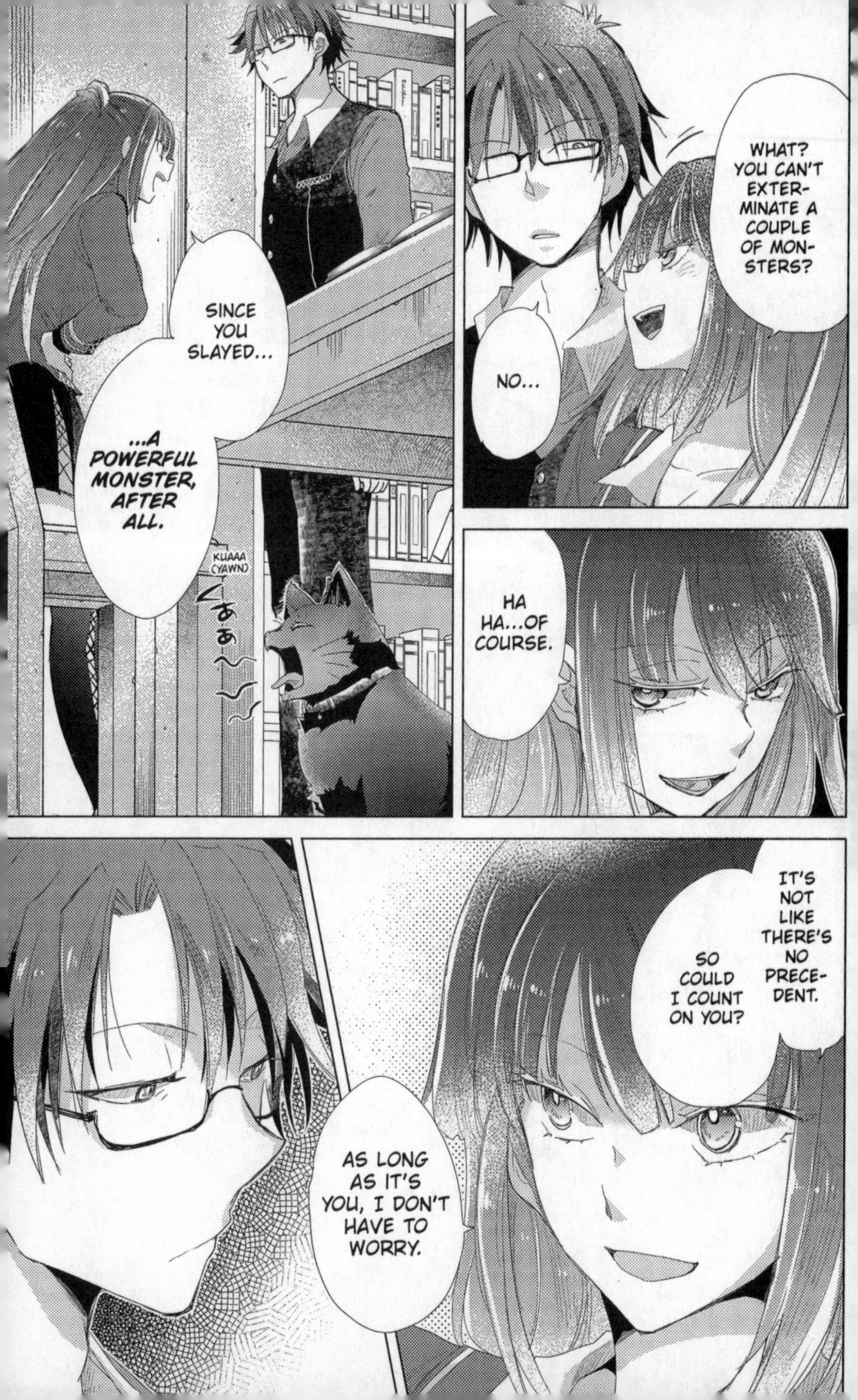
WHAT? YOU CAN'T EXTER-MINATE A COUPLE OF MON-STERS?
NO...
HA HA...OF COURSE.
SINCE YOU SLAYED...
...A POWERFUL MONSTER, AFTER ALL.
KUAAA (YAWN)
くあぁ〜
IT'S NOT LIKE THERE'S NO PRECE-DENT.
SO COULD I COUNT ON YOU?
AS LONG AS IT'S YOU, I DON'T HAVE TO WORRY.

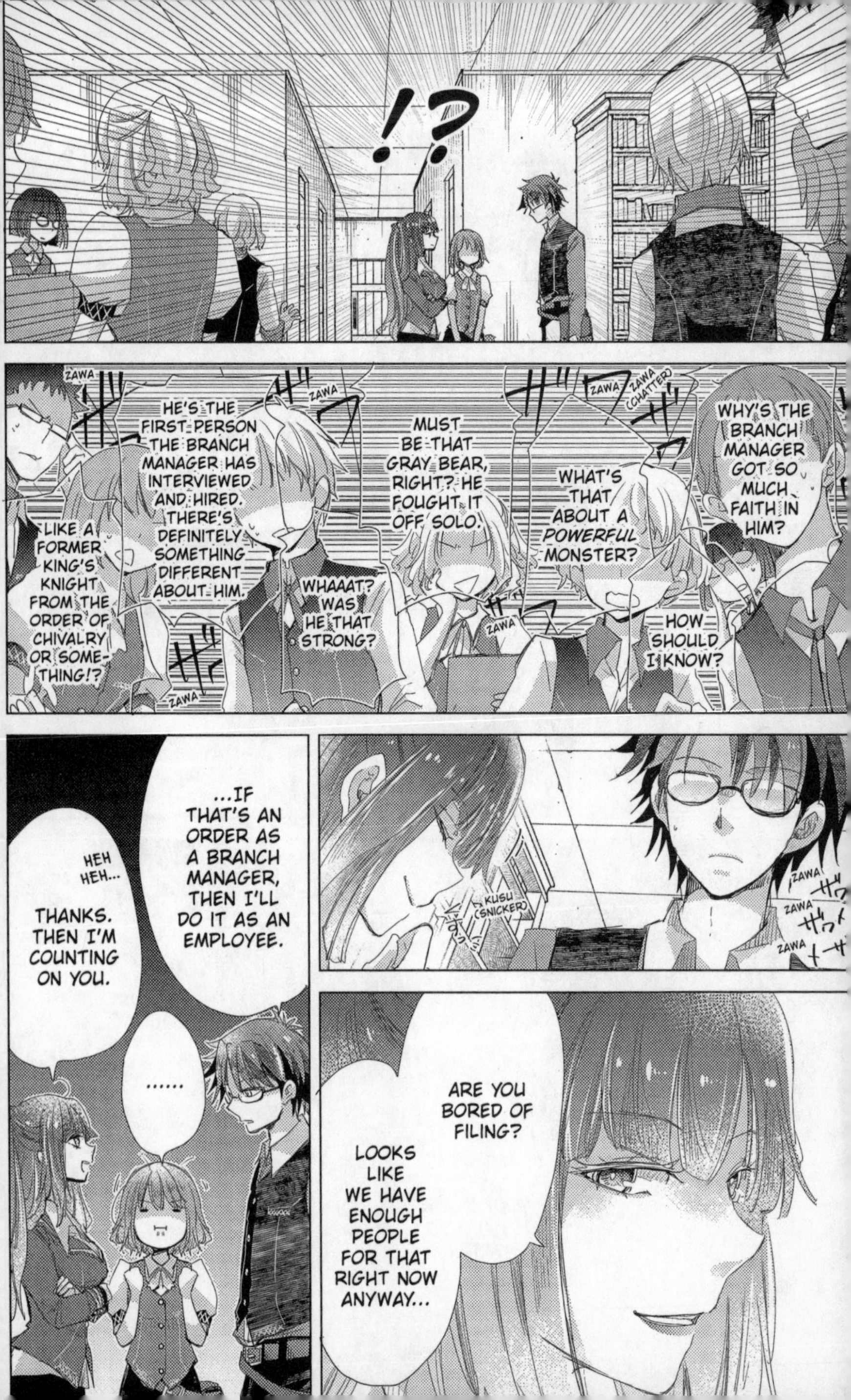
!?
ZAWA
ZAWA (CHATTER)
WHY'S THE BRANCH MANAGER GOT SO MUCH FAITH IN HIM?
HOW SHOULD I KNOW?
WHAT'S THAT ABOUT A POWERFUL MONSTER?
ZAWA
MUST BE THAT GRAY BEAR, RIGHT? HE FOUGHT IT OFF SOLO.
WHAAAT? WAS HE THAT STRONG?
ZAWA
HE'S THE FIRST PERSON THE BRANCH MANAGER HAS INTERVIEWED AND HIRED. THERE'S DEFINITELY SOMETHING DIFFERENT ABOUT HIM.
ZAWA
LIKE A FORMER KING'S KNIGHT FROM THE ORDER OF CHIVALRY OR SOMETHING!?
ZAWA
ZAWA
ZAWA
ZAWA
KUSU (SNICKER)
ARE YOU BORED OF FILING?
LOOKS LIKE WE HAVE ENOUGH PEOPLE FOR THAT RIGHT NOW ANYWAY...
...IF THAT'S AN ORDER AS A BRANCH MANAGER, THEN I'LL DO IT AS AN EMPLOYEE.
HEH HEH...
THANKS. THEN I'M COUNTING ON YOU.
......

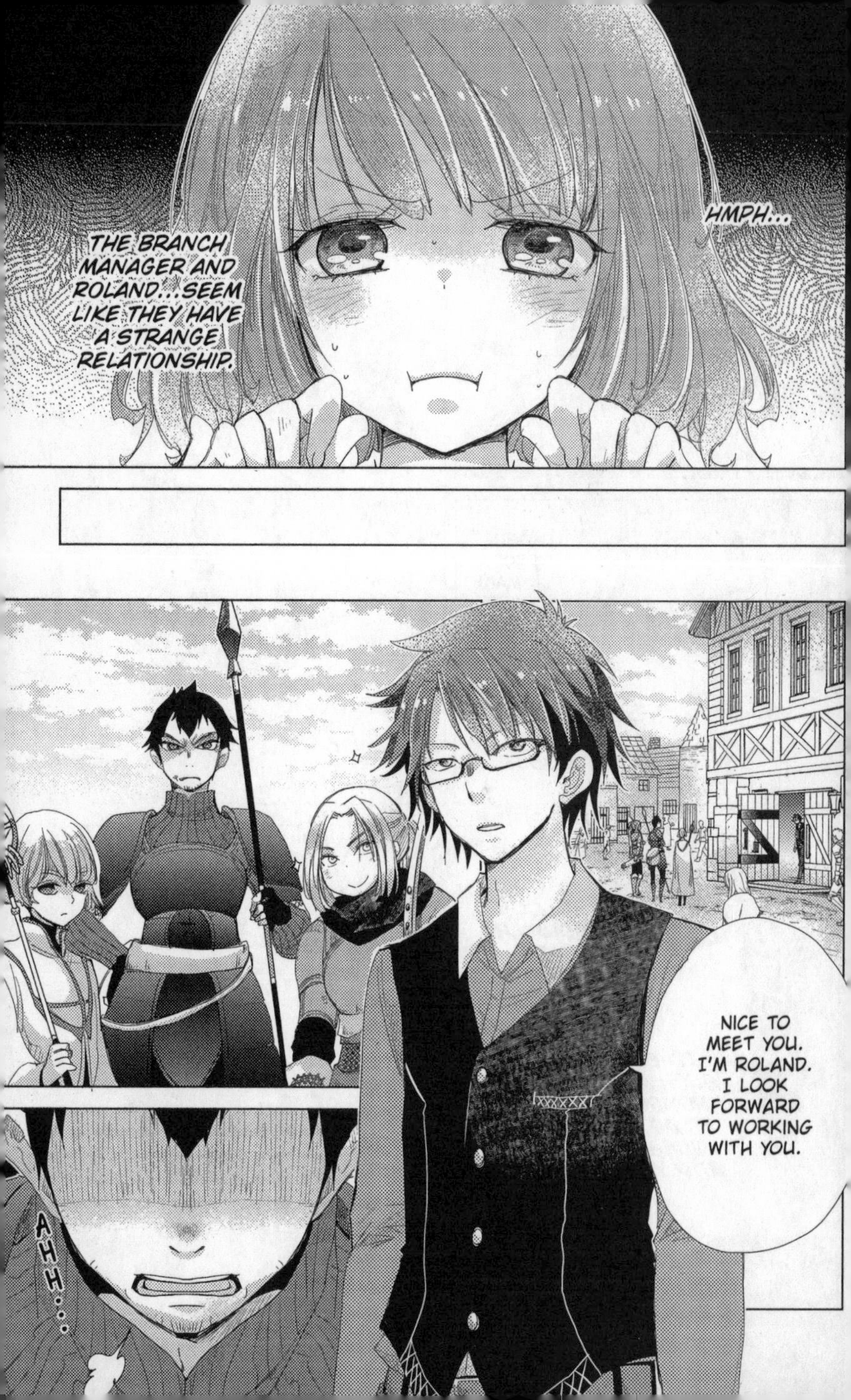
HMPH...
THE BRANCH MANAGER AND ROLAND...SEEM LIKE THEY HAVE A STRANGE RELATIONSHIP.
NICE TO MEET YOU. I'M ROLAND. I LOOK FORWARD TO WORKING WITH YOU.
AHH...

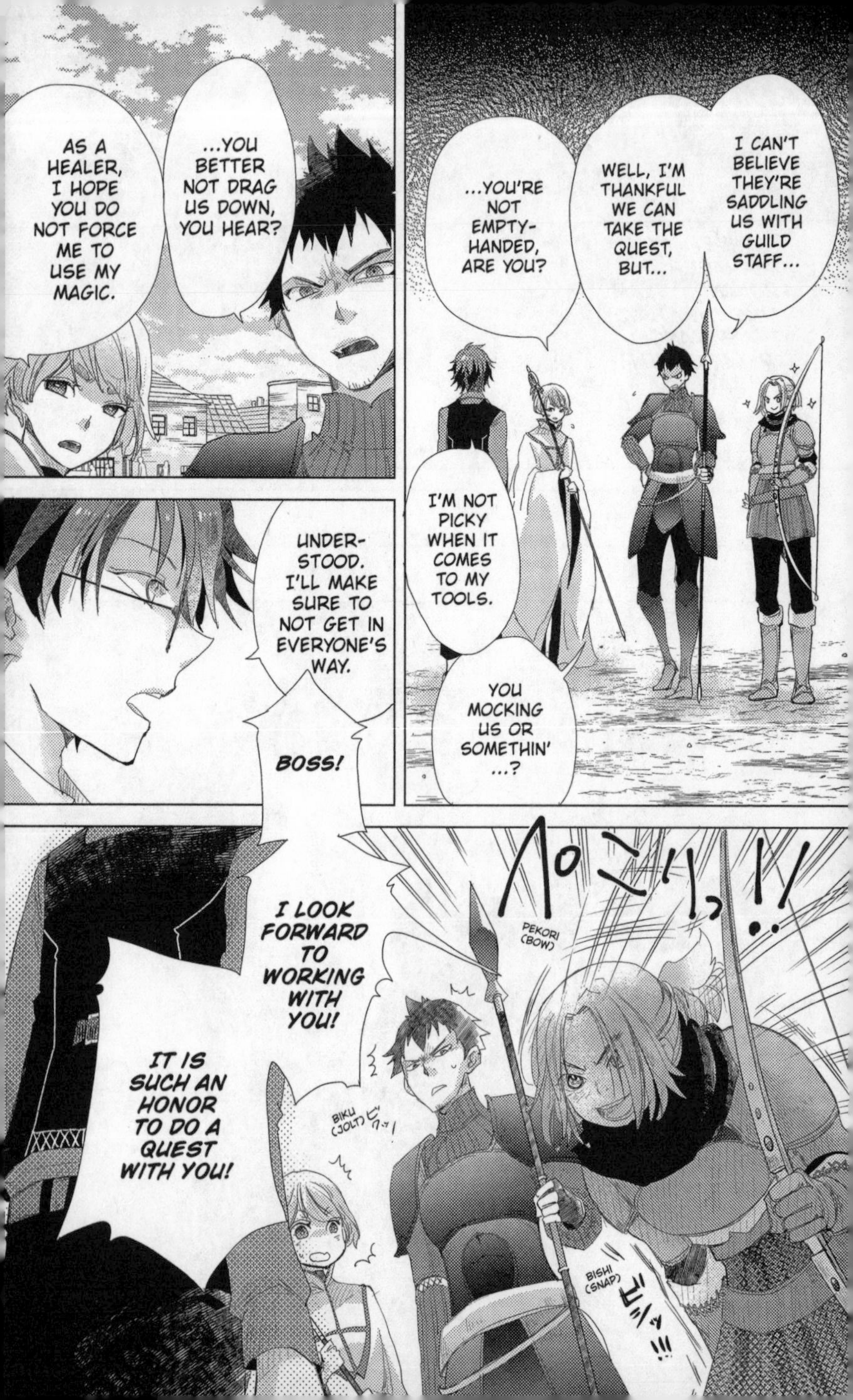
I CAN'T BELIEVE THEY'RE SADDLING US WITH GUILD STAFF...
WELL, I'M THANKFUL WE CAN TAKE THE QUEST, BUT...
...YOU'RE NOT EMPTY-HANDED, ARE YOU?
I'M NOT PICKY WHEN IT COMES TO MY TOOLS.
YOU MOCKING US OR SOMETHIN' ...?
...YOU BETTER NOT DRAG US DOWN, YOU HEAR?
AS A HEALER, I HOPE YOU DO NOT FORCE ME TO USE MY MAGIC.
UNDER-STOOD. I'LL MAKE SURE TO NOT GET IN EVERYONE'S WAY.
BOSS!
PEKORI (BOW)
I LOOK FORWARD TO WORKING WITH YOU!
BIKU (JOLT)
IT IS SUCH AN HONOR TO DO A QUEST WITH YOU!
BISHI (SNAP)

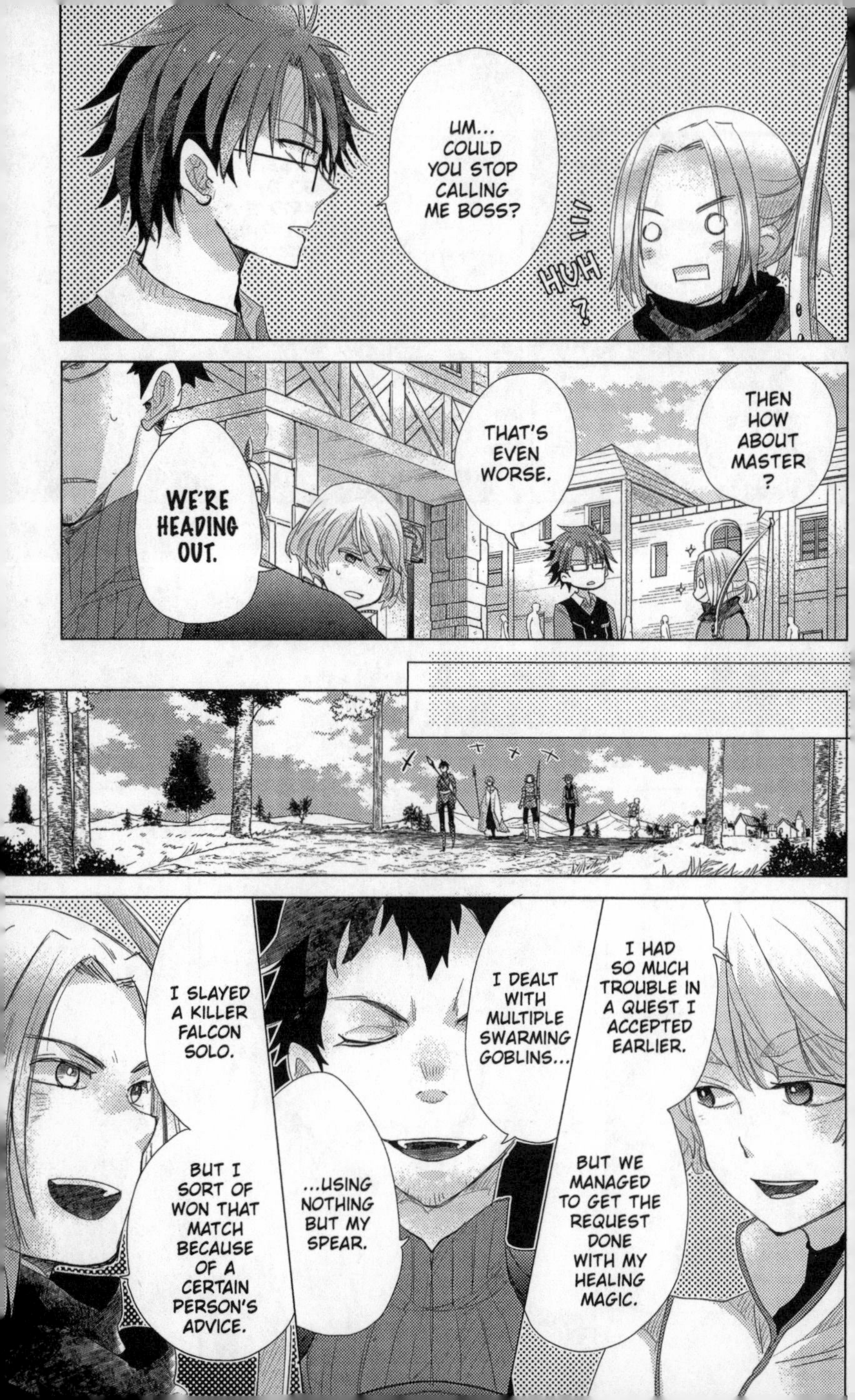
UM... COULD YOU STOP CALLING ME BOSS?
HUH?!!
THEN HOW ABOUT MASTER?
THAT'S EVEN WORSE.
WE'RE HEADING OUT.
I HAD SO MUCH TROUBLE IN A QUEST I ACCEPTED EARLIER.
BUT WE MANAGED TO GET THE REQUEST DONE WITH MY HEALING MAGIC.
I DEALT WITH MULTIPLE SWARMING GOBLINS...
...USING NOTHING BUT MY SPEAR.
I SLAYED A KILLER FALCON SOLO.
BUT I SORT OF WON THAT MATCH BECAUSE OF A CERTAIN PERSON'S ADVICE.

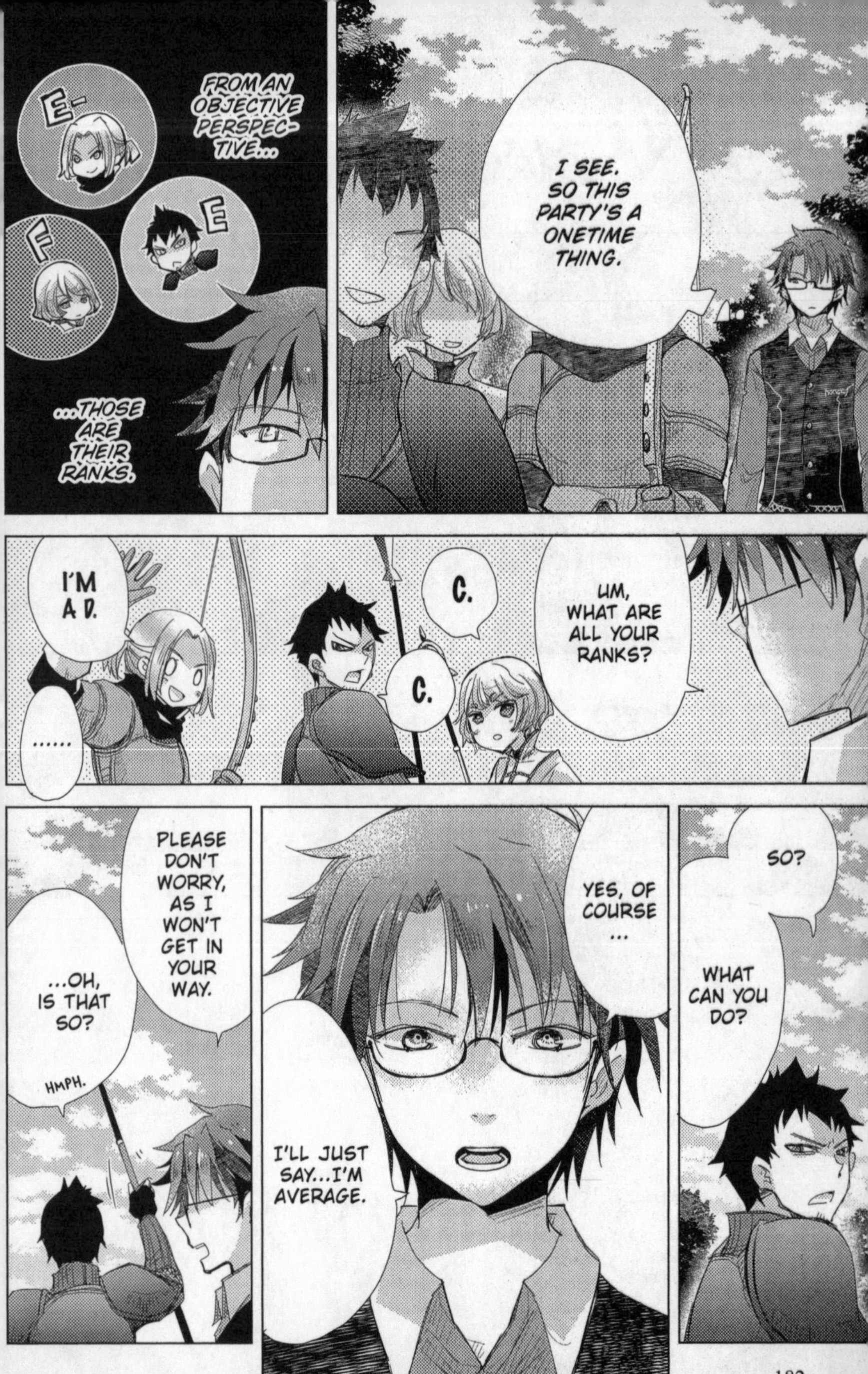
I SEE. SO THIS PARTY'S A ONETIME THING.
FROM AN OBJECTIVE PERSPEC-TIVE...
E-
E
F
...THOSE ARE THEIR RANKS.
UM, WHAT ARE ALL YOUR RANKS?
C.
C.
I'M A D.
......
SO?
WHAT CAN YOU DO?
YES, OF COURSE ...
I'LL JUST SAY...I'M AVERAGE.
PLEASE DON'T WORRY, AS I WON'T GET IN YOUR WAY.
...OH, IS THAT SO?
HMPH.

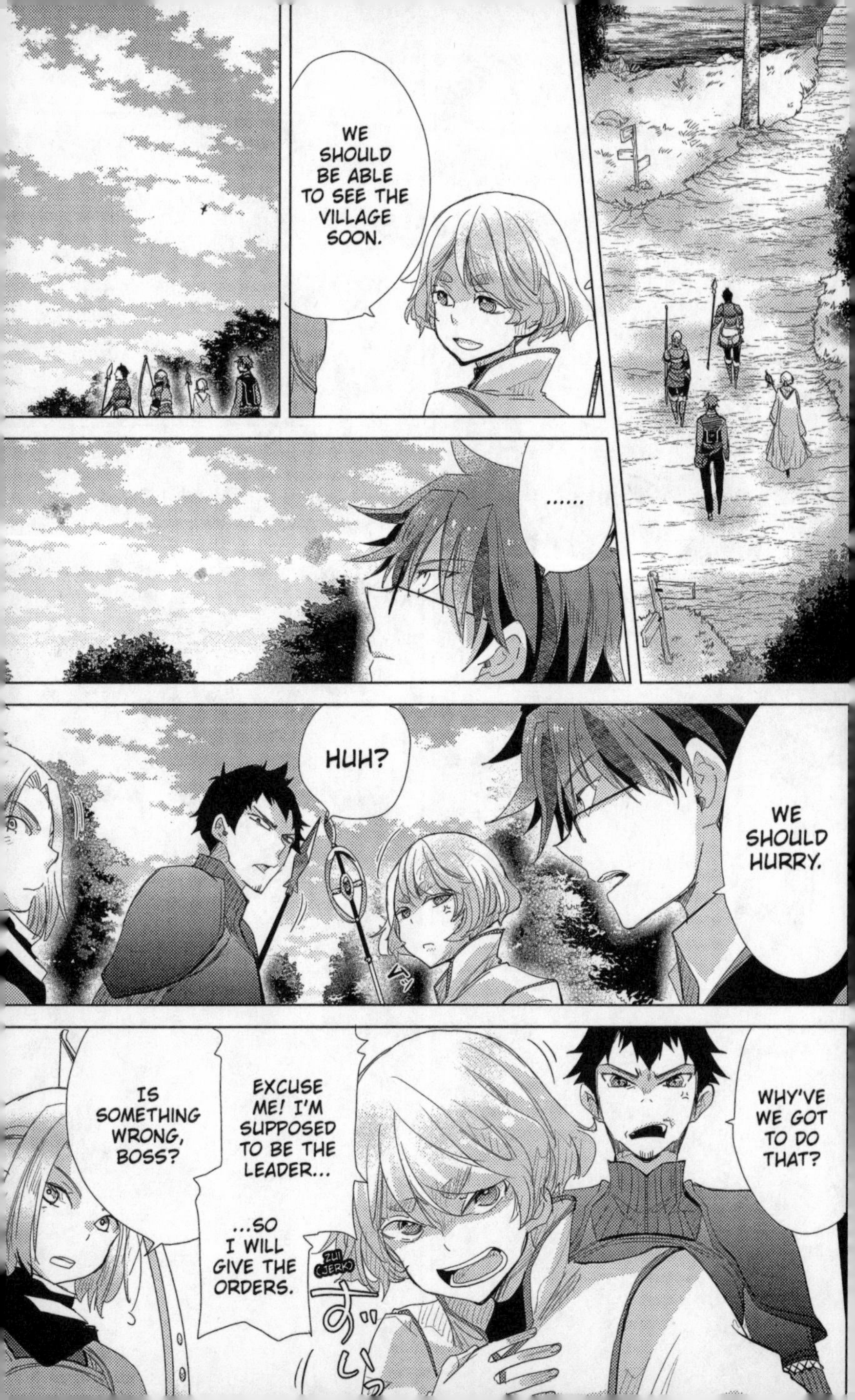
WE SHOULD BE ABLE TO SEE THE VILLAGE SOON.
......
WE SHOULD HURRY.
HUH?
WHY'VE WE GOT TO DO THAT?
IS SOMETHING WRONG, BOSS?
EXCUSE ME! I'M SUPPOSED TO BE THE LEADER...
...SO I WILL GIVE THE ORDERS.
ZUI (JERK)

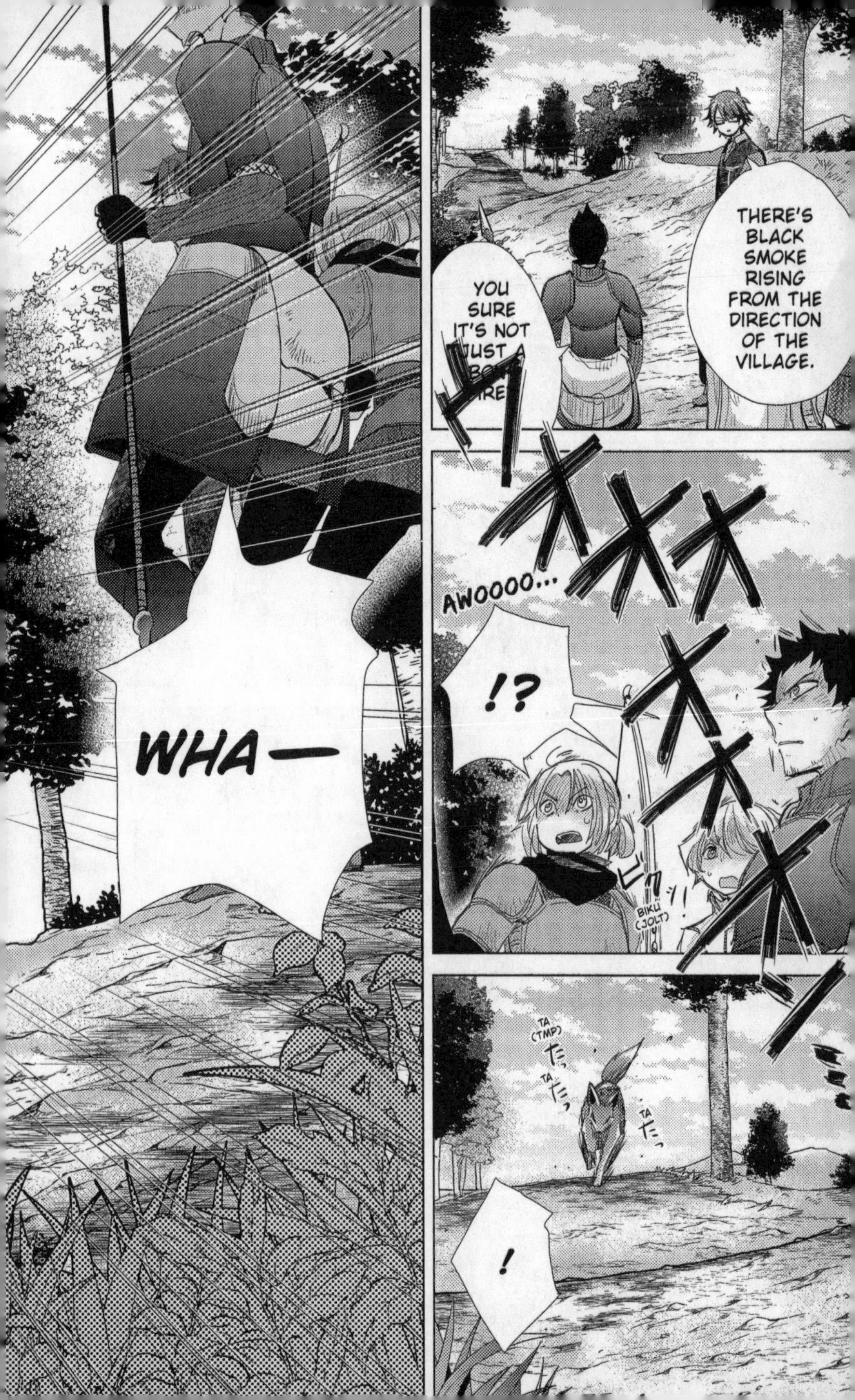
THERE'S BLACK SMOKE RISING FROM THE DIRECTION OF THE VILLAGE.
YOU SURE IT'S NOT JUST A BONFIRE
AWOOOO...
!?
BIKU (JOLT)
TA (TMP)
TA
TA
!
WHA—

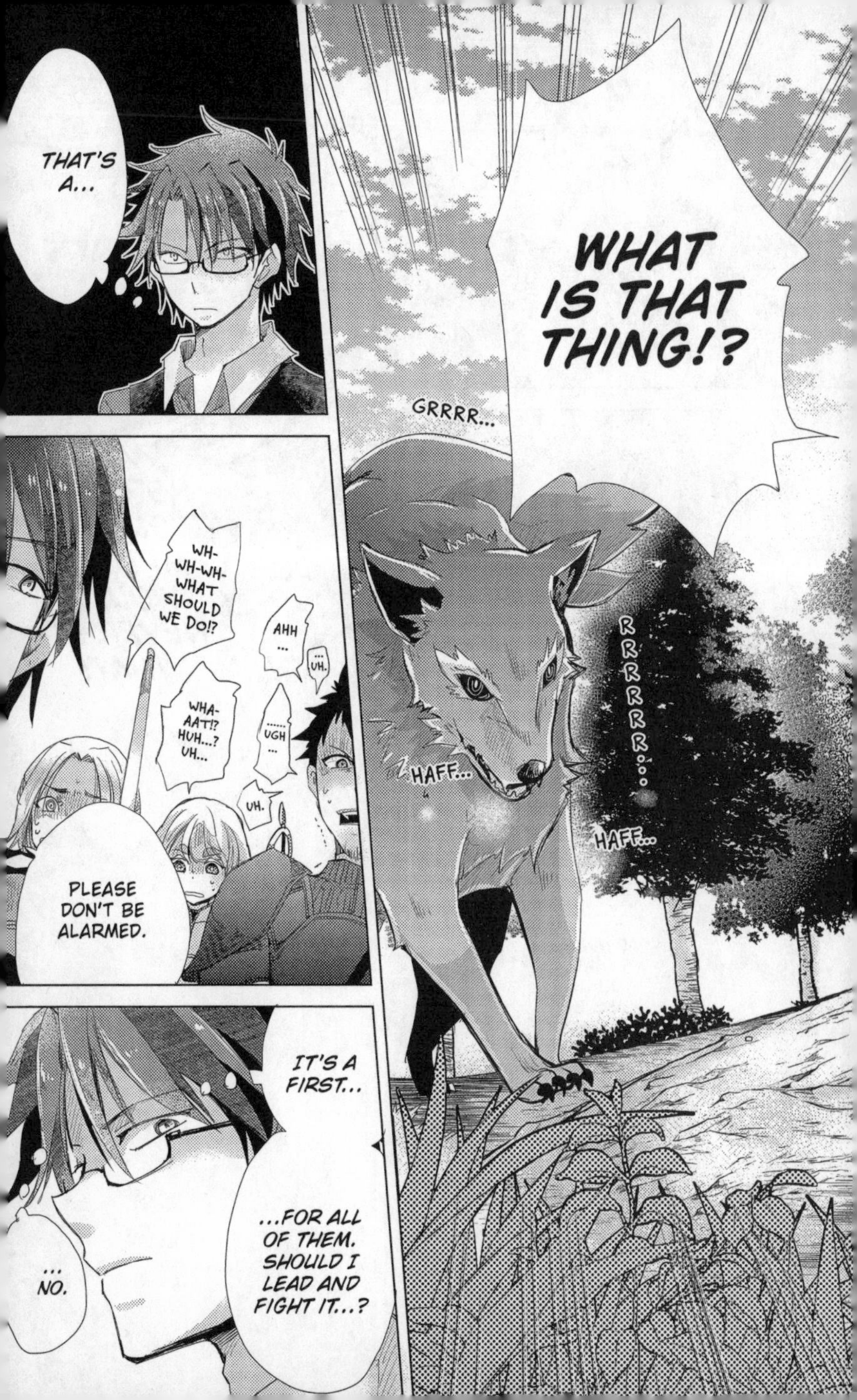
WHAT IS THAT THING!?
GRRRR...
RRRRRR...
HAFF...
HAFF...
THAT'S A...
...UH.
AHH...
WH-WH-WH-WHAT SHOULD WE DO!?
......UGH...
WHA-AAT!? HUH...? UH...
UH.
PLEASE DON'T BE ALARMED.
IT'S A FIRST...
...FOR ALL OF THEM. SHOULD I LEAD AND FIGHT IT...?
... NO.

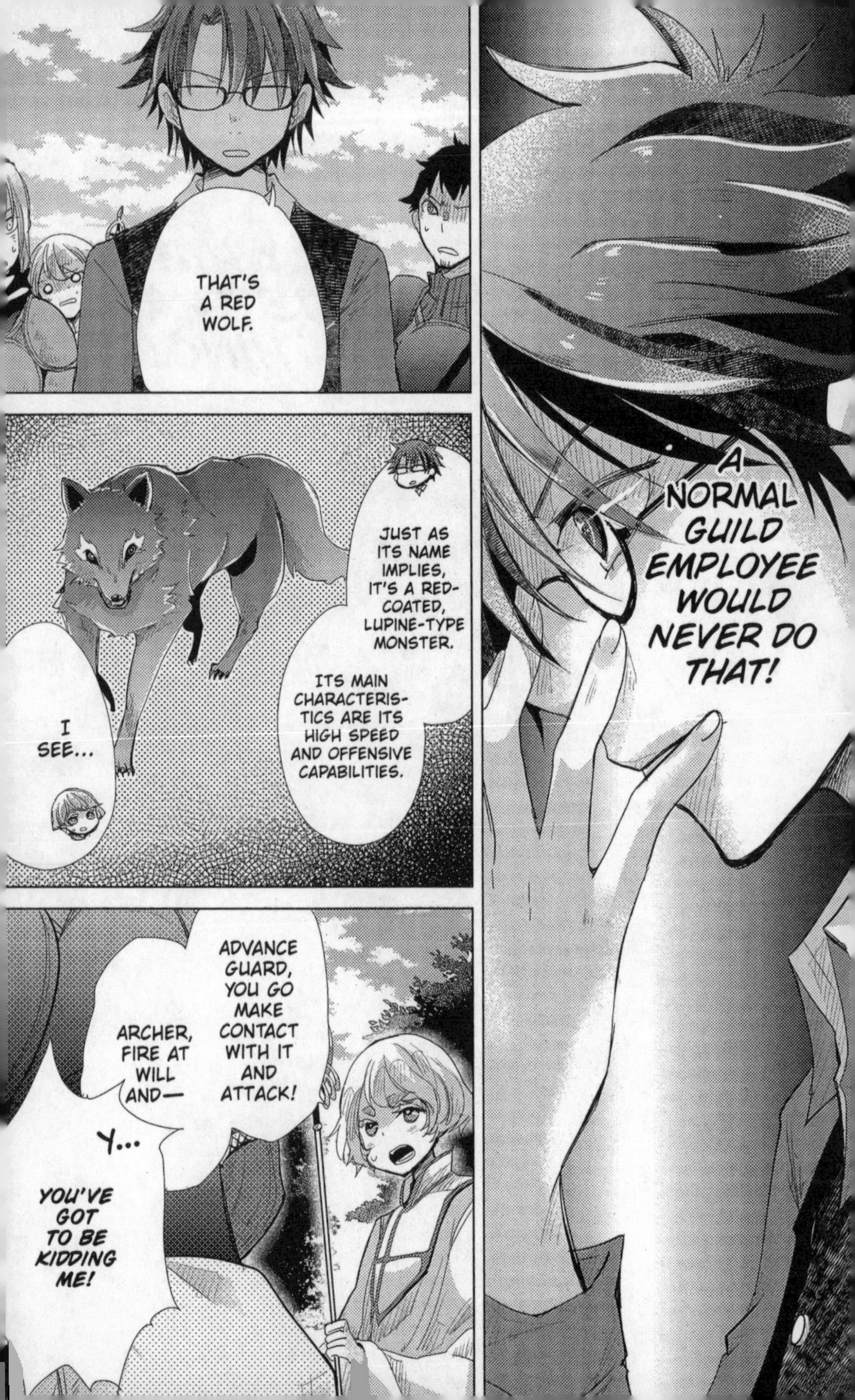
A NORMAL GUILD EMPLOYEE WOULD NEVER DO THAT!
THAT'S A RED WOLF.
JUST AS ITS NAME IMPLIES, IT'S A RED-COATED, LUPINE-TYPE MONSTER.
ITS MAIN CHARACTERIS-TICS ARE ITS HIGH SPEED AND OFFENSIVE CAPABILITIES.
I SEE...
ADVANCE GUARD, YOU GO MAKE CONTACT WITH IT AND ATTACK!
ARCHER, FIRE AT WILL AND—
Y...
YOU'VE GOT TO BE KIDDING ME!

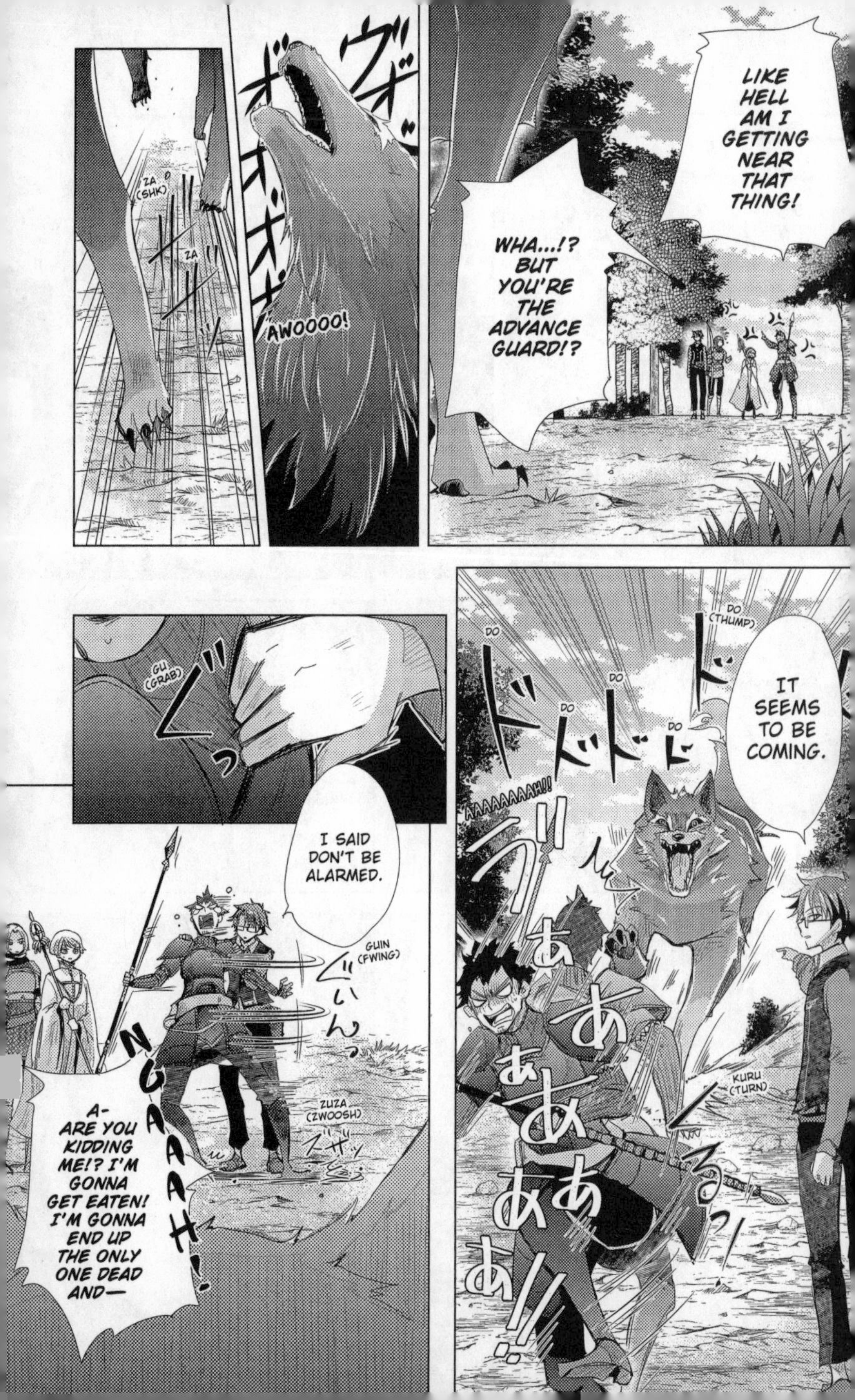
LIKE HELL AM I GETTING NEAR THAT THING!
WHA...!? BUT YOU'RE THE ADVANCE GUARD!?
AWOOOO!
ZA (SHK)
ZA
DO (THUMP)
IT SEEMS TO BE COMING.
DO
DO
DO
DO
AAAAAAAAH!!
KURU (TURN)
GU (GRAB)
I SAID DON'T BE ALARMED.
GUIN (FWING)
NUAAAAH!
ZUZA (ZWOOSH)
A- ARE YOU KIDDING ME!? I'M GONNA GET EATEN! I'M GONNA END UP THE ONLY ONE DEAD AND—

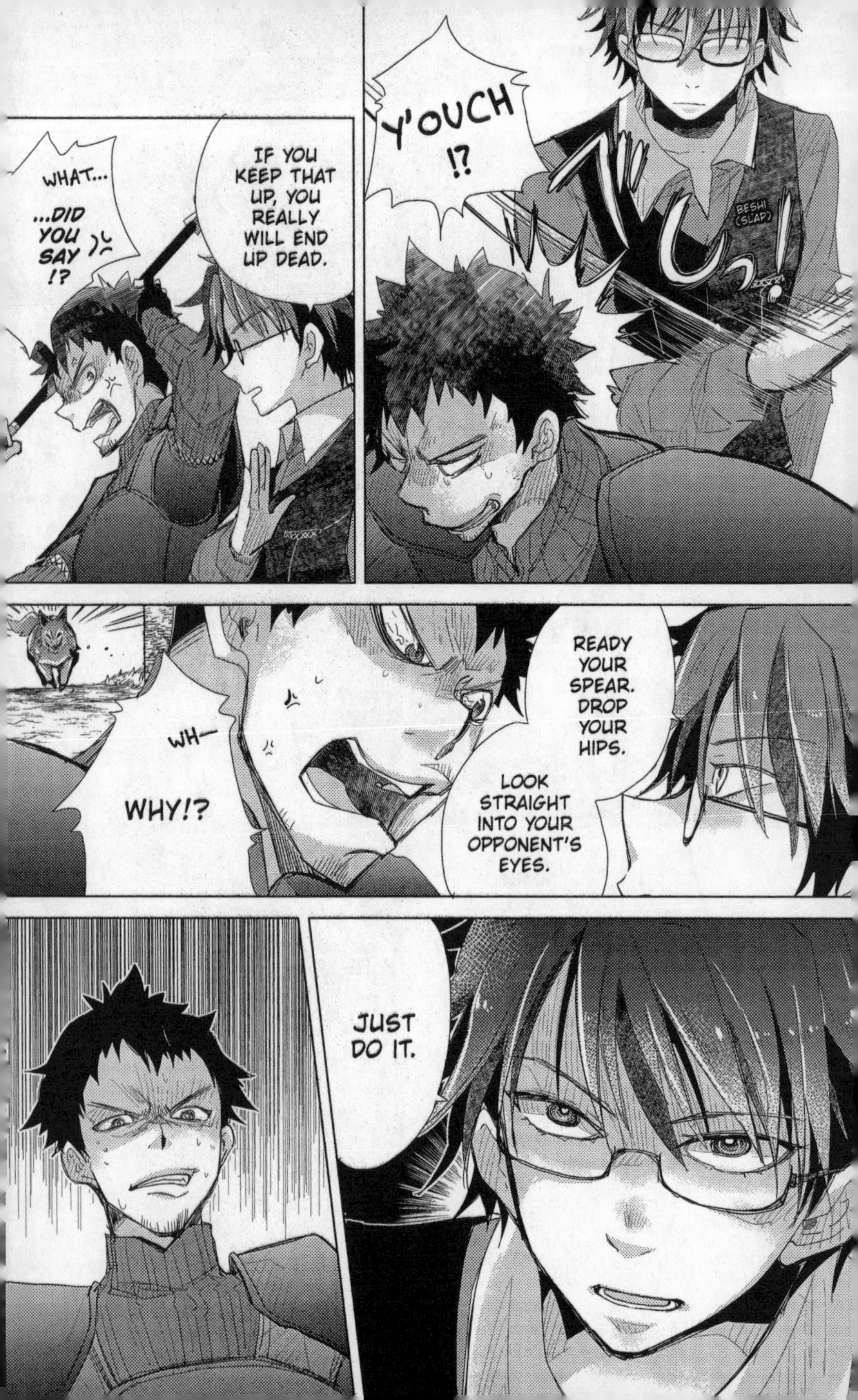
Y'OUCH !?
BESHI (SLAP)
IF YOU KEEP THAT UP, YOU REALLY WILL END UP DEAD.
WHAT...
...DID YOU SAY !?
READY YOUR SPEAR. DROP YOUR HIPS.
LOOK STRAIGHT INTO YOUR OPPONENT'S EYES.
WH—
WHY!?
JUST DO IT.

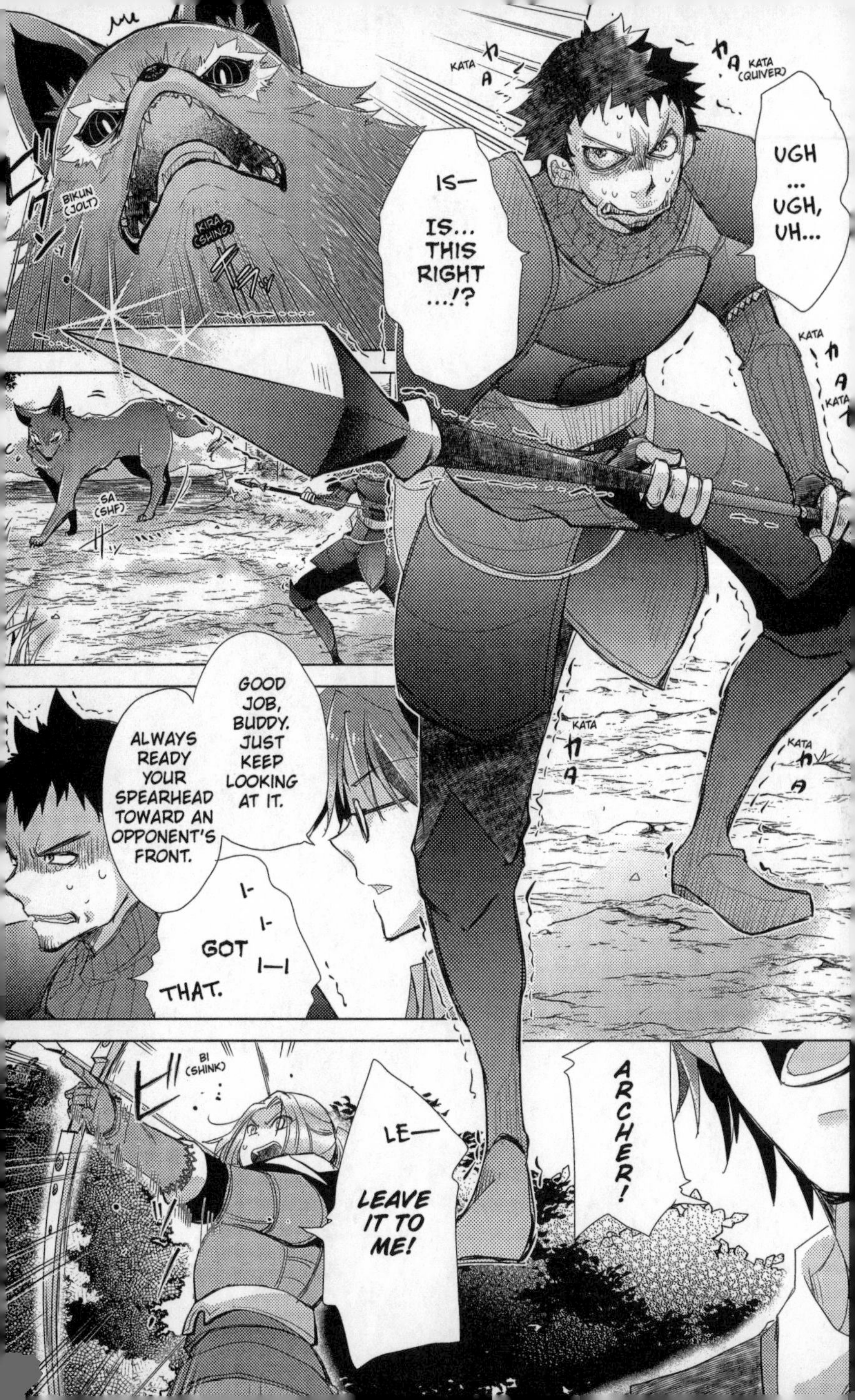
KATA (QUIVER)
KATA
UGH ... UGH, UH...
IS— IS... THIS RIGHT ...!?
KIRA (SHING)
BIKUN (JOLT)
KATA KATA
SA (SHF)
KATA
KATA
GOOD JOB, BUDDY. JUST KEEP LOOKING AT IT.
ALWAYS READY YOUR SPEARHEAD TOWARD AN OPPONENT'S FRONT.
I- I- GOT I—I THAT.
ARCHER!
LE— LEAVE IT TO ME!
BI (SHINK)

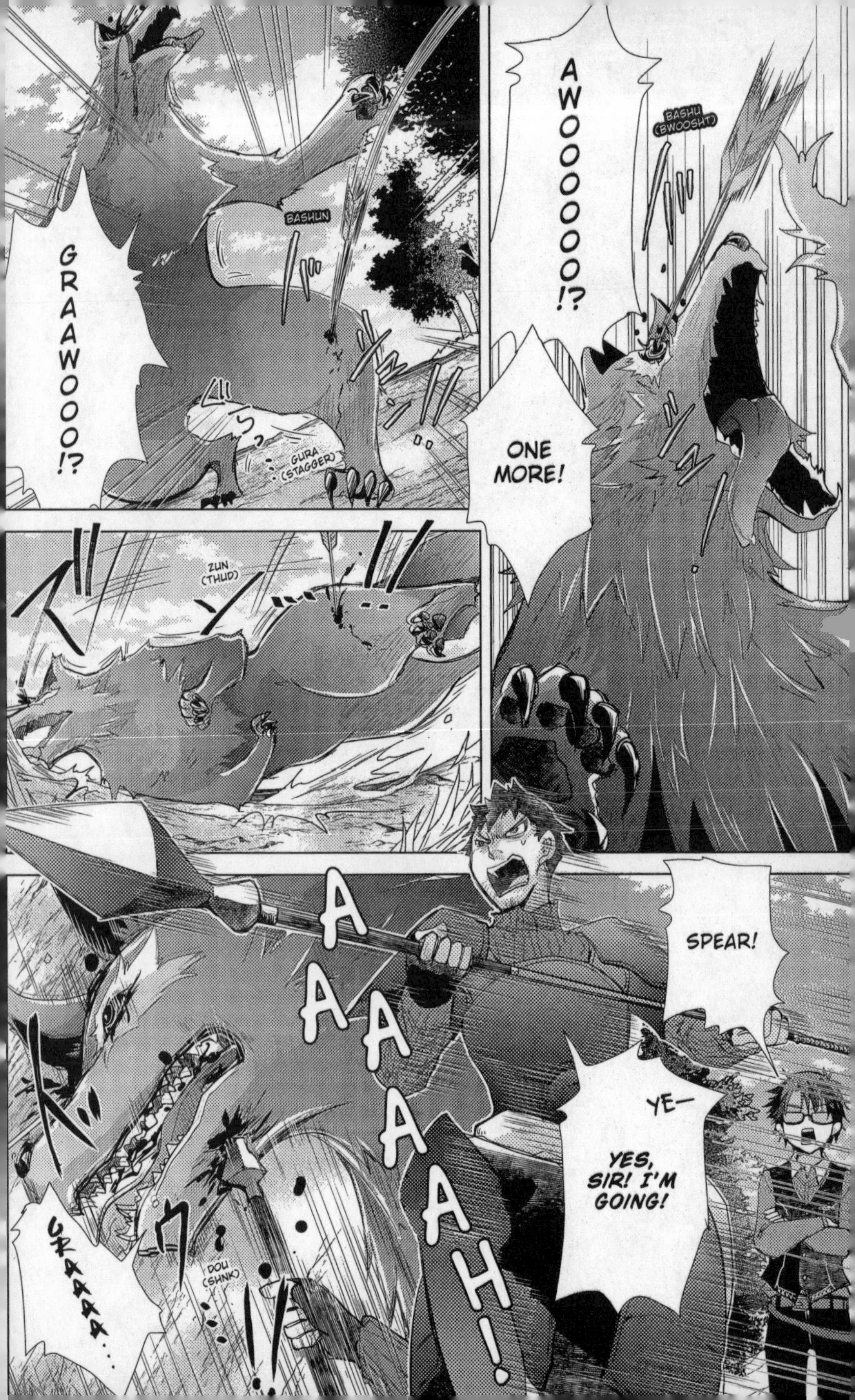
AWOOOOOOO!?
BASHU (BWOOSHT)
ONE MORE!
BASHUN
GRAAWOOOO!?
GURA (STAGGER)
ZUN (THUD)
SPEAR!
YE—
YES, SIR! I'M GOING!
AAAAAH!
DOU (SHNK)
URAAAA...

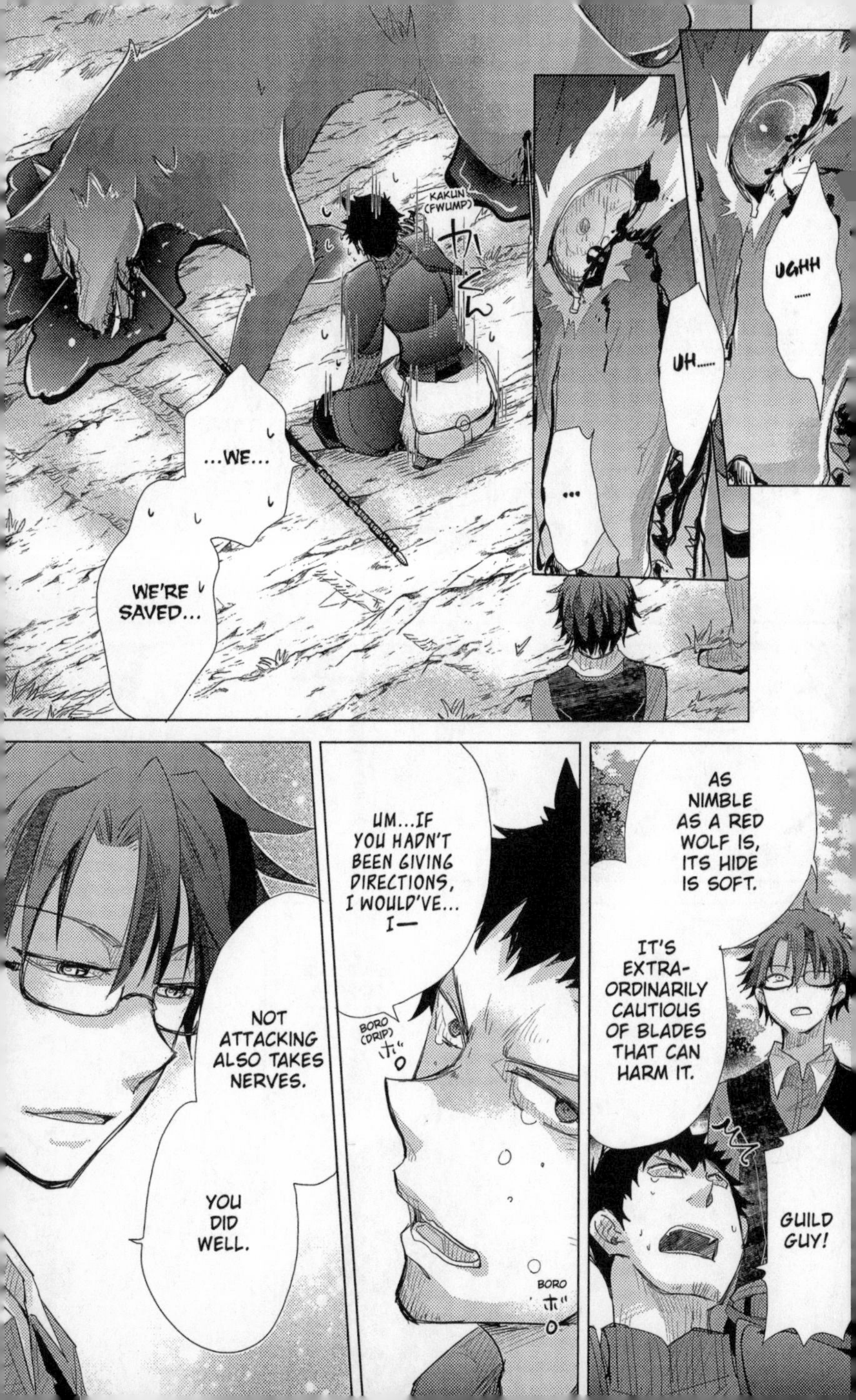
UGHH ......
UH......
...
KAKUN (FWUMP)
...WE...
WE'RE SAVED...
AS NIMBLE AS A RED WOLF IS, ITS HIDE IS SOFT.
IT'S EXTRA-ORDINARILY CAUTIOUS OF BLADES THAT CAN HARM IT.
GUILD GUY!
UM...IF YOU HADN'T BEEN GIVING DIRECTIONS, I WOULD'VE... I—
BORO (DRIP)
BORO
NOT ATTACKING ALSO TAKES NERVES.
YOU DID WELL.

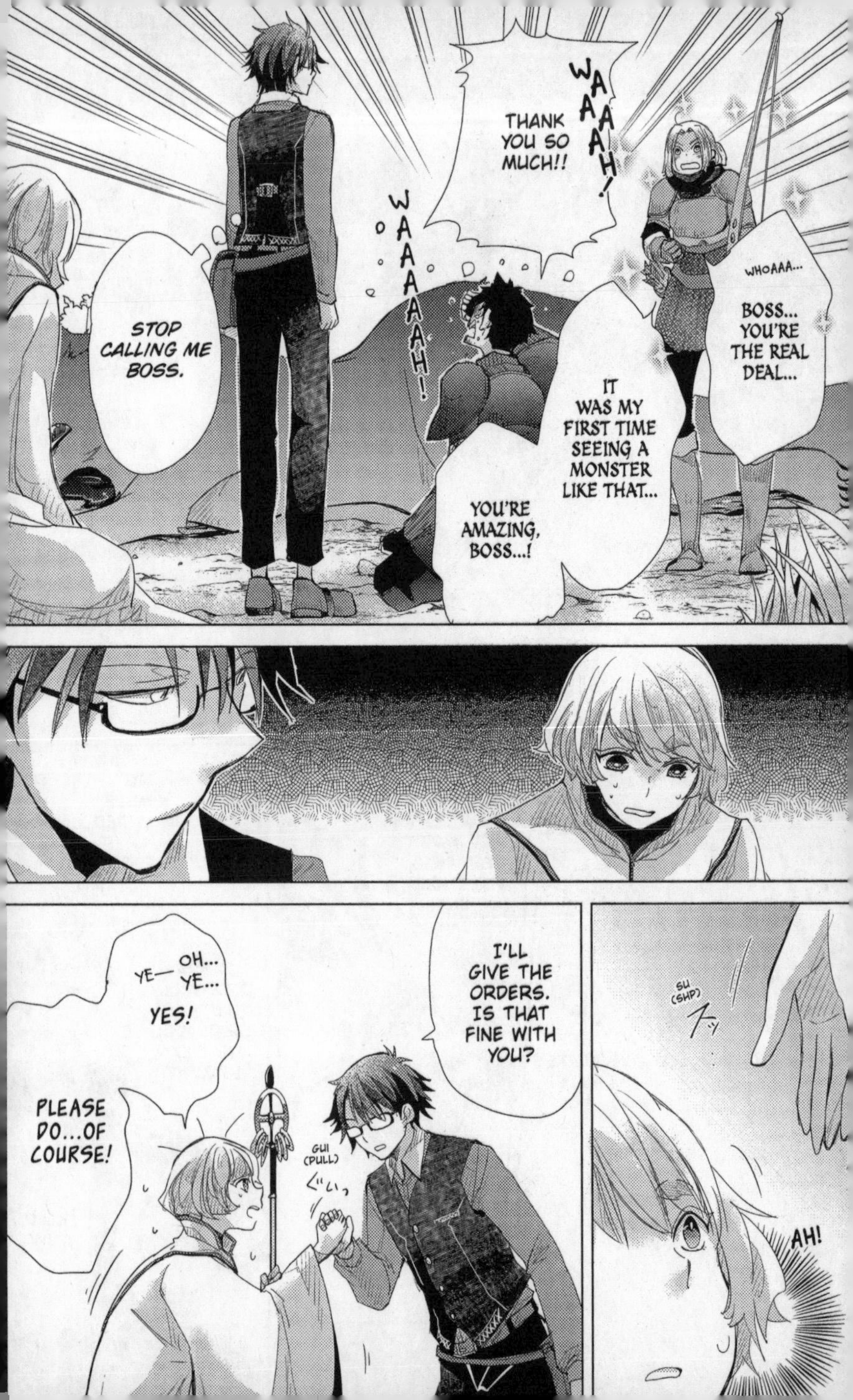
WHOAAA...
BOSS... YOU'RE THE REAL DEAL...
WAAAAH!
THANK YOU SO MUCH!!
WAAAAAAH!
IT WAS MY FIRST TIME SEEING A MONSTER LIKE THAT...
YOU'RE AMAZING, BOSS...!
STOP CALLING ME BOSS.
SU (SHP)
スッ
AH!
I'LL GIVE THE ORDERS. IS THAT FINE WITH YOU?
YE— OH... YE... YES!
GUI (PULL)
ぐいっ
PLEASE DO...OF COURSE!

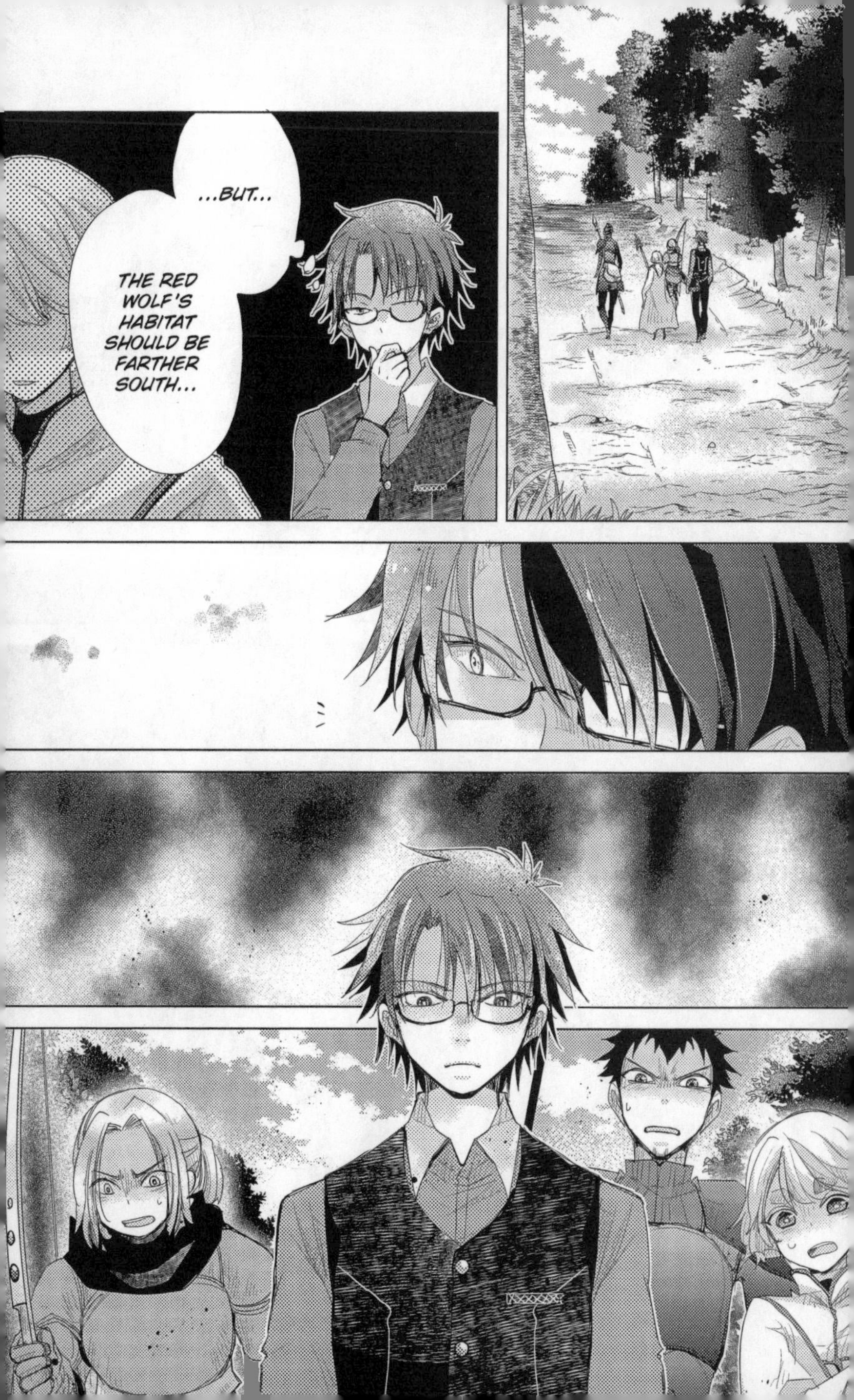
...BUT...
THE RED WOLF'S HABITAT SHOULD BE FARTHER SOUTH...

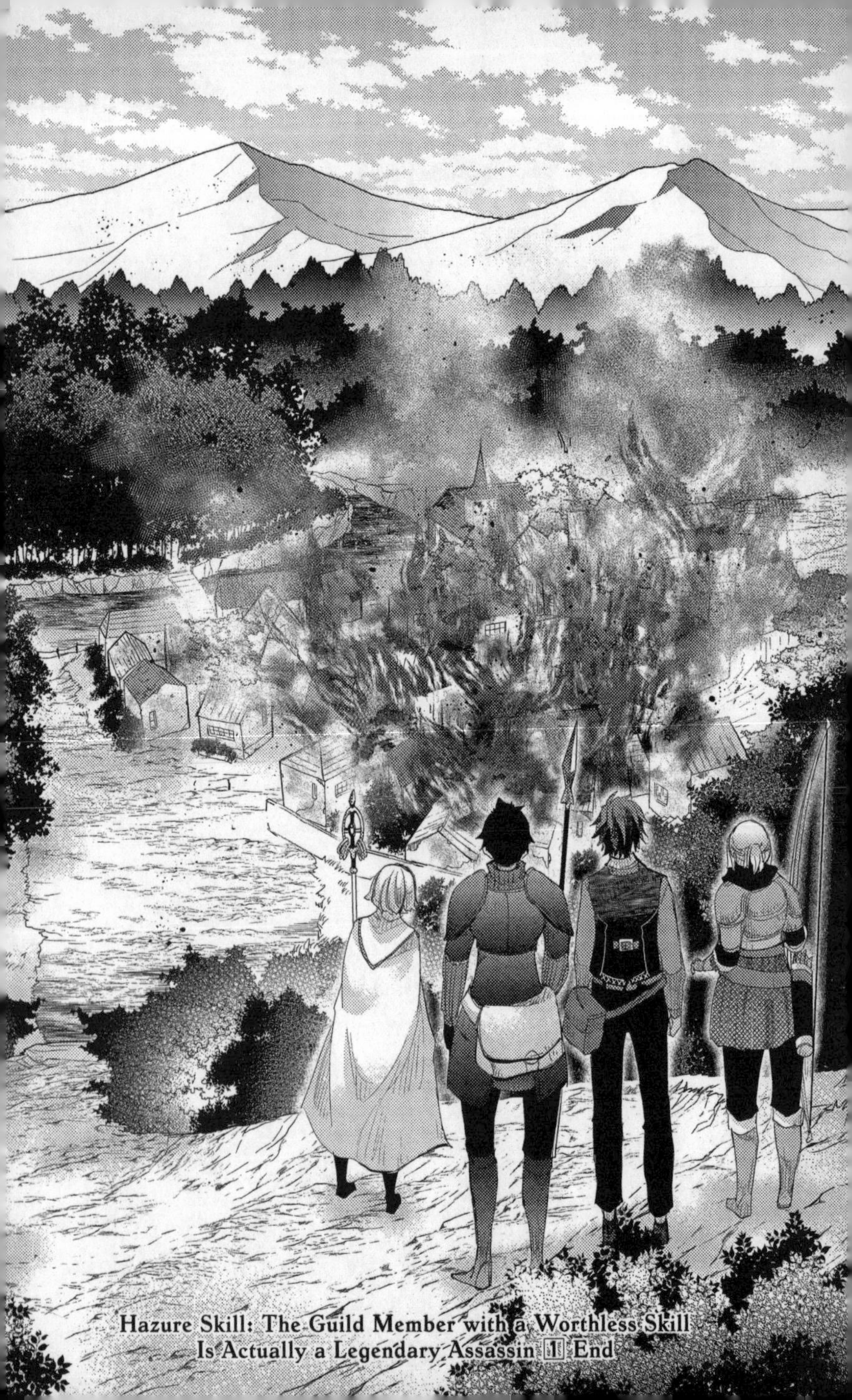
Hazure Skill: The Guild Member with a Worthless Skill
Is Actually a Legendary Assassin 1 End

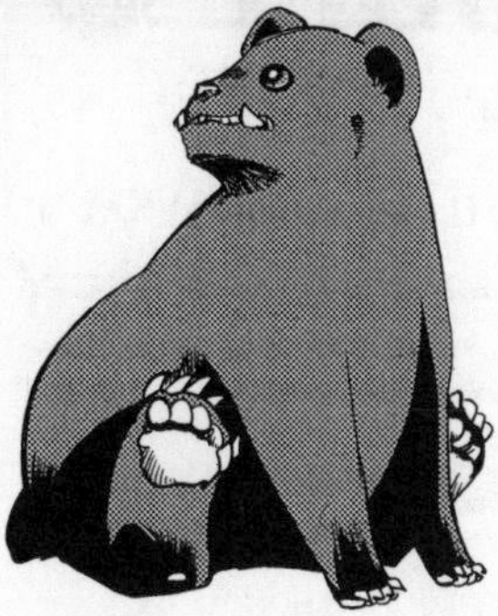

AFTERWORD

THANK YOU FOR PICKING UP THE FIRST VOLUME!

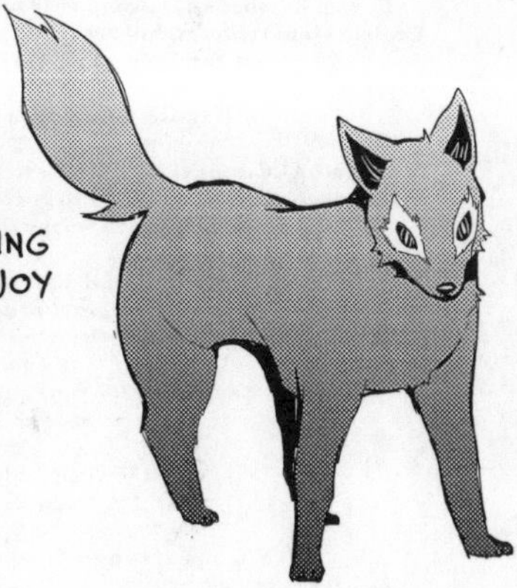

I HOPE THE READERS WHO KNOW THIS SERIES FROM THE ORIGINAL BOOK AND THOSE WHO ARE READING IT FOR THE FIRST TIME ALIKE ENJOY THIS MANGA.

I HOPE TO SEE YOU AGAIN IN THE NEXT VOLUME.

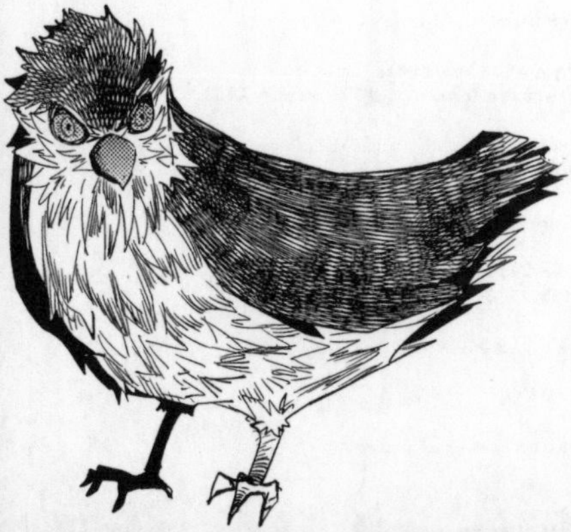

SPECIAL THANKS

OSAKI-SAN
TORIO-SAN
MOTO-SAN
SUMIKA-SAN

MY EDITOR

KENNOJI-SENSEI
KWKM-SENSEI

HAZURE SKILL 1

THE GUILD MEMBER WITH A WORTHLESS SKILL IS ACTUALLY A LEGENDARY ASSASSIN

Fuh Araki   ORIGINAL STORY **Kennoji**   CHARACTER DESIGN **KWKM**

TRANSLATION **Jan Mitsuko Cash**   ✹   LETTERING **Chiho Christie**

HAZURE SKILL "KAGE GA USUI" WO MOTSU GUILD SHOKUIN GA,
JITSUWA DENSETSU NO ANSATSUSHA Vol. 1
©Fuh Araki 2019
©Kennoji, KWKM 2019
First published in Japan in 2019 by KADOKAWA CORPORATION, Tokyo.
English translation rights arranged with KADOKAWA CORPORATION, Tokyo
and Yen Press, LLC through Tuttle-Mori Agency, Inc.

English translation © 2021 by Yen Press, LLC

Yen Press
150 West 30th Street, 19th Floor
New York, NY 10001

Visit us at yenpress.com † facebook.com/yenpress †
twitter.com/yenpress † yenpress.tumblr.com † instagram.com/yenpress

First Yen Press Edition: May 2021

Yen Press is an imprint of Yen Press, LLC.
The Yen Press name and logo are trademarks of Yen Press, LLC.

The publisher is not responsible for websites (or their content)
that are not owned by the publisher.

Library of Congress Control Number: 2021930391

ISBNs: 978-1-9753-2437-7 (paperback)
978-1-9753-2438-4 (ebook)

10 9 8 7 6 5 4 3 2 1

BVG

Printed in the United States of America